The American West in the Twentieth Century

The American West in the Twentieth Century

A Short History of an Urban Oasis

Gerald D. Nash

UNIVERSITY OF NEW MEXICO PRESS

Albuquerque

Library of Congress Cataloging in Publication Data

Nash, Gerald D
    The American West in the twentieth century.

    Bibliography: p.
    Includes index.
    1. The West—History—1848–1950.   2.   The West—
1951–   I.   Title
[F595.N37 1977]   978'.03   77-81981
ISBN 0-8263-0464-8

Manufactured in the United States of America.
Library of Congress Catalog Card Number 77-81981.
International Standard Book Number 0-8263-0464-8.

Third printing, University of New Mexico Press, 1985

To the Memory of John D. Hicks

Contents

Preface

This is a little book about a big subject. Designed primarily as a work of synthesis, it seeks to provide a framework for interpreting and understanding the American West in the twentieth century. Many books and articles have been written about the modern West—by historians, journalists, social scientists, travelers, and others—yet much of this literature is widely scattered. Like many others, I have long felt the need for a comprehensive overview that would provide historical perspective on many aspects of the western experience in the twentieth century. Such a volume might serve much as a road map does in charting terrain that, although not wholly unfamiliar, is in many aspects still largely untraversed. So I ask the reader to join me in putting on seven-league boots and to take a long look at the outlines of the historical development of a land that is as big as the western sky.

I hope that future years will see the appearance of comprehensive works about the twentieth-century West. My own purpose is more modest in this volume. I have attempted to digest the voluminous literature on many special aspects of the western experience and to provide a survey for the general reader rather than the specialist, emphasizing some of the most significant aspects of western development since 1890. In short, this book is designed to provide a clear and simple introduction to one of the most significant events in twentieth-century America—the maturation of the trans-Mississippi West.

In a way this work is not only about the West, but about an area that encompasses almost one-half of the continental United States. The history of the West is not merely the history of a region, but a major aspect of the entire American experience. And so I tend to view the history of the West not only as regional lore, but as an integral part of the history of the United States. To be sure, broad generalizations for this vast area are difficult to sustain. For the purposes of this book we will therefore focus on five sub-regions, including California, the Pacific Northwest, the Rocky Mountain states, the Southwest, and the Plains. In formulating generalizations for the entire region I have drawn illustrations and examples from one or another of the sub-regions. I invite readers to test the validity of these generalizations in regard to the history of their own particular locality. Of all the western states, California receives more emphasis than any other because since 1900 its national as well as regional influence has been preeminent. Moreover, since 1900 it has harbored approximately two-fifths of the population of the trans-Mississippi West, and I feel that such emphasis is justified.

Much of the inspiration for this book came from my late mentor, John D. Hicks, to whose memory it is dedicated. The fraternity of men and women interested in the history of the West—professional as well as amateur—is an especially congenial one. So many of them have contributed to the completion of this volume that, rather than single out any individual, I wish to express my appreciation to all of them collectively. My gratitude also extends to my wife and family for help and understanding.

Introduction:
The American West
in the Twentieth Century

Is there a twentieth-century West? To pose the question is to open a
Pandora's box that yields some uncertainties, and perhaps even negative
responses. Thanks to Frederick Jackson Turner and his devoted band of
disciples over the last seventy-five years, we know much more about the
West before 1890 than thereafter. The Turner thesis—that the frontier
constituted a dominant influence on American civilization until 1890—has
been an invaluable guide to understanding the American experience up
until that time. Some Turnerians even claimed that the very absence of a
frontier in the twentieth century profoundly affected the development of
the United States in the more modern period. Others felt that the West
disappeared by 1890, that the years since then have been an anticlimax
for the West—a pale and lusterless end to the most significant phase of
western development during the nineteenth century and before.

But it can be argued that the frontier hypothesis of Frederick Jackson
Turner is not very applicable, nor indeed relevant, to an understanding of
the American West after 1890. In fact, Turner himself in his later years,
during the 1920s, came to feel this way as he witnessed the rise of
industrial America with some dismay. And so we might step outside the
Turnerian framework, and the interesting debate it has engendered, and
deal with the twentieth-century West on its own terms. Other ap-
proaches, such as the findings of social scientists, provide insights and
understanding about the area west of the Mississippi River. For the twentieth century did not constitute an inglorious end to a glorious process—
frontier development—but represented one of the most significant phases
in the transit of civilization in America. During the Great Age of Discovery in the fifteenth century, civilization moved from Europe to the West;
from then until the nineteenth century civilization moved westward across
the continent of North America, where it modified cultural life-styles; and
in the twentieth century the transit of civilization was reversed as the

1

life-styles of the American West were exported to the East, to Europe, and to many other portions of the world. Thus, in answer to the question posed earlier: Is there a twentieth-century West? I would maintain, most emphatically: Yes, there is a twentieth-century West, and it is alive and well. In fact, the history of the West in the twentieth century may very well constitute the most significant era in the entire history of the region.

What were the major influences that shaped the American West in the twentieth century? Let us point out at the outset that the combined influence of cultural traits and institutions, on the one hand, and environment, on the other, provided a crucible for western growth. Now, the dynamic forces that shaped western development after 1890 were somewhat different from those described by Turner for the preceding period. Turner assigned great weight to the impact of environment in shaping characteristics of personal behavior, as well as western politics, economic life, and values. But after 1890 cultural influences may very well have become more significant than environment in setting the life-styles of people in the West. Then, technological advances provided increasingly for greater human control over the environment. This is not to say that the peculiarities of the western natural environment ceased to play a significant role in shaping the civilization of the West in the course of the twentieth century. They continued to exert a significant influence, but more often than not were subdued by cultural factors. Culture (in the broad German sense of *Kultur*) and environment thus have been the two great formative factors in the development of the twentieth-century West. As the distinguished geographer Carl O. Sauer once wrote, if culture was an agent, and the natural area a medium, then the cultural landscape was the result.[1]

Let us examine some of the major cultural forces that shaped the twentieth-century West more closely. Obviously, the modern West was not born in a vacuum; its development was closely tied to the growth of the rest of the United States at particular stages of its history. The reciprocal relationship between older and newer regions was always close, and so the history of the West must be viewed within the broader context of the whole American experience. Into the trans-Mississippi area poured more than 40 million Americans and at least 8 million foreigners in the three-quarters of a century after 1898. If they did not bring their culture in knapsacks—like the settlers of earlier years—they did bring the distinctive traits of civilization in the United States east of the Mississippi River with them. The dominant Anglo-Saxon majority carried with it conceptions of social status, ethnic minorities, and accepted behavior patterns for young and old. Above all, they brought with them the American faith in science and technology, with which they hoped to modify the new environment. Their supreme confidence in the superiority of their values led them to look somewhat askance at existing cultures in the region, those of the Indians, Spanish-Americans, and Mexicans. They came also with the desire for material gain, for wealth, and for the utmost exploitation of whatever natural resources they might find. In most instances the new western migrant in the twentieth century carried along his political inheritance—a desire to transplant the political institutions with which he had been familiar in the older regions—the Northeast, the Middle West, and the South. And he usually sought to re-create the cultural life he had known in his home community. Whether this base mass of people who migrated westward after 1898 was of higher intelligence than those who stayed behind is difficult to establish, but very likely they constituted an especially aggressive group. In the twentieth century, therefore, we witness a transit of American civilization from East to West, a transplantation of American culture east of the Mississippi River to the vast stretches beyond. Obviously, that eastern culture was to undergo considerable change in the process of movement. But the cultural patterns developed in the eastern United States by 1898 were to exercise a dominant influence in shaping the cultural landscape of the West.

Let us briefly reiterate this summary of major cultural influences on the twentieth-century West. The predominant value system brought by a majority of new settlers embraced a profound faith in science and technology, a belief closely related to the desire for material gain. They also brought know-how with them—entrepreneurial skills that enabled them to undertake a phenomenally rapid development of the region. Western growth was further shaped by selective patterns of migration. And crises—whether wars or depressions—also exercised a significant impact on the course of western expansion after 1898. Values, technology, entrepreneurship, migration patterns, and crises thus were among the dominant influences on the West during the twentieth century.

As we have already mentioned, however, environmental influences did not wholly cease to affect the particular directions of western growth in these years. Land may no longer have been the dominant force that it had been in the nineteenth century. Environmental factors in this later period were more varied, including not only land, but climate, an increasingly wide range of natural resources, wilderness areas, and open (including air) spaces.

Over the years, geographers, regional scientists, and sociologists have developed literally dozens of classifications of the physiographic features in the region west of the Mississippi River. Many of these are ingenious, but for purposes of our discussion here let us adopt a very simple scheme. Let us view the West as a series of dry as well as humid regions. The entire area west of the Mississippi River contains an enormous variety of terrain, climates, and topography. But let us assume that there is a Dry West and a Wet West. Certainly the Great Plains can be regarded as a Great American Desert, much as the early nineteenth-century explorers like Lewis and Clark or Zebulon Pike saw it. This Great American Desert is bounded by wet areas on the east, as well as on the West Coast. It is almost like an island in the sea. Throughout much of its history, indeed, it has been as dependent on its eastern and western neighbors as an isolated island in an ocean.

As Walter Prescott Webb pointed out some years ago, we cannot understand the American West unless we recognize what for many Americans—especially easterners—is an unappealing fact, that the desert dominates almost two-thirds of the West, and one-third of the entire United States.[2] Most Americans have tended to view deserts unsympathetically. Even our language reflects some of the aversions that we feel. We speak of arid, semi-arid, and sub-humid lands to describe relative degrees of dryness.

But the desert will not wilt away, despite our aversions. Technology and human ingenuity may modify it, may tame it, may make it more amenable—but it will not fade. Having existed for millions of years, it seems to possess a peculiar sense of timelessness and vastness. If it does not always overpower its human conquerors, nevertheless it often affects them in a thousand different ways. The well-known literary critic Edmund Wilson once noted, after a visit to the West, that visitors from the East feel a strange sense of unreality toward the West that seems to make human existence appear hollow. For in the West everything seems to be out in the open, instead of being underground, as in the older and more densely populated areas. Wilson thought that climate and landscape combined to convey such strange feelings. The empty sun, the rare torrential rains, the dry mountains, and the vast voids of landscape, the hypnotic rhythms of day and night that revolve with unblurred uniformity —undoubtedly these left an emotional and psychological impact on the human beings who poured into these great open spaces.[3]

The Dry West (Montana, Wyoming, Utah, New Mexico, West Texas, Nevada, Colorado, Arizona) includes eight states whose average annual rainfall is 12 inches or less. If these states were relatively poor, if their populations were generally sparse, their economies underdeveloped, and their cultural life restricted, this was in part because of the nature of their geographical environment. This is not to say that cultural factors did not also operate to shape their unique characteristics. But from the beginning physical influences channeled selective patterns of migration and continued to affect settlers after they arrived. Aridity of the environment continued to influence them even in the midst of the sophisticated technology of the twentieth century. Just because physical obstacles to growth presented by desert environments in the past were important does not imply that such obstacles might not be conquered in the future.

The Wet West includes the eastern rim states, on one side, and the Pacific Coast, on the other. Kansas, Nebraska, the Dakotas, Oklahoma, and Texas in the east, and California, Oregon, Washington, and Idaho on the west form the boundaries of the Great American Desert. The key to differences between the varied regions of the West was water. In the Wet West annual average precipitation fluctuated between 24 and 30 inches.

In the course of the twentieth century, technology was able to arrange a kind of marriage between the Dry West and the Wet West. Whether by windmill, cloud-seeding, or deep water well, by dry farming, or huge new hydroelectric dams, several generations of westerners utilized technology to bring water to the arid regions. And once the Dry West and the Wet West were joined in a closer union, they begot new offspring, born in part because of greater human controls over water supplies and climates.

This offspring was a new oasis civilization that clustered almost exclusively in towns and cities. Let us designate it as an urban oasis. In the Northeast and Middle West travelers found cities as well as genuine rural areas dotted by farms and countryside in which human and animal life were plainly visible, but a different aspect faced them in the West. There they could see few rural areas to speak of. Instead, they were confronted with vast empty stretches, dominated by plains, deserts, and mountains, often devoid of human habitation. The only vestiges of life could be found in towns and cities that served as oases—centers of human activity in the midst of the seemingly endless sea of nothingness.

And so the American West in the twentieth century came to be primarily an urban civilization whose foundation was based on the expansion of its oases, which were also its major population centers. Most of the great western cities—Los Angeles, San Francisco, Portland, Seattle, Phoenix, Denver, Salt Lake City, and Houston—or scores of smaller cities like Rapid City, Tucson, Albuquerque, and El Paso have been located near a river or some other body of water, constituting oases for a large part of the territory around them.[4] The American West of the twentieth century was an urban West in which more than two-thirds of its inhabitants were urban dwellers, with some exception in Montana, Wyoming, and Idaho.

So the peculiar environment west of the Mississippi River blended with the complexities of American culture as it had developed by 1898 to create a new derivative civilization—the American West of the twentieth century. This civilization was not primarily a frontier society. Born of a highly complex industrial and urban United States, the modern West was rarely rural. Indeed, its urban aspect was one of its prime characteristics, for the cities set among its vast distances, its plains and mountains, were the centers of its life. This was the urban oasis, a new civilization that was to exercise an increasingly important influence on almost every aspect of American life in the twentieth century.

In the course of the twentieth century, the development of the West passed through at least two stages. Between 1898 and 1941 the relationship of the West to the East was not unlike that of a young colony and its mother country. That arrangement did not wholly cease by the time of World War II but the conflict helped to transform the West so that in the succeeding three decades the region became a pacesetter for the nation.

During much of the first half of the twentieth century the American West constituted a colonial society in its relationship to the older areas of the United States east of the 98th meridian. As an underdeveloped region, it was largely dependent on the eastern regions for virtually every aspect of its development.[5] The East was where a majority of new potential settlers could be found; where western farmers and manufacturers could find immediate markets and where they could secure the many manufactured goods they needed to exploit the resources of their new land; where established cultural values and institutions could be secured and transplanted; and where many of the sources of political power lay that would help to facilitate rapid development of their region. This heavy dependence of the West on the East also cultivated a state of mind among westerners, a psychological outlook that had many of the earmarks of a love-hate relationship. On the one hand, most westerners were clearly aware of their dependence; on the other, they frequently resented it and sought to assert more independence. In many aspects, they exhibited typical characteristics of colonials. And like Americans in 1776, westerners between 1898 and 1941 strove continuously for more independence, a goal toward which they had moved closer on the eve of World War II.

With the advent of World War II westerners gradually accustomed themselves to a new role—pacesetters for the rest of the nation. The war accelerated change everywhere in the United States, and in few regions more so than in the West. The area was virtually transformed by the conflict. To be sure, perhaps the liberation was not yet complete. But the changed role of the American West in the three decades after 1941 revealed the extent of the transformation. Instead of being an imitator, a follower of the East, the West had become a pacesetter for American society, a model that much of the rest of the nation copied slavishly, for social mores and customs as well as for the economy, politics, and manifestations of culture, whether serious or popular. Between 1941 and 1971 it was possible to say that the West today was America tomorrow. Western life reflected characteristics that the rest of the United States was to adopt only a decade or so later. In its successes as well as in its failures, the West had become America's barometer.

And so, let us begin the story of the twentieth-century West. The major theme underlying its development is one of rapid growth—of the cities as well as less populated areas. I ask the reader to explore with me the nature of that growth, how people went West and what life-styles they adopted there, what changes they wrought in exploiting the economy, the problems they reflected in their political behavior, and their efforts to build a distinctive cultural life. In a book so brief we can do no more than to sketch broad themes and trends. But let us hope that this modest prospectus of western history during the twentieth century, by providing a historical context for a wide range of western developments, will provide a useful introduction to the rich heritage of the region.

NOTES

1. Carl O. Sauer, "The Morphology of Landscape," in *Publications in Geography*, II, No. 2 (Berkeley: University of California Press, 1925), p. 53.

2. Walter Prescott Webb, "The American West: A Perpetual Mirage," *Harper's Magazine*, 214 (May, 1957), pp. 25–31. See also Hans Huth, *Nature and the American* (Berkeley: University of California Press, 1957).

3. Edmund Wilson, *The American Jitters: A Year of the Slump* (New York: Charles Scribner's Sons, 1932), especially his comments on Los Angeles, pp. 224–244.

4. An early effort to view the West from an urban perspective came from a group of writers. See Duncan Aikman, ed., *Taming of the Frontier*, Essay Index Reprint Series (New York: Books for Libraries, 1925).

5. This point was persuasively made by Walter Prescott Webb, *Divided We Stand: The Crisis of a Frontierless Democracy* (New York: Farrar & Rinehart, 1937).

PART ONE

The Colonial Society, 1898–1941

1

The West in the Progressive Era, 1898–1941

The opening of the twentieth century saw westerners slowly recovering from the hard times that had characterized most of the Gay Nineties. The pace of western growth had slackened somewhat during that difficult decade and with the return of prosperity westerners resumed their main passion—the rapid development of their as yet sparsely populated region. And so the years between 1898 and 1914 witnessed another major surge of new immigration into the West, but to its towns and cities rather than to its more remote areas. In the cities the new migrants—like true colonials—attempted to reestablish life-styles they had known in their eastern or midwestern homes. But the impact of the western environment altered some of their established ways so that western urban life in the Progressive era already reflected some innovation and novelty. The colonial aspect of the West was also clearly discernible in its economic life. It was still primarily a producer of raw materials for the industrial East. And such ties to the older sections also explain the nature of western politics during these years. Derivative rather than original, westerners followed the progressive reform programs of their eastern cousins. As a relatively new region, however, the West still offered greater opportunities for experimentation than the East and westerners did make some contributions to the cause of reform in the Progressive era. Meanwhile, they were strenuously seeking to develop the cultural life of the region. Depending largely on the culture they had known in their former homes, they nevertheless strove to build a new cultural life west of the Mississippi River. In short, between 1898 and 1914 the West was still a colony of the East, but it was growing rapidly, and beginning to show signs of independence.

Peopling The Western Cities

At the turn of the century the West was on the threshold of another major population boom. More than 8 million newcomers poured across the

11

Mississippi River to people various portions of the region. What was the pattern of this population influx? What were the origins of the new settlers? What kind of people were they? And what life-styles did they develop in their new homes? These questions deserve a closer look.

Patterns of Migration

Most of the new western immigrants during these years tended to come in waves, or cycles. Western migration had doubled in the 1870s, more than tripled in the 1880s, but grew by only 51 per cent in the depression-ridden 1890s. Then, during the first decade of the century, it grew by 147 per cent and then again slowed to 78 per cent between 1910 and 1920. Population increases therefore were not constant, but came fitfully in spurts and cycles. The spurts came approximately once in each decade, the major upsurges approximately every 18 years. The peak year of 1887 did not repeat itself until 1906. Owing to their cyclical nature, western population increases created booms and busts. Thus, many western cities found it difficult to consolidate their population gains or quickly to integrate newcomers into their existing societies because the influx tended to be so rapid. So these surges often created social havoc in particular areas and rapid institutional changes.

The Affluent Migrants

Who were the individuals who came west during the Progressive era? They tended to be very unlike the frontiersmen of the nineteenth century. Two waves in particular were evident. Between 1895 and 1905 wealthy individuals were one prominent group. They were followed sometime about 1905 by another wave of migrants, composed to a considerable degree of affluent middle-class people, many of them comfortably situated in the Middle West, who were seeking retirement havens in the Southwest or on the Pacific Coast.

Collectively, this western migration was very different from the ones that had preceded it. As Charles F. Lummis, the famous contemporary western writer, pointed out, if earlier western pioneers had often been motivated by sheer adventure, these migrants represented a reasoned migration. If the earlier migration was of men, the wave in the Progressive era was one of families. Gold lured the '49ers; climate prompted the exodus of the early twentieth-century settlers. If they were not a heroic migration, they were extremely judicious. They came, not empty handed, but with new capital for investment. They brought not brawn, but brains. Instead of coming in

An urban oasis in the early years of the twentieth century: Phoenix, Arizona. Source: *Arizona Highways.*

prairie schooners, they arrived comfortably on trains. And instead of building shacks or cabins, they moved into elegant hotels, comfortable apartment houses, or built beautiful homes in a variety of styles.

The wealthy migrants who came between 1895 and 1905 had a great deal to offer. If the West grew rapidly during this period it was due in large measure to the influx of so many wealthy and intelligent newcomers. A noteworthy feature of the incoming population, wrote J. P. Widney, an observer in southern California in 1888, was that it was composed almost entirely of the well-to-do—those who brought intelligence and money with them. In addition, many showed above average enterprise, talent, intellect, and culture, and they had a civic vision. Unlike earlier pioneers, who were often farmers, a majority of these individuals came from cities. They came from stores, counting houses, shops, and offices in eastern states. They brought religious values with them, a belief in temperance and education, and they yearned passionately for the refinements of civilized life.

Many of these "Boosters," as they were called, also brought cunning, shrewdness, and calculation to the West. They became successful promoters, real estate agents, and developers. They were go-getters who built their expansionist plans wherever they happened to settle. They gave western society much of its forward thrust during this period. In California Henry L. Huntington, the streetcar magnate; John D. and Rudolph Spreckels, of the "Sugar King" family; and E. L. Doheny, the oil tycoon, were representative of this group, as were the Smiley Brothers in Riverside. Similar personalities could be found elsewhere in the West, such as the

Evans family in Denver, for example, or the Ilfelds of New Mexico. Such people, as we have mentioned, came west in Pullman cars, not covered wagons, and in larger numbers than earlier settlers. And since the railroad companies largely had stepped aside as colonizing and promotion agents by 1890, this new generation of Boosters undertook even more aggressive and systematic promotion campaigns to develop their new homeland. Chambers of commerce became major spokesmen for business leaders of western communities, enthusiastic agents who propagandized the nation in their penchant for further western growth.

After 1905 the nature of westward settlement changed appreciably as it came to be dominated by the migration of more elderly people. In the years between 1905 and 1915 a large proportion of new western settlers was composed of well-to-do middle-aged or older retired middle-class people, mostly from the Middle West. They came not to boost, but to retire, not to strive, but to relax and to enjoy their new life of leisure. Some were health seekers, tuberculars or asthmatics who came west to regain their vigor. Arriving in large numbers, they gave a new character to the communities to which they were drawn. In fact, some communities, such as Long Beach, California, Seattle, and Tucson, were inundated by them. Their presence was reflected in a variety of ways. These cities tended to emphasize the development of hospitals and medical facilities, for example. It has been pointed out also that in southern California the prevalence of pet establishments and pet cemeteries was another reflection of the influx of the aged, for childless couples tend to keep domestic animals. The typical westerner of these years was therefore not riding on his horse heading for a roundup; he was likely to be boarding a trolley car on his way to the nearest pet shop.

The census returns also revealed a great deal about the changing origins of western settlers during this period. During the last three decades of the nineteenth century a large number of new westerners had come from the New England states as well as from New York. The sturdy sons and daughters of Maine and Massachusetts, especially, became the makers of much western history during these years. The founder of California's citrus industry, for example, C. C. Teague, was born in Maine. But after 1900 New England's contribution to the stream of western settlement declined. In the years between 1900 and 1914 middle-western states became a major source. By 1910 Illinois, Ohio, Missouri, and Iowa contributed the bulk of new western settlers, although significant numbers arrived from New York and Pennsylvania. Thus, the origins of western settlers shifted steadily westward during these years, presaging a trend that was to be dominant throughout much of the twentieth century.

Iowa became one of the major jumping-off places for new migrants, of course, resuming the role Council Bluffs had played in the early nineteenth

A western entrepreneur in the early twentieth century: Charles Ilfeld of
New Mexico. Source: Charles Ilfeld Company.

A western business tycoon:
Claus Spreckels. Source:
Denver Public Library,
Western History Depart-
ment.

century. By the turn of the century most of the good cheap lands of Iowa were gone. It was then that rural population growth there began to decline. To a large extent, farm prosperity was also responsible for the Iowa migration. Many Iowans earned large profits from the enormous increase in land prices during the preceding three decades. As rail transportation placed the entire West within reach of Iowans, they cast their eyes westward and became peculiarly susceptible to the propaganda spread nationwide by the California Boosters. As Carey McWilliams once asked, if you look west of Iowa what do you see? Arid plains, mountains, inter-mountain deserts, and still more mountains. Some Iowans tried their hand at farming in Kansas, and Colorado; but the majority moved on to southern California and the West Coast, where fertile lands such as they had known in Iowa were beckoning and where climate promised a retirement haven for the elderly. With some justice, Iowa newspapers by 1914 were referring to southern California as New Iowa.[1] By 1930, one-third of the persons who had lived in Iowa in 1900 were living in some other state, and the vast majority of these had moved into the trans-Mississippi West.

Although white Anglo-Saxon immigrants constituted a majority of newcomers to the West during the Progressive era, there was also a continuing flow of minorities, including at least 80,000 Japanese. The remarkable success of the Japanese and their adaptability quickly resulted in a nativist reaction against them—as dramatized by the efforts of the San Francisco school board in 1906 to segregate Oriental children. More than 10,000 Filipinos also came to the Pacific Coast during this period, since American annexation of their homeland permitted them free entry. From India came as many as 10,000 laborers, who tilled many of California's large corporate farms, while bearing the brunt of intensive prejudice against them. As yet black Americans did not join the great westward trek in any appreciable number. Fewer than 20,000 moved into the trans-Mississippi West during this era. As for Mexican newcomers, their great migrations also still lay in the future.[2] Nevertheless, the great diversity of peoples who came west in the Progressive era laid the foundations for a multiracial and multiethnic rather than a homogeneous society.

Western Life-Styles in the Progressive Era

The influx of older citizens from the Middle West between 1898 and 1914 helped to change the life-styles of the region. Many western cities during these years took on a decided middle-western look. Emphasizing the conservative values of their Protestant founders, they stressed abstinence, church attendance, frugality, neighborliness, and conformity. Certainly this was true of Los Angeles, Portland, Seattle, Denver, Salt Lake City, and

Albuquerque. That veteran California observer, Carey McWilliams, felt that a glacial dullness engulfed southern California between 1898 and 1914, after middle westerners had arrived in droves. By 1896 the city fathers of Los Angeles closed the gambling houses, and ten years later restricted the number of saloons to 200. Clergymen in southern California boasted that Los Angeles had more churches than any comparable city in the United States. A caustic contemporary critic (Willard H. Wright in the *The Smart Set*) complained in early 1913 that the character of Los Angeles was being formed by the

> rural pietist obsessed with the spirit of village fellowship, of suburban respectability. . . . You will look in vain for the flashing eye, the painted cheek, the silken ankle. The city's lights go out at twelve, and so does the drummer's hope. And there is a good old medieval superstition afloat in Los Angeles that all those things which charm by their grace and beauty are wiles of the devil, and that only those things are decent which are depressing. Hence the recent illumination and guarding of all public parks lest spooning, that lewd pastime, become prevalent. Hence the Quakerish regulation of the public dance halls. Hence a stupid censorship so incredibly puerile that even Boston will have to take second place.

This development, he went on, was due to the middle-western migration, to inhabitants

> from the smaller cities of the Middle West, "leading citizens" from Wichita; honorary pallbearers from Emmetsburg: Good Templars from Sedalia, honest spinsters from Grundy Center—all commonplace people, many of them with small competencies made from the sale of farm lands or from the life-long-savings of small mercantile business. These good folks brought with them a complete stock of rural beliefs, pieties, superstitions and habits—the Middle West bed hours,. . . the church bells, *Munsey's* magazine, union suits, and missionary societies. They brought also a complacent and intransigent aversion to late dinners, malt liquor, grand opera and hussies. They still retain memories of the milk can, the newmown hay, the Chautauqua lecturers. . . . There are other evidences in Los Angeles of the village spirit. There is her large and inextinguishable army of quid-nuncs. Everyone is interested in everyone else. Snooping is the popular pastime, gossiping the popular practice. Privacy is impossible. This village democracy naturally invades the social life of Los Angeles.[3]

The middle-western migrants also affected the physical aspect of western cities by giving them a squat appearance and a somewhat flattened-out form in various neighborhoods. A visitor during these years to Seattle, Portland,

and Los Angeles, to Phoenix, Tucson, Albuquerque, Denver, and Salt Lake City, as well as scores of smaller towns and cities, would see the pattern repeated again and again. Middle-western settlers were interested not in building a cosmopolitan city such as San Francisco, but in a series of connecting villages or communities. They wanted homes, not tenements, houses, not apartment buildings. Indeed, a city like Seattle had virtually no apartment buildings until World War II. Homes meant villages or villagelike neighborhoods. Thus, the grouping of houses as well as land use in most western towns and cities during these years was determined not so much by industrial conditions as by the home-owning impulse of a vast majority of newcomers. They built mammoth villages and undertook the suburbanization of the West. Few realized at this time that this western pattern would engulf the entire nation in the years after World War II. In the Progressive era, and indeed, until World War II, San Francisco alone among western cities remained one of the great cosmopolitan urban centers of the nation.

As in the nineteenth century, western society during the Progressive era was in a condition of great flux. Large waves of newcomers engulfed most western cities, bringing with them new talent, new capital, and new cultural backgrounds. While seeking to adapt to the life-styles that they found, these newcomers also left their own imprint. And so, much of the West during the Progressive era gave the appearance of being the Middle West transplanted—in its people, its cities, and its manners. Only the growing number of racial and ethnic minorities served as a reminder that, after all, this was not really the Middle West or the South, or New England, or even a conglomerate of these regions, but a distinct society emerging with unique traits all its own.

The Colonial Economy

The influx of new settlers sparked a decade and a half of rapid western economic growth. It was during these years that the region's transportation network was rapidly expanded, it became the major source of raw materials for the industrialized east, and westerners developed some infant industries of their own and began to lay the groundwork for economic independence. Clearly, the West was an economic colony of the East. But in the midst of the frenzied pace of the national economic growth during this period, the West made many gains of its own.

Developing a Transportation Grid

The key to much of the economic development that took place in the West between 1898 and 1914 was the development of transportation.[4] Just as a spider spins a web, so westerners fostered the expansion of railroads, roads and highways, and new harbors, and agitated for the completion of the Panama Canal. Such arteries of transportation drew the West together while extending its contacts with the East, and the outside world.

Until 1914 railroads were still the major instrument for economic development of the region. By 1914 at least one-third of all the railroad mileage in the West had been built in the twentieth century. It was then that the Santa Fe, the Denver and Rio Grande, the Union Pacific, the Northern Pacific, and the Great Northern finally completed many of their lines. Only after the turn of the century was the Western Pacific extended from San Francisco to Salt Lake City. The railroads did more than bring people to the West, however; they also stimulated the region's economic growth. Especially significant was the development of refrigerator car service by the Santa Fe, Union Pacific, and Southern Pacific railroads, which carried fruits and vegetables from the West Coast to eastern urban centers. The Santa Fe also carried large tonnages of mineral ores eastward for processing. So important had the export of California fruits and vegetables eastward become in 1906 that both the Union Pacific and the Southern Pacific railroads pooled their resources to organize the Pacific Fruit Express, a joint fleet of refrigerator cars that carried the bulk of the Pacific produce eastward. By 1910 this company was already responsible for expediting more than 40,000 cars annually. More than any other means of transportation during this period, the railroads brought the West close to profitable markets.

Panama-California Exposition, San Diego, 1915, showing Spanish-colonial architectural styles. Source: Title Insurance and Trust Company, San Diego.

The railroads also lessened the isolation—physical and mental—of many westerners. Before the proliferation of railway lines in 1900, westerners outside urban centers usually made only one or two yearly trips to a general store in the nearest town or city. There they would purchase goods in large quantities, often from a limited selection. But as the railroads introduced a greater variety of goods, shopkeepers established a larger number of specialty stores in towns and cities that served as points of distribution. This development, in addition to increasing ease of transportation, led ranchers to make more frequent trips to town, bringing them into closer contact with urban life there. For to the cities the railroads brought newspapers and magazines—from the East, and from every corner of the world—acquainting westerners with life in New York, London, Paris, or perhaps Denver and San Francisco. The urban impact on the West was extended in 1912 when Congress authorized parcel post service, which stimulated the mail order business and brought the newest fashions from New York to even the most isolated ranch in no time.

To no one's surprise, the extension of railroads stimulated increasing demands for better roads and highways to connect city and country, and to serve as feeders for the railroads. Westerners, in view of the vastness of their physical surroundings, became especially avid supporters of the good roads movement of this era. In 1900 many railroads, such as the Southern Pacific in California, supported the good roads crusade, as did many farm organizations. By 1910 they found powerful support from chambers of commerce and new organizations formed by automobile drivers in the West. Car owners in California formed the California State Automobile Association in 1900, and the Automobile Club of Southern California, and in the ensuing decade these became prototypes for similar organizations in most western states. Aware of the economic potentials of greater automobile travel, the powerful individuals who led these new associations persuaded the California legislature in 1909 to authorize bond issues for constructing a systematic paved state highway system. By 1914 almost every western state legislature had taken a similar step. Meanwhile, private businessmen took the initiative to stimulate transcontinental travel by car. In 1912 they organized the Lincoln Highway Association, whose prime goal was to secure the building of a graveled, all-weather, coast-to-coast highway stretching from New York City to San Francisco. Automobile clubs throughout the West, chambers of commerce, and automobile dealers along the route contributed financial support for the project. The highway followed the old Overland Trail out of Council Bluffs, Iowa, across Nebraska to Laramie, Wyoming, on to Salt Lake City, across Nevada to Reno, and across the Sierras into San Francisco. By 1915 sufficient portions of the highway—at best a euphemism at the time—had been completed so that a five-car cavalcade could wend its way tortuously from New York to the San Francisco

Panama Pacific International Exposition, in the midst of considerable fanfare. But Los Angeles merchants protested their exclusion so noisily that the Association hastily authorized an alternate route from Ely, Nevada, into Los Angeles. The whole experiment was far more successful than some of its promoters had dared to dream, for it inaugurated the era of long-distance auto travel in the West and heralded a new period in western development.

Meanwhile, the surge of population into the West during these years also resulted in a significant expansion of its harbors. Between 1900 and 1914 San Francisco was still the Queen of the Pacific, dominating trade with Hawaii, Japan, and China. But many newer harbors were effectively vying for trade as the entire West began looking out upon the world. Seattle became the most serious challenger, and soon began to dominate commerce with Alaska, to funnel Pacific Northwest grain and fish exports, and to secure a portion of the China traffic. Further south, Los Angeles in 1900 had just completed construction of its new port at San Pedro, which was designed to challenge the commercial primacy of its larger neighbors to the north. Within a decade San Pedro had become California's major outlet for oil exports. Smaller ports, such as San Diego and Monterey, served the fishing industry. The West's major inland harbor was at Stockton on the Sacramento River, which served as an important distribution point.

But perhaps the most significant development in western transportation—in the eyes of many westerners—was the opening of the Panama Canal. This event signaled the real end of the frontier in the West, a genuine coming of age. The canal, westerners hoped, would inaugurate a new era of economic self-sufficiency, would bring an end to the colonialism

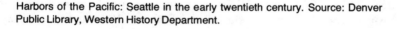

Harbors of the Pacific: Seattle in the early twentieth century. Source: Denver Public Library, Western History Department.

under which they had chafed so long by bringing the West into direct contact with the Far East, with Latin America, with the eastern United States, and with Europe. As railroads had brought the West closer into the mainstream of American life in the nineteenth century, so the Panama Canal would bring them into close touch with the world in the twentieth. At least such were the hopes of countless westerners in 1914.

And they reflected their hopes in the resplendent expositions with which they heralded the great event. Most impressive were San Diego's Panama Exposition of 1915 and San Francisco's spectacular Panama Pacific International Exposition the following year, where pavilions were erected representing not only the Pacific Coast region but the Mountain states and the Southwest. Whatever their immediate merit, these expositions also had a symbolic function. They crystallized the hopes and dreams of millions of westerners, and foreshadowed a new stage in the economic development of the region.

The expansion of transportation, therefore, was an important aspect of western economic growth, for without it the region had few hopes of shedding its colonial status. Transportation was the key to greater economic maturity, and between 1900 and 1914 westerners used it well in undertaking a significant expansion of the region's economic life.

Farmers, Cattlemen, and the Fisheries

Western raw materials producers were especially active in seeking better transportation, for they hoped that it would result in the immediate expansion of their markets.

Already by 1900 western agriculture was highly commercialized. Wherever a traveler looked in the West, whether in Washington, Oregon, or California, in Idaho, Utah, Colorado, or Arizona, whether he visited vast cattle ranges in Wyoming, Nevada, New Mexico, Texas, and Montana, or gazed on the vast plains of Kansas and Nebraska—although topography and climate varied greatly everywhere, the nature of western agriculture was the same—primarily commercial. Most westerners produced for markets rather than for their own use. And the diversity of western farming was perhaps unequaled elsewhere in the nation. The Pacific Coast was becoming the fruit basket of America, producing an astonishing array of peaches and pears, berries and cherries, apples, oranges, and grapefruits. Its incredible production of vegetables for the nation's cities was also just beginning in these years. At the same time Colorado, Utah, Idaho, and California were becoming the nation's largest beet sugar producers. In addition the West was contributing one-half of the country's cattle and sheep. No less significant was the area's substantial grain production, including wheat, corn, and barley. By 1914 the West clearly had become the food purveyor of industrial America.

If westerners were able to make a garden of the region once known as the Great American Desert, it was largely owing to their ingenuity in applying technology to modify their new environment. Of course, they had already begun in the nineteenth century to adapt tractors, combines, automatic milking machines, and countless other tools to the particular western environments in order to facilitate large-scale production, a process they continued in the twentieth century. But perhaps their most significant adaptation during these years was irrigation, which made the deserts bloom. Where there was water there were profits. Farmers on the Pacific Coast had the highest per capita returns in the nation, followed closely by producers utilizing irrigation in the Mountain states and the Red River Valley of the Dakotas. Irrigated lands also made possible highly efficient modes of production, especially for fruits and vegetables, increasingly in demand by the teeming populations of the nation's towns and cities. Technological efficiency made western farmers the most productive in the nation.

In every section of the West farmers were busily engaged between 1900 and 1914 in boosting their production. In California farmers were making the Central and Imperial valleys into America's hothouses by demonstrating the possibilities of year-round production, and of extensive citrus culture. In the Pacific Northwest they were in the midst of replacing extensive wheat farming with more intensive forms of fruit culture, and with developing profitable dairy and ranching enterprises. The dry states of the Mountain West were not so fruitful, but even there irrigated oases in Arizona, Colorado, Utah, and Idaho stimulated the growth of small towns and cities. The Plains states continued to serve as a breadbasket, suited as they were for wheat and corn. As for the semi-arid stretches of Wyoming, Montana, Texas, New Mexico, and Arizona, they seemed peculiarly suitable for cattle grazing.

The Progressive era witnessed the emergence of California as the nation's leading agricultural producer.[5] Here the marriage between technology and farming was closer than anywhere else. California's great valleys and varieties of climates made it peculiarly susceptible to economic exploitation by a people who understood the skillful application of technology to extract much of its hidden wealth. By 1914 the value of California's agricultural production already exceeded $100 million, the result of the most mechanized agricultural practices in the world. Here were few family-size farms; instead, giant ranches owned by corporations were characteristic, typified by the Hotchkiss Ranch in the San Joaquin Valley, or the fruit ranch of the DiGiorgios in Sonoma. Here were vast irrigation works, complicated machinery, and rows and rows of warehouses, all requiring large capital investments. These years saw the further expansion of what Carey

McWilliams has aptly termed "factories in the fields," large, highly rationalized corporate farms relying on intricate machinery as well as on a corps of cheap migratory laborers.

This high degree of specialization gave the state a curious aspect. Visitors found an unfamiliar landscape—vast stretches of irrigated and intensively cultivated lands with few human beings in sight. Nor could they see many signs of settled communities such as schools, churches, or neatly painted homes, as in the Middle West. Here and there one might spy a group of barracks, a bunkhouse, or a dilapidated decommissioned railroad freight car that served as home for migratory workers who tilled the fields. But the richness of the land and the poverty of some of its inhabitants made for a stark contrast.

Newcomers to California marveled at the agricultural miracle. By World War I California had become the nation's largest citrus producer. The oranges and lemons of southern California—nationally advertised under the *Sunkist* label by the California Fruit Growers Exchange—found ready new markets in urban centers everywhere. California farms also became major purveyors of vegetables to the nation. On the foundations laid by Ágoston Haraszthy during the Civil War period many Italian-American immigrants made the state a leading wine producer. At the same time, shrewd Armenian immigrants in the Fresno area made that part of the state America's raisin capital. And enterprising newcomers from the American South were already exploiting its capacities for cotton culture, destined to become a major crop in later years. In the entire United States there was not a single state that could match California in the variety or quantity of its agricultural production.

Specialized farming was also becoming characteristic of the Pacific Northwest during the Progressive era, prompted by mechanization and improved transportation facilities. This region contained some of the nation's most prosperous farms. In 1910 wheat and cereals still accounted for one-half of the Pacific Northwest's farm production. The wheat barons of Walla Walla, Palouse, and Adams counties in Washington owned estates covering thousands of acres. Washingtonians shipped much of their wheat directly to Liverpool via Pacific Coast ports, although some of it was milled in Portland or Tacoma for export to Alaska and the Orient. Increasingly important, however, was fruit, which small farmers grew in the river valleys of Oregon and Washington. Hardly less significant were the efforts of apple ranchers in the Yakima country, who increased their production tenfold between 1890 and 1914. By then Washington had become the nation's leading apple producer. And Puyallup County in Oregon had become the major berry exporter in the nation. The Pacific Northwest was also emerging as a major vegetable producer. Irrigated farms reached new production records between 1898 and 1914, finding ready markets in the East as well as in the region's own growing towns. Taking advantage of favorable soil conditions, farmers in southern Idaho increasingly specialized in potatoes, in addition to sugar beets and hops. And soon after the turn of the century enterprising horticulturists such as Charles Lilly in the Puget Sound region began producing bulbs and flower seeds that found national and worldwide markets.[6]

In the more arid regions of the Rocky Mountains, the Southwest, and the Plains, agriculture was far less significant, amounting to less than 10 per cent of total national production. Where there was water, however, farmers were usually not far off. One could find irrigated oases in southern Arizona, northern and central Utah, southeastern Colorado, and portions of Montana. In these areas yields of fruits and vegetables were high, usually supplying regional urban market areas. Beet-sugar producers were an exception, since they supplied the bulk of national production. This region was home also to thousands of marginal self-sufficient farmers, often living in poverty in the small Spanish-American towns of New Mexico and Arizona, on the Indian reservations of the Southwest, and among the once ambitious homesteaders in West Texas. Profitable farming was possible in some areas of the arid regions, but it was a risky and often heartbreaking business.[7]

It was to help farmers in the more arid regions that Senator Francis Newlands of Nevada after 1900 urged federal assistance. Year after year he reiterated his demand, which was also taken up by the National Irrigation Congress, a potent pressure group composed of interested westerners. In 1900 both the Democratic and Republic national platforms contained demands for federal aid to persons seeking to reclaim and irrigate dry lands. President Theodore Roosevelt quickly sensed the popularity of this issue in the West and prodded Congress into action. The result was the Newlands Act of 1902, which created a new reclamation fund established from the income secured by the sale of federal lands west of the 100th meridian. The act provided loans for private individuals who undertook reclamation. In the ensuing dozen years the U.S. Reclamation Service in the Department of the Interior, which administered the program, focused its energies on hundreds of small projects west of the Continental Divide. One of its prize examples was the Uncompahgre Project in southwestern Colorado—the first successful Newlands project in Colorado—which transformed arid desert lands into rich lettuce and onion fields, and later, into lucrative apple orchards.

On the Plains, wheat growers predominated. The vast flatlands of the Dakotas, Kansas, and Nebraska produced more than one-third of all the nation's wheat. Large corporate farms, as in the Red River Valley, often reaped the largest profits. But even the smaller farmers during this period experienced good years, for this was one of the prosperous eras for American farmers in the twentieth century.

Agriculture, then, was the West's major industry during the Progressive era. Altogether, the region west of the 98th meridian produced more than one-half of the nation's food supplies and so played a significant role in the developing specialized national economy that was emerging in America during these years. But westerners still complained about their colonial relationship to the East, and they became impatient and incorrigible boosters of the economic diversification of their region.

Some of their energies were invested in the cattle industry, for every portion of the West contained some semi-arid lands that were not wholly suitable for agriculture. And the growth of towns and cities opened up new markets for cattlemen.[8] Between 1900 and 1914 Americans ate more beef than at any other time in their history, as much as 75 pounds per person yearly. To be sure, the western cattle industry never regained the preeminence it had attained in the decades after the Civil War. Nevertheless, between 1900 and 1914 western cattlemen supplied the nation with about one-half of its beef requirements. Thus, it became an important auxiliary industry in the increasingly diversified western economy.

Despite the romantic image of the cattle industry projected by dime novels and popular magazines during these years, the lives of many western cattle growers were difficult. Fluctuating prices, shortage of credit, animal diseases, and harsh weather often made the going hard. Although Americans ate more beef than ever between 1900 and 1910, cattle prices did not reflect the demand. Meanwhile, production costs climbed higher and higher, as did the interest rates charged by many eastern bankers. These were also years of rampant cattle diseases such as tick and hoof and mouth disease. The epidemics of 1902 and 1908 took an especially heavy toll on the western cattle ranges. The influx of cars and trucks added a new dimension to cattle rustling. The twentieth-century cattle thief would pull up to a corral in a shiny truck during the dark of night, load up, and make a quick getaway.

Western cattlemen sought to deal with their major problems by increasing their efficiency and by seeking government aid. The quality of American cattle improved immeasurably prior to World War I largely because of scientific breeding methods and range management. Most of the successful cattle growers abandoned grazing their animals on the open range. Instead, they established ranch farms where they fed animals sorghum grains and other scientifically developed feeds, which soon replaced corn as the main crop in the semi-arid regions. They also did much to improve their breeds. Herefords came to dominate the Great Plains. At the Saint Louis Exposition of 1904 Carl Hagenbeck, a German breeder, exhibited sacred Brahman cattle from India, a breed soon widely adopted by Texans. In fact, in 1906 President Theodore Roosevelt personally intervened to allow O. P. Borden (of the Borden Milk Company) to import more Brahman cattle for his herds.

Higher quality usually increased the value of the animals, thus allowing many cattle growers to profit despite sagging prices.

Increasingly, western cattlemen turned to Washington for help. It was largely at the behest of the National Cattlemen's Association that in 1901 the U.S. Department of Agriculture established the Division of Animal Husbandry, primarily to aid the cattle industry. In ensuing years it established rigorous quarantines that helped cattlemen control epidemics. At the same time it encouraged the introduction of new breeds and new breeding methods. It was less successful in establishing new grazing policies, which the National Cattlemen's Association demanded in 1900. The Association hoped that Congress would permit the leasing of the shrinking public domain to cattle growers. But until passage of the Taylor Grazing Act in 1934 Congress was unresponsive to this demand, so many a western cattleman continued to graze animals on federal lands, without express permission yet virtually free of any federal presence.

In a sense, the importance of the cattle industry on the Great Plains was matched by the emergence of a major fishing industry on the Pacific Coast.[9] After 1900, as the population increase in the trans-Mississippi West created new markets, the western fisheries were more fully exploited, not only by New England Yankees, but by colonies of Portuguese, Greeks, and Italians in California, and Chinese and Japanese up and down the coast from Alaska to Lower California. Although the Pacific fisheries were responsible for a catch as varied as any in the world, intensive commercial exploitation centered on salmon and halibut in Alaska and the Pacific Northwest, and on tuna off California.

If urbanization gave a decided boost to the fishing industry on the Pacific Coast, western cities also played a major role in its development. It was there that the capital could be found for this increasingly mechanized new industry. As Boston, Salem, and New York had once dominated the Atlantic fisheries, so between 1898 and 1914 Los Angeles, San Francisco, Seattle, and Anchorage became the major centers of the western fishing industry.

In the Pacific Northwest the salmon fisheries became the basis of the new industry. The main grounds were the waters off Alaska, the coasts of British Columbia and Washington, and Puget Sound. The ocean waters, as well as the mouths of many rivers such as the Columbia and the Fraser, yielded a variety of salmon. Although considerable amounts of salmon were sold fresh in western cities, and some was salted, smoked, or frozen, the bulk of the catch was canned. The first decade of the twentieth century witnessed an extraordinary growth in canneries in the Pacific Northwest and Alaska. By 1914 Alaska had already become the major source of the world's salmon, followed closely by Washington and Oregon.

If not so lucrative as salmon, Pacific halibut nevertheless became a major element in the western fishing industry during the Progressive era. Whether fresh or frozen, halibut has long been considered one of the world's tastiest fish and the demand for it was lively. Halibut fishing in the Pacific was begun in earnest by a group of New England fishermen in Washington, north of Cape Flattery, in 1888. The major transcontinental railroads were just then completing their main lines, thus bringing eastern market centers within the reach of westerners. At first Bostonians and other easterners turned up their noses at Pacific halibut and refused to buy them. But as the Atlantic halibut fisheries became increasingly exhausted by 1900—and as urban growth and immigration created increased demands—Pacific halibut secured a hold in eastern markets. Western fishermen mechanized far more than their eastern counterparts, and extended their operations more than 2,000 miles to the distant fishing banks off Alaska. By 1914 their yearly catch exceeded 50 million pounds, making the Pacific halibut industry the largest in the world. Seattle emerged as the major center, although smaller towns in the Pacific Northwest, as well as Prince Rupert in British Columbia and some Alaskan towns, also built extensive processing facilities.

In the eighteenth and nineteenth centuries fishermen out of California sought the sea otter and the whale. Now, in the early years of the twentieth century they roamed the California coast and the Pacific for the ubiquitous albacore, or tuna. To be sure, California's salmon fisheries on the Sacramento River continued to be important until about 1910. But increasingly during this period the tuna fish became the major catch. Portuguese and Japanese fishermen in southern California became particularly active in expanding the tuna industry and making canned tuna a California staple. Tuna still offered great opportunities for small enterprisers. Each year a large fleet composed of thousands of small inexpensive motor boats, each usually manned by three men, would set out from California ports in search of tuna. Mostly they stayed within about 50 miles of the shore. By 1914 California's tuna grounds extended from the Mexican boundary to Point Concepcion, about 200 miles north of los Angeles. By then California fishermen were bringing in an annual catch of over 200 million pounds, valued at more than $25 million. From what had been a minor economic pursuit in 1900, the Pacific fishing industry in these years developed into a major natural resource industry for the entire West.

Miners and Lumbermen

As westerners mined the sea, so also they mined their forests and their earth. Between 1898 and 1914 the western lumber industry became a major element in the nation's economy and provided many of the raw materials needed for building urban America—East, South, North, and West.

California's forests were vast. In 1900 about 15 per cent of the nation's

Fishing for halibut in the Pacific. Source: Thompson and Freeman, *Pacific Halibut Fishery.*

Hauling logs by train in the Pacific Northwest at the beginning of the twentieth century. Source: University of Washington Library.

total timber stand was in California and by 1900 lumbering had become a prime source of income for the state. As population growth stimulated widespread construction, the state's timber producers began cutting more than 2 billion board feet annually. Even so, this was inadequate to satisfy California's housing needs, and builders imported vast quantities of lumber from Washington and Oregon. Much of this import was processed by northern California mills (in Siskiyou, Lassen, and Butte counties). Humboldt and Mendocino counties produced almost all the redwood processed in the United States.

Lumbering was the major industry in the Pacific Northwest next to farming. The economies of most towns and cities depended on it. In 1914 lumbering accounted for 38 per cent of the value of all manufactures, and for 55 per cent of all payrolls. As population expansion stimulated a building boom throughout the West, new markets for timber and timber products appeared. By 1900 the forests of the East and Middle West had been largely exhausted, and those in the South and the West assumed a new national importance. In fact, many lumber operators from the Middle West migrated to the Pacific Coast during these years. Typical were Ben Healy of Wisconsin, Alfred H. Anderson, and Chauncey W. Griggs, who did much to develop the lumber industry of the Pacific Northwest. But the giant among them all was Frederick Weyerhaeuser from Minneapolis. In 1900 he bought 900,000 acres of timber from the Northern Pacific Railroad. Thirteen years later he owned 26 per cent of all timberlands in the state of Washington, and almost 20 per cent of those in Oregon. The Northern Pacific Railroad itself counted 30 per cent of all timberlands in Montana within its own holdings. Such purchases resulted in rampant speculation in timberlands between 1898 and 1914, not only by the large owners in the region, but by more than 20,000 small operators in the area.

The influx of new lumbermen into the Pacific Northwest triggered a surge in production. Washington became the leading lumber-producing state in the nation by 1914, almost doubling its output of 3 billion board feet in 1902 within a decade. Oregon and Idaho tripled their production between 1898 and 1914. Much of this increase was effected through extensive mechanization of production methods, by the introduction of new machinery, and through carefully planned and integrated sawmills. The extension of steam railroads into remote logging camps also helped revolutionize the industry. By 1911 western lumber operators formed the West Coast Lumbermen's Association, which established industry-wide standards and marketing practices, reflecting the increasing maturity of the industry.

The great expansion of lumbering in the Pacific Northwest was dependent to a degree on a steady supply of migratory labor for mills and logging camps. As a result, an active labor movement developed in the region. As early as

1903 lumber mill workers formed the International Shingle Weavers' Union of America, affiliated with the American Federation of Labor. Although it led strikes in 1906 and 1913, the union's influence had declined by World War I because it had failed in its main objective—the unionization of all workers in the industry. More dramatic was the rise of the International Workers of the World (IWW), organized in 1905 as a much more militant union, one that also attracted anarchists and radicals. Committed to class warfare and revolution, its membership in the logging camps did not exceed 3,000 during this period, but its influence was more pervasive than such numbers might suggest. Through strikes, speeches, and industrial sabotage the IWW made itself the most feared and hated labor organization in the West.

While the Pacific Coast supplied the nation with significant amounts of timber, the Mountain states provided it with essential minerals. Nature had endowed the American West with more than 90 per cent of all the metal reserves in the United States. Millions of years ago, during the last Ice Age, much of the continental United States west of the 98th meridian was covered by a thick sheet of ice. And as the great layers of ice subsequently melted, countless minerals were dissolved in the waters of huge lakes left by the retreating ice sheet. During arid periods that followed, the waters evaporated. Desiccation set in to create the arid portions of America, depositing minerals and sediments at the bottom of these erstwhile lakes that were to become the mountains, valleys, and deserts of the West. The bounties of nature enabled western miners in 1914 to produce 90 per cent of the nation's copper, a significant portion of its lead, and most of its gold and silver. Moreover, the West produced a wide variety of ores used as industrial alloys, such as tungsten, molybdenum, vanadium, manganese, zinc, and mercury. New Mexico provided 90 per cent of the nation's potash needs. As yet petroleum was not significant as an energy resource, but it, too, was later found primarily in the West. Mining tended to be an urban industry. Wherever minerals were found, towns and cities sprang up, if not for the processing of raw materials, then for providing services for the thousands who usually flocked to the scene of mining operations.

A mining map of the West during these years would clearly reveal the great diversity and abundance of western ores. Copper—its most important mineral between 1900 and 1914—was produced in Arizona, Utah, Montana, and New Mexico. What gold was still mined in these years came from California, with smaller amounts from Utah, Arizona, Nevada, Colorado, and New Mexico. Silver—often a by-product of other ores—came largely from Utah, with Nevada, Idaho, Colorado, Arizona, California, and New Mexico contributing smaller amounts. As for petroleum, California, Texas, and Oklahoma were proven during these years to contain large and lucrative reserves.[10]

To the western visitor during these years the great open-pit copper mines must have been nothing less than spectacular. One of the largest in the world was the Bingham Copper mine just outside Salt Lake City. Measuring several miles across its east-west rim, it was first developed by the remarkable Guggenheim family between 1903 and 1910. Then it passed into the ownership of the Kennecott Copper Company. Aptly designated "the richest hole on earth," by 1914 it already had produced copper valued at more than $1 billion. In addition, its owners also extracted significant amounts of zinc, gold, silver, and molybdenite. The Bingham Mine was crucial in western development because the new mass-production techniques that its engineers developed during this period were quickly adapted throughout the entire West—indeed, throughout the world. Especially significant was the perfection of open-cut mining methods, which made possible large-scale commercial exploitation of low-grade ores that previously had been unprofitable. It has been said that such a technological breakthrough was hardly less important for the mining industry in the twentieth century than the development of the factory system was for the industrial revolution of the nineteenth century. In mining, as in so many other spheres of the economy, westerners used technology to conquer nature.

The spectacular developments at Bingham were repeated elsewhere in the West, if not quite so dramatically or on so large a scale. In 1910 the Kennecott Copper Company purchased the Santa Rita copper mine in southern New Mexico, which it transformed into one of the great open-pit mining operations in the region. Meanwhile, both Phelps-Dodge and the Anaconda Corporation secured valuable copper mining properties in southern Arizona. Towns like Globe and Bisbee became the new Eldorados of the western world, and Arizona, the nation's major producer of copper. Montana—if not quite so significant a producer as Arizona—was dominated by Anaconda. Although the Guggenheims, who controlled Anaconda, had their general offices in New York City, they were in a sense the real rulers of Montana, guiding (and misguiding) the state's destinies during much of the twentieth century. Perhaps Montana, more so than most western states, exemplified the region's colonial status in its relationship to the industrial East.

If other metals were singly not so important in the western economy, as a group they were significant. After 1900 the annual value of gold mined rarely exceeded $5 million. California produced more than one-half of this amount with Utah, Colorado, and Arizona contributing the rest. Much of this gold was secured as a by-product of lead or copper. Silver was another major product of the western mines, in demand not only for coins, but for dental uses, for the expanding electrical industries, in photography, and for ornamental purposes. Although Utah was a leading producer, new discoveries in Nevada brought back echoes of the glories of the Comstock Lode. Colorado, California, and New Mexico mined smaller amounts. Utah also became the nation's chief lead producer in these years, partly because of the highly sophisticated application of new flotation processes.

The opening of the twentieth century coincided with the emergence of petroleum as one of the leading energy resources of industrial America. Between 1898 and 1914 many new finds were made in California, Texas, and Oklahoma. In California various enterprisers like E. L. Doheny struck it rich in the southern portion of the state, near Los Angeles and in Kern County. The speculative fever accompanying oil exploration affected thousands of hopeful prospectors there during these years. Many were disappointed, especially by President William Howard Taft's executive order of 1909 withdrawing many federally owned California oil lands from immediate exploitation. Even so, the state's petroleum production soared—from 5 million barrels in 1900 to 15 million barrels in 1914. Meanwhile, the Texas oil boom was sparked by the remarkable oil discoveries at Spindletop in 1901, which set off a flurry of exploration in Texas involving thousands of persons and corporations. During these same years the admission of Oklahoma to statehood (1907) resulted in active petroleum drilling in that state, making it a major new source of oil.

Throughout the West, then, the extractive natural resource industries were the very foundation of the economy. Much like any other under-developed area, the West was valuable because of its natural resources. Lacking the population, the capital, and the skill to develop many of these resources itself during the Progressive era, the West became prey to the more highly industrial East, which had the capital, the markets, and the skills needed to use many of the region's natural riches. Thus, there was much justice in the complaint of many westerners that they were in effect a colony of Wall Street, a dependency of the industrial Northeast, which extracted most of the wealth to be had in the West but offered little in return.

Manufacturing and Service Industries

Small wonder, therefore, that a major objective of many westerners in these years was to diversify their economy and to secure greater self-sufficiency. This attitude was especially true of recent immigrants, who aggressively sought to boost the economic potential of their new home. Thus, in the Progressive era westerners strove to expand their manufacturing, their service industries, and their financial institutions. By World War I they had not yet achieved their much desired economic independence, but they had made giant strides toward their goal.

In the years between 1900 and 1914 western manufacturing was still in its infancy. Its total annual value in 1914, for example, was $80 million, less than 5 per cent of the national total. By and large, the West still had to import most of the manufactured goods it needed while shipping large quantities of raw materials to other areas. What manufacturing there was in the West related either to the processing of raw materials or to small-scale diversified manufactures for local markets. Thus its major industries included food and meat processing, lumber milling, sugar refining and flour milling, and also foundries, printing, and a multitude of small-scale operations. Most of the mannfacturing establishments were located in urban centers along the Pacific Coast and in Colorado, Utah, and Texas. Local conditions varied, of course, but in the entire region the number of manufacturing establishments more than doubled in the years between 1900 and 1914 while capital invested more than quadrupled. The growth in manufacturing during these years can be traced partly to the frenzied building of towns and cities in the West, which created new demands for goods and services. Throughout the region, metropolitan centers were replacing the frontier.

After some decline during the depression of the 1890s California's manufacturing industries underwent an impressive revival in the decade after 1900. Doubling the value of their output between 1900 and 1914, California's manufacturers wrought their greatest gains between 1900 and 1909, with the pace slowing somewhat thereafter. They supplied not only the state's own rapidly expanding population with goods, but also much of the population of the Pacific Coast, the Rocky Mountain area, and the Southwest. In 1900 San Francisco was still the major manufacturing center in California and the West. But the earthquake of 1906 seriously damaged San Francisco's primacy. By 1914 many manufacturers had moved across the Bay to Oakland. Meanwhile, Los Angeles was emerging as a major new rival.

California's manufacturing industries were closely tied to processing raw materials and to small-scale fabrication for local markets. The leading source of manufacturing income came from lumber mills, which produced timber, sash, and doors, and similar items needed by builders. Meat-packing plants and the numerous fruit and vegetable canneries added significantly to the state's total income, as did Claus Spreckels' sugar refineries. As for fabricated goods, foundries and printing plants provided the bulk of that type of manufacture.

In the Pacific Northwest the pattern of manufacturing was similar, if on a smaller scale. Here, too, the value of manufactures doubled between 1900 and 1914, and was beginning to exceed that of agricultural products. And, even more than in California, the lumber industry was king. By 1910 the belching smoke of Seattle's numerous lumber mills was giving that city a decided industrial appearance. Similar mills were also found in large numbers in Portland and Tacoma as well as in more isolated areas. Establishments such as the Wheeler-Osgood sash and door factory in Tacoma were among the most modern of their kind in the nation. They also produced furniture, wooden packing boxes, paper, and wood pulp. The region also developed an extensive canning industry, not only for fruits and vegetables, but for fish. Some of the largest eastern meat packers began to establish western branches here during these years, such as the new Swift plant in Portland. The shipbuilding industry operated on a small scale only because it was as yet unable to compete with the older and more established East Coast yards. Thus, most of the ships plying Pacific waters were not built in the West. Nevertheless, by 1910 Washingtonians pointed with pride to Moran's modern shipyard in Seattle, which had secured a federal contract for building the United States battleship *Nebraska*. Visitors would notice various other small manufacturing establishments, including many foundries and printing plants. If the level of manufacturing activities in Pacific Northwest towns was only about one-third that in older eastern cities, this period nevertheless saw very real and rapid growth.

At the beginning of the twentieth century manufacturing was still in its infancy in the Rocky Mountain states, the Southwest, and Texas. Mining and cattle were the major props of the economy. Here and there one could find a small foundry supplying local needs. As elsewhere in the West, most of these small establishments converted raw materials into semi-finished products, and were concerned with processing rather than with fabrication. The most extensive manufacturing in the region was in Denver, Colorado, the home of numerous food-processing establishments. By the turn of the century thick polluted clouds of smog and pollution already evoked an outcry from conservationists. The presence of coal and iron ores in Colorado and Utah led to the establishment of the West's only major steel manufacturing center in Pueblo. There the Colorado Fuel and Iron Company, under the control of the Guggenheims, produced between 1900 and 1914 a significant amount of finished steel, which made Pueblo the Pittsburgh of the Rockies. Otherwise, as Governor Sayers of Texas lamented in 1899, the West sorely lacked facilities for large-scale manufacturing.

Why were westerners so slow in developing manufacturing during these years when they so eagerly desired it? As a region, the West had many handicaps to overcome. Its relatively sparse population meant that large markets were not yet readily available. Moreover, well-established eastern manufacturers provided keen competition, which new western industrialists found hard to meet. Such a situation tended to deter new investments in western manufacturing, especially since exploitation of new natural resources promised much quicker, and larger, profits. In addition, transportation costs were often prohibitive, in part because of the distance of the West from population centers in the East but also to some degree because of discriminatory rate policies of the railroads, usually dominated by eastern financiers. These men were quite content to discourage western manufacturers, not only to prevent competition with better established eastern companies, but to maintain the West as a source of cheap raw materials to supply factories elsewhere.

Why, then, in spite of these obstacles, did westerners succeed between

A western luxury hotel: The Coronado in San Diego, California. Source: Denver Public Library, Western History Department.

A western luxury hotel: The Broadmoor in Colorado Springs, Colorado. Source: Denver Public Library, Western History Department.

1900 and 1914 in expanding their manufacturing activities? In view of the steady westward migration of people, it appeared most unlikely that manufacturing development could long be impeded. The shift of population was bound to stimulate an eventual westward movement of manufacturing, even if time lags did occur. Westerners had to conquer distance, lack of know-how, capital shortages, and eastern discrimination. But the population boom in new cities—the urban oases—in itself generated new forces that began to break down existing obstacles to manufacturing. Increasingly the new settlers created new markets, and also provided an increasingly diverse array of skilled and unskilled labor. The extremely high cost of imported manufactures as well as the long time often required for their delivery also tended to hasten the further development of some forms of manufacturing in the West.

To a greater extent than elsewhere in the nation, service industries in the West assumed an important position in the economy, even early in the century. Included were transportation companies, banks, real estate sales, medicine, law, and entertainment. But perhaps the most distinctive service industry to emerge during these years was tourism. By this time the West was well on its way toward becoming the playground of America.[11]

The reasons for the growth of tourism are not hard to find. Many potential settlers first visited the region as tourists. They liked what they saw, and they stayed. Among affluent Americans an increasingly large number found an outlet for their leisure time in domestic as well as in overseas travel. Before World War I these included many upper-class Americans, and also the new industrial elite. But already a growing number of western tourists were of middle-class backgrounds. Retired eastern shopkeepers or professional men as well as comfortably situated middle-western farmers who retired early because of profits made from land poured westward after 1900. California and the Southwest became their Mecca. Indeed, what other region than the American West could boast such natural wonders as the Grand Canyon in Arizona, Yosemite and Yellowstone, the breathtaking beauty of Mt. Rainier in Washington or Crater Lake in Oregon, the serene mesas of New Mexico, and the majestic Rockies of Colorado? Where else could Americans become acquainted with such a collection of ancient as well as living cultures, including those of the western Indians and the Spanish-Americans? In addition to the scenery, the West offered some of the best, and most healthful, climates in the world. In fact, it was the salubrious weather that brought whole caravans of health seekers, the "wheelchair brigade," to the West, men and women who hoped to regain their physical well being (like Theodore Roosevelt) or who hoped to make their sufferings more endurable. After 1900 thousands and thousands of persons stricken with tuberculosis, respiratory ailments, and other illnesses went west,

A luxury hotel in the West: The Montezuma Hotel (built 1886) in Las Vegas, New Mexico. Source: *New Mexico Magazine.*

to be healed, to recuperate, or just to rest, gazing on scenic wonders in the midst of balmy climes.

Of course, if American tourists from various backgrounds went west during this period it was because of western initiatives in providing improved transportation facilities as well as excellent hotel and resort accommodations. The western railroads published a flood of promotional materials designed to stimulate travel in the West. "Come West and regain your Health," declared a Southern Pacific brochure in 1901. Among new western vacation centers, San Diego, Santa Barbara, Monterey, and Berkeley were popular. Tucson, Denver, Colorado Springs, Albuquerque, and El Paso also developed an active tourist trade. In these new resorts ambitious businessmen built some of the most elegant hotels in the America of that day. This was the luxury era of American hotels, when the standard was set by the world famous Coronado Hotel in San Diego. A year-round resort, it boasted 750 magnificent private rooms, dazzling in their elegance. Its public rooms and halls were exquisitely paneled, its 17 acres of carpets muffled unseemly sounds. About it were vast parks and gardens, some in the style of Versailles, and the hotel provided a railroad spur for those guests who came in their private railroad cars. Thomas Edison himself came to install the electric lighting system, the largest in any western building. Joseph Pulitzer swore that the magnificence of the Coronado could not be matched anywhere in the world. To some degree its splendor was matched by the Del Monte Hotel in Monterey, for as the Southern Pacific told dubious easterners, it provided its guests with "the best means of deriving the highest benefits from the natural charms of California." The Montezuma

Hotel in Las Vegas, New Mexico, was another distinguished Victorian palace in its day. In Colorado Springs the Broadmoor held sway as a distinguished national hostelry for the well-to-do. It was founded as a gambling casino in 1892; its promoters decided by 1907 to convert it into a health resort, and so added a lavish ballroom as well as distinguished dining halls. Other cities tried to compete for the tourist trade, and thus Tucson spawned the Camelback Inn, Denver boasted the Brown Palace, and San Antonio the Menger. Even outside the cities, near particular scenic attractions, westerners built fine hotels during these years. By the turn of the century Yellowstone Park boasted seven hotels, of which the Mammoth Hot Springs was best known.

Western tourism was also facilitated by the Innkeeper of the West, Fred Harvey. Perhaps he was one of the most authentic heroes of the twentieth-century West. An Englishman who came to the United States in 1851, after a varied career as a cook he became aware of the need for good food at reasonable prices at train depots throughout the West. When he discussed his plans for a chain of restaurants along train routes with executives of the Burlington Railroad in 1875 they rejected his proposal. Harvey then presented his ideas to officials of the Santa Fe Railway. They accepted his concept, and the famous "Harvey Houses" were born. After 1886 he began to build a chain of attractive and immaculate restaurants at Santa Fe stops where he served appetizing and moderately priced meals. Moreover, he hired a corps of well-dressed and superbly trained waitresses whom he regarded as civilization's advance guard in the West. Under the supervision of a matron these legendary Harvey Girls provided excellent food service. By 1900 Harvey had developed a system whereby train engineers wired ahead to the next Harvey House. There all was in readiness when the passengers arrived, to their great mystification, for few expected all the accoutrements of civilization in even the most remote wilderness. Harvey Girls soon acquired as exalted a place in the mythology of American womanhood as airline stewardesses of a later age. Many of them married leading citizens of the West and so brought their early training into thousands of the best western homes. Between 1900 and 1914 Harvey took over operation of all dining services on the Santa Fe lines and operated some of its hotels, such as the Alvarado in Abuquerque. He also fostered the construction of the Bright Angel and El Tovar lodges at the Grand Canyon in Arizona in 1904, which his management made into one of the stellar tourist attractions in the United States. More than any other person, Fred Harvey brought good food to the West and pioneered the region's development as one of America's major tourist attractions.[12]

The establishment of national and state parks to display the scenic wonders of the West also augmented the expansion of tourism during this period. To be sure, before the organization of the National Park Service in

1917, national parks were still scattered and largely neglected. Even before World War I, however, Yosemite and Yellowstone parks had already become important tourist attractions. Congress had authorized establishment of the Yellowstone area in 1872 and allowed its superintendent to grant leases to private persons to provide hotels and tourist facilities. After 1885 one of these lessees, W. W. Wylie, became famous for his ten-day tours in the park and the establishment of popular tourist camps in the area. Owing to the persistent lobbying in California of the well-known naturalist John Muir, Congress established Yosemite Park in 1890. The state of California itself built the Stoneman House there, which housed 150 guests. Other tourist camps and facilities were established by lessees. It was Muir's influence, also, that prevailed in congressional creation of Mt. Rainier National Park in 1899 in Washington. President Theodore Roosevelt, as might be expected, was enthusiastic about creation of more national parks and furthered establishment of Crater Lake in Oregon in 1902 and Mesa Verde in Colorado, site of ancient Indian cliff dwellings, in 1906. In addition, in 1906 he persuaded Congress to create national monuments to preserve historical or archaeological ruins, most of which had already been heavily vandalized. They included thousands of cliff dwellings in Colorado, New Mexico, and Arizona, old Spanish missions in California and Arizona, petrified forests, natural bridges, and the like.[13] The preservation of these wonders by national and state governments not only protected a priceless heritage, but contributed significantly toward making the West a major attraction for tourists from everywhere. And in view of its economic development at this period, tourism became an important element in the still young economy of the West.

Perhaps no segment of the western economy—whether the extractive or service industries, manufacturing or transportation—could have developed as rapidly as it did had it not been for the maturation of western banks and financial institutions. It was they who channeled much needed capital into the various growth enterprises. Between 1900 and 1914 the number of banks in the trans-Mississippi West increased more than threefold. Reflecting to some extent their distrust of Wall Street and eastern financiers, westerners tended to favor the formation of state-chartered rather than national banks.

In most areas of the West new banks were one of the most visible manifestations of economic growth. The turn of the century coincided with economic recovery from the serious depression of the 1890s in the West as elsewhere. Not only did most Main Streets contain three times as many banks in 1914 as in 1900, but their resources increased at an even greater rate. The increasing strength of western banks was shown clearly by those in San Francisco after the great earthquake of 1906 when they were able to carry on successfully without many failures. The financial panic of 1907 did affect western banks more severely and led many western state legislatures between 1907 and 1914 to embark on reform of banking regulation in order to strengthen state supervision. This sentiment was reflected in western support of the Federal Reserve Act of 1914, which many western bankers hoped would lessen the centralization of capital in the East. Banking growth was even more striking in the Pacific Northwest, where bank assets grew almost tenfold.

In addition, most western towns and cities boasted trust companies, building and loan associations, and other specialized financial institutions that provided capital for building western cities and all kinds of new enterprises. It would not be accurate to say that the West had achieved financial independence by 1914. But it was rapidly establishing the institutional framework needed to finance its own economic growth without colonial dependence on the East, and on Europe.

So, by 1914 westerners could look back with some satisfaction on a period of constructive economic growth. They had secured an appreciable increase of population that generated the development of a more elaborate transportation system, growth of the extractive industries, and of manufacturing, trades, and finance. To be sure, the West was not yet economically as self-sufficient as many westerners might have desired; its

A western political leader of the Progressive era: Governor Hiram Johnson of California. Source: University of California Library.

colonial status had not been ended. But it had made great strides in attaining a more balanced economy characterized by increasing diversification. Such economic growth was not without its problems, however, some of which were reflected in western politics of these years.

Western Politics in the Progressive Era

Sooner or later the aspirations, hopes, and frustrations that westerners experienced in developing their region were reflected in politics. For they yearned to grow, to throw off their image as a pale reflection of the East, and to build new cities that would provide a model for all America. It is not surprising that they became concerned with what appeared to them as obstacles to the growth they so much desired. Like other Americans, westerners confronted various problems that stemmed from the industrial- ization of America. Three of these came to be of immediate concern. As a colonial or underdeveloped region, they were particularly sensitive to abuses stemming from corporate domination—and monopoly. And they were much concerned with inefficiency as well as corruption in governments at all levels. In the West, more than elsewhere, despite loud protestations of individualism, government had a crucial role to play in the further development of the country.[14]

Political Problems in the West

Wherever one traveled in the West at the turn of the century one could hear widespread complaints about "the company." It mattered not whether one talked to westerners on the Pacific Coast, in the Rocky Mountain states, or in the Southwest. The details might vary, but their concern over the appearance of monopoly was the same. In California it was the Southern Pacific Railroad that was the villain, with its viselike grip (until 1911) on state and local politics. Bill Herrin, its legal counsel after 1880, well fitted the villain's role. In the state of Washington the Great Northern Railroad's J. D. Farrell exercized potent influence among both Republicans and Democrats alike. Even in states barely touched by industrialization the specter of monopoly arose. The Wyoming Stock-Growers' Association exercised an influence over politics in the state rarely equaled by large corporations elsewhere. Major cattle associations also played a powerful role in New Mexico and Colorado. Standard Oil was accused of manipulating Kansas politics in 1910, although the accusations perhaps outweighed realities.

Perhaps the most flagrant example of corporate control over politics occurred in Montana, where the Anaconda Mining Company—the Guggenheims and their Wall Street allies—ruthlessly extended its influence into almost every aspect of the state's politics.

If the Southern Pacific's California machine was not typical of the entire West, neither was it unique. More or less, other large corporations influenced political life in similar ways. Through assiduous use of campaign contributions Herrin exercised considerable control over state legislators, the congressional delegation, and administrators in state government. Businessmen's organizations, such as the San Francisco Chamber of Commerce, often accused the SP of stifling the state's economic development through high rates and blatant discrimination. Reform groups such as the Lincoln-Roosevelt Republican League (which had many imitators in other states between 1907 and 1914) charged the SP with undermining democratic political processes through its undue influence over state and national affairs. No wonder that Hiram Johnson, the progressive Republican gubernatorial candidate in 1910, reiterated his single theme: "Kick the Southern Pacific out of politics." It was a refrain in which millions of Californians joined with enthusiasm.

Throughout the West, between 1900 and 1914, complaints about the extraordinary influence of special economic interest groups were rife. For these special interests, whether business, agriculture, or mining, threatened the nature of the region's growth in every respect. The social structure,

A western Progressive: William S. U'Ren of Oregon. Source: *American Magazine.*

economic development, cultural life, and politics of the region all stood to suffer if the special interests had their way.

In many instances undue influence by special economic interests was reflected in political corruption. It affected state capitals, city governments, and localities. Everywhere in the West state legislators and administrators were susceptible to bribery, graft, and other irregularities. Lincoln Steffens, the famous urban reformer, in his *Autobiography* reported that William Herrin had once told him that "we have to let these little skates get theirs, we have to sit by and see them run riot and take risks that risk our interests, too."

One of the most glaring instances of corruption came to light in San Francisco, where Boss Abe Rueff was the power behind the throne of puppet Mayor Eugene Schmitz (1901–1906), a former band leader. Rueff collected bribes, blackmailed legitimate business establishments by threatening law suits or by direct police harassment, and extorted graft through various protection rackets. Many times Rueff collected his graft under the guise of legal fees. He also forced gambling houses and "French restaurants" (houses of prostitution) to purchase liquor and other special licenses from the city government. Municipal streetcar employees as well as workers for the Pacific Gas and Electric Company were shaken down for political contributions to the Rueff regime. Ironically, Schmitz had been elected as a "reform" candidate to displace the political power of the Southern Pacific Railroad acting in concert with Pacific Gas and Electric. Rueff was ultimately exposed by crusading journalist Fremont Older in 1908 and sent to prison, but the depth of his corruption shook the faith of many westerners in democratic government.[15]

With local variations California's political corruption was reflected elsewhere in the West. Seattle after 1890 was also beset with recurrent political irregularities. There the ruling political bosses also created a close alliance with saloons, brothels, and gambling halls, often supported by local business leaders. Portland, Oregon, faced similar problems. In the election of 1896, for example, strong-armed hoods in the pay of local political bosses actually pulled voters out of line at polling places and pushed paid hirelings into the polling booths to cast votes for the machine. Many of these ruffians had been imported from San Francisco. Nor did the Rocky Mountain states escape. Denver was dominated by a series of corrupt city governments between 1890 and 1910, which forged close alliances with local tramway companies, with the private electric and gas utilities, and with various types of franchised businesses. Open corruption in Denver elections was common, and vote buying or ballot stuffing not at all unusual. And if details varied in many other smaller western towns and cities, the general pattern of corruption in the region was the same.

A third major political problem was the inefficiency of western governments at all levels. This was, as we have mentioned, a period of very rapid population growth and urban development, and existing political institutions often proved inadequate for new challenges, geared as they were to a sparsely populated and more rural society. The growth of western cities during these years triggered a demand for many new services such as water and public utilities, gas, electricity, transportation, and improved sanitation. The urban dwellers of the West also demanded new social and recreational facilities and new hospital and public health services. And with the rush of newcomers also came an increased number of indigents, who placed severe strains on charity and welfare agencies. Life in the Progressive era, therefore, put new demands on governments at every level, demands to which they were often slow to respond.

Perhaps it should be said that the political constituencies in the West between 1900 and 1914 tended to be better educated, more urbane, and more sophisticated than in other regions of the nation. Census statistics reveal that the percentage of professionals and skilled workers tended to be higher in the West than elsewhere, particularly on the Pacific Coast. The West had one of the lowest illiteracy rates in the nation (if states with Indian reservations are excluded). And, as pointed out, a high percentage of new migrants to the West during this period were of middle-class origins with some educational background. Of course, the West had a much smaller number of recently arrived immigrants and ethnic minorities than other regions, and consequently, a relatively homogeneous electorate.

Progressive Reform in Western Cities

The Progressive movement was in part an effort to deal with such problems as corporate domination and governmental corruption and inefficiency. National in scope, it nevertheless grew out of particular local conditions. If the reform impulse did not originate in the West, westerners made important contributions to it. As one of the nation's youngest and most recently settled areas, the West was more prone to undertake political experimentation than older regions. Thus, the reform urge was perhaps strongest on the Pacific Coast, but was also potent in the Rocky Mountain states and the Southwest. In city and state politics, westerners were actively engaged in extensive political, economic, and social reforms of the society they were building.

After 1900, urban reformers rose to prominence in every section of the West. San Francisco boasted a large number, including James D. Phelan and millionaire Adolph Sutro. Seattle's reform mayor after 1910 was Reginald

Thompson, who pushed through a long list of changes. In Denver a succession of reformers such as John A. Rush, J. Warner Mills, and Thomas S. McMurray attempted to deal with pressing issues. In large cities as in small during the Progressive era, reform-minded men in both parties were elected to positions of political prominence and leadership.

These new leaders attempted a variety of political, economic, and social reforms. To eliminate corruption many of them called for home rule (greater self-government) for their cities. Between 1900 and 1914 home rule was adopted almost everywhere in the West—in Los Angeles, San Francisco, Seattle, Denver, El Paso, and in many smaller communities. Some reformers felt that entirely new forms of municipal government were needed. They embraced the "Galveston Plan," involving city rule by a commission rather than by a mayor and a city council. This idea had grown out of the great disaster at Galveston in 1900 when a tidal wave had destroyed large portions of the city. When in ensuing months the corrupt mayor and his administration were unable to accomplish significant reconstruction, the voters decided to appoint a commission of experts for the task. The commission worked so well that it came to be adopted by more than 400 other cities during the ensuing decade.

The economic reforms of urban progressives often centered on the improvement of public utility services. In Los Angeles and San Francisco the reformers were intent on imposing stricter regulation on what already had become a jumble of street car and trolley lines. Rate regulation of electric light and gas companies was a prime issue in San Francisco and Seattle, and in scores of smaller cities, and was generally accomplished by World War I.

In a region in which water was scarce it might be expected that the availability of water for the cities would become a major political issue. It became most heated, perhaps, in two of the largest cities in the West, Los Angeles and San Francisco.

Already at the turn of the century the bulging population of Los Angeles led the city fathers there to fix their gaze far out beyond the horizon in their search for water. Between 1900 and 1905 the number of the city's inhabitants grew from 102,000 to 250,000. The idea of securing some of the needed water from the Owens River belonged to former city engineer Fred Heaton, who also served as mayor from 1899 to 1901. His close friend at this time was city engineer William Mulholland, who became a strong advocate for constructing a new city aqueduct in the Owens Valley. The plan secured the support of powerful businessmen in the city, including Harrison G. Otis (of the Los Angeles *Times*) and streetcar magnate Henry E. Huntington. In view of very severe water shortages in 1904, and again in 1905, the voters of Los Angeles approved a bond issue for developing the project, much to the dismay of farmers in the valley. President Theodore Roosevelt and Gifford Pinchot, head of the U.S. Forest Service, supported the city authorities, however, and in 1908 Mulholland began to supervise the building of a 233-mile aqueduct to bring water to the city. The project took five years to complete, and at the time was considered an engineering feat second only to the construction of the Panama Canal.

Meanwhile, San Francisco, too, was searching for new supplies of water. The city's new charter of 1900 empowered municipal authorities to assume direct responsibilities for supplying water to the burgeoning population. After various investigations city engineer C. E. Grunsky reported that the best source was the beautiful, scenic, and remote Hetch Hetchy Valley in Yosemite National Park. Thereupon, Mayor James D. Phelan applied to the U.S. Secretary of the Interior for permission to construct a reservoir there. But he had not reckoned with the violent reaction of enraged conservationists, led by the already legendary John Muir. It was true that Hetch Hetchy was scenic, but it was also so inaccessible that less than a dozen persons had ever been able to explore the valley. The conservationists secured much favorable publicity and were able to hold up the project for more than a dozen years. In 1908, with Gifford Pinchot's advice, President Theodore Roosevelt approved the application of San Francisco city authorities, but Richard Ballinger, President Taft's Secretary of the Interior, revoked the permit. Finally, in the administration of Woodrow Wilson, Secretary of the Interior Franklin K. Lane, a former attorney for the city of San Francisco, approved construction, soon also to be supported by a congressional appropriation. The entire system took many years to build and was not completed until 1934, when it provided much needed new water for the still increasing urban and suburban populations in the metropolitan area of San Francisco.[16]

Many other western cities also spent large sums for improving their water systems. They completely rebuilt their streets, extended new trolley lines into suburbs, built miles and miles of sewers, constructed new electric power plants, and on the Pacific Coast built virtually new port facilities.

Western urban reformers in addition undertook a variety of social measures. Most of them extended their municipal public health services (as visiting nurses) and hospitals and enacted municipal ordinances to prevent contagion. Denver's Judge Ben Lindsey pioneered with the establishment of special courts and counseling facilities for juvenile offenders, a model that was widely copied throughout the nation. Much of the reformers' energies went into providing improved recreational facilities for western city dwellers. San Francisco, Los Angeles, and Denver built very impressive new park systems. San Francisco's Golden Gate Park, completed by World War I, attracted worldwide attention. Seattle and Portland hired the famous landscape architects, the Olmsted Brothers, in 1908 to design their extensive new park systems. In Denver, progressive reformer Robert Speer in 1905 became the first mayor elected under the new council form of government under home rule. In a few years he greatly altered that city's appearance by expanding the parks and by laying out broad boulevards and parkways. His administration also built the first modern storm sewers in Denver. His accomplishments were perhaps crystallized with the construction of a new civic auditorium in Denver, which became host to the Democratic National Convention of 1908, the only presidential convention ever to be held in that city.

Progressive Reform in Western States.

The reform impulse also reached state governments in the West. In fact, many of the most distinguished political leaders of the Progressive era were westerners. Hiram Johnson, whom Californians elected as their progressive governor in 1910, also enjoyed national prominence as the vice-presidential candidate of the Progressive party in 1912, reflecting the increasing political power of the West. Rudolph Spreckels, the millionaire sugar heir, Congressman William Kent, and Meyer Lissner were other prominent California progressives. In Oregon, William S. U'Ren made that state almost synonymous with reform during his tenure (1906–1911). In Colorado progressives looked to Henry Buchtel and John F. Shafroth. Other western states, especially Idaho, New Mexico, Kansas, and the Dakotas, had strong progressive factions in both the major parties. Of those who were nationally known, Bronson Cutting in New Mexico, Edward P. Costigan in Colorado, William Borah of Idaho, and Arthur Capper of Kansas were most often in the news.

On the Pacific Coast, in the Rockies, in the Southwest, and on the Plains, progressive state reformers attempted political reforms that they hoped would make governments more responsive to the diversified populations in the West. Their reforms were not unique, but reflected those adopted elsewhere. They included the initiative and referendum, the recall of public officers, the secret ballot, the direct primary, and a wide range of measures to modernize governmental administration. Wyoming pioneered in 1890 with women's suffrage, because western states—often beset by a shortage of the gentler sex—felt it necessary to provide special attractions for them.

Of the various western state reformers, perhaps William S. U'Ren became the most admired national model, with the possible exception of Robert La Follette in Wisconsin. U'Ren's primary interest was in the use of direct legislation through the initiative and referendum—as a tool to solve most of the outstanding domestic problems of the time. A Democrat with Populist leanings, U'Ren worked through the People's Power League, a nonpartisan group that in 1902 secured adoption of the initiative and referendum in Oregon. In the ensuing decade U'Ren made Oregon a laboratory of political democracy as he fostered the adoption of a wide range of political reforms. His program became known as the "Oregon System," and was widely admired and copied throughout the United States.[17]

Progressive reformers in the western states also became concerned with economic and social measures. In all of the western states tighter controls were secured over railroads and public utilities, over banks, insurance companies, and corporations. Indeed, Kansas pioneered with its Blue Sky Law of 1914, which set a national pattern for state regulation of corporate securities. Depending on their degree of industrialization, western state legislatures also enacted laws regulating child labor, working hours of women (the Oregon statute of 1905 was a pioneer), providing for the eight-hour day, the mediation of labor disputes, and factory inspection. Since the Women's Christian Temperance Union and the Anti-Saloon League were strong in the West, most states during this period adopted some form of temperance or prohibition legislation. Thus, the West was in the forefront of state reform during the Progressive era and in some ways provided a model that other regions of the United States were to follow.

In the Progressive era westerners did not provide conspicuous leadership in national affairs. True, Hiram Johnson was chosen as the vice-presidential candidate of the Progressive party, and William Borah of Idaho was becoming an important national figure in the Senate. But just as the West still had a colonial status in regard to older regions, so its spokesmen tended to be the junior partners in the national establishment. And in Congress westerners did not usually vote as a conscious regional bloc but tended rather to follow their special interests. Only if the region's special interests were at stake, as in the case of the Newlands Reclamation Act of 1902 or the Federal Reserve Act of 1913, did westerners reveal some similarity in their voting patterns. Although heavily dependent on the federal government for financial aid—in internal improvements, tariffs, and military expenditures—most westerners nevertheless expressed a distrust of overly great federal power. Their distance from the nation's capital bred a measure of independence in them that led to a suspicion of federal authority. Thus, western political attitudes were a curious blend of dependence and independence, of collective action and individualism, that sprang from the peculiarities of the western experience at the opening of the twentieth century.

Struggling to Build a New Culture

Westerners in the Progressive era did more than throw all their energies into politics or economic development, however. They were also concerned with developing the accoutrements of civilization, with stimulating a lively cultural life in the West. To be sure, they were often self-conscious in their efforts and felt much like colonials who were seeking to imitate the culture of their homeland, in their case the East. During these years, therefore, western cultural life tended to be largely derivative and eclectic rather than unique or original. Westerners were followers rather than leaders. They were seeking to establish some of the best features of the cultural life they had known back home—whether East or South. Yet the products of New England or New York could never be duplicated exactly in the natural environment of the West, for its newness encouraged flexibility and experimentation. Very slowly, almost imperceptibly, the West began to develop a cultural life of its own.

The cultural expression of westerners during these years took varied forms. A distinctive western literature emerged that attracted national attention. Wealthy newcomers to the West after 1900 also fostered a flurry of activity in art and architecture as well as in music. And it was during this period that the West was developing an educational system with innovations that were watched and sometimes imitated in other regions. Western culture had not yet come of age, but between 1900 and 1914 it displayed a vitality that placed it on the threshold of new sophistication and maturity.

The Flowering of Western Literature

The expansion of population and consequent economic development of the West during this period found a clear expression in literary activity. Westerners were a people on the move, many of them recent migrants to the region who—being somewhat footloose—had experienced many insecurities that led them to sink their roots in something. Certainly the trend toward romanticism and nostalgia that was so prominent in western literature during these years had its origins in this search for identity. The focus on the Spanish-American heritage in California and the Southwest was one effort to manufacture a new western identity almost overnight. At the same time many easterners, under the stress of quickening industrialization, yearned for a return to simpler rural America, and looked on the West as the last remnant of what many believed had been a golden age. So they too, shared in the nostalgia for a West which was soon to be never more. To be sure, western literature also had its realists, representatives of a national tradition that sought to view western life realistically and without sentiment. Together, the romanticists and the realists between 1900 and 1914 created a very respectable body of literature that reflected the increasing maturation of cultural life along the erstwhile frontier.[18]

Perhaps most widely read in East and West were the western romanticists who emerged during this period. Some of them were like the medieval

A western writer of the early twentieth century: Charles F. Lummis. Source: Denver Public Library, Western History Department.

troubadors, singing the virtues of their western life for all to hear. And being eminently practical, some supported themselves by gravitating to the new luxury tourist hotels of the region, which sought to stimulate western tourist traffic. Perhaps best known was Charles Fletcher Lummis, a New Englander (and Harvard graduate) of impeccable background. Walking westward across the continent in 1885, he was greeted at the El Monte Hotel in Los Angeles by Harrison Gray Otis, the famous owner of the Los Angeles *Times*. For the rest of his life Lummis became an eloquent booster of California and the Southwest in hundreds of articles, novels, poems, and essays. In 1894 he became editor of *The Land Of Sunshine*, a new western literary periodical devoted to boosting the virtues of the region. Around this journal Lummis founded a literary cultural circle that attracted many well-known western writers such as David Starr Jordan, Mary Hallock Foote, John Vance Cheney, Edwin Markham, Mary Austin, Frederick Webb Hodge, Theodore S. Van Dyke, and Charles D. Willard. As Carey McWilliams has said, it was Lummis who discovered the Southwest for American culture and who proclaimed loudly (and prophetically) that the center of American culture was destined to shift westward.

Lummis' central themes were the celebration of nature in the West, the aborigines, and Spanish-American civilization in the Southwest. In developing these themes Lummis freely mixed fact and fiction, but his facile pen succeeded in fastening a mythology of a past western golden age on

Americans. Newly arrived immigrants in the West hungrily soaked it up in their eagerness to adjust to the life-style of their new land. Lummis provided them with an instant sense of identity—no matter how artificial it may have been—and made them feel a little less strange in their new surroundings.

Similar to Lummis, if less talented, was George Wharton James. An Englishman and former Methodist minister who migrated to southern California in 1881, James devoted much of his career until 1923 to boosting the virtues of the West. More of a publicist than a serious writer, his prodigious output of more than 40 books nevertheless did much to develop the romantic tradition in western literature by catering to the broad public interest in western history, emphasizing especially the old Spanish missions in California and the Southwest. He did much to develop the stereotype of American Indians as "noble savages." James was widely read not only in the West but throughout the nation and was important in arousing interest in the supposed origins of the West.

If Lummis was the best known of the romanticists, he was not necessarily the most talented. Other writers in the tradition included Mary Austin, Stewart E. White, Gertrude Atherton, and Charles F. Saunders. Mary Austin was especially skilled in capturing the feelings of newly arrived westerners who were awed by the majesty of nature in the West. With much sympathy for Indians, she conveyed their feelings for the rawness of nature, which differed so from those of white men. A prolific writer, in her *Land of Little Rain* (the southern Sierras) she acquainted Americans with the Dry West (1903) as no other writer had. In her novel *The Ford* she decried, in

A popular western writer in the twentieth-century West: Owen Wister. Source: Denver Public Library, Western History Department.

fictional form, the destruction of the pristine West by Los Angeles' Owens Valley project. Her novels *Isidro* (1905) and *The Flock* (1906) were similar in theme. White, too, was an incorrigible romantic. He described the haunting beauty of the West, its wildlife, and its natives. Not a major writer like Austin, he was popular in his time. Many of his stories appeared in *The Saturday Evening Post*. In *The Blazed Trail* (1902), *The Cabin* (1910), and *Gold* (1913), White indulged the national yearning for nostalgia by writing of the western wilderness, the deserts, mountains, its natives, badmen and heroes, and heroines. He glorified the Catholic-mission past and made Spanish dons (never Mexican peasants) his heroes. Indians, too, he romanticized. His novels were read by millions and were important in giving birth to a highly diversified cultural movement that was reflected in restorations, revivals, and pageants, plays, paintings, and museum collections. That the mythical past they were designed to celebrate never existed in reality did not disturb the majority of new westerners. The romanticists provided them an escape from the problems of the present, from feelings of insecurity and alienation that beset many of the newcomers.

Gertrude Atherton, a wealthy native San Franciscan and popular novelist, was also prolific. She used western motifs in many of her books. Among her best sellers were *The Splendid Idle Forties* (1902), which, like most of the romanticists' output, echoed the myth of an idyllic past in California and the Spanish Southwest. *The Californians* (1898) was her superficial novel about the confrontation between Spanish California society and Yankee newcomers.

The nostalgia for the Old West was reflected also in much popular literature, folklore, and the founding of historical societies. "Westerns" became one of the major forms of popular literature during the Progressive era. Emerson Hough's *The Story of the Cowboy* (1895) bemoaned the passing of the Old West. Even more widely read was Owen Wister, a Philadelphia lawyer who visited Wyoming for his health in the 1890s and became so enamored of the country that he devoted his remaining years to writing western stories. One of his greatest successes was *The Virginian* (1902), which romanticized life in Wyoming between 1874 and 1890. Dozens of other successful westerns streamed from the pen of his fellow easterner Zane Grey, a dentist whose flair for popular writing made him a virtual national pastime in the three decades after the appearance of his first work in 1904. Less skilled but widely read "western" authors of these years included Harold Bell Wright, *Their Yesterdays* (1912), B. M. Bowers, *Chip at the Flying U* (1910) and other Flying U stories, E. M. Rhodes, *Bransford in Arcadia* (1914), and H. H. Knibbs, *Songs of the Outlands* (1914).

All these writers had their counterparts in professional historians like Theodore Roosevelt, Frederick Jackson Turner, and Frederick Logan Paxson. For those wishing more diluted fare, these years saw the appearance of new magazines such as *Frontier Stories*, *West*, and *Pioneer*, which catered to the yearnings of urban Americans for a simpler society of the past. The Progressive era also witnessed the founding of historical societies in almost every one of the states in the trans-Mississippi West, which devoted themselves to collecting data, folklore, ballads, and Indian music.

Not all western writers romanticized the region. Three of the most widely read nationally were Frank Norris, Jack London, and Ambrose Bierce. Norris, a native of Chicago who came to San Francisco when he was 14, was a pioneer of American naturalism who used California as a scene for many of his writings. Reflecting the influence of Emile Zola, Norris wrote *McTeague* in 1899, using the locale of San Francisco as a framework for a searing story of human degradation. Tempering his brutal analysis of people with a measure of the romanticism so craved by the reading public, in 1906 Norris published his muckracking *The Octopus*, an indictment of the Southern Pacific Railroad's control over California politics. His bitterness was matched by Jack London, a native of San Francisco. By 1900 London was writing exciting stories about western life, and the recent Klondike Alaska gold rush for the *Overland Monthly*, the West's most distinguished literary magazine. His most famous work, *The Call of the Wild* (1903), was set in Alaska. A convinced socialist and sharp critic of American society of his day, London condemned what he considered to be its authoritarian nature in *The Iron Heel* (1907). London's starkly realistic style made him extraordinarily popular between 1900 and 1914, when he was perhaps the highest paid writer in the world.

Not quite as talented was Ambrose Bierce, a regular San Francisco columnist who was known for disliking everything and everybody he ever came in contact with. Although he was never able to produce a book, he wrote hundreds of widely read essays after the turn of the century, for William Randolph Hearst's San Francisco *Examiner*. Since his stories, such as those published *In The Midst of Life*, often had a melancholy quality, he reminded many readers of Edgar Allan Poe.

The West also produced a variety of poets. True, few of them were of major stature, but their works contributed to the developing cultural life of the region. Of those who used a western setting for their work, Joaquin Miller, Edwin Markham, and George Ella Sterling were among the most widely read. Miller was already a California institution by the turn of the century. Probably born in Indiana, he came west soon after the Gold Rush. In 1869 he published a wretched poem, "Joaquin," glorifying the Mexican bandit Joaquín Murietta, whom he described rather ineptly as a lineal descendant of Montezuma. But if Miller had scant talent, he had much showmanship. On a trip to England the following year he became known as "the poet of the Sierras." This title may have been dubious, but it stuck until World War I. Thus, although his poetry had little literary merit, he did much to acquaint easterners as well as Europeans with the rudiments of the emerging cultural life of the West. Far more talented was Edwin Markham, a school teacher in Oakland, California, whose "The Man with the Hoe" (1898) attracted considerable attention in American literary circles everywhere. Sterling, a friend of Jack London's, and a protégé of Ambrose Bierce, was a young New Yorker of uneven talent. After settling in Carmel, California, in 1908, he wrote some of his better works, including "The City by the Sea," which portrayed the beauties of San Francisco.

Although most western towns and cities encouraged amateur or professional drama, only San Francisco during these years was able to rival New York and Boston in the number of annual performances and in the maintenance of a professional theater on a large scale. Traditional repertoire featuring Shakespeare and other classics was common, but western plays such as Bret Harte's *Two Men of Sandy Bar* and Joaquin Miller's *The Danites in the Sierras* were also produced with some frequency. The development of the theater during this period was not so impressive as it had been in the second half of the nineteenth century, perhaps because western settlers during these years, from small-town middle-western backgrounds, had no great appreciation for the stage. Perhaps also, the development of motion pictures adversely affected expansion of theatrical production.

Art, Architecture, and Music

That the cultural life of the region was flowering was reflected also in the growth of western art.[19] Most of the larger western towns and cities were beginning to establish art museums by the turn of the century. An example was set by the California writer Charles Lummis, who in 1896 helped to establish the Southwest Museum at Los Angeles. His hope was that it would provide a showplace for western artists and would help to conserve the artistic heritage of the West. Moreover, he anticipated that it would promote a cultural awareness in westerners that would foster pride and forge a sense of identity with the region. Obviously, art flourished where there was wealth, and where patrons encouraged artists to express themselves on canvas. Few western cities in 1900 had wealth available for artistic endeavor or an art-conscious elite to encourage native artists. San Francisco was an exception. As early as 1871 the San Francisco Art Association was established to support younger painters. Among well-known artists Albert Bierstadt was prominent. His work included many canvases of California landscapes and of Yosemite. First coming west in 1858 with a government exploring expedition, Bierstadt painted exquisite pictures of animals in the mountains, plains, and forests of the trans-Mississippi West. At his death in 1902 he was perhaps the West's outstanding painter and had contributed to development of the romantic image of the region. Romanticism was tinged with precise realism by William Keith, active between 1865 and 1911, who became famous for his almost photographic paintings of sierra scenes. A friend of John Muir, the naturalist, and a lover of nature himself, Keith also produced a variety of western pastoral landscapes that sought to convey a mood of romantic mysticism. Before World War I Chris Jorgensen was another of the more talented western landscape artists. His use of rich colors and stark contrasts created a brisk demand for his canvases. After 1908, a new arrival in Los Angeles, William Wendt, turned out a series of landscapes in the colorful romantic vein that his predecessors had pioneered.

The unique scenery of the West and its old cultures long held a special attraction for photographers. Carleton E. Watkins first gained fame for his photographs of Yosemite in Civil War days. In the ensuing half century he traveled into virtually every section of the West to record striking scenes of western life and the West's natural wonders. Most of his plates were lost in the San Francisco Earthquake of 1906, and shock over the loss led to his commitment in the Napa state hospital in 1910. His prominent colleague, German-born Arnold Genthe, set up a studio in San Francisco in 1898. Perhaps he captured the disaster of the 1906 San Francisco earthquake better than any other photographer. His innovative techniques made him nationally famous, and in 1911 he moved to New York City.

Western architecture of these years was a testament to the developing culture of the trans-Mississippi region. Perhaps it was the natural grandeur of the West that drew various architects to it over the years. To be sure, western architectural styles during the Progressive era could be considered colonial as was so much else in the West, inasmuch as they tended to imitate popular styles in the East. But in adapting these familiar styles to the West, architects of the region added their own innovative, functional touches drawn from the natural environment of the region as well as from its history. Thus, western architects of this period worked in the national popular Gothic style, but varied their designs skillfully to reflect western climate, the Mission style in California, and the Pueblo architecture of the Southwest.

Most of the best-known western architects made their homes in California. They included Willis Polk, Bernard Maybeck, and John Galen Howard in San Francisco; the Greene Brothers in Pasadena in the Los Angeles area; and Irving Gill in San Diego. Polk tended to work with traditional classic and Gothic styles. The Ferry Building in San Francisco (1896) and the Civic Center there were some of the better examples of his work. He was responsible for rebuilding many important buildings in the city after the earthquake and fire in 1906, most in the Gothic style. However, he also contributed to the new vogue of mission architecture in California by his restoration of the Mission Dolores, the oldest building of its kind in San Francisco. Somewhat more innovative was Bernard Maybeck.

Bertram Goodhue's Spanish-colonial architectural style: The Panama-Pacific Exposition in San Diego, 1915. Source: Title Insurance and Trust Company, San Diego.

Although many of his buildings were executed in Romanesque and Gothic styles, he concentrated on giving them a western touch. Between 1901 and 1914 he designed dozens of spacious residences in Berkeley and San Francisco that were a distinctive blend of Gothic Revival with Bay Region Redwood Shingle. These "Maybecks" reflected western stirrings for architectural independence. Maybeck also designed the neo-classical Palace of Fine Arts for the Panama Pacific International Exposition of 1915 that reflected more traditional styles.

In Pasadena the Greene Brothers were developing a unique western style with their California Bungalow, a simple house designed for functional indoor-outdoor living well suited to the western climate. The Greenes built their first redwood bungalow in 1903, drawing somewhat on the plans of early nineteenth-century California adobe homes. The patio became a sort of outdoor living room, reflecting the spaciousness of the western natural environment. These bungalows enjoyed great popularity in California and throughout the West, where the Greenes had numerous imitators. And by World War I easterners were paying them the ultimate compliment —imitation.

The Mission style in California and the Pueblo style in the Spanish Southwest received wide publicity and exposure from San Diego's Panama Pacific Exposition in 1915. The city fathers, intent on illuminating the

historical background of San Diego, entrusted the architectural planning to
Bertram Goodhue of New York, who had recently written a book on Spanish
colonial architecture in Mexico. Goodhue adopted the dominant Spanish and
Mexican seventeenth- and eighteenth-century styles associated with José
Churriguera for many of the buildings at the Exposition. In succeeding years
this influence was to be profound, for the style was copied for hundreds of
private and public buildings in the West. In New Mexico, Arizona, and
Texas the Mission style was modified by Pueblo architecture, sometimes
derived directly from Goodhue's influence. Architectural experts have
argued the merits and weaknesses of these respective styles for years, but in
the broader context of western cultural development they reflected decided
progress in skillful adaptation of older and traditional styles as well as
experimentation with new or derivative architecture in efforts to develop a
distinctive western style.[20]

As early as the nineteenth century, westerners had shown a strong interest
in music, serious as well as popular. Most western towns and cities after 1900
made at least some efforts to promote symphonic music, concerts, and, less
often, opera. Of all western cities San Francisco was the most sophisticated.
Enthusiastic audiences packed its Tivoli Theater to listen to visiting artists.
Among those performers who appeared were the world famous soprano
Adelina Patti, the Lieder singer Lotte Lehmann, and divas Nellie Melba and

Spanish-colonial architectural
styles in Southern California dur-
ing World War I: The Beverly Hills
Hotel, Beverly Hills, California.
Source: First National Bank of Los
Angeles.

Luisa Tetrazzini. On the night of the San Francisco earthquake of 1906 the great Italian tenor Enrico Caruso was performing in Bizet's *Carmen*. Orchestral performers were usually ensured large audiences in San Francisco, as the young Italian conductor Arturo Toscanini discovered. And in 1911 San Francisco was the first city in the nation to provide regular public funds for its symphony orchestra. The inhabitants of the city were also enthusiastic opera lovers, and San Francisco was one of the few American cities in 1900 to support a regular opera season. Between 1879 and 1904 the Tivoli Theater and opera house there presented a twelve-month season, with less frequent performances until it closed in 1913. The first reputed performance of Pietro Mascagni's *Cavalleria Rusticana* was given there in 1890. In fact, the musical life of San Francisco was far more sophisticated than that of most American cities of this period.

Other western cities could not match San Francisco, but this is not to say that they did not encourage musical activities, although they were more amateurish.[21]

Education and Science

How were the cultural traditions of the West to be transmitted to future generations? This obvious concern led westerners during the Progressive era to take a special interest in expanding their colleges and universities, schools, and other educational facilities. In higher education, the New England influence of the nineteenth century was now reinforced by the millions of middle westerners who went west between 1900 and 1914. Unlike the migrants from the East Coast, who reflected a decided preference for private colleges, the middle westerners were confirmed believers in state and public institutions. In fact, Stanford University, founded in 1891, was the only large private university west of the Mississippi River. Every other western state and territory during this period increased its appropriations for higher education, but the money went to state-supported colleges and universities and normal schools. One of the leading state universities in the West by 1914 was the University of California, which, under the leadership of Presidents John LeConte and Benjamin Ide Wheeler, had already achieved a national reputation. The curriculum in western institutions emphasized practical subjects that would be useful in developing the region. The preference for public universities was shared by private benefactors like Leland Stanford, who had originally hoped, in 1882, to make a large bequest to the University of California. Only after the California state senate—controlled by Democrats—refused to confirm his nomination as a regent did he turn to the idea of founding a private university to bear the family name. The dynamic first president of Stanford, David Starr Jordan, an erstwhile president of Indiana University, pointed out many times that he believed the future of higher education in the United States to be with state universities.

The expansion of public education was slower in the West than in the East during the Progressive era, largely because of the limited tax base of most western communities and states, which were struggling to build a more diversified economy. Even California was not able to require compulsory education until 1874, and free textbooks were not available until 1912. The state had fewer than forty high schools at the turn of the century. The other western states lagged behind California in providing textbooks and post-elementary school training. Most western towns also experienced considerable difficulties in securing good teachers. Many of the best educators in the East were loath to venture westward into the colonial "provinces," and were especially reluctant to move into remote areas.[22]

It was not surprising, then, that the West was not as yet particularly distinguished in science, although the Pacific Coast did exercise some attractions for oceanographers and astronomers. During these years the newspaper magnate E. W. Scripps made a large donation to the University of California for establishment of the Scripps Institute of Oceanography at La Jolla, which established itself as one of the leading research centers of its kind by World War I. The University of California also extended its facilities at the Lick Observatory (first established in 1874) to make this one of the distinguished astronomy research centers in the nation. By 1917 the world's largest telescope was installed at the Mt. Wilson Observatory, enormously boosting research in astronomy at nearby Throop College of Technology (soon to be renamed California Institute of Technology), a rather obscure institution up until then that was soon to be transformed into one of the country's most famous scientific centers. And in Flagstaff, Arizona, the Lowell Observatory, administered by Harvard University, established itself as a leading facility for planetary research.

By 1914, then, the West had completed a decade and a half of rapid cultural development. In quantity as well as quality, these years witnessed a greater literary outpouring than during any equivalent period in the western past. In their search for roots, westerners were developing a respectable foundation for a regional tradition that found a receptive audience throughout the nation. And writers like Jack London and Frank Norris enjoyed national stature. Similarly, during this period the West was home for an increasing number of talented artists. If their work was not as imposing as that of major figures in the East, nevertheless they represented beginnings that were to yield fruit in later years. And in the realm of architecture westerners were already innovating with new styles that represented the first genuine creative efforts in twentieth-century American architecture. At the same time, the strengthening of universities and scientific research centers in the West during the Progressive era provided the institutional framework for cultural experimentation in the future. Even if their dependence on eastern models is still evident, westerners significantly made great progress in expanding and diversifying their cultural life in these early years of the twentieth century.

On the eve of World War I westerners could look back upon their progress since the turn of the century with pride and satisfaction. They had transformed their erstwhile frontier environment into an emerging urban civilization, except for some of the remoter areas. More than 8 million persons had come to settle in the region during this period, more than 90 per cent in towns and cities. The metamorphosis of Los Angeles from a country town of less than 100,000 to a city of almost half a million was not atypical. These newcomers set new records in economic development, not only in the production of raw materials, but in stimulating manufacturing and service industries. Many of the problems accompanying this tremendous growth became political issues, leading to reform movements in the West that, although not always innovative, attracted national attention. The cultural life of the West, especially its literature and architecture, developed as population and wealth increased. Newcomers added to the literate reading public and demanded improved taste in design of homes and public buildings. To be sure, in many phases of its life the West was still a colony of the East between 1898 and 1914, but the rapid pace of western growth in the Progressive era indicated that this relationship would become increasingly impermanent. And World War I tended to accelerate the pace of change.

NOTES

1 Carey McWilliams, *Southern California Country* (New York: Duell, Sloan and Pearce, 1946).

2 On Japanese, see Yamato Ichihashi, *Japanese in the United States* (Stanford: Stanford University Press, 1932); other minorities are discussed in Varden Fuller, "The Supply of Agricultural Labor as a Factor in the Evolution of Farm Organization in California," in U.S. Senate Committee on Education and Labor, *Violations of Free Speech and Rights of Labor Hearings*, Part 54 (Washington: U.S. Government Printing Office, 1940); also a Ph.D. dissertation (1939) at University of California.

3. Quoted in McWilliams, *Southern California Country*, pp. 158–159.

4. On this, and other phases of western economic growth during the era, C. R. Niklason, *Commercial Survey of the Pacific Southwest* (Washington: U.S. Government Printing Office, 1930), a United States Department of Commerce Publication, is instructive.

5 Readers who wish to delve into California's economic development in greater detail can consult Robert G. Cleland and Osgood Hardy, *The March of Industry* (Los Angeles: Powell Publishing Co., 1929), and Gerald D. Nash, *State Government and Economic Development: A History of Administrative Policies in California 1849–1933* (Berkeley: University of California, Institute of Governmental Studies, 1964).

6. See Dorothy Johansen and Charles M. Gates, *Empire of the Columbia: A History of the Pacific Northwest*, 2d ed. (New York: Harper and Row, 1967).

7. Eugene W. Hollon, *The Southwest, Old and New* (New York: Alfred A. Knopf, 1961); Alvin T. Steinel, *History of Agriculture in Colorado* (Fort Collins: Colorado State Agricultural College, 1926).

8. A standard work on the cattle industry is John T. Schlebecker, *Cattle Raising on the Plains, 1900–1961* (Lincoln: University of Nebraska Press, 1963).

9. Informative on the Pacific fisheries is Jozo Tomasevich, *International Agreements on Conservation of Marine Resources, with Special Reference to the North Pacific* (Stanford: Stanford University Press, 1943).

10. Thomas A. Rickard, *A History of American Mining* (New York: Johnson Reprints, 1932), and Carl Coke Rister, *Oil: Titan of the Southwest* (Norman: University of Oklahoma Press, 1949), are informative for the general reader. Russell R. Elliott, *Nevada's Twentieth Century Mining Booms* (Reno: University of Nevada Press, 1966), and Leonard J. Arrington, *The Richest Hole on Earth: A History of the Bingham Copper Mine* (Logan: Utah State University, 1963), deal with particular areas.

11. Tourism in the nineteenth century is discussed in Earl S. Pomeroy, *In Search of the Golden West* (New York: Alfred A. Knopf, 1957).

12. Since no definitive book on Harvey has appeared, interested readers are referred to James L. Marshall, *Santa Fe: The Railroad That Built an Empire* (New York: Random House, 1945).

13. John Ise, *Our National Park Policy: A Critical History* (Baltimore: Resources for the Future, 1961), is invaluable on the subject.

14. The history of western politics since 1900 is still a virgin field. My discussion is based on books and articles concerning individual states and cities. Earl S. Pomeroy, *The Pacific Slope* (New York: Alfred A. Knopf, 1965), and George E. Mowry, *The California Progressives* (Chicago: Quadrangle Books, 1963), are helpful.

15. Walton Bean, *Boss Rueff's San Francisco* (Berkeley: University of California Press, 1952), discusses the regime in detail.

16. The struggle over Owens Valley is described by Remi Nadeau, *The Water Seekers* (Garden City, N.Y.: Doubleday, 1950), and Vincent Ostrom, *Water and Politics: A Study of Water Policies and Administration in the Development of Los Angeles* (Los Angeles: Haynes Foundation, 1953). Elmo R. Richardson, *The Politics of Conservation: Crusades and Controversies, 1897–1913* (Berkeley: University of California Press, 1962), probes the Hetch-Hetchy dispute.

17. Lincoln Steffens provided a fascinating glimpse of U'Ren in *Upbuilders* (New York: Doubleday, Page and Co., 1909).

18. Until a cultural history of the West is written, interested students must search for fragments. On literary activities of these years, Franklin D. Walker, *A Literary History of Southern California* (Berkeley: University of California Press, 1950) is helpful, as are the works of individual authors.

19. Eugen Neuhaus, *History and Ideals of American Art* (Stanford: Stanford University Press, 1931), and this painter's *Drawn From Memory: A Self-Portrait* (Los Angeles: Pacific Books, 1964), afford insights into the development of western art.

20. Readers seeking to pursue this subject further should consult Harold Kirker, *California's Architectural Frontier* (San Marino, Cal.: Huntington Library, 1960), Esther McCoy, *Five California Architects* (New York: Reinhold, 1960), and David Gebhard and Robert Winter, *A Guide to Architecture in Southern California* (Los Angeles: Los Angeles County Art Museum, 1965), which also provides a self-guided tour.

21. Consult Howard Swan, *History of Music in the Southwest, 1825–1950* (San Marino, Cal.: Huntington Library, 1952), and Ronald L. Davis, *A History of Opera in The American West* (Englewood Cliffs, N.J.: Prentice-Hall, 1965).

22. On this subject detailed studies for individual states and localities are available, of which William W. Ferrier, *Ninety Years of Education in California, 1846–1936* (Berkeley: Sather Gate Book Shop, 1937), is illustrative.

2

From War to Depression, 1914–1929

In the years between World War I and the onset of the Great Depression the development of the West accelerated. To be sure, the growth was uneven in the region. Expansion occurred mainly in towns, cities, and the larger urban centers, especially on the Pacific Coast and in some portions of the Southwest. Thinly populated areas on the Plains or in the Rocky Mountain states barely held their own in population, and in many cases lost native sons and daughters who were drawn to metropolitan centers in other parts of the nation. Viewed as an entity, however, the trans-Mississippi West made giant strides during this period and was moving from a position of colonial dependence on the East toward a much greater degree of self-sufficiency. Its population grew rapidly, its economic life became increasingly diversified, and its political influence was becoming more potent. The cultural expression of westerners was beginning to have an impact on the entire nation. The Great Crash of 1929 temporarily ended this phase of western development, but the great progress that had been made in the preceding fifteen years left ardent western boosters to hope for still more to come.

World War I

World War I was to have a profound impact on the West, as on all other regions in the United States. It did much to accelerate the flow of new settlers to the region, who often were lured by the promise of new wartime jobs. To be sure, at the end of the conflict many westerners faced serious problems of readjustment and retrenchment. But the war created new plateaus of productivity. During the 1920s expansion was based on the accelerated levels created in wartime. And a larger population, combined with an expanding economy, meant that the West would exert greater influence on national affairs. The election of 1916 in many ways dramatized this increasing political power of Americans living west of the Mississippi River. We can conclude, therefore, that although World War I did not inaugurate a new chapter in the annals of the West, it did a great deal to accelerate the region's growth and to hasten its transition from colony to self-sufficiency.

Although it is difficult to measure population flows into the trans-Mississippi West between 1914 and 1919 precisely, available U.S. census statistics do indicate the influx was large during this period. The rate of increase was probably less than it had been in the decade from 1900 to 1910, or than it would be during the 1920s. Nevertheless, it amounted to somewhere around 70 per cent. Drawn by the war-created jobs, a cross-section of America moved west and often stayed. The new arrivals included middle westerners from the vast farmlands at the center of the North American continent, black tenant farmers from the South, and for the first time, Mexicans in appreciable numbers. Most of the newcomers migrated to towns and cities, hoping for jobs in the new aircraft factories in Los Angeles, the shipyards of San Francisco and Seattle and Portland, or in smaller manufacturing establishments in Denver and other western cities. Mexicans tended to seek work on the large farms along the Pacific Coast and in Texas, where they became an important segment of the migratory labor forces. Unprecedented wartime demands for vastly increased food supplies led to a sharp increase of western farm production and a consequent shortage of farm labor, which Mexicans filled ably and well. West Coast states secured a larger share of the newcomers than other portions of the West. Despite dislocations, therefore, the war brought a new influx of people in search of opportunity.

And there were opportunities galore as westerners braced themselves for an all-out effort in behalf of the national mobilization program. With its vast potential as a storehouse of natural resources, the West was indispensable to President Wilson's goal of maximum production. Westerners almost doubled their agricultural output, expanded the cattle industry, increased the flow of minerals from their varied mines, and developed a variety of new manufactures. In fact, the outbreak of war in Europe significantly affected western manufacturing. When intercoastal shipping was withdrawn to meet the urgent needs of the Atlantic trade, rail facilities in the West became increasingly overtaxed. As overland shipments became more uncertain, and as both rail and water rates increased after 1914, westerners were willy-nilly thrown back on their own ingenuity, since they were frequently cut off from the industrial centers of the East. Consequently, western industry was stimulated by these disruptions in the nation's transportation system, much in the same way that the War of 1812 had once stimulated the growth of manufacturing in New England.

The war started an economic boom in the Pacific Coast states. In California, farmers were well equipped to expand their production quickly, for they had already developed one of the most highly mechanized types of agriculture in the nation. Between 1914 and 1918 they virtually doubled their output of fruits and vegetables, prompted not only by seemingly unlimited new European markets, but also by the subsidies paid by the U.S. Food Administration. That federal agency was headed by Herbert Hoover, himself an adopted westerner, who showed special consideration for California and the West in many of his policies. Responding to his slogan that "Food Will Win the War," California grain growers doubled their output. In addition, wartime prices prompted the increased cultivation of various new crops. Of these cotton was the most important. Innovative farmers found the Imperial Valley to be admirably suited for the growth of cotton, needed for army uniforms, and within a few years California became one of the nation's leading producers. California farmers had no trouble finding the labor to implement their output. Beginning in 1914 they began to import an increasingly larger number of Mexican *braceros* for the various seasonal harvests. Although the growers usually urged these workers to return to Mexico after their labors were completed, an increasing number decided to stay, forming the nucleus of the emerging *barrios* in Los Angeles and some of the smaller cities of the Central Valley. Californians doubled their agricultural production within a few short years and contributed more than a third of the nation's total wartime food production. Many an Allied soldier opening up a can of fruits, vegetables, meat, or fish could be fairly sure that it had come from the American West.

California's fishermen became prime beneficiaries of America's meat shortage after 1917. German and Allied mine fields in the North Sea drastically reduced the catch of European fishermen and virtually eliminated their competition. And Hoover's program of "meatless Fridays" for Americans created vast new markets for fish in the United States. California's fishermen more than doubled their catch between 1914 and 1919, not only of the popular tuna but of a new variety, the Pacific sardine. As the North Sea sardine catch dwindled during the war, Californians brought in a catch of more than 200 million pounds annually. The California sardine industry was thus a direct outgrowth of World War I.

California's mining and lumber operators also sought to rise to the challenge. Obviously, they could not overnight boost the production of gold and silver. But they did expand vastly the production of various less glamorous minerals that were urgently needed for maximum wartime production, especially in the construction and chemical industries. Thus, high prices induced individual miners as well as corporations to increase their outputs of salt, soda, potash, cement, and quicksilver. In almost every instance such increases were secured by imaginative technological innovations and the development of more efficient production techniques. The Navy's urgent need for petroleum also prompted California's producers to increase their total output by 50 per cent between 1917 and 1919. This they did by new drilling methods and by inaugurating offshore drilling operations near Long Beach. Meanwhile, soaring lumber prices encouraged California's lumbermen to double their output between 1914 and 1919 as the demand for millions of wooden shipping crates and the construction of hundreds of new army camps created a veritable timber boom.

Wartime demands led California's manufacturers also to double their production in the short five-year period between 1914 and 1919. Many of these gains were made in existing industries such as canneries, meat-packing plants, flour mills, foundries, and printing establishments. In addition, a number of eastern manufacturers began to establish branch offices and factories in California, usually in the San Francisco area, to serve western local markets. But the war also stimulated new industries such as airplane manufacturing in Los Angeles and San Diego. Although most aircraft engines at this time were still made in Detroit, the assembly of parts and the fuselage began to be centered in southern California. Airplane manufacturers chose it as a desirable location because of the mild year-round climate that allowed testing in virtually all seasons.

In the Pacific Northwest the influence of the war on the economy was somewhat similar to California's experience. In response to Herbert Hoover's appeal for more wheat, growers in the Northwest doubled their harvests within two years. Apple growers brought in record crops and made Washington the nation's number-one apple producer. Fishermen in the Pacific Northwest likewise increased their catch significantly, with the largest gains being made by the Alaska salmon fishermen, who raised their take by more than 70 per cent in the war years. But perhaps no industry was stimulated as much by wartime demands as lumbering, the region's most important (52 per cent) source of income. In the state of Washington production of timber increased threefold, providing employment for 2 out of every 5 Washingtonians. Oregon's spruce producers quadrupled their output between 1914 and 1919. To be sure, not all of these gains should be attributed to the influence of the war, for the opening of the Panama Canal in 1914 made it possible for western lumber to reach eastern and European ports more cheaply and more quickly than it had ever reached them before. Indeed, many of the giant companies in the region, such as Weyerhaeuser, Pope and Talbot, and the Charles McCormick Lumber Company, had their own ships built at this time to take advantage of lucrative new markets.

More shortlived was war-inspired manufacturing activity in Washington and Oregon. As might be expected, the war initiated a real boom in American shipbuilding, with the West Coast as a natural beneficiary. Between 1914 and 1918 western shipyards hired more than 50,000 men to meet a flurry of new orders. And the need for speed in construction drove wage rates up to levels that were significantly higher than in the rest of the nation. As orders poured in from western lumber companies requiring new ships for the Panama Canal traffic, from the Allies, and from the U.S. government, Seattle shipyards hummed. By 1916 the French and Norwegian governments had placed significant orders with Pacific Coast shipyards. Soon the U.S. Emergency Fleet Corporation awarded contracts to as many as twenty-eight shipyards in the Pacific Northwest for wooden schooners, also underwriting the expense of expanding existing shipbuilding facilities. In addition, nine major shipyards in the region concentrated on the building of steel vessels. The largest of these was the Seattle firm of Skinner and Eddy, which achieved worldwide renown in 1919 by launching new ships in less than sixty days. Altogether, the shipyards of the Pacific Northwest delivered 297 vessels totaling 1,792,000 tons and costing $458 million. This constituted a significant shot in the arm for an economy based largely on the exploitation of natural resources. But, unfortunately, the boom collapsed as quickly as it had arisen. In 1919 the Emergency Fleet Corporation canceled almost all its orders, and within two years the western shipbuilding industry was reduced to less than 10 per cent of its wartime capacity.

Let us not assume, however, that rapid western economic expansion always proceeded smoothly, for labor problems plagued the region, especially the Pacific Northwest. United States entry into the war, and resulting labor shortages, were bound to result in some friction between management and labor, and the outbreak of strikes. This was particularly true of the logging industry, where in the summer of 1917 both the International Workers of the World as well as the American Federation of Labor sought to take advantage of the situation to increase their membership. Both unions demanded the adoption of an eight-hour day by the industry and also improved living conditions in the lumber camps. But lumber operators were equally tough. By July of 1917 they had organized themselves into the Lumbermen's Protective Association, which rejected all union demands. In fact, they even refused to negotiate. Thus, on August 1, 1917, the IWW and the AF of L logging unions decided to call a strike that idled more than 50,000 men that month. When they felt the pressure of hostile public opinion, however, the AF of L members began to flock back to work within a few weeks. The Wobblies, on the other hand, refused and began to advocate sabotage. Working closely together with the U.S. Department of Justice and the National War Labor Board, the Lumbermen's Protective Association proposed creation of a government-approved company union—the Loyal Legion of Loggers and Lumbermen. By the end of 1917 more than 100,000 men in the industry had joined this organization which secured acceptance of the eight-hour day and maintained harmony between the employers and workers until the end of the war. As for the uncompromising nucleus of Wobblies in the loggin; camps, they were reduced to impotence. Their opposition to the war had branded them as traitors, and the federal government's official sanction of the Loyal Legion deprived them of much of their potential membership. The IWW never recovered from this blow and after World War I lost all influence in the logging camps.[1]

The economic contributions of the Rocky Mountain and southwestern states to the war effort lay mainly in their production of minerals and cattle. To be sure, where profitable farming existed in this region, the growers performed remarkably. Colorado wheat farmers, for example, tripled their total crop between 1913 and 1919. But the major wealth of the states in this area was in their mines. The high prices for copper, which were stimulated by war manufactures, led to a vast increase of production at the giant plants in Arizona, Utah, Colorado, New Mexico, and elsewhere. Some companies, such as the Kennecott Copper Corporation, also opened up new mines. At Tyrone, in western New Mexico, Kennecott built an entire new company town to exploit the rich ores in the vicinity. Since construction was not completed until 1919, when copper prices took a huge dip, Kennecott immediately abandoned the property. Tyrone became the quickest ghost town in the West, not to be resurrected until 1968. Near the famous old mining town of Leadville in Colorado the Climax Company in 1917 opened the world's largest molybdenum mine, a metal essential to the production of high-grade steel. Another steel alloy, vanadium, was mined in the Paradox Valley of western Colorado. And high prices stimulated the mining of tungsten at Nederland in Boulder County, Colorado. Virtually all of these mines were abandoned at the end of the war as demand slackened.

From its beginning in 1914 World War I stimulated the western cattle industry, for suddenly stockmen saw new markets opening that had not been available to them before. In 1914 they had been virtually unable to compete in world markets. American beef exports were less than 6 million pounds in that year. But then came the war and its dislocations and by 1918 American beef exports exceeded 500 million pounds. In addition, high wartime wages enabled city dwellers throughout the United States to eat more meat. And so cattle prices doubled in this period, prompting a vast expansion in western cattle production. Stock growers were able to boost their herds so significantly because of various emergency measures they undertook. One helping hand was extended to them by the federal government, which opened up its national forests to allow more grazing. In addition, many more cattle growers shifted to ranch farming (rather than letting animals run loose), which gave them greater control over their operations. The result of all of these measures was to enable the United States not only to supply Great Britain and the Allies with sizable quantities of meat, but to provide adequate meat supplies for America's armed forces. In war as in peace, the West was one of the bulwarks of America's food supplies.

Westerners undertook this vast economic expansion despite widespread reluctance for direct American involvement in the war. Europe was too remote in the minds of many westerners. They were more concerned with domestic rather than foreign issues. This sentiment was strongly reflected in the election of 1916, in which the western states cast the deciding votes for Woodrow Wilson. In that year the main theme of Wilson's supporters was that "he kept us out of war." With that theme westerners were in wholehearted agreement. During the fall of 1916 William Jennings Bryan barnstormed through many of the trans-Mississippi states, reiterating the slogan before many receptive and enthusiastic audiences. So close was the division with the American people on the issue of war, however, that only California's ballots on election night guaranteed Wilson's victory. His small majority in California enabled him to retain the presidency by a clear sectional alignment between the West and South. With the exception of New Hampshire and Ohio, Wilson failed to carry any eastern states. On the other hand he secured the votes of all of the states west of the Mississippi River with the exception of South Dakota and Oregon, where German-Americans voted Republican. To a considerable extent, therefore, Wilson was elected president because the West united behind him in his efforts to keep the United States out of World War I.

During the war western nationalism also found an outlet in nativism and suppression of dissent. Anti-German and anti-foreign sentiment was as strong in the West as anywhere. Rumors of sabotage ran through many a western community. Such apprehensions were fueled further by fear of radicals. In the public mind, aliens and radicals were cut from the same cloth. One incident around which such feelings crystallized was the case of Joe Hill in Salt Lake City during 1914 and 1915. Hill was an itinerant Swedish drifter who was also an outstanding song writer for the IWW. In 1914 he was arrested for armed robbery of a grocery store in Salt Lake City and the murder of the proprietor and his son. Whether or not Hill was guilty of the crime was never definitely determined, but public opinion and the local courts expressed considerable hostility to him. In 1915 the Utah Supreme Court upheld his conviction and execution by a firing squad.[2] Irrespective of the particular issues in the trial, the case aroused national and international attention. Rightly or wrongly his execution was widely interpreted as expressing western hostility towards foreigners and radicals.

The case of Tom Mooney in California during the next year followed a similar pattern. During a Preparedness Day parade down Market Street in San Francisco on July 22, 1916, an explosion of unknown origins disrupted the march, killing ten persons and wounding forty others. No one knew precisely who was responsible for the action, but the San Francisco police chief as well as the newspapers quickly blamed radicals for the crime. Among the persons they accused was Mooney, an obscure anarchist of Irish antecedents who had been acquainted with various radicals in California over the years. Mooney and the others were convicted by state courts despite lack of clear evidence concerning their guilt. In fact, Mooney was condemned to die, but Governor Stephens commuted his sentence to life imprisonment.[3]

But to many westerners perhaps the most hated symbol of dissent during World War I was the IWW. The exigencies of war were used throughout the region to suppress the union, even though a variety of motives may have inspired its opponents. Outright violence against IWW organizations broke out in Everett, Washington, on May Day, 1916, when the city fathers and a hastily assembled band of vigilantes shot at a boatload of IWW organizers who were attempting to land at Everett to recruit new members. The posse turned them back, but not before killing seven men. During the early months of 1917 the governors of Washington, Oregon, and Montana were beginning to take steps to drive the IWW out of their states. Then came the great western strikes during the summer of 1917, not only in the lumber camps of the Northwest, but also in the copper mines of Montana, Arizona, and elsewhere. The reaction of western state and local authorities was swift, encouraged by President Wilson and the Department of Justice. The strike of copper mines in Butte, Montana, ended in September as the National Guard occupied the town. Vigilante action in cooperation with local police forces and posses was also effective in Arizona in July 1917. There, at Bisbee, the local law enforcement officers herded more than 1,200 striking miners on a freight train, threatening them with violence should they dare to return. At other major Arizona copper mines, at Jerome, Globe, and Douglas, vigilante groups used violence to intimidate strikers and IWW officials, hastening their departure. Then, in the middle of July, the governors of California, Arizona, Utah, Nevada, Idaho, Colorado, Oregon, and Wyoming together formulated a plan of common action to rid themselves of the IWW and its members. They felt that federal action to supplement the local repression already under way would be most effective. Attorney General A. Mitchell Palmer happily complied with their request, and so on September 5, 1917, the Department of Justice raided IWW offices in Omaha, Tulsa, Spokane, and Seattle to arrest union leaders to charge them with obstructing the war effort under the Sedition Act of 1917. The combined force of federal, state, and local authorities was more than the IWW could withstand, and it never recovered from these blows. These actions were widely applauded in the West and defended as necessary for the successful prosecution of the war effort.

Western support for the war effort also expressed itself in legislative action to foster patriotism and to suppress opposition to the war. Many state legislatures acted along the lines of the Texas lawmakers who met in 1918, determined to have Texas signal its support of the war effort. In the special session of that year they enacted a loyalty act that provided punishment for persons critical of government policies of American involvement in the war. A legislative committee meanwhile recommended that state officials investigate all books in the state library and undertake to destroy or remove all of those that contained references to German greatness. At the same time the Texas lawmakers denied aliens the right to vote and stipulated that all classes in the public schools be conducted in the English language. In addition, they required that teachers devote ten minutes each day to the teaching of patriotism. Of course, details varied in each state, but as a region the West sought to give wholehearted support to the American cause, even at the price of civil liberties.

Thus, the West united in giving strong support to the national mobilization effort. And in turn, the wartime experience had a decided impact on the region, accelerating its growth. For the war tended to diversify western population, especially by hastening the influx of minority groups such as Mexicans and black Americans. It expanded western urban centers and broadened the horizons of westerners everywhere. Perhaps even more significant was the influence of the conflict on the western economy. It revealed the untapped potential of many spheres of western economic life, and it gave considerable impetus to new forms of manufacturing.

The wartime experience also created stresses. Some of these strains were reflected in the politics of this period, particularly in the suppression of dissent and the desire to drive radical or alien elements from the West. If this effort was partially successful, however, it was not entirely because of suppression. The exigencies of war also created new opportunities for labor to secure long-wanted rights, including the eight-hour day, improved working conditions, and collective bargaining. The achievement of some of these demands in wartime partially explains the failure of radicals to rally support for their causes more effectively. The adoption of some IWW demands, for example, indicated that perhaps not all of its agitation had been in vain. And so the war left the West more populous, more prosperous, and perhaps a more sober region in 1919 than it had been five years before. Like many Americans in 1919 westerners wondered what the return of peace would mean for the next decade.

Postwar Adjustments, 1919–1921

The end of the war did not create the millennium that many westerners had been led to believe would come with peace. Instead, the postwar period was one of crises, anguish, and tribulations. Many persons undoubtedly welcomed an end to the fighting, yet they were beset by many tensions and frustrations for which they sought outlets. The cessation of hostilities disrupted the lives of many in the West, who were forced to adjust their wartime mentality or occupations to peaceful pursuits. And those who had come westward to work in newly created jobs suddenly found themselves displaced and footloose with the abrupt end of the war. Thus, the uncertainties of postwar readjustments that faced Americans everywhere in 1919 had an especially unsettling impact in the West, a new, less structured, and less stable society than the region east of the Mississippi River.

These insecurities found an outlet in various social crises that plagued the West and the nation. Unemployment and strikes, fear of radicals, aliens, and foreigners, and racial tensions were only some of the manifestations. Throughout 1919 thousands and thousands of men and women lost their jobs as wartime activities ceased abruptly. More than 100,000 war jobs disappeared virtually overnight on the Pacific Coast alone. In addition, hundreds of thousands of returning former servicemen reentered the job market. So former veterans, shipyards workers, miners in Colorado, Arizona, and Montana, lumbermen in the Pacific Northwest, and migrant farm laborers throughout the West joined the ranks of the unemployed, whose discontent was revealed in a rash of strikes in 1919 and 1920. And these strikes greatly unnerved many lower-middle-class westerners with rural backgrounds who, not entirely secure in their new environment, feared the dissolution of society. Of all the strikes perhaps the Seattle general strike in February 1919 attracted the greatest national attention. There the citizenry believed that Bolsheviks had persuaded the city's workers to cooperate in a complete cessation of all work activities, perhaps as a prelude to revolution. Hard hit by the closing of shipyards, the AF of L unions voted to support the general strike, set for February 6, 1919. On that day the city became strangely quiet. Streetcars stopped, taxi cabs and vendors disappeared from the streets. Restaurants closed their doors, hotels cut their services, and department stores did no business. The usually bustling waterfront was strangely quiet. Was this the prelude to revolution? The Seattle *Union Record* declared that the strike "will lead NO ONE KNOWS WHERE." Mayor Ole Hanson demanded that the unions call off their strike by eight the next morning and hinted at the use of troops, although there had been no violence. The threat worked. The Seattle *Times* declared jubilantly that "Attempted Revolution is Defeated." By February 10 workers had returned to their jobs and the city hummed again, only the shipyard laborers holding out for their wage demands. Mayor Hanson was hailed throughout the country for his resolute stand against "would be destroyers of law and order," and the citizens of Seattle breathed more easily.[4]

In one way or another, the bitter feelings toward strikers and radicals that had surfaced in Seattle were reflected in various other communities throughout the West. On Armistice Day 1919, in Centralia, Washington, a group of American Legionnaires and some other war veterans beat up a group of Wobblies and stormed the local offices of the IWW. When they left, at least one of the union men lay dead.

At the same time the California legislature met to deal with disloyalty. One solution, the lawmakers believed, was the enactment of syndicalism laws. Legislators in Nevada, Idaho, Colorado, Arizona, and other western states passed similar laws within the next two years. Under the California statute mere membership in any organization committed to the destruction of the American form of government was a crime, and made a person so accused subject to criminal prosecution. The legislators were taking aim not only at cells of the newly organized American Communist party, but also at the scattered remnants of such few IWW chapters as had managed to survive. Between 1919 and 1927 the California attorney general secured 521 indictments under the law, and 168 convictions. Those convicted were usually obscure persons; some already were serving jail terms. Of the more prominent persons indicted, Charlotte Anita Whitney of California was best known. A prominent social worker and philanthropist from a distinguished California family, Miss Whitney was able to retain distinguished lawyers to represent her. The U.S. Supreme Court upheld her conviction, although she remained free on bail. Governor C. C. Young in 1927 granted her a pardon.

In other western states the criminal syndicalism laws were not administered so stringently as in California. Neither Arizona nor Montana authorities ever used the laws in their respective jurisdictions. In the state of Washington juries refused to convict persons charged with violation of its criminal syndicalist act. In South Dakota, Oklahoma, Wyoming, Nevada, Utah, and Colorado enforcement was desultory. In Idaho, on the other hand, sentiment against the IWW was still strong. Prompted by the demands of big lumber companies in the northern part of the state, authorities imprisoned 31 men under the syndicalist act, in the process effectively destroying the last vestiges of the union's influence. With the exception of California and Idaho, enthusiasm for criminal syndicalist laws waned sharply within a year after the Armistice.[5]

The West did escape the race riots that in 1919 were rampant east of the Mississippi River. The serious disturbances at Longview, Texas, were an exception. If westerners did not reflect the same tensions that erupted elsewhere in the United States, this was largely because the black population west of the 98th meridian was still extremely small, less than 3 per cent of the total population. As for Mexicans or Orientals, they had been cowed through legal or informal ways. Moreover, they too constituted a very small minority in the communities in which they lived.

To a considerable extent the fears of westerners after the war were fueled by the economic depression that settled on the region between 1919 and 1921. Most westerners were affected by it, whether they were farmers, cattlemen, miners, or manufacturers. The first to feel the cancellation of war orders were manufacturers and businessmen. Meanwhile, western farmers bore the brunt of shrinking markets and plummeting prices. The wheat farmers on the Plains, in the Rocky Mountain states, and on the West Coast saw the price of wheat decline 100 per cent in the first year after the Armistice. The drastic decline for other crops was similar, whether corn, barley, cotton, or hay. The fall in prices for fruits and vegetables was not as drastic, but sufficiently severe to wreak havoc among smaller growers. And fishermen up and down the Pacific Coast saw their income shrink to less than one-half of 1919 levels in just a few months. Not only did their European markets disappear, but as meat again became more readily available, many Americans turned away from fish. However, even western cattlemen suffered during the postwar years. Prices for beef and hogs dropped to one-half of the wartime levels, plunging thousands of cattlemen on the Plains and on the Coast into bankruptcy. Doubtless other thousands would have faced the same fate had not the War Finance Corporation extended them special emergency loans to tide them over the crisis.[6] The large protest vote when Americans went to the polls in 1920 indicated the general unrest.

The years between 1919 and 1921, then, were difficult for westerners as for Americans elsewhere. Emotional readjustment for a people who seemed perpetually on the move posed problems, problems rendered more difficult by economic hardship. Nevertheless, although these years saw widespread retrenchment in the western economy, economic activity did not return to its pre-1914 levels, but reached plateaus that were significantly higher than in earlier years. After 1919, levels of production were still the highest in the peacetime history of the region. And as the nation and the West recovered from depression in 1921 they entered another extraordinary period of growth that would once again transform many aspects of western life.

The 1920s

The decade of the twenties saw a vigorous expansion in population, economic activity, and cultural life. To be sure, this growth was not the same in all areas encompassed by the region. It was evident in California, and to a lesser extent in the Pacific Northwest. It was moderate in the Southwest. In the Rocky Mountain states and the Plains there was less change, and some of the states in this region even lost population. As in the middle of the nineteenth century, so in the 1920s the westward surge of population leapfrogged. It skipped from the Mississippi River directly on to the Pacific

Coast, from the Wet East to the Wet West. Perhaps scholars felt that they had put the myth of The Great American Desert to rest. But in the popular mind that myth was still very much reality in the 1920s. Millions of settlers bypassed the Dry West in their frenzied race to the Pacific Coast, very much as their forerunners had a century before.

Thus the Pacific Coast witnessed the most impressive growth of any western region in the twenties. There the large cities, towns, and smaller urban centers often doubled their population in the decade, experienced an appreciable economic development, and supported a flowering of cultural activities that was unmatched elsewhere in the West. In 1929 many westerners still felt that they were colonials, but the lively growth of the Pacific Coast during the decade indicated that the ending of colonial status was not far off.

New Waves of Settlers, 1921–1929

Here we shall take a close look at the people who went to the West in the 1920s, at their origins, social status, ethnic backgrounds, and ultimate destinations. Then we shall examine the new life-styles they developed, especially the suburbanization of western cities.

During the twenties the nature of western settlers changed, both as to their points of origin and their social status. This was the third great wave of migrants in the twentieth century. The first, you will remember, consisted of wealthy persons from the East (1890–1906); the second (1906–1917) was composed largely of retired middle-class people from the Middle West; in the twenties most western migrants were of lower-middle-class background, usually from the Middle West but also from southern and border states. To be sure, the steady flow of affluent, retired, middle-class middle westerners continued. Like earlier immigrants, the newcomers sought the benefits of western climate, and the joys of its scenery and outdoor living. But they also went westward in search of better economic opportunities. The migration of the twenties also included a sizable number of eccentrics and nonconformists to California, drawn by the glitter of Hollywood, just then emerging as a major film center. Some spilled over into Arizona, Nevada, and New Mexico, wherever films were made. To be sure, they were not all dwarfs, one-eyed sailors, or stage-struck teen-agers, but they did include large numbers of professional gamblers, racketeers, confidence men, and mystics, as well as assorted dropouts from American society. In addition, poor people began to be quite visible in Los Angeles and many other western cities as the growth of slums presaged problems that would become nationwide during the sixties and beyond. In Los Angeles the increasingly large influx of

Mexicans resulted in the growth of a *barrio,* while certain suburbs came to be occupied by other distinctive groups. Bell Gardens came to be known as home of the Okies, while Monterey Park was acknowledged to be the western terminus for the Arkies. These people poured into the state so rapidly and in such great numbers during the 1920s that there appeared to be constant turmoil and social havoc where they settled. Almost all of them (96 per cent) went to live in cities. To a considerable extent their exodus was facilitated by the completion of highways that made possible all-weather travel on transcontinental roads. Indeed, the development of western highways in the 1920s had the same relation to the population boom on the West Coast during these years as the completion of the Santa Fe Railroad had on the growth of southern California in the 1880s. This was the first great migration of the automobile age. In this single decade, California's population actually doubled, reaching a total of almost 6 million in 1929.

The origins of these people lay primarily in the Middle West. Illinois, Missouri, Iowa, and Ohio were the starting points for the majority of newcomers. As yet, southerners and easterners were not moving to California in significant numbers. If the younger sons and daughters of large middle-western farm families moved to the Pacific Coast, they did so partly because of the increasing difficulty of securing reasonably good farm lands in their home states. On the other hand, some of their parents, having acquired comfortable estates because of a succession of good crop years up until 1914 and from wartime profits, sought peaceful retirement in the midst of spectacular scenery and balmy climates. And so the Main Streets of Middle America moved westward in the twenties. One could find a Middletown in Los Angeles as readily as in Indiana.

Somewhat smaller contingents moved to the Pacific Northwest. Here too, as in California, the bulk of newcomers tended to be of lower-middle-class background from the Middle West and also from the South. A higher percentage of southerners went to Washington and Oregon than to California. Most of the newcomers were born in Illinois, with Missouri and Texas not far behind as "mother states." A sizable number were from Appalachia, drawn by the promise of jobs in the lumber camps and surrounding towns. It was no accident that the Ku Klux Klan had a brief flurry of success in Oregon between 1920 and 1922. André Siegfried, the French traveler and social critic, pointed out in 1927 that the atmosphere of Portland, Oregon, as well as of Los Angeles, and the biases and attitudes of many of their people, reminded him of what he had observed in his southern travels. The Pacific Northwest and southern California thus constituted the Bible Belt of the West, much like the South and border area east of the Mississippi River.

Still fewer migrants settled in the cities of the intramontane region. There they sought to reestablish some of the characteristics of the culture they had known in the Middle West. It was not accidental, therefore, that sections of western cities such as Denver, Salt Lake City, Albuquerque, and Phoenix had a distinctive middle-western atmosphere. Houses and streets were planned and constructed in the middle-western style of the early twentieth century, and the habits of the people who lived in them matched their physical surroundings.

Thus, in every portion of the West, the middle-western migration of the twenties significantly altered the character of many of its cities. Although the newcomers settled in urban areas, they usually retained many of the values of rural America, whence they came. With the exception of San Francisco, therefore, most western cities lacked a cosmopolitan atmosphere. Instead, irrespective of their size, they retained a distinctly rural or small-town aspect. Consequently, the conflict between town and country, between rural and urban values, that characterized American society during the 1920s had a different coloration in the West, where cities contained both of these elements. The rural-urban conflict here was more intense because of the constant influx of newcomers. Every day western city dwellers were beset by the gap between the ideal of a rural Arcadia that they had come seeking and the reality of a growing metropolitan society.

In many respects the twenties brought the rural-urban conflict into the midst of everyday life. This change was brilliantly described by Louis Adamic in 1925 when he wrote that Los Angeles was still an enormous village, but was beginning to change. As he pointed out,

> the people on the top in Los Angeles, the Big Men are the business men, the Babbitts. They are the promoters, who are blowing down the city's windpipe with all their might, hoping to inflate the place to a size that will be reckoned the largest in the country—in the world. These men are the high priests of the Chamber of Commerce whose religion is Climate and Profits. They are—some of them—grim, inhuman individuals with a great terrifying singleness of purpose. They see a tremendous opportunity to enrich themselves beyond anything they could have hoped for ten or even five years ago, and they mean to make the most of it. . . . And trailing after the Big Boys is a mob of lesser fellows . . . thousands of minor realtors, boomers, promoters, contractors, agents, salesmen, bunko-men, officeholders, lawyers and preachers—all driven by the same motives of wealth, power, and personal glory. . . . They exploit the "come-ons" and one another, envy the big boys, their wives gather in women's clubs, listen to swamis and yogis and English lecturers, join "love cults" and Coue clubs in Hollywood and Pasadena, and their children jazz and drink and rush around in roadsters. Then there are the Folks . . . they are retired farmers, grocers, Ford agents, hardware merchants, and shoe merchants from the Middle West or wherever they used to live, and

now they are here in California—sunny California—to rest and regain their vigor, enjoy climate, look at pretty scenery, live in little bungalows with a palm-tree or banana plant in front, and eat in cafeterias. Toil-broken and bleached out, they flock to Los Angeles, fugitives from the simple, inexorable justice of life, from hard labor and drudgery, from cold winters and blistering summers of the prairies. [7]

This mingling of rural dwellers with urban types created the new surburban culture of the West, a sort of compromise between conflicting value systems of the twenties.

Another characteristic of westerners in the 1920s was their ethnic diversity. The trans-Mississippi region was not peopled entirely by the native born. No less than the great cities of the East in the first three decades of the twentieth century, the West contained a significant percentage of foreigners. In the 1920s their numbers totaled about 28 per cent of the general population, exceeding the national average. California had the largest Oriental settlement in the U.S. In some states, such as North Dakota, two-thirds of the people there in the twenties had been born outside the state, whereas one-fourth were foreign immigrants, largely Scandinavians, Germans, Russians, and Englishmen. In the Southwest, New Mexico and Arizona had significant Indian and Chicano groups, totaling more than one-third of their populations. One-fourth of all Texans were of Mexican or Chicano descent. The twentieth-century West, therefore, no less than the East, contained a diverse array of immigrants from every quarter of the globe.

During the decade of the twenties the largest single influx of newcomers to the West was that of Mexicans into California. These immigrants were not to be confused with "old" Californians, the relatively small number of old families who prided themselves on descent from early Spanish settlers. More than a quarter of a million Mexicans entered the state between 1919 and 1929, most of them as migratory field laborers. On the eve of the Great Depression 368,000 persons born in Mexico or having parents born in Mexico lived in California, compared to just 8,000 at the turn of the century. They would come in time for the harvest season and then follow the crops through the southern and central portions of the state. At the end of the season California farmers hoped that they would go back to Mexico. Instead, many of the migrants wintered in Los Angeles and smaller towns. By 1925 they constituted 7 per cent of the population of Los Angeles, 27 per cent of its relief cases, and 54 per cent of its hospital cases. Already by 1929 Californians were complaining of their "Mexican problem." Within a few years Los Angeles came to be the largest Mexican urban community outside of Mexico City itself.

The Mexican immigrants who came during these years did not integrate as easily into the American community as other migrants. Not only did they face prejudice, but language proved to be a barrier to acculturation and they clung tenaciously to their imported folk culture. Because of proximity to Mexico and its Spanish heritage, neither Texas nor California appeared a completely foreign land to many, and so they persisted in their ways. And since predominantly American communities were not willing in this period to recognize "bi-culturality," to respect Mexican folk culture on a par with American culture, on its own terms, the Mexican and the Chicano populations lived a somewhat isolated and self-contained existence in the teeming *barrios* that mushroomed in Los Angeles, El Paso, San Antonio, and other California and southwestern towns.[8]

A somewhat smaller minority were the Japanese, who settled up and down the Pacific Coast, although their largest communities were in California. In 1900 there were perhaps no more than 500 Japanese in the West. Then came a trickle of about 15,000 during the next decade, increasing to around 50,000 in the twenties. The center of Japanese life was in Los Angeles, which became known in these years as Little Tokyo. The Japanese first worked for the railroads but by World War I were moving rapidly into the citrus industry. Unlike other minorities the Japanese were not content to remain farm laborers. Despite the alien land acts in many states, which forbade land ownership by aliens, by 1925 they had attained an important position both in citrus and in California produce farming. In Los Angeles County they controlled 90 per cent of truck crops by the end of the decade. Moreover, they quickly established themselves as the most skilled landscape gardeners in the West. And they also gained a significant foothold in the western fishing industry. Despite prejudice and various forms of discrimination, Japanese immigrants succeeded in establishing an important position for themselves in many aspects of western life.

These years also saw the growth of black communities in the West, of which Watts, in Los Angeles, became the largest. Elsewhere, the number of black citizens rarely exceeded 5 per cent of the total population. At the turn of the century Los Angeles counted about 2,800 black citizens, 7,600 in 1910, 19,000 in 1920, and about 31,000 in 1930. Before World War I most black Angelenos were pullman car porters from the East or the Middle West. It was said in the twenties that most black migrants made a better adjustment to Los Angeles than to any other American city, perhaps because Mexicans and Japanese bore the brunt of prevailing racial prejudices. In any case, after 1916 the first sizable southern migration of rural black people from Mississippi, Georgia, and Alabama arrived. They settled on what was then the outskirts of Los Angeles, Mud Town, or Watts, and by 1925 were moving into the Central Avenue district. In view of the extraordinary growth of southern California during these years, job opportunities for skilled and unskilled workers were greater than in most other sections of the nation.

Most of the black community of Los Angeles during this decade was engaged in a variety of unskilled jobs and in household services.[9]

The great migration of the twenties brought an increasingly higher percentage of older persons over 50 to California, and also to many other parts of the West, thus altering the social structure of the region. The median age of persons under 30 years of age had always been higher west of the Mississippi than in the East, for until 1900 the West beckoned mainly to young men and young families. But if Horace Greeley had advised Americans to "go west, young man," in the Civil War era, perhaps his advice in the twenties had filtered down to older Americans, judging from the census statistics. Between 1919 and 1929 the percentage of older persons in the population of most western states increased steadily. In 1929 Los Angeles had the highest percentage of persons over 45 of any of the ten largest cities in the nation. In relation to their size, much the same was true of Phoenix and Tucson, and to a lesser extent of Denver and Albuquerque. In 1929 there were as many people in Los Angeles between 65 and 69 as in the 35–39 age range in San Francisco. Especially in those parts of the West where the climate was moderate, along the Pacific Coast and in the Southwest, the percentage of older persons was higher than the national average.

The growth of a significant community of older persons tended to shape life-styles in many parts of the West. In the 1920s the presence of a large number of retired people was reflected by the growth of the state societies of the period, the invention of cafeterias—the twentieth-century version of the old western saloon—and the prominence of cemeteries and businesses catering to the dead. And, as pointed out earlier, the undue emphasis on pets and their care was another reflection of the needs of large numbers of childless persons. In one way or another, these institutions grew to serve the needs of older people and to provide them with some sense of community.

One expression of the yearning for a sense of community came in the organization of the state societies in the 1920s. These societies were a modern version of the immigrant-aid societies that had been long established in eastern urban centers. California had the largest number, but they flourished also in other western states. They were organizations of persons from a particular state, be it Iowa, Illinois, or Arkansas, who assisted newcomers in making adjustments to their new home. California had as many societies as there were states. They helped to alleviate loneliness in many ways, especially through their mammoth annual picnics. In the two decades after 1921 as many as 150,000 people annually attended the Iowa Picnic alone. The guiding father of the societies during these years was C. H. Parsons, who in 1909 organized the Federation of State Societies, which he led until World War II. Its membership exceeded half a million persons. On the day of the picnic, Parsons wrote in his reminiscences, it was a thrilling experience for thousands of uprooted lonely individuals to hear "the tramp of Iowa's mustered hosts." The picnic grounds were organized according to towns and counties so that erstwhile native sons could mingle with others from their own locality. "I've seen a lot of thrilling scenes," Parsons wrote, "of brother meeting brother for the first time in years; of friends standing, hands clasped, tears on their cheeks, greeting each other for the first time in ten, twenty, thirty or forty years." The state societies were an important agency of acculturation, primarily for older migrants.

The development of cafeterias in the West during the twenties was another manifestation of "the aging of the West." Cafeterias were peculiarly well suited for older, mobile, rootless people of lower-middle-class, rural background. Very probably the cafeteria had its origins in Los Angeles, where in 1912 the Boos Brothers opened the first large self-service restaurant. Soon cafeterias became the hub of social life for the over-50 group of westerners. Why? Perhaps, because cafeterias were friendlier eating places than restaurants, and certainly more informal. The possibility of meeting someone there was greater than in a restaurant. And since many of the older middle westerners were "drys," they eschewed bars. The informality of cafeterias was especially appealing to ex-farmers or small townsmen, for in the twenties many cafeterias exhibited all the aspects of an indoor picnic. Moreover, retired people on limited budgets appreciated the relatively low cost of food and the opportunity to linger in the search for companionship. So, the cafeteria was born out of the needs of older people in the West, although in ensuing years it became popular throughout the nation.

The natural concern of many older persons with death and dying was well reflected in the West during this decade. The number of funeral parlors and embalming establishments was considerably higher in southern California and other western towns than the nationwide average. It was no accident that the most famous cemetery in twentieth-century America was established in the West. This was Forest Lawn Memorial Park in Los Angeles, founded in 1917 by Dr. Hubert Eaton. Assuming a surrealistic pseudo-Hellenistic atmosphere, this huge establishment featured beautifully kept walks flanked by dazzling and colorful arrays of flowers that hid amplifiers from which soothing music emanated. Eaton also put in an art gallery to give his park the appearance of a cultural center in which it would be a veritable joy to die. And in order to use his establishment to the fullest Eaton also provided three marriage chapels, assuring with great efficiency that bridal processions and funeral corteges would not get in one another's way.

The presence of a large number of older persons without young children may have contributed to a decided emphasis on pets and their care in Los Angeles, Tucson, and other western cities. Childless people often found that domestic animals satisfied some of their emotional cravings. Thus, it was not accidental that visitors to Los Angeles and to other western cities often found a large number of well-equipped dog and cat hospitals, training schools, rest homes, dog resorts, and cemeteries. The Hollywood Pet Cemetery became the most famous of its kind in the nation.[10] In short, as the Spanish conquistadors had left marks of their trail in the sand, so the high percentage of older people left a mark on the social landscape of the West during the 1920s and thereafter.

But the most important influence on the life-styles of westerners in the twenties was the automobile. It made possible the growth of suburbs, and the development of a new kind of metropolitan area that spawned ring upon ring of new suburbs in seemingly endless procession. To these suburbs came the young, the old, and all those who were disenchanted with American life elsewhere and had come to start anew. Whatever their background, most new westerners had a special sense of loneliness, of alienation, of uprootedness, which sprang largely from their great mobility. Not only had they pulled up roots to move westwards; after they had arrived the automobile provided them with a means to remain in constant motion. Suburbanization, indeed, often forced movement on this new type of city dweller. The West was becoming a civilization on wheels, the herald of a new age in America. To be sure, southern California more than any other portion of the West reflected this new living style, but other areas of the West were also beginning to reveal similar characteristics, if in more subdued form. These years, then, witnessed the development of a new American life-style in the West based on extensive mobility.

It would be difficult indeed to overestimate the social impact of the automobile on the West, beginning with the twenties. Over the next half century motor cars were to exercise a dominant influence in determining the configuration of western cities and their life-styles. The urban sprawl that was already developing in Los Angeles by 1925 set a pattern to be followed by all of America in the future. Middle westerners of these years wanted homes, not apartments, and in the West they still found the space to indulge their whim and to realize their ideal. As the automobile thus made possible the construction of outlying areas around towns and cities, real estate developers pounced upon relatively cheap lands to generate a succession of real and artificial booms. No plan, no systematic order dominated their vision, nothing but immediate and short-term profit. And many of the resultant communities in their garish and impermanent and unlovely aspect reflected this headlong rush to build. A look at any western city in the twentieth century—Los Angeles, San Francisco, Seattle, Portland, Denver, Albuquerque, El Paso, Phoenix, Tucson, Dallas, Houston—will reveal the "Los Angeles pattern" first developed in the 1920s. To a considerable extent the pattern developed not only because of the automobile, but also because the great majority of new western settlers after World War I came from rural areas of the Middle West, and to a lesser extent from the South. Thus, they were flat-land dwellers, addicted to openness and broad horizons. No skyscrapers for them, as for easterners, no congested tenements or apartment houses. Perhaps they were chronic or eternal villagers, as Carey McWilliams has suggested, but whether consciously or not, they sought to re-create the village pattern of the rural regions whence they came in this new metropolitan western environment. They hoped to have the country in the city, to create the best possible of two different worlds. And the automobile provided the means whereby this goal could be achieved, even if imperfectly.

And so Los Angeles by 1929, like other, later western cities, became a city without a center, a collection of suburbs (née villages) knit together by automobiles. The sense of community that city and town dwellers had once felt was bound to disintegrate in this new type of automobile culture. No longer was there a relation between one's residence and one's place of employment. On the eve of the Great Depression Los Angeles already had a higher per capita ownership of automobiles than any other city in the nation—one car per family. With more than 800,000 automobiles in Los Angeles, there were more police assigned to traffic work than there were men on the entire force in San Francisco. And widespread use of cars tended to abort the growth of other types of transportation or mass transit and fostered the constructions of "strips" of highways extending in all directcs. During this period Los Angeles became America's first city on wheels, its first automobile metropolis, to be emulated by other cities in the West, and ultimately, throughout the nation.

Automobiles also played a significant role in the less densely populated regions of the West. In the remoter areas of the Rocky Mountain states, the Southwest, and the Plains, the automobile was crucial in ending the isolation that many westerners had long felt. Hamlin Garland in his books before World War I captured that sense of loneliness better than most other writers. After 1919, however, westerners everywhere were shedding some of that isolation. Their physical remoteness was greatly reduced by the use of cars; emotional isolation was lessened as automobiles brought them a larger measure of human contacts, and their intellectual isolation was diminished as travel to towns to take advantage of cultural attractions—whether libraries, movies, art exhibits, or musical performances—became increasingly common. Obviously, the development of radio in the twenties further narrowed the gap between city and country dwellers. Life on the ranch was becoming not much different than life in the city had been a generation earlier. The new Home on the Range differed markedly from the old one. An old cowboy, commenting on this great change in 1927, said:

> Most of the cow ranches I've seen lately was like a big farm. A bungalow with all modern improvements, a big red barn that holds white-faced bulls an' hornless milk cows. The corrals are full of fancy

chickens, there's a big garage filled with all kinds of cars, and at the bunkhouse that sets back where the owner and his family can't see or hear them, are the hands.

You might see a man with a big hat, boots and spurs—he's the fence rider—but most of them wear bib overalls. The boss wears puttees and a golf cap.

The bungalow, that's got electric lights an' hot and cold water. There's a piana [sic] that you play with your feet, and a radio, a Mah Jong set, and a phonograph.

Some westerners did not have to move to the city to enjoy its advantages; the city moved to them![11]

And yet the automobile created a paradox. By increasing mobility, it created a new kind of loneliness, a new kind of maladjustment rooted in a loss of a sense of community. This was truer of recently arrived westerners in the twenties than it was of "old" second- and third-generation westerners. In the new suburbs that sprang into being people living on the same side of the same street in the same block in the same neighborhood were often complete strangers. And this loneliness within the crowd often erupted into various forms of social or personal maladjustment. In the twenties, the divorce rate in Los Angeles was twice as high as the national average; the number of suicides was relatively high; and juvenile delinquency and crime rates were higher than in the East. As one sociologist, Charles N. Reynolds, pointed out, in communities where there were large numbers of newcomers "social control agencies such as the opinion of neighbors, friends or relatives are weakened or absent and the law itself fails to function as it should." Status systems were largely absent, and even if painfully established, were quickly overturned by a new avalanche of migrants. And so, although the automobile brought new freedom, it also carried the germ of alienation. But who could surmise in 1929 that the life patterns first developed in Los Angeles would be repeated a thousandfold throughout the United States in the course of the next half century?

The fact that the West had a relatively rootless population in the twenties as well as a low density of settlement explains its attraction to cultists. The attraction of such a restless country for fakers, dreamers, or dropouts from society was irresistible. Consequently, California and the West became the home of a diverse array of cults or experiments in living. Southern California became a favorite spot, not only because it was at the end of a continent, but also because of its mild winters. A succession of eccentrics descended on the area and left their indelible imprint on the land. This is not the place to expand on their various experiences, but only to indicate that they contributed to making the western social fabric. One of the earliest settlements was the Point Loma Theosophical Community, founded in 1900 by Katherine Tingley, the Purple Mother, near San Diego. Until her departure in 1923, the Purple Mother had a significant role in introducing southern Californians to Yoga. She, too, was a western pioneer. Her theosophical teachings were adapted in 1911 by a retired Virginia lawyer, Albert Powell Warrington, who established the Krotona community in the middle of present-day Hollywood. He was deeply interested in the occult and psychotherapy, but also sponsored concerts, literary readings and lectures, and drama. Krotona stimulated the formation of a Theater Arts Alliance in Los Angeles in 1919, which led to the famous Hollywood Bowl concerts of a later day. In addition to these well-known sects, literally thousands of small faddist movements sprang into being during the twenties, including vegetarians, faith healers, and nudists. "In All the World No Strip Like This" declared a sign over the entrance of the nudist Land of Moo in southern California.[12]

As an extremely mobile people, the inhabitants of this automobile culture displayed a mixture of rural as well as urban beliefs. In view of the large-scale exodus of middle westerners to the Pacific Coast at this time, it is not surprising that they brought some of their values with them. As Lincoln Steffens noted in 1927, on returning to California from Europe: "California today is not a western, it is a middle western, State." Steffens was exaggerating, but his statement contained a germ of truth. Often rural and urban values existed side by side, but sometimes they came into conflict. The rural influence was revealed in nativism, in strong support of prohibition, and in the popularity of religious orthodoxy in the form of fundamentalism. Yet these values were superimposed on those of native sons or "old westerners" in urban communities who exhibited a cosmopolitan tolerance, a laxity toward self-indulgence such as drink, and a rather loose adherence to formal religous observances.

It cannot be said that the Ku Klux Klan commanded any particular following in the West during the twenties, although there were some exceptions. The Klan had a brief measure of success in Oregon and Texas between 1920 and 1922, but was deeply rooted only in Oklahoma. In Oregon the Klan supported a public school attendance law in 1923 that was aimed at the destruction of parochial schools. But two years later, before this law became operative, the United States Supreme Court declared it unconstitutional. Voting statistics indicate that the major support for this measure came from recent arrivals in Portland and other towns. The electorate in the rural areas of Oregon, composed mostly of stable "old Westerners," showed little sympathy for the Klan. The Oregon legislature of 1923 also enacted an alien land law in imitation of California's 1913 statute prohibiting land ownership by aliens. After 1925 such prejudices subsided, however. The rural prejudices of the newcomers to the West were reflected in their anti-labor attitude. Employers organized hundreds of open-shop associations during the decade, of which California's Civil Liberties Bureau, the California Better America Federation (composed of Los Angeles merchants), and the San Francisco Industrial Relations Committee were among the most effective.

Prohibition was one of the issues closest to the hearts of the many westerners who had but recently come from the Middle West and the South. It also attracted support from former urban progressive reformers who considered it unfinished business left over from the great reform era before World War I. These groups regarded prohibition as an essential aspect of moral regeneration. On the other hand, big-city dwellers, ethnic groups, and a variety of social critics, in addition to many young people, resented this effort to impose standards of private morality by law. Throughout the West these conflicting tendencies could be observed, related directly to the composition of the population in a particular western community. In those western cities that had relatively large foreign populations, and which treasured their reputations for sophistication—notably San Francisco and Seattle—the inhabitants consistently voted against prohibition. But those urban areas that contained large blocs of middle-western and southern migrants—such as Los Angeles and Portland—supported prohibition. Elsewhere in the West divisions on this issue were common, especially in view of the fluidity of their social structure. Phoenix, Tucson, Denver, El Paso, and Albuquerque did not vote overwhelmingly for the Eighteenth Amendment (prohibition), whereas Salt Lake City did, primarily because of the Mormon influence.

The rural Protestant lower-middle-class background of so many new westerners in the twenties found expression in their support of religious orthodoxy. Southern California became one of the centers for revivalism in the region, although by no means the only one. One of the most dramatic revivalists of the decade was Aimee Semple McPherson, or Sister Aimee, as her followers were wont to call her. The widow of a Baptist preacher, in 1918 she arrived in San Diego in an old car with two children and $100. Sensing the needs of many of her fellow migrants, she decided to emphasize faith healing and developed the Four Square Gospel (conversion, healing, the Second Coming, redemption). Although her early revival meetings were held in a boxing arena, she had by 1922 collected enough money to build the magnificent gleaming white Angelus Temple in Los Angeles with a 5,300-seat auditorium. There she presented elaborately staged pageants with a flair for showmanship that rivaled Hollywood. Once seen, Sister Aimee—attired in spotless white, prancing on stage with a pitchfork aimed at the devil—could never be forgotten. All this to the accompaniment of the mighty organ which she had installed, elaborate choirs, stage props, and lighting devices, while outside, airplanes showered religious tracts on the thousands who had been unable to gain admission. These spectacles, combined with her passionately delivered sermons, provided color for the drab lives of the thousands of uprooted and insecure people who became her followers, and provided them with a form of emotional release that perhaps had therapeutic value. Her influence waned after 1926 when she disappeared temporarily, either to be resurrected from the dead or to escape to a love tryst with the church organist.[13] More austere and traditional was the Reverend Robert P. (Fighting Bob) Schuler, a Methodist minister who in 1920 came to Los Angeles from the South. Inveighing against sin, drink, and evolution, Shuler had become a major political power in Los Angeles by 1929. According to Edmund Wilson, he was the real boss of Los Angeles. His radio audience in the twenties was reputed to be the largest in the world. He unseated a mayor, a district attorney, police chiefs, and was himself nearly elected to the United States Senate.

The twenties, then, were a time for great changes in parts of the West.

The Western Economy, 1921–1929

The heavy influx of people into the West during the twenties provided a great stimulus to the expansion of the regional economy.

Despite the post–World War I depression, the level of western economic activity in 1921 was considerably higher than it And it continued to expand significantly in the era of Harding and Coolidge. During these years the automobile as well as radio and communication improvements further integrated the West as a region and facilitated its contacts with the East. The West was still primarily a raw-materials producing area, however, and its prosperity was selective. Farmers, cattle growers, and fishermen experienced many ups and downs during the decade, as did miners and lumbermen. On the other hand, western manufacturing grew steadily during these years and the service industries boomed. Meanwhile, quietly and unobtrusively, western financiers were laying the foundations for a financial system that greatly lessened their dependence on Eastern and foreign capital, thus providing a greater measure of economic self-sufficiency.[14] The West may still have been a colony of the East in 1929, but it was far less a colony than it had been thirty years earlier.

Transportation

Instrumental in western economic growth were new modes of transportation. And none had a more revolutionary impact on the West than the automobile. What the railroads did for the opening up of the West in the nineteenth century, motor cars and trucks did for its development in the twentieth. For centuries many of the major problems of the West had been closely related to its geographical peculiarities, particularly its isolation from the population centers of the United States. The automobile changed all that after World War I. Automobiles not only provided cheap and easy communication between East and West; they also led directly to the development of new routes in the West. Cars ended western isolation. If the automobile was more significant for the West than the East, it was partly because it could reach areas where railroads had not yet been built. And the vast open spaces of the West provided unlimited opportunities for the development of auto travel.

It was not surprising, therefore, that in the 1920s westerners rushed to acquire automobiles, as in no other section of the nation. This was the great era of highway building in the West, comparable to the great internal improvements craze during the first half of the nineteenth century. Between 1919 and 1929 the western states, with the help of federal funds provided in the Highway acts of 1916 and 1921, built over 1 million miles of new highways suitable for cars. In matching federal grants, the states of the trans-Mississippi West issued a flood of highway bonds during the twenties and then, when these funds proved inadequate, followed the pioneering lead of Oregon in 1919 in imposing a gasoline tax to pay for roads. And so highway travel boomed after World War I. Already by 1925 more western tourists traveled by car than by rail, and westerners themselves took to automobiles more readily than their ancestors had taken to horses. Automobile ownership and registration were higher in the West than in any other section, about twice the national average. California alone had 10 per cent of the nation's 23 million cars and trucks in 1929, as many as all the other western states combined. California as a state, and Los Angeles as a city, in 1929 had the highest automobile registration per capita in the nation. The population of Los Angeles doubled in the decade after 1919, but car ownership quintupled.

The economic impact of the auto on the West was immediate. As the President's Research Committee on Social Trends pointed out in 1930: "No invention of such farreaching importance was ever diffused with such rapidity, or so quickly exerted influences that ramified throughout the national culture." As Los Angeles revealed by 1929, the automobile created a new kind of city, a series of suburban clusters that marked the birth of the megalopolis. Now it was possible for a citizen to work in one place, and to have his residence in another, which meant that megalopolis would have a high degree of individual home ownership and a relatively low density of population. Clusters of small homes in suburbia in turn generated a revolution in retail distribution as real estate developers began to build "shopping centers" geared to customers who came by car rather than on foot. The ubiquitous American supermarket was born in Los Angeles in the 1920s. One of the first was constructed by A. W. Ross, a Los Angeles realtor, in

1925 on the empty stretches of Wilshire Boulevard, which he turned into the "Miracle Mile," geared especially to shopping by automobile. Automobiles also created a myriad of auxiliary service industries in California during the 1920s—repair shops, cheap eating establishments, motor courts, and gasoline stations. Perhaps the first gasoline station in the United States was established by Earl B. Gilmore in Los Angeles in 1909 when he placed a gasoline tank on a farm wagon, painted it bright red and yellow, and parked at the corner of Wilshire Boulevard and LaBrea Avenue. Meanwhile, Detroit auto manufacturers, especially Ford and Chrysler, by 1929 had established assembly plants in California, providing further manufacturing employment. Yet westerners were reminded of their colonial status by the fact that most automobile parts were still manufactured in the East.

Increasing competition from car and truck unfortunately weakened the condition of western railroads in the twenties. The railroads were getting an increasingly smaller share of the passenger and freight traffic during the decade. Of course, the impact of water transportation also cannot be ignored, for Panama Canal traffic grew steadily during these years. Bulk commodities such as petroleum and lumber went east by sea rather than by rail. In 1914 virtually all western freight moved east by railroad; ten years later at least one-half went by ship. Such vigorous new competition led the western railroads between 1918 and 1929 to undertake a drastic revision of their rate schedules. Year after year, but especially in 1921 and 1924, they filed hundreds of new reduced-rate schedules with the Interstate Commerce Commission and also lessened their discriminatory rates against western towns and cities of the interior. Such discrimination had prevented many localities in the Rocky Mountain and southwestern regions from competing effectively with coastal cities as jobbing and distribution centers. These more equitable rates enabled merchants of the interior to expand their trade in the 1920s and so contributed to urban growth in these less-heavily populated areas.

Nevertheless, like the South, the entire trans-Mississippi West vigorously protested the basing point system—long in use by the railroads—which they formally adopted in 1924 with ICC approval. Despite its great economic progress, the West in the twenties was still an economic colony of the East, a producer of raw materials that the East fabricated for its own profit. As late as 1929 east-bound tonnage from the West was three times as great as the westward flow. But in 1924, in an effort to systematize the nation's railroad rate patterns, the Interstate Commerce Commission divided the nation into four districts, and then stipulated freight rates on distance from "basing points," major eastern manufacturing centers. The price of steel, for example, no matter where produced or how delivered, was fixed at a sum equal to the base price at Pittsburgh, plus rail charges from Pittsburgh to the point of delivery.

With their concern over the conquest of distance, it is not surprising that westerners early played a prominent role in the development of aviation. During World War I Los Angeles and San Diego became aircraft manufacturing centers. Although during these years airplane engines were still made mainly in Detroit, the twenties saw the rise of plants in the West to fabricate fuselages, parts, and to perform some assembly. Climate was a major reason for the location of airplane manufacturing in southern California, for year-round mildness permitted testing throughout the year. During the same time the Boeing Aircraft Company was establishing itself in Seattle, largely because that city was the founder's place of residence. By 1929, however, Boeing had built up one of the most technically proficient airplane factories in the United States and had become a significant factor in the economy of the Pacific Northwest. Together, Los Angeles and Seattle made the West one of the leading aircraft manufacturing areas in the nation.

Westerners embraced flying with almost as much enthusiasm as they did the motor car. In fact, the first successful air passenger run was inaugurated in 1919 between Los Angeles and San Diego. By 1925 four transcontinental air lines were operating from the Pacific Coast. And throughout the trans-Mississippi West a disproportionately large number of persons rushed to secure pilot's licenses. Californians led the nation, for of 10,215 registered pilots in 1929, 2,076 were from the Golden State. And as for aircraft, Californians registered 1,222 out of a total of 7,840 in the entire country. In other western states there were fewer planes and pilots, but more than Americans elsewhere westerners quickly grasped the opportunities to conquer distance that air travel presented to them.

So the expansion of the western transportation system in the twenties provided a sound foundation for the growth of the economy in many areas. This economy was even then one based primarily on the extraction of raw materials. Thus, agriculture, ranching, fishing, mining, and lumbering still constituted the major industries of the West. And, in one way or another, each of these industries was based on the availability of water. In the Dry West—whether arid or semi-arid—water continued to be the key to greater prosperity.

Water

Where population grew much faster than the supply of water, serious problems were bound to arise. Such a dilemma beset southern California in the twenties, then in the midst of one of the greatest population surges in its history. Each year 100,000 new residents poured into Los Angeles—in addition to the 2 million already there—seriously taxing the city's water resources. It was reported that the city fathers were so desperate that they consulted occult rain makers, scientific rain makers, and Indian medicine men, but could not find a plausible solution.

Where was new water to be found? Throughout the decade the city of Los Angeles expanded its controversial Owens Valley project, despite vociferous protests from settlers there. In 1923, on three separate occasions, these settlers gripped their rifles in an unsuccessful effort to stop diversion of water into the Los Angeles Aqueduct. Protests became much louder in 1928 when a dam in the San Francisquito Canyon—a part of the project—gave way. Its collapse on March 12, 1928, brought an avalanche of water rushing down into the Santa Clara Valley, sweeping before it trees, houses, bridges, and railroad tracks. When the bodies were counted, public authorities discovered that the flood had taken the lives of 385 people, making it one of the greatest natural disasters in the United States during this decade.[15] The Owens Valley tragedy pointed up the desperate need for new and safe sources of water for burgeoning cities in the West.

Already the city fathers of Los Angeles were looking outside California for new supplies, especially to the Colorado River. As early as 1904 Arthur Powell Davis, a distinguished engineer and nephew of John Wesley Powell, conceived a plan for the comprehensive development of the Colorado River, a plan that was widely discussed in ensuing years. Then, between 1916 and 1922, Davis became director of the U.S. Reclamation Service and secured the support of Secretary of the Interior Albert Fall. The most avid supporter of the Boulder Dam Project was Congressman Phil Swing of California who, along with Senator Hiram Johnson, sponsored appropriate legislation. Considerable opposition to federal water development grew in Congress, from private power companies, from the Harry Chandler interests, and also from the state of Arizona, which feared diversion would be harmful to its own economic growth. In view of this acrimony Secretary of Commerce Herbert Hoover in 1922 called a conference of western states to meet in Santa Fe, New Mexico, to formulate an interstate compact to apportion the water of the Colorado. At this meeting representatives from California, Colorado, Wyoming, Utah, New Mexico, Arizona, and Nevada formulated a compact to provide for development of the Colorado River basin for the common benefit of the participating states. The plan provided for the equitable division of water between upper-basin states (Wyoming, Colorado, Utah, New Mexico) and lower-basin states (California, Arizona, Nevada). Eventually all of them ratified the compact, except Arizona.

Nevertheless, the western states needed federal aid if the Colorado River compact was to be made effective. For years the advocates and opponents of the project in Congress fought to a standstill. Not until 1928 did its proponents have the strength to secure its enactment. In that year Congress authorized the construction of Boulder (later designated Hoover) Dam near Las Vegas, Nevada, to harness the Colorado River. This project provided for

Majestic Hoover Dam. Source: U.S. Bureau of Reclamation. Photo by E. E. Hertzog.

Power for the West: Grand Coulee Dam in Washington, at dusk. Source: Denver Public Library, Western History Department.

State-owned grain mill and elevator, Grand Forks, North Dakota, built in the 1920s. Source: State Historical Society of North Dakota.

effective flood control for California's Imperial Valley, augmented the water supply of Los Angeles, and created a multistate water reserve, in addition to providing for the generation of hydroelectric energy for the entire Southwest. Under President Hoover's prodding, construction began in 1930, not to be finished until five years later. When completed, Boulder Dam was the largest in the world in its day. Without it, the expansion of Los Angeles and hundreds of other smaller western towns and cities in the West would have been seriously retarded.

Within the states, legislators were also embarking on their own water projects. During the twenties every one of the western states authorized some form of water development within its borders. The most ambitious plans were in California, where several progressives, such as Rudolph Spreckels, advocated a Central Valley Project, a coordinated public water and power development scheme for the entire state. Private power interests, especially the Pacific Gas and Electric Company, strongly opposed this proposal, and prevented its legislative enactment in 1924 and 1926. In 1929, however, the California legislature did authorize a study of the plan's feasibility. The history of public water development plans in other western states followed somewhat similar patterns, despite differences of detail.[16]

Agriculture, Livestock, and the Fisheries

The availability of water was especially crucial for the expansion of agriculture. California in the twenties became not only the leading farm state of the West, but of the nation, producing a variety of crops whose annual value approximated $1 billion. Its agricultural diversity was unmatched anywhere. California became the major purveyor of fruits and vegetables for the large urban centers of America; its citrus fruits found ready markets throughout the world; and by 1929 it had also became the country's largest producer of cotton. By that year it was shipping more than 250,000 carloads of produce yearly to markets throughout the nation. It was estimated that Californians then produced more than 180 specialty crops, mainly through the application of mass-production techniques to farming. Sophisticated use of irrigation works in deserts such as the Imperial or San Joaquin valleys, combined with scientific farming methods, made such production records possible. Moreover, California agriculture came to be dominated even more by giant corporations in the image of Miller and Lux or the Di Giorgio Brothers. These companies practiced a high degree of specialization and were able to exploit seasonal migratory labor, especially Mexican *braceros* first brought into the state during the twenties. And through shrewd utilization of irrigation they changed deserts into orchards, and converted wastelands into gardens. By 1929, it seemed as if in California, man had triumphed over nature.

And yet, the predominance of corporate farming in California aroused considerable unrest. To be sure, the problem was not new. Henry George had protested against land monopoly in California half a century earlier. By the 1920s, however, it was clear that time was running out on Californians. Either they would make another sincere effort to implement the concept of family farming, or the dominance of big corporations over the state's agriculture was likely to endure. And so, during and after World War I, a group of land reformers led by Elwood P. Mead, former state engineer (and director of the U.S. Bureau of Reclamation, 1922–1936), the Commonwealth Club of California, and others prevailed on the California legislature to authorize the establishment of two experimental cooperative farming communities. These pilot projects were designed to demonstrate that small-scale farming along the lines of rural cooperatives was feasible. In view of the unemployment situation and the large numbers of returning war veterans, the lawmakers were agreeable to this experiment and in 1919 appropriated more than $100,000 for it. Under Mead's direction farming communities were established at Lehi and at Durham. Despite high hopes, much enthusiasm, and idealism, these ventures in agricultural cooperation soon encountered many difficulties, from the settlers themselves as well as from increasingly unfriendly legislators who looked askance at experiments in "socialism." By 1929 the colonies were considered failures, and the legislature decreed their dissolution.

In the Pacific Northwest agriculture also continued to be an important source of income. Farmers were subject to the same fluctuations there as elsewhere, experiencing wartime boom, the postwar depression from 1919 to 1921, rising prices until 1925, another decline, and then some improvement from 1927 to 1929. Fruit production became increasingly more important than grains during this decade and farmers in this area—like the Californians—fared somewhat better than their counterparts in the grain or cotton regions.

The least prosperous of western farmers in the twenties were those in the Rocky Mountain states, the Southwest, and the Plains. Where there was water in the Rockies, profits from farming could be made. In Colorado, for example, large-scale fruit, vegetable, and beet sugar producers did not fare badly. But many small farmers on the dry lands of eastern Colorado—who had been lured into wheat and grain production by high prices during World War I—could not survive the price slump after the Armistice and faced bankruptcy. Indeed, farm tenancy in Colorado increased from 23 per cent in 1920 to 35 per cent ten years later. The larger farmers managed to survive, partly by strengthening cooperative marketing associations to stabilize production and increase prices, very much like their colleagues in California. Poverty became the lot of many small farmers in the Southwest, in remote villages or on Indian reservations, throughout the twenties. And, for the Plains farmers, especially for the grain farmers of Kansas, Nebraska, and Oklahoma, the entire decade was difficult. Falling prices and increasing costs confronted many with mortgage foreclosures and bankruptcy. Some of the younger sons gave up farming in the 1920s and moved to urban centers to find jobs.

Western agriculture was becoming more commercial, and much like big business, in the twenties. Its spectacular success was traceable to the adaptation of technology and mass-production methods and to economies of scale. These methods were usually employed most successfully by giant corporations, but even medium-sized farmers found in this decade that they could survive by organizing farm cooperatives that could rival corporations in size as well as effectiveness. By 1929 it was clear that farmers would have to band together to stabilize production and prices, and that in all likelihood, they would need the aid of the national government to help them attain these twin goals.

Like the farmers, western cattlemen experienced hard times in the twenties, especially in the Rocky Mountain states, the Southwest, and on the Plains. The postwar depression persisted in these areas until about 1923, when meat prices began to recover somewhat. American cattlemen lost their European and world markets and watched meat consumption at home decline, partly because of heavy unemployment. And so prices dropped—and dropped. Whereas the price for cattle had been $14.50/hundredweight in 1918, it was down to $6.00/hundredweight in 1922. And yet overhead and expenses remained the same. Thus, thousands upon thousands of cattlemen between 1919 and 1925 were forced to sell their stock, their land, their equipment, and even their personal belongings simply to declare bankruptcy. Thousands of others were barely saved by emergency loans extended by the War Finance Corporation, which President Harding revived in 1921 to help cattlemen and farmers. And disease and drought caused additional problems. In 1921 and 1922 Montana and Wyoming were beset by such severe grasshopper plagues that cattle there had to be moved elsewhere. Although disease control became remarkably effective during the 1920s, the year 1924 saw the spread of the dreaded hoof and mouth disease throughout the western states, leading to the imposition of a regional quarantine. Conditions improved after 1926 as increased ranch farming and scientific breeding enabled remaining cattle growers to improve their efficiency.[17]

Times were not too good for the commercial fishermen of the West in the twenties. Certainly their production records were remarkable, for they doubled their catch between 1919 and 1929: But prices for fish plummeted in direct relation to the increase in production. The increase was secured by the use of larger boats and more highly mechanized equipment. Moreover, after 1919 Pacific fishermen ranged farther than ever. During the decade they combed the seas from Alaska down to the coasts of South America and often ventured more than 2,000 miles westward into the Pacific.

California's fishermen between 1914 and 1929 developed the largest sardine fishing industry in the world. Their annual catch during this period exceeded 300 million pounds. But the market for canned sardines simply was not large enough to absorb this huge quantity, and many of the fish were converted into fertilizer, fish oil, and other by-products. But by continuing to bring in a catch that was vastly in excess of demand, the California fishermen were by 1923 coming into conflict with the conservation policies of the California Fish and Game Commission. Throughout the decade the Commission tried, not very successfully, to limit the amount of fish caught, but it found enforcement difficult.

During the decade the tuna fishermen were also bringing in large catches, but as prices steadily declined this industry too entered a slump. As for salmon, by 1919 the schools had already been so greatly depleted in California that the industry shrank to insignificant proportions. In addition, river pollution and hydroelectric power projects seriously diminished the few spawning grounds still left in California.

In the Pacific Northwest these years saw a modest expansion in the salmon and halibut fisheries. At no time until 1929 did the demand for salmon reach World War I levels. In addition, American salmon fishermen had to meet stiff competition from Japanese, Canadians, and Russians in export markets. As Americans increased the intensity of their fishing they also raised the specter of exhaustion. The conservation problem became so serious that in 1930 the United States and Canada signed the Sockeye Salmon Convention to create an International Pacific Salmon Fisheries Commission to regulate seasons and the total annual catch. Meanwhile, the Pacific halibut fisheries continued to be the world's largest, although they did not increase their production in the twenties. Nevertheless, the issue of conservation arose during World War I and led eventually to an American-Canadian Fisheries Conference in 1918. As a result of further discussions both countries agreed to the creation of an International Fisheries Commission in 1924, which was to recommend conservation policies. Not until a new treaty of 1930, however, did the two governments grant the Commission more effective regulatory powers.[18]

Like farmers and cattlemen, therefore, western fishermen faced difficult times during the 1920s. Despite the efficiency of their production methods, shrinking markets depressed prices for their products. And increasingly, their rapid exploitation of fish resources brought them into conflict with conservationists—in government and out—and led to the imposition of further restrictions on their activities.

Minerals

Other raw materials producers also encountered major problems in the twenties. Since mining was more important than agriculture in the Rocky Mountain states, the health of the industry to some extent affected the entire regional economy. Between 1919 and 1921 prices of most minerals sagged, driving out many of the smaller operators. Production of copper fell sharply until 1923, when it began a slow rise, along with lead, zinc, and coal. The economies of Arizona, Utah, and Montana, and to a lesser extent, Nevada, Colorado, and New Mexico, felt the shock as thousands of unemployed miners flocked to towns and cities in search of jobs. Even after the recovery of mining prices in 1923 employment in the mines lagged because most producers had mechanized. By also utilizing new metallurgical processes, which made the exploitation of low-grade ores profitable, some mine operators were able to weather the severe price fluctuations. As they cut wages, they sometimes encountered labor troubles, as in the 1927 strike at the Cripple Creek, Colorado, coal mines. Copper was clearly the West's most important mineral in the 1920s. Gold production continued to decline during these years, although silver mining, in Nevada and Utah, increased significantly. Production of alloy metals that had been profitably mined during World Ward I—such as tungsten, molybdenum, and vanadium —stagnated in the 1920s because of competition from Chinese and Belgian Congo producers. During the 1920s California's Death Valley continued to be the nation's major source of borax, and New Mexico emerged as the preeminent potash producer in the United States. By 1929, the West produced 90 per cent of all minerals (other than coal) in the United States and thus played a crucial role in the American economy.

Without doubt, however, the most glamorous mineral of the West during the twenties was petroleum. It was on the vast oil fields of the West that great fortunes were made and lost during these years. As the rapid increase in automobiles generated entirely new markets for gasoline, oil, lubricants, and related products, the petroleum industry experienced the greatest boom in its history. And almost all the new petroleum discoveries of this period were in the West, in California, Texas, and Oklahoma, with lesser but significant finds in Wyoming, Kansas, New Mexico, and Montana.

Between 1919 and 1925 Californians learned of a series of spectacular discoveries in their state, in the San Joaquin Valley as well as in the Bakersfield area and southern California. Such names as Elk Hills, Kettleman Hills, Santa Fe Springs (Union Oil), Signal Hill (Shell Oil), and Huntington Beach (Standard Oil of California) conjured up visions of unlimited wealth. These finds made California the leading oil producer in the United States in 1929, producing 250 million barrels of oil annually, worth more than $500 million. In fact, the value of petroleum produced in California during the 1920s exceeded $2.5 billion, worth more than all the gold mined in the state since the glorious days of '49. And concomitantly, petroleum refining became the state's largest manufacturing industry. What gold was to the West in 1849, petroleum was in 1929.

By the end of the twenties the center of petroleum production was already shifting to the Southwest. Oklahoma had been a significant oil producer since the early days of statehood (1907). But the discoveries of new fields, especially the Oklahoma City field in 1927, raised its output enormously. And at the same time, vast new reserves were found in Texas. There the discoveries at Ranger in 1917, and at Big Lake in Reagan County after 1923, had augmented an already impressive production. But all previous wells were dwarfed by Dad Joiner's discovery of the fabulous East Texas field in 1930, one of the richest in the world. By that time the glut of petroleum in American as well as world markets had already plunged the industry into a severe depression.[19] Yet the development of the industry in the preceding decade had been little short of miraculous. On the eve of the Great Depression, the American West had come to supply America with yet another basic resource—petroleum.

Meanwhile, the boom in construction throughout the United States generated ample markets for lumber producers in the West. Yet, like other producers of raw materials, they experienced many vagaries and price fluctuations during the decade. Between 1919 and 1923 the industry tended to be depressed, but thereafter California as well as Pacific Northwest lumbermen enjoyed higher prices. In addition to fluctuating markets, timber producers were becoming increasingly conscious of conservation. The speed-up of lumber utilization during the World War I had again dramatized the dangers of rapid forest depletion. Gifford Pinchot continued to be a leading spokesman for conservationists, pointing out in 1921 that the destruction of forests then was about four times as great as their replenishment. Large lumber companies were not insensitive to such warnings. In 1924 they joined other groups in encouraging Congress to improve fire protection. Under the Clarke-McNary Act of that year Congress authorized cooperative reforestation as well as fire-control programs with the Forest Service, federal and state agencies, and private timber operators cooperating. The Sweeney-McNary Act of 1928 extended this program by authorizing creation of forest experiment stations to be administered cooperatively by public as well as private agencies. Meanwhile, lumbermen themselves, through their various trade associations, attempted to limit production to stabilize prices and to prevent ruinous competition and waste. Thus, both federal and state governments as well as private lumber interests were developing a common interest in restricting timber cutting and in fostering reforestation. As some westerners saw it, greater control over production and prices on their part would diminish eastern control of the industry.

Manufacturing and Service Industries

Although westerners were still primarily raw-materials producers in the twenties, this period saw them make further strides in developing manufacturing. By 1929 the western economy was certainly far more diversified than it had been in 1914. Not all areas of the West showed the same rate of progress, however. As might be expected, California made the greatest gains in manufacturing, with a more modest showing in the Pacific Northwest. The Rocky Mountain states and the Southwest, on the other hand, remained largely static in their industrial development. The growth of manufacturing thus revealed the same pattern as the growth of population—namely, a leapfrogging from the 98th meridian westward to the Pacific Coast.

To a considerable extent, California's accession to the number-eight spot among the nation's manufacturing states was generated by the remarkable growth of the automobile industry. By 1929, all manufactures contributed one-third of the state's income. Petroleum refining suddenly became the leading source of manufacturing income, and Richmond one of the nation's major refining centers. And the unprecedented demand for road-building materials was caused by the large-scale highway construction program stemming from widespread ownership of cars and trucks. But other industries also grew significantly during the decade. Food processing developed on an increasingly larger scale in California. In addition, the size and scale of many machine fabrication plants expanded considerably in this decade. Increasingly, eastern manufacturers were establishing branch factories on the Pacific Coast. Ford, General Motors, and the Chrysler Corporation built assembly plants and Akron tire manufacturers like B.F. Goodrich established West Coast plants. Many of these newer industrial plants arose in southern California as by 1929, for the first time, Los Angeles became the state's leading manufacturing center, overtaking San Francisco and Oakland.

It was in the twenties, therefore, that Californians finally achieved the necessary conditions for manufacturing success. Raw materials in themselves had not been sufficient to generate industrial growth. Markets had been desperately needed, and now the population growth during the decade was providing them. More than any other means of transportation the automobile was binding the state together as an integrated economic unit, facilitating easy distribution of manufactured goods. And petroleum and electric power were overcoming California's erstwhile lack of coal, and providing it with the twentieth-century's major energy resources. Taken together, these new conditions made California an important source of manufactures, not only to supply its own swarming population, but that of the entire trans-Mississippi West.

Industrial expansion proceeded at a much slower pace in the Pacific Northwest. Between 1919 and 1921, in fact, manufacturing output declined to one-half of its wartime peak. Thereafter a slow recovery took place until in 1929 manufacturing output slightly exceeded World War I levels. The lumber industry and food processing continued to be major sources of manufacturing income, with some development in furniture and paper industries. Shipbuilding shrank to insignificant proportions between the two world wars. Construction industries were significant in most of the larger towns and cities. Nevertheless, although more slowly than Californians, businessmen in this region began to diversify their products. This diversification was reflected in a significant expansion of clothing manufactures, and also printing plants in the Pacific Northwest. By the end of the decade, however, the Pacific Northwest was still preeminently a lumbering and agricultural region.

The expansion of manufacturing on the Pacific Coast was not equaled elsewhere in the West. In the Rocky Mountains states, the Southwest, and the Plains, manufactures were still in their infancy, largely because of sparse population and discriminatory railway freight rates. In a few selected areas the construction of new oil refineries, as in Texas, provided a flurry of activity. On the other hand, some smaller local manufacturers found it difficult to compete with national companies that were invading their markets, and went out of business. On the whole, the West Coast excepted, manufacturing activity remained static in the trans-Mississippi region.

Not manufacturing but service industries in the twenties came to provide a significant new source of income for the West. Of these, tourism was one of the most significant. And tourism was revolutionized by the automobile during this decade. Until World War I tourism had been primarily the prerogative of the well-to-do; thereafter it became a common leisure activity. More than 3 million travelers annually came to sojourn in the West during these years, and after 1925 the majority came by car. This influx created a whole new complex of service industries in the West, encompassing gasoline service stations and repair shops, roadside restaurants, camp grounds, and new auto or tourist courts. As the magnificent great western hotels had served the wealthy before 1914, so the new plebeian establishments now served the multitudes. Like the gasoline station, the auto court was a western innovation. Consisting of a few simple wooden cabins or bungalows on a roadside tract with parking space for cars, it provided modest and inexpensive accommodations at low cost, less than even second-rate hotels. It had a special appeal to motorists, situated as it was adjacent to a highway, often with a small cooking facility, requiring no tipping or change of clothes. Easy to enter, easy to leave, the auto court was superbly geared to life on wheels, a life now followed by millions of new travelers on limited budgets. The invasion of the West by more than 40 million tourists in the twenties made tourism a major source of income for most states in the region.

Of course, the less numerous wealthy travelers did not wholly forsake the West during this period. The great resort hotels built at the turn of the century continued to draw large crowds, although some were losing the splendor of their early days. A larger percentage of their guests were now over 50 years of age. Increasingly, the younger generation of the "idle rich," the "flaming youth" of the twenties, now journeyed westward not to stay in grandiose hostelries built on eastern or European models, but to frequent dude ranches, a new type of western accommodation developed during this period. Understandably, city dwellers in the increasingly congested metropolitan centers of the East and Middle West hankered for a "return to nature," with all modern conveniences, of course. Such a yearning for the wide-open spaces was often mingled with a romantic nostalgia for a simpler and less complicated mode of life, one without many of the pressures of modern urban existence. The West provided an ideal setting for the temporary fulfillment of such dreams, and the dude ranch served as the vehicle for their realization. By 1919 several enterprising ranch owners in California, Arizona, Nevada, New Mexico, and Colorado decided to profit commercially from eastern interest in "life on the range." Some of them merely accepted paying guests; others built luxurious guest accommodations for the dudes, who dressed in western wear and were otherwise reminded of what the earlier West had been like. They were offered activities such as horseback riding, hiking, hunting, and other recreational attractions. Between the two World Wars the dude ranch became one of the most distinctive tourist attractions in the West, designed for a generation of big-city Americans for whom the region provided not only physical relaxation, but emotional release.

The heavy western tourist traffic of the 1920s stimulated new "cultural awareness" industries in the region. Businessmen were quick to capitalize on the sudden popularity of western wear and sports clothes, which many tourists affected. In the Southwest, Spanish-American or Chicano foods, traditions, and architecture were prominently emphasized, especially by Fred Harvey restaurants and gift shops, to attract tourists. And the widespread movement to publicize Indian culture that mushroomed after World War I, particularly as it related to Indian art, rugs, pottery, and jewelry, as well as basketwork, was in part a direct response to western tourism.

Without doubt, the development of the tourist industry in the West was enormously boosted by the extension of the National Park system. In 1916 Congress finally authorized establishment of the National Park Service to administer and augment this precious national heritage. Under the strong leadership of its first, and legendary, director, Steve Mather (1917–1928), the National Park Service made many more facilities available to tourists during the twenties. It also took an aggressive role in developing tours, national monuments, and historic sites. In 1919 only 1 million visitors came to the national parks; ten years later that number had increased more than tenfold. As Americans became an urban people with increased leisure time, they found in the automobile one of their last links with nature.

Tourism thus became an important industry in the West during the postwar decade. The increasing density of population east of the Mississippi River, the spread of automobiles and good roads, greater leisure for the many, and the majestic western scenery and climate combined to draw millions of visitors.[20] Moreover, nativism and nationalism were often intertwined, and old Americans as well as a new group of first-generation Americans found "See America First" campaigns of the National Park Service and the railroads congenial with their outlook. In that sense, tourism in the West was a manifestation of national pride, of the search of Americans for roots.

Not all tourists went west to see the wonders of nature in the twenties, however. Some went because they wanted to see the new movie capital of America arising on the Pacific Coast—Hollywood. Indeed, the motion picture industry was rapidly emerging as one of the most important in California, and as *the* major industry of southern California. Certainly it was well suited to the economic and physical features of that region, for it required no raw materials, was unaffected by discriminatory freight rates, and could draw on an ample pool of labor skills for the 100,000 persons which, in 1929, it required. By that time its expenditures exceeded $150 million annually, providing a reservoir of purchasing power that stimulated a host of other industries. Although estimates were not precise, contemporaries thought that more than a quarter of a million tourists were drawn to Hollywood each year.

In California the movie industry emerged at an appropriate stage of the state's economic growth. Less subject to business fluctuations than other industries, motion pictures provided a cushion for the state's economy. Moreover, since Hollywood produced 90 per cent of all motion pictures in the United States it was not disturbed much by competition. Nonseasonal and nonpolluting, the movie industry spawned hundreds of subsidiary pursuits. A studio such as that of the Warner Brothers boasted 108 auxiliary companies, including a radio manufacturer, a lithograph concern, real estate companies, music publishing houses, radio stations, and recording studios. Many professions received an enormous impetus from Hollywood, which also made Los Angeles America's newest fashion center, primarily for sportswear. Almost overnight, between 1919 and 1929, motion pictures became the nation's number-ten industry and a major contributor to western economic growth.[21]

Far less glamorous, but not insignificant, was the income that western states received from federal installations—especially army posts—within their borders. Given the underdeveloped nature of their economies in the twenties, as in the preceding half century, the expenditures by the national government constituted a significant portion of the states' total income. In sparsely settled states such as Arizona, New Mexico, Utah, the Dakotas, and Montana, such payments amounted to more than 15 per cent of the total annual gross state product. In fact, westerners in these years received a larger amount of federal monies than they paid to Washington in taxes. This apparent inflow of federal funds aroused much protest among some easterners. Yet this condition was not new; it had existed since the first settlement of the West. As an underdeveloped region the West desperately required capital, especially for large-scale projects such as internal improvements. When private enterprise was unable or unwilling to undertake development, westerners turned to the national government for help. This was as true in the 1920s as it had been a century before. To a considerable extent, therefore, the West was a creature of the federal government, and this dependence did not lessen during the course of the twentieth century.

If western industries grew substantially in the 1920s this was also partly because of the increasing maturation of its financial institutions. It would be inaccurate to say that in these years westerners freed themselves completely from their dependence on eastern capital. But they made remarkable progress in building a stronger banking system and so were able to provide themselves with a larger proportion of their capital needs than had the preceding generation.

Much of the credit for the western financial revolution of the twenties belonged to a man who emerged as the leading banker of the West in the twentieth century, A. P. Gianninni. Born in 1880, he started life as a fruit merchant in San Francisco, retiring in 1901 as a wealthy man. But Gianninni's restless energy did not allow him to remain retired for long. In 1904 he organized the Bank of Italy, depending on his friends and acquaintances in North Beach, then San Francisco's Italian quarter, for business. His foresight during the San Francisco earthquake and fire in 1906—when he whisked away his institution's funds to a place outside the city for safekeeping—aroused much favorable attention, and by 1912 he had opened two new branches. Unlike many of his fellow bankers, Gianninni took special interest in small borrowers and depositors and actively sought their business. To the disdain of his peers he advertised for customers and even sent out aggressive salesmen to drum up business. At the same time he provided many new services such as free counseling for small businessmen and installment loans. Gianninni sensed early what most other bankers were to grasp only a generation later; namely, that in an industrial mass society the accumulation of capital drawn from millions of small depositors could be at least as significant as dependence on syndicates composed of wealthy individuals and corporations.

But no banker could reach the multitudes by maintaining one centralized banking house in an austere downtown location. Instead, Gianninni decided to go where the people were. And so he was determined to open small and friendly branch banks in the midst of city and suburban neighborhoods. Gianninni conceived of the device of branch banking as the major tool for his expansion, combining the advantages of centralized banking direction and decentralized operation. Between 1910 and 1920 he opened twenty-four new branches and made the Bank of Italy the largest in the state. But the real burst of expansion came in the twenties when, after some bitter political battles with state banking superintendents, he secured permission to establish 150 new branches and to consolidate them into one comprehensive system. On the eve of the Great Crash, Gianninni had built the greatest bank in the West, destined to become one of the largest in the United States, and, indeed, the world.[22] Controlling more than 40 per cent of California's banking capital in 1929, Gianninni was able to supply much of the credit needed to undertake California's economic growth, and that of many neighboring western states as well.

If Gianninni was the captain of western banking, he was not the only prominent financier in California. In southern California Joseph Sartori was hardly less significant. It was he who arranged the merger between the First National Bank of Los Angeles and the Security National Bank in 1929, thereby creating one of the largest banks in the United States, second only to the Bank of Italy in the West. Much of the construction boom in southern

California during the twenties was financed by the Sartori empire. Many lesser mergers and consolidations characterized the state banking picture in these years. The total resources of California banks increased from $1.7 billion in 1917 to more than $4 billion in 1929. In short, by that time Californians no longer had to look outside their state for money to finance their expansion. Their own banks and insurance companies were now fully capable of providing large-scale credit to sustain rapid economic growth.

A somewhat more moderate expansion characterized banking development in the Pacific Northwest during the twenties. By and large, however, that region, too, became a creditor rather than a debtor, now able to finance much of its own economic development. The per capita resources of banks in Washington and Oregon were among the highest in the nation. And between 1919 and 1929 the number of banks there quadrupled. No one bank dominated the region as the Bank of Italy did in California, but the big Seattle and Portland institutions took the place of eastern financiers in handling investments and other business for the smaller country banks. Increasing self-sufficiency, therefore, characterized banking in this region, in contrast to other portions of the West, where the nature of the banking system did not change as appreciably during the decade of the twenties.

To sum up, the western economy made giant strides during this decade. To be sure, growth was greatest where the population was—and that meant California and the Pacific Coast. The Rocky Mountain states, the Southwest, and the Plains were not affected by the boom. Nor had the West by 1929 thrown off all vestiges of economic colonialism. It was still the nation's major producer of raw materials, dependent for its manufactures on the older East. But in the twenties westerners undertook a striking diversification of the economy, reflected not only in the growth in the output of raw materials but also in the development of manufacturing, the increasingly important service industries, and financial institutions. By 1929 the West was clearly growing up.

The Politics of Moderate Reform

The rapid but uneven economic growth of the West and the increase of population on the Pacific Coast provided the major issues of western politics in the twenties. But no simple generalizations aptly describe the political life of the West during these years, in view of extraordinary diversity. Most westerners, of whatever political persuasion, felt that further growth of the region was desirable. Hence they were disinclined toward political extremes. Rather, they tended to be middle-of-the-roaders, cautious advocates of modified reform. These were years of consolidation—not unlike the 1950s, when reform and conservatism coexisted in the programs of both major and minor parties. In order to describe western politics of the 1920s aptly, let us call this a period of muted reform.

Patterns of Western Politics

Throughout the 1920s reform continued to be a political issue in every western state, as many progressives sought to finish the unfinished business left suspended by World War I. To be sure, the mood of the twenties was more muted, less frantic, and less emotional than at the opening of the century. Much had happened since 1900. But progressives were still concerned about passing prohibition, a long-standing demand of a whole generation of reformers before 1914, and thereafter. On this issue they were joined by conservative elements. Progressives had also long demanded efficiency in government and had been among the foremost advocates of "scientific management" or administrative reorganization of state and local governments. They had also been strong supporters of the extension of a variety of public social services. Meanwhile, out on the Plains, the agricultural radicals—the neo-Populists—were demanding public ownership and operation of essential economic services. During the twenties the reformers achieved all of these proposals and turned their dreams into reality.

Far more significant of political trends, however, was the fact that the expenditures of western state governments between 1919 and 1929 and of western towns and cities, with a few exceptions, almost doubled, reflecting a national trend. In 1913 western state expenditures totaled about $100 million; in 1921 they were $220 million; in 1929 they were close to $336 million. State governments were making increasing appropriations for highways, for education, and for social services, despite widespread talk about the need for economy and retrenchment.

Conservative aspects of western politics in this era were reflected in a mood of moderation, in a desire to implement existing programs, but not to inaugurate many new ones. This was obviously a reform mood different from the one that had captured the imagination of many westerners in the decade before the war. Nativist laws and the Ku Klux Klan were manifestations mainly of the immediate postwar years, however, and much less of the years after 1921. By 1923 the Ku Klux Klan had lost all power in every state of the trans-Mississippi region. And most western courts refused to enforce nativist laws that came up to them for review, or to convict persons indicted under them. It is erroneous, therefore, to consider the appearance of the Klan, or nativism, as characteristic of the entire decade, when actually their influence was confined to the short period between 1919 and 1921. Rather, the conservatism of the decade was revealed more in the mood to implement —almost never to repeal—reforms of the preceding decade, but not to develop ambitious new programs.

Why, then, were political lines generally blurred in most western state and local politics of this period? To a large extent, this may have been because of extensive migration into the trans-Mississippi West, as well as considerable internal migration within the region. When people move, they often take their voting habits with them. The elaborate statistical computer analyses of political behavior made in recent years by the University of Michigan's Survey Research Center indicate that party loyalty has been an important determinant in influencing the vote of the average person. When more than 2 million small-town or rural middle westerners moved to the Pacific Coast in the 1920s they took their Republican voting preferences with them, as well as a desire to maintain the *status quo*. The experience of moving 2,000 miles, not to speak of the problems of adjusting to a new and strange environment, almost a foreign land, had been disruptive enough. Many of the Rocky Mountain states and the states of the Southwest lost population during the twenties. The dissatisfied, those seeking change, departed to seek greener pastures elsewhere, leaving behind their more placid or more successful neighbors who were not touched significantly by social, economic, or cultural changes during the period. Such large-scale migrations explain in part the blurring of political party lines during the decade.

It was different on the Plains. There, violent economic changes spawned an agricultural depression and bred political cohesion. There, political radicalism, articulated through the Non-Partisan League in North Dakota and elsewhere, had repercussions throughout the West.

Demographic patterns, then, aid us in understanding the diversity of politics in the West during the 1920s. If the conflict between city and country was more muted in the West than elsewhere, this was only because large numbers of rural dwellers moved to western cities, especially those on the West Coast, where they continued to practice the rural voting habits to which they were accustomed. And the exodus from the Rocky Mountain and southwestern states, combined with agricultural depression on the Plains, help to explain the political behavior of those regions.[23]

California

California's politics during the 1920s were a good illustration of blurred party lines. More than any other western state, California was the recipient of newcomers—2 million of them, most from rural backgrounds. It was no accident that Los Angeles resembled a huge village or that fundamentalist preacher Robert P. Schuler became the city's political "boss" during the decade. The city's political outlook—reflected in many issues—tended to become small-town middle western. At the same time, political confusion was compounded by a historical accident—the cross-filing system whereby a candidate for office could become a nominee of more than one political party. Republicans could file in Democratic primaries and vice-versa. This sytem had been advocated by Hiram Johnson and other progressive reformers in 1913 who hoped to destroy political bossism and existing political parties, not without an eye to strengthening their own rule. Yet Johnson and his supporters had not foreseen that cross-filing might destroy the party system and party responsibility. In the twenties, cross-filing allowed incumbents to manipulate thousands and thousands of ill-informed or recently arrived voters.

The influx of middle westerners contributed to the collapse of the Democratic party in California during the 1920s, where it had long been a power. Registered Republicans now came to outnumber Democrats by a ratio of 4 to 1. Republicans filed in Democratic primaries and so tended to dominate both houses of the state legislature during the 1920s. And the middle-western influence in the state was starkly revealed in the election of James Rolph, Jr., as governor in 1934. Many former governors had been native sons, but Rolph had been a member of the "Iowa Migration," and thus in a way emerged as the symbolic spokesman of the new migrants to California.

Despite political confusion and the blurring of party lines, the major trend of state policies during the twenties was one of muted reform. As elsewhere in the West, most Californians were concerned with finishing the unfinished business of the Progressive era. Prohibition was thus high on their list of priorities. The northern part of the state—containing many native sons, immigrants, Catholics, and other settlers who prided themselves on their cosmopolitanism—tended to oppose prohibition and consistently voted against it. San Francisco became known as the second "wettest" city in the U.S., next to New York City. Not so southern California which, as already pointed out, contained large numbers of native American Protestants of rural middle-western backgrounds. Los Angeles was the center of the "drys" in the state although "wets" were by no means without influence. In the enforcement of prohibition, California reflected many of the same divisions as other parts of the United States. Residents of most of the cities and larger towns tended to be unfavorable (with the exception of Los Angeles), whereas less-densely populated areas provided staunch support.

Administrative reform of state government was another old progressive issue that saw fruition in the 1920s. In November of 1918 progressive

Governor William D. Stephens appointed a committee on efficiency and economy to develop a reorganization plan to improve the effectiveness of state government. The proposals of this group were not acted on by the 1919 legislature, but two years later it adopted a modified scheme by which 112 state agencies were merged into five major new departments, greatly simplifying the structure of state government. The demand for further consolidation arose during the budget-cutting regime of Governor Friend W. Richardson (1923–1926) but was not prosecuted very vigorously until reform-minded Governor C. C. Young helped secure adoption of the comprehensive Administrative Reorganization Plan of 1927. New social functions being assumed by the state because of its expanding population led Governor Young to create additional state agencies two years later, after the major task of administrative reform was largely completed.

The various governors of California during the twenties also supported other measures urged by reformers. After a vigorous fight against corporate lobbies in 1921, Governor Stephens was able to finance his vast expansion of social services by securing legislative approval of an increase of 35 per cent in corporate taxation. The expansion of social services was being advocated vigorously by the Progressive Voter's League, a new organization formed in 1923 by progressives in many walks of life. Within two years its influence led to a vast expansion of state appropriations for public education and to broadened activities for the State Board of Charities and Corrections, which administered state hospitals and prisons. The state legislature in 1925 also overwhelmingly ratified the child labor prohibition amendment to the United States Constitution. Meanwhile, the Progressive Voter's League secured the election of C. C. Young to the governorship. Young's support of the Central Valley Project and public power and hydroelectric development was reflected in his appointment of the Central Valley Investigating Commission in 1929. By then the state was providing aid for the needy, physically handicapped, and the needy blind, and had began to establish an old-age pension system. With an eye toward population growth, Young also developed a long-range building program for social welfare institutions. In short, much of the work of state government in California during the 1920s gladdened the hearts of reformers and implemented many of the programs originally advocated by progressives before the First World War.

The Pacific Northwest

In the Pacific Northwest the political mood was also one of mild reform during the 1920s. Here, too, the influx of middle westerners tended to strengthen the Republicans, who had substantial majorities in congressional delegations and in state and local administrations. Congressmen from this region tended to become virtual fixtures in Washington. Willis Hawley of Oregon served in the House for thirteen terms (1907–1933); his colleague Nicholas Sinnott served from 1912 to 1928. Idaho voters sent William J. Borah to the United States Senate from 1907 to 1940, Congressmen Burton French from 1903 to 1933, and Addison Smith from 1912 to 1932.

Reform issues were one of the main ingredients of the region's political life during the decade. Support for prohibition was widespread, stronger in the rural areas than in the cities. Portland alone of the larger towns and cities favored prohibition, largely because of a large number of new lower-middle-class settlers from the rural Middle West or the rural border states and South. Seattle, on the other hand, priding itself on being a cosmopolitan seaport, and with a significant number of the foreign born, tended to be a "wet" center in the region.

Administrative reorganization was also a major political concern in each of the states in this area. As a result of the progressive political reforms of the preceding decade, administrative reorganization came before the voters of Washington as an initiative and referendum issue. Governor Louis Hart sought to imitate the example of progressive Governor Frank Lowden of Illinois in 1921 by proposing a comprehensive reorganization of state agencies. With only a few slight changes, the legislators enacted this comprehensive administrative code, which abolished more than seventy-five existing agencies and integrated them into ten new major departments. When Governor Roland H. Hartley assumed office in 1925, he furthered these administrative changes in the hope of attaining more efficiency in the face of rapidly expanding state functions.

Oregonians were far less decisive on state administrative reorganization, although the issue first had been proposed by William S. U'Ren and his People's Power League in 1909 and 1911. In 1917 a special investigating committee appointed by the legislature prepared a state reorganization plan, but neither in 1919 nor in 1923 was the legislature willing to enact it. The 1929 legislature submitted another proposal to the voters in 1930, who decisively defeated it. Consolidation of some state agencies was begun with legislative approval in 1929, however, so that Oregon undertook a fragmented form of administrative reorganization.

Idaho reformers were more determined. In 1919 the legislature accepted the recommendations of Governor D. W. Davis for the abolition of more than 50 state agencies and their consolidation into nine major departments. Many reformers were discouraged by the fact that administrative reform did not necessarily substitute efficiency for political patronage, but they were learning, if only from hard-won experience.[24]

Other reform issues became prominent in the region. Inasmuch as agriculture was so important in the area, it is not surprising that farm protest was endemic throughout the twenties. Reflecting the activities of the militant Non-Partisan League in North Dakota, the Farmer-Labor party in Idaho during the off-year election of 1922 secured a very significant minority vote. In the state of Washington the votes of discontented farmers affiliated with the Non-Partisan League in 1922 helped to send a progressive Democrat, Clarence Dill, to the United States Senate. Throughout this period the League was able to secure initiatives and referenda on issues it considered important. Meanwhile agrarian unrest was also reflected in Oregon in the 1922 gubernatorial victory of Walter Pierce, a dirt farmer. Although the Ku Klux Klan claimed credit for his election, he always disavowed sympathy for the Klan and publicly rejected its support. Much agrarian discontent was also shown in the strong support the Pacific Northwest gave Robert M. LaFollette, presidential candidate of the Progressive party in 1924. His candidacy cut by as much as one-half the Democratic vote total in the 1920 election and made significant inroads into the Republican column as well. Idaho cast almost as many votes for the Progressives in 1924 as for Republicans. And as many urban dwellers in the Pacific Northwest voted the Progressive ticket as did those in rural areas.

On the national scene Oregon's Senator Charles McNary was the co-sponsor of the McNary-Haugen Bill to raise farm prices through overseas exports. The bill became the major hope of American farmers for relief from the terrible depression that had gripped them since the close of the war. McNary was a recognized spokesman for grain interests in the Pacific Northwest and the nation. In 1928 he was able to rally most of the congressional delegations from the region to vote for the McNary-Haugen Bill, although it succumbed to President Coolidge's veto.

Perhaps more than other westerners, the citizens of the Pacific Northwest were outspokenly in favor of another progressive program—federal, state, and municipal regulation of public utilities. Public power became a heated political issue here in the twenties. In 1920 sharp conflict broke out involving Seattle, Portland, and Tacoma, which had municipally owned utilities, and Stone and Webster, a private power company based in Boston, and the Washington Water and Power Company. The private utility companies vigorously opposed expansion of public power facilities and spared no funds to fight them. Issuing a blizzard of propaganda—booklets, speakers, materials for use in the public schools—they attacked public ownership as socialistic. In addition, they made large contributions to both political parties, while maintaining strong lobbies in the state capitals. The issue of public power expansion crystallized in many towns and cities of the Pacific Northwest during the twenties, but reached a climax in Portland, where a progressive Republican state legislator, George Joseph, became the leader in the fight against the private power interests. His efforts prevented a merger between the Portland Electric Power Company and the Northwestern Electric Company, which would have threatened the city with a private power monopoly. Joseph became so popular that in 1930 he set out to win the Republican nomination for governor and embarked on a vigorous campaign. Unfortunately, his efforts ruined his health and he died a few weeks after his victory. During the crisis one of his closest friends, Portland's merchant prince, Julius Meier, stepped in to take his place. Reemphasizing the need for public power, he went on to win in the general election. In 1930, also, Oregon voters approved a measure that Joseph had advocated for many years—state authorization for establishment of public power districts by localities.

In neighboring Washington reformers also succeeded in making political capital out of public power. There, Homer T. Bone, who in 1911 had been the legal counsel for the city of Tacoma, became its leading political advocate. A Socialist in 1912, a Progressive in 1924, and then a Republican until 1932, when he switched to the Democrats, Bone was a direct link between prewar and postwar reform. He achieved one of his prime aims in 1930 when the Washington legislature enacted a public utility district law that he had advocated for more than a decade.[25]

The Rocky Mountains and Southwest

Moderate reform also characterized politics in the Rocky Mountain states and the Southwest, affecting both Democrats and Republicans. Between 1911 and 1929 the governorship of Arizona was dominated by the reform-minded George W. Hunt. In New Mexico, progressives under the able leadership of Bronson Cutting held the balance of power in state politics and swung their support now to one, now to another of the major parties. In Texas there were strong reform elements within the Democratic party. Progressive Democrat Pat Neff became governor in 1919, advocating prohibition, administrative reorganization, highway expansion, and tax reform. He was defeated by Earle Mayfield in 1922, who openly espoused Klan support. But Mayfield was defeated by "Ma" Ferguson in 1924, who vigorously denounced the Klan. Her successor was the most outspoken Texas reform governor of the decade, Dan Moody, who at 33 years of age became the youngest chief executive in Texas history. Moody relentlessly prosecuted the Klan, undertook extensive administrative reorganization, effectively reformed the prison system, and fought for the extension of civil service. And although Texas cast its electoral votes for Hoover in 1928, this was less because of religious prejudice against Al Smith than for Hoover's espousal of prohibition. In that same election Texans voted for Tom Connally as senator against the one-time defender of the Ku Klux Klan, former Governor Mayfield. In fact, with the exception of Mayfield, the governors of Texas during the twenties supported reform programs originally proposed by progressives before World War I.

As relatively sparsely populated areas, the Rocky Mountain states and the Southwest tended to favor prohibition. However, opinion was often divided. The larger cities and towns, such as Denver, Albuquerque, El Paso, and Houston, opposed prohibition. Only Salt Lake City, where Mormon influence was strong, was enthusiastic for the Eighteenth Amendment. The outlying areas, sparsely populated, generally favored prohibition . And since they tended to dominate the legislatures, their attitude was reflected in official actions taken by their respective states.

Since they were not affected by the widespread population increases characteristic of the Pacific Coast, state legislatures in this region were slow in undertaking administrative reform of their governments. In 1921 Arizona Governor Thomas E. Campbell proposed such a reorganization and submitted a specific plan. It was approved in the state senate but failed by one vote in the lower house. Six years later State Representative Elijah Allen reintroduced the measure, but this time the senate turned it back. Not until 1933, under the spur of depression, did Arizona reorganize its state government. Meanwhile, in 1921 the New Mexico legislature refused to submit a proposal of the Taxpayer's Association to the voters proposing the appointment of administrative officers by the governor. Again in 1927 a plan for some integration of state agencies was revived, but no action was taken by the legislature until six years later. This pattern was not unlike what occurred in Colorado. There, a special committee of the legislature recommended a reorganization plan in 1917, but only one aspect, a budget system, was adopted, and that not until two years later. Governor William E. Sweet sponsored another administrative reform plan in 1923, but it aroused considerable storm in the legislature. No reorganization took place until 1933, when the exigencies of depression provided the impetus for a substantial reorganization of the state government. Without the same pressures of burgeoning populations and expanding state activities, the Rocky Mountain and southwestern states were by no means opposed to reform, merely lackadaisical in its enactment.

Moderation was a key to understanding many political issues in these regions during the twenties. Of the six states that ratified the Constitutional amendment to prohibit child labor, five were in the West, including California, Washington, Arizona, Colorado, and Montana. These were all states with heavy concentrations of migratory field workers, and reformers were especially anxious to eliminate the exploitation of migrant children as farm laborers. Some of the states, like New Mexico, in 1929, belatedly enacted workmen's compensation laws. Most of the states in the area increased their appropriations for social welfare institutions and made efforts to improve conditions in their prisons. The use of convicts to work on highways was largely eliminated. Western states were also receptive to old-age pension schemes in these years. Montana in 1923 was followed by

California, Nevada, Colorado, Idaho, and Wyoming in providing compensation—very minimal, to be sure, but compensation nonetheless—for persons over 70 years of age. This is not the place for a comprehensive listing of reforms originally proposed by progressives, which state legislatures in the West enacted during the 1920s. Such an analysis would reveal what a few highly selective examples only indicate—that, far from being a decade of reaction, the political life of the twenties in the West was characterized by moderate reform.

Great Plains

Such a characterization is not wholly true of the Great Plains, however, where the Non-Partisan League was stoking a political prairie fire, as one historian has described it.[26] The Non-Partisan League—despite its name—was an agrarian reform party, founded in North Dakota in 1915 by A. N. Townley. The fate of North Dakota farmers had for years been dominated by a tight oligarchy of railroad and grain milling interests located in Minneapolis. Farm protests had surfaced in 1892 through the Populist party; they were revived in 1906 when a protégé of Robert M. LaFollette, John Burke, was elected governor. He pushed through a progressive reform program in the state until he left office in 1912. But the complaints of North Dakota farmers against middlemen did not cease. They argued that fees for using grain elevators were too high, that dockage rates at terminals were exorbitant, that fraud inspired the low grades assigned to grain by the milling companies, that interest rates were usurious, and that railroad rate charges robbed them of their well-deserved profits.

It was within this context that Townley, a former grain farmer himself, organized the Non-Partisan League. Townley was born and raised on a farm in Brown's Valley, Minnesota. He read widely on politics and economics under the tutelage of a radical tailor; then, in 1907, he began to farm near Beach, North Dakota. After five years of hard work he found himself bankrupt and bitter. Now a convinced socialist, he became an organizer for the party in the next year. But his failure to follow orders led to his dismissal and he decided to build his own organization. The League dominated state politics until 1923, although in the half dozen years thereafter it was still a potent influence. Strictly speaking, the League was nonpartisan in the sense that it supported any candidates—national, state, or local—who supported its program. That program was formulated by Townley and the leaders of the League, all of whom were convinced and militant socialists. North Dakota had a large number of Scandinavians and Germans who either were socialists themselves or were well acquainted with various forms of government ownership and operation in the context of European precedents. The League found strong support among such groups. Between 1915 and 1923 it elected more than one governor, controlled both houses of the legislature, and saw enactment of many phases of its program.

The program of the League was avowedly socialistic. Townley himself never ceased to preach class warfare and hatred of business interests. As an intensely practical man, he also had immediate aims. The League advocated state ownership of terminal elevators, flour mills, packing houses, and cold storage plants. Its platform also included a demand for state grain inspection, state hail insurance, and new rural credit banks to provide low-interest loans. Exemption of farm improvements from taxation was another frequent demand of League members. In an area dominated by agriculture, during a decade of persistent agricultural depression, the League's program had widespread appeal.

Townley and his organizers lost little time in beginning their drive to secure control of the state government to implement their program. Between 1915 and 1919 the League upped its membership to more than 50,000 and in the elections of 1919 it gained control of most state offices and the support of the state's newspapers. It aggressively pushed through its program as in 1919 when the legislature created an industrial commission to manage all state-owned business enterprises. It founded the Bank of North Dakota, in part to provide low-cost rural credits, and created the North Dakota Mill and Elevator Association, which was to create a system of warehouses, elevators, flour mills, and factories. In addition, North Dakota lawmakers approved a graduated income tax, hail insurance, and a state fire and tornado fund. As the Grand Forks *Herald* noted: "The State is now the Socialistic laboratory of the country."

During the next decade the success of these enterprises was mixed. S. A. Olness, a prominent supporter of the League, was responsible for carrying out many phases of the program. Although challenged by private insurance companies, the state-owned and operated enterprises were supported by the courts and operated throughout the decade, although with varying degrees of effectiveness. Townley's influence waned during the twenties while that of William Lemke and William L. Langer grew. Although the Mill and Elevator Association and the Bank of North Dakota were the most successful public enterprises, they did not greatly ameliorate the vulnerable position of North Dakota farmers. In many ways they were still subject to exploitation by middlemen and the vagaries of world grain markets, over which they had little control. By 1929 more of the state's farmers were looking to the federal government for aid rather than to political action. And so the influence of the Non-Partisan League waned, although it continued to exert some influence over state politics.

Prairie rebel: Arthur N. Townley, the founder of the Non-Partisan League of North Dakota. Source: Pioneer-Dispatch Press.

During its heyday, however, the League's impact was felt throughout much of the West. It was the major impetus behind the formation of te Farmer-Labor Party in Minnesota, which came to be a dominant political force in that state for half a century. The League enjoyed widespread support in Colorado and in Idaho during the early twenties, as well as in Oregon, Washington, Montana, and South Dakota. Militant socialism in an agrarian setting was therefore a significant trend of western politics in the twenties. And if in succeeding years the federal government assumed increasing responsibility for farmers on the Plains after 1929, this was to some extent a direct result of the League's agitation. The decline of agrarian radicalism and the expansion of federal farm programs were intimately related.

Cultural Growth

In view of deep-seated feelings of colonialism among many westerners—a sense of intellectual inferiority in relation to the East—it is not surprising that so many of the cultural currents in the West during the twenties focused on a quest for national or regional identity. If this nationalism, this search for identity, at times found an expression in nativism, it also found a more positive outlet in the development of a variety of intellectual endeavors—in literature, art, architecture, and to a lesser extent, in music. At the same time, the relatively low density of population in the West made it an attractive home for members of the "Lost Generation," those men and women who rejected the dominant values of an idustrialized, materialistic America and sought succor in the wilderness. Much as seventeenth-century Europeans had fled from their Babylon to the New Jerusalem in America, so a substantial group of eastern intellectuals made their way to the West in the 1920s in search of a new society.

The regionalism that characterized so much of western cultural life during this period was not peculiar to the West, but was a national, even international, phenomenon. During this same period an important group of southern regionalists was beginning its work, and intellectuals were undertaking a far-reaching reexamination of New England culture. Regionalism was also an important trend in Italian literature during the decade, as it was in France, where Henri Pourrat was its foremost advocate. Another group of European intellectuals were advocating a continental nationalism, including Massimo Bontempelli and Paul Valéry. In short, the reemergence of regionalism in western cultural life was a part of wider intellectual currents in Europe and America as a whole.[27]

Literature

In literature, western regionalists in the twenties were a distinct group. Perhaps one of their ablest spokesmen was B. A. Botkin who, in his introduction to *Folk-Say: A Regional Miscellany* (Norman, 1929), outlined the philosophy of the movement. The basis of the regionalism of the 1920s lay in the relation of folklore to literature, on relating historical retrospection. It was not merely an effort to provide local color. Writers of this decade sought to go beyond Walt Whitman, beyond the pastoralism of James Whitcomb Riley, beyond the sentimentalism of John Fox, Jr., or the idealism of William Allen White or Ed Howe. "The first flush of romantic local color paled before a steadily encroaching realism," wrote Botkin " 'reeking of the soil,' as in Hamlin Garland, and growing more depressing in the 'village virus' of *Spoon River Anthology* and *Main Street,* until, with the added impetus of the war, the balance swung back to romanticism." This new regionalism sought grounding in historical roots, and a new feeling for locality because "for all of its sense of mystery, inspired by legend and superstition [it] has its feet on the ground and its hands in the soil." It sought to be critical, detached, and objective. American artists, Botkin proclaimed, must find their roots in native soil. They must create a genuine American Myth. "Whether naturalistic, supernatural, or both, this literature bases its appeal primarily on the ideal of a Golden Age, of which the folk and the frontier are the last depository."[28] The mission of western regionalism was to provide deep-seated roots for all American culture.

An impressive group of writers was attracted to the movement. On the West Coast Robinson Jeffers, Willa Cather, Walter E. Kidd, Eugene Manlove Rhodes, and Ruth Suckow were but a few of the more prominent. In the Southwest there were Andy Adams, Mary Austin, Witter Bynner, J. Frank Dobie, Harvey Fergusson, and Stanley Vestal. Few critics would argue that the western writers of this period combined all the elements of greatness. But their great achievement was to bring American literature back to its roots in the heartland of America. At the turn of the century there were few literary centers in the United States other than Boston and New York. But these cities were regionally unidentified with America, for John Gould Fletcher, one literary critic, noted that culture existed in New York, but in a void, out of relation to what the rest of America may do or think. It had as few roots in the soil as the carefully tended and yet feeble specimens in Central Park.[29] To make a literary reputation in 1900 it was enough to quote foreign names—Strindberg, Nietzsche, d'Annunzio, or Balzac. By 1929 the western regionalists had created a new body of literature that, rooted in the context of American traditions (including Indian and Spanish-Southwestern), was sufficiently meritorious to warrant critical appraisal.

Nevertheless, it may be legitimate to ask why the accomplishments of western writers during these years were not more impressive than they were. In response, one would have to point to the problems faced by artists seeking to adjust to a new environment. It was hard to grasp something for which one had little feeling of familiarity. And so, instead of pondering over the uniqueness of their new environment, western writers sometimes fell back to describing it in familiar terms they had used elsewhere. As a contemporary critic, Hildegarde Flanner, pointed out in 1930, when men and women seek to find themselves at home in a new place, they re-create their exterior world in the image of old truths and convictions they brought with them. Thus they make the new world familiar,.and affirm it in the name of art. This blending of old and new also created a certain cultural confusion in the West, which eastern critics were not slow to notice. But population growth on the West Coast in the twenties was so explosive that it allowed little time for adjustment. Many newcomers knew relatively little about their new home, and a certain incongruity marked many aspects of their writing, and the culture.

Easterners still tended to look down on western literary efforts in the twenties (as in later years) and to consider them as the products of not very good upstart colonials. A good example of this provincial snobbery that was widespread east of the Mississippi River was an address by Stuart P. Sherman at the University of Chicago on May 9, 1922, in which he said: "There are little glens of Eden along the eastern coast, there is a narrow strip of Paradise along the western coast. . . . But for thousands of miles between these oases through wide wastes of grey [sic] sagebrush and sand, through ghastly white reaches of salt, one hears only the lowlands murmuring heavily, 'In the sweat of thy brow shalt thou eat bread' and the barren desert replying, 'All is vanity and vexation of spirit.' " Like many other eastern literary critics, Sherman was not merely wrong; he was uninformed.

The American West during this decade nurtured many literary oases. Along the Pacific Coast cultural activities tended to cluster in San Francisco, with important communities in Carmel, Laguna Beach, and Santa Barbara. Seattle had a much smaller and less significant cultural community. Another major cultural center arose in New Mexico, where Taos and Santa Fe became important literary and artists' communities in the 1920s. In the Rocky Mountain states, the Southwest, and the Plains, smaller cultural clusters sprang up during these years. What the Paris salon of Gertrude Stein was to the expatriates who frequented it, the Carmel home of Robinson Jeffers, the Taos adobe of Mabel Dodge Luhan, and the ranch of D. H. Lawrence were to a talented group of literati who went west to find themselves as individuals and as artists.

Easily the dominant figure in the California group was the poet Robinson Jeffers. In Carmel, Jeffers built his stone house with his own hands, there to meditate and hold court for other intellectuals during the rest of his life. Profoundly influenced by the nobility and beauty of the Carmel coastline, he contrasted it with the depravity of man in various major works, including *Roan Stallion* (1925) and, in the same year, *Be Angry at the Sun.* His poems revealed an effort to capture the rhythms of nature and to blend with them. Far less distinguished was his close friend, the poet George Sterling, who killed himself in 1926 in San Francisco's Bohemian Club.[30] The beauty and climate of southern California attracted thousands of mediocre poets. A contemporary estimate of approximately 3,000 suggested that this part of the country had more poets per square mile than any other.

Other literati were attracted to California during these years. Some of the major figures in the realist school of American writing went there, but produced little that was worthy. Hamlin Garland settled in Hollywood where, in 1930, he wrote *Roadside Meetings.* Theodore Dreiser was also there, and the very productive Upton Sinclair. In the realm of less distinguished but profitable "westerns," California also hosted well-known writers. Perhaps Zane Grey, author of *Riders of the Purple Sage* (1912), was the best known, for he published about two books each year in his undeviating style. A popular mass producer of this genre was Harold Bell Wright, whose *The Eyes of the World* (1914) was set in southern California. Wright used his meager literary talents to emphasize the grandeur of nature and the puniness of man, a theme that found an avid reception among millions of his readers. Mrs. Gene Stratton Porter was another of the best-selling "western" writers who won fortune, although less fame. Los Angeles and its environs was the scene and inspiration for her novels, and for some not very distinguished poetry. A prolific contributor to another realm of popular American literature—the mystery story—was Erle Stanley Gardner. A lawyer who was admitted to the California bar in 1911, Gardner became best known as the creator of Perry Mason, a detective-lawyer operating in California, who captured the imagination of Americans everywhere in the half century after World War I. Mason was America's Sherlock Holmes. In serious as well as popular literature, then, the West in the twenties was exerting a national impact.

The accomplishments of writers in the Pacific Northwest were less impressive. No major novelists or poets emerged during these years. Most of the minor poets, such as the popular Ella Higgenson, Homer Balch, and Christian Binkley sought, not too successfully, to utilize scenic grandeur and the poverty of the human spirit in their work. But most did not transcend mediocrity. *The American Mercury* published a collection of western verse from Oregon in 1926, and a number of smaller poetry magazines, such as Albert R. Wetjen's *The Spectator, Oregon Magazine*, or Colonel Hofer's *The Lariat*, provided outlets for dozens of local writers. Like most western states, Oregon had an active writer's league as well as a poetry society. Probably the best known literary figure of the region was the critic Vernon L. Parrington, who in 1928 won a Pulitzer Prize for his *Main Currents in American Thought*. This critical history of American literature from a Jeffersonian perspective had a distinct western orientation and came out of the context of the new regionalism that captured the imagination of so many intellectuals in the West during the 1920s.

Perhaps more distinguished than the cultural oases of California were the cultural centers of Taos and Santa Fe, New Mexico, which mushroomed during the post–World War I decade. Considering the various attributes of Taos and Santa Fe in the 1920s, it is not surprising that they became a haven for disillusioned urban intellectuals who sought to escape from what they considered the crassness of American civilization, while still seeking roots. In these years Taos and Santa Fe were as yet rather isolated, without major railroad lines or good roads. Living costs were cheap, with three-room houses available for as little as $10 monthly. But there was more. Here writers and artists could find cultures old in time, and yet genuinely American in place, cultures that had been largely neglected by the Anglophiles who had ruled American culture for so long. What a delight to discover the richness of Indian and Spanish-American civilizations that antedated Plymouth Rock. And here was a land that was strangely beautiful, dry and sunbaked, embedded between vast horizons that stretched for hundreds and hundreds of miles, unbroken except for serene mesas interspersed with sagebrush. And what a riot of colors this panorama presented! Here was a spectacular blending of red, purple, and yellow sands. Here man and nature were not at war as in the great eastern cities but blended to produce serenity.[31]

The writers who gathered in this land of enchantment after World War I were a distinguished group. Some of them had already been to Europe and had been bored; others, for one reason or another, could not or would not go abroad. But most of them were rebels against American society, which they hoped to escape. But more than simply escape, they were searching for new roots. As Malcolm Cowley wrote in *Exile's Return*, his generation had been wrenched from its moorings and knew little local history. And so they felt lost and uprooted, without attachment to a region or a tradition. In the Southwest some of them found both. Perhaps their reaction was not unique, for as the philosopher Arthur O. Lovejoy once noted, cultural primitivism was a not unusual expression of discontent by men and women living in a complex society, yearning for a simpler and less sophisticated mode of life. The New Mexico group was a good example. One of the founders of the Santa Fe circle was Alice Corbin Henderson, formerly associate editor of *Poetry*, a Chicago magazine. In addition to her own books, such as *Brothers of Light*, an account of the primitive Penitente religious sect in the remote mountain villages of northern New Mexico, she edited the first distinguished anthology of southwestern poetry, *The Turquoise Trail*. In her Santa Fe home she had entertained many of the nation's distinguished literary figures of the period, and some of these contributed to her anthology. They included, among others, John Galsworthy, Willa Cather, Harriet Monroe, Carl Sandburg, and Stanley Vestal.

Henderson's anthology set a new standard for regional literature and became nationally known. It owed some of its high quality to the inclusion of Willa Cather's writings, for Miss Cather was then at the height of her career. Two of her best novels, *The Professor's House* (1925) and *Death Comes for the Archbishop* (1927), were written in Santa Fe. Often expressing jealousy of Miss Cather at the frequent literary gatherings of Santa Fe's literati was Mary Austin, who fancied herself the undisputed queen of the circle. Enchanted with the Southwest, Mary Austin attempted to base her writings on the natural as well as cultural environment of the region. In *Land of Journey's Ending* (1924) she compared the Pueblo culture of the southwestern Indians with American life, with the latter suffering in comparison. And in *The American Rhythm* (1931) and *Starry Adventure* (1931) she further developed the theme that literature should be deeply rooted in environment if it was to be genuine and have meaning. Perhaps her talents were not as great as those of Willa Cather, but her contribution to regionalism directed the attention of Americans to the West and emphasized the significance of both Indian and native cultures, hitherto largely ignored in the United States as indigenous, deeply rooted American cultures.

Other accomplished writers included Witter Bynner and Oliver La Farge. Bynner sought to convey the rhythm of Indian life to his readers, seeking to explore the blending of Indian values with the cycles of nature. His *Indian Earth* was one of his most successful efforts. Oliver La Farge, of distinguished New England background, created something of a literary sensation in 1929 with his *Laughing Boy*, which won him a Pulitzer Prize that year. La Farge dealt with the same general theme with which the New Mexico group was concerned—namely, the conflict of cultural values in the United States, as reflected in the clash between industrialism and primitivism. Perhaps better than any member of the circle La Farge explained the Indian's dilemma to a wide circle of American readers while at the same time severely indicting the dominant value system of American society.

No more than forty miles north of Santa Fe, Mabel Dodge Luhan established a literary and artistic salon at Taos. Leaving her lower Fifth Avenue salon in New York City in 1919, this wealthy socialite threw herself into the life and traditions of the Southwest and sought to make her spacious home in Taos one of the cultural gathering places of the nation. Perhaps she did not achieve her rather grandiose dreams, but she did serve to stimulate a rather lively traffic of intellectuals in the region. Her prize acquisition, she was often wont to boast, was D. H. Lawrence, who came in 1924 and stayed for three years. Disillusioned with English and American society, Lawrence sought escape, and for a while his restless soul found some sustenance in New Mexico. As he noted; "New Mexico was the greatest experience from the outside world that I have ever had. It certainly changed me forever. Curious as it may sound, it was New Mexico that liberated me from the present era of civilization, the great era of material and mechanical development." During his sojourn he wrote *Reflections on the Death of a Porcupine* and *Mornings in Mexico*. Lawrence's presence served to attract a host of lesser writers while making Mabel Dodge Luhan's salon a favorite stopping-off place for major writers traveling through the country.[32]

If other literary oases in the West could not match the dazzle of Santa Fe and Taos, nevertheless they bore testimony to much activity. In the Southwest Texans revealed considerable interest in folklore and regionalism. There, L. W. Payne founded the Texas Folklore Society in 1909, whose publications included such well-known national writers as J. Frank Dobie. Periodicals such as the *Texas Review*, 1915–1924, after 1924 the *Southwest Review*, provided an outlet for regional literature. In Oklahoma regionalism was actively fostered by the well-known folklorist Stanley Vestal. Works of younger Oklahoma poets appeared in the May 1926 issue of *The American Mercury*.

The Echo Anthology, edited by David Rafflelock, was a collection of Colorado verse. D. Maitland Bushby, editor of *Tom-Tom*, a regional magazine published in Arizona, put together yet another anthology titled *Southwest Verse*. H. G. Merriam, editor of *The Frontier* in Montana, made that publication widely known for the excellent fiction it carried. South Dakota's poetry society numbered more than 200 persons in the twenties. Some of its work was published in *Pasque Petals*, a little magazine, and some of its best selections were collected in an anthology by J. C. Lindberg and Gertrude B. Gunderson and titled *An Anthology of South Dakota Poetry*.

Art

As in literature, westerners displayed an increasing sense of sophistication in art during the twenties. Many of the artists during these years lived in "colonies," or oases in close proximity to writers. Thus, California had a number of significant artists' colonies at Carmel, Santa Barbara, and Laguna Beach. Taos, New Mexico, became the home of several dozen prominent painters, and other smaller colonies were scattered throughout the West.

During the twenties California was slowly becoming one of the art centers of the nation. These years saw the founding of distinguished art institutes in southern California, such as the Otis Institute, Chouinard Art School, and the Los Angeles Art Center School. The Huntington Art Gallery in San Marino was building its famous English Renaissance collection during this decade, and the Southwest Museum in Los Angeles was displaying one of the finest aboriginal Indian collections in the nation. Further north, the rival city of San Francisco was trying hard to maintain its reputation as art center of the West. Its major art museum was the M. H. de Young Memorial Museum in Golden Gate Park, established in 1926. Some of the collections in the California Palace of the Legion of Honor, founded in 1924, rivaled those of the de Young. Even smaller cities in California boasted fine collections, such as the Crocker Gallery housed in Sacramento, revealing an increasing appreciation as well as support for art by the community.

California artists, like many in the West, understandably became interested in light, and thus in post-Expressionism. As one eastern artist, Fernand Lungren, pointed out, "I had to unlearn most of what I had understood as light and color." Another early artist, J. Bond Francisco, said he discovered only late in life that "light was the thing in Southern California; that the light actually changes the texture and shape of the hills." During the 1920s California painters had grasped the need for working in a western context. Milford Zornes, Barse Miller, Phil Dyke, Tom Craig, Maxwell Armfield, George Post, Dong Kingman, and Millard Sheets were among the most talented. Later, Sheets became director of the Los Angeles County Art Institute, where he was responsible for much experimentation with color.

In the Southwest, even more than in California, regionalism flourished. The first artists to settle in Taos in 1916 were Bert Phillips and Ernest L. Blumenschein. They were entranced by the Indians, the Spanish-Americans, and the landscape, and they wrote their friends about the area. Within a few years they were joined by Walter Ufer, E. Irving Couse, Victor Higgins, and Oscar Berninghaus. Some of these men had been members of the Ashcan School, and now turned from urban scenes to the wilderness, founding something like an "American Scene" school in the process. As one contemporary art critic, Rose Henderson, wrote in *The Outlook* (August 1, 1923): "The color and atmosphere make the place a painter's paradise. It is like a sunny corner of Old Spain, with a dash of Parisian life, and the desert and Indian thrown in as a distinctly American asset." These painters founded the Taos Society of Artists during World War I, whose showings were accorded an enthusiastic national reception. Their exhibition at the Corcoran Gallery in Washington, D. C., in 1922 gained them a wide circle of admirers and a secure place in the world of American art.

Another distinguished group of painters made Santa Fe their home. There they tended to cluster on the Camino del Monte Sol, a hill overlooking Santa Fe, where Alice Henderson, the writer, earlier had built her impressive adobe home. In many ways the atmosphere here was reminiscent of Greenwich Village in New York City. Here there gathered a galaxy of talents who found the southwestern life-style congenial. Many of them were post-Impressionists seeking individual expression, but using Cézanne as a model. In New Mexico they found new subject matter, brilliant colors, and striking ambiances of light. They included Andrew Dasburg, a leading exponent of cubism; Marsden Hartley, a disciple of Kandinsky; and Russell Cheney. One of the first artists to settle in Santa Fe had been Robert Henri, a well-known member of the Ashcan School, and it was he, in part, who persuaded John Sloan to move to Santa Fe. Sloan came in 1921. Having portrayed the common man in New York City, Sloan now turned his attention to the Indian of New Mexico, convinced that he was a living representation of the merger between art and nature. Sloan lived not too far from John Marin, one of the foremost experimenters with color in the American art world of the 1920s. Marin was impressed by the poetic aspects of weather. And where else could the dramatic battles between the elements be observed better than the West? The environment also drew another of the great twentieth-century American painters to New Mexico—Georgia O'Keeffe, who arrived shortly after World War I. Wife of the famous photographer Alfred Stieglitz, O'Keeffe found inspiration in the spaciousness and isolation of the region. Some of her paintings that stemmed from the regional environment included *Black Cross, New Mexico*, and the famous *Ranchos de Taos Church*, for she was also much impressed by the simplicity and economy of design as well as lack of ornamentation in southwestern mission architecture. To her mind, it reflected a fine blend of man and nature, an adaptation that American society had yet to achieve.

The southwestern communities of artists during this decade also encouraged Indian painters. Indian painters found receptive audiences during these years, in part because of the vogue of Primitivism in the American art world. Moreover, their use of symbolism, their freedom from exactitude, their delicate colors, and their intense individualism were the very qualities sought so avidly by the Expressionists and Cubists of this period. Among some of the better known Indian artists of this decade were

Awa Tsireh, Vehino Shije, and Fred Kabotie. Largely at John Sloan's insistence, Kabotie and Tsireh exhibited their works in New York City in 1920 and received a favorable reception. Critics then and later debated whether Indian artists painted what they thought the white man might like to see, or whether they were giving full expression to themselves and their culture. Whatever the case may be, the rapid growth of western art colonies in the twenties acquainted Americans with a dimension of native culture hitherto hidden to most people in the United States—Indian art.

Architecture

Regionalism was also a major trend among western architects who were searching for new directions in this period. The neo-Spanish colonial style developed by Bertam Goodhue continued to be popular in California. When William Randolph Hearst decided to build his famous castle at San Simeon, he retained Goodhue to design his towers. By 1925 Goodhue was experimenting with more functional styles, however, as the completion of his design for the Los Angeles Public Library clearly indicated. But the Spanish colonial style was widely used by builders of small homes in the twenties. Southern California was Hispanicized as houses, apartments, flats, store buildings, post offices and public structures, filling stations, and hotels aped the mission style. After the earthquake of 1925 in Santa Barbara, that city was rebuilt almost entirely in this fashion, as was the exclusive new suburban community of San Clemente. California also revealed a bewildering—and often tasteless—mixture of Venetian, Norman, Old Plantation, Italian, Queen Anne, and Elizabethan styles, without any sense of order or reason. Such cultural confusion reflected the pell-mell settlement of California in the twenties and the passionate search of many of the newcomers for identity.

Two major architects did emerge from the architectural experimentation that characterized California during this period. One was Irving Gill, a student of Louis Sullivan at the turn of the century, when he came to San Diego. After experimenting with various traditional styles Gill started, by World War I, to experiment with a new "California Modern" style that would be well suited to the physical and cultural environment. By the twenties he was designing homes that anticipated the ranch house style several decades later. At the same time he innovated with apartment buildings by adapting the idea of a "bungalow court," a southern California innovation. These apartment dwellings were designed so that each tenant had his own entrances, halls, and gardens, and their interiors were planned to capture the unique exterior light common in that area. Bella Vista Terrace in Sierra Madre was a fine example of his work.

Gill's views on western architecture at the time of World War I were remarkably perceptive. As he wrote in 1916: "The west has an opportunity unparalleled in the history of the world, for it is the newest white page turned for registration. The west unfortunately has been and is building too hastily, carelessly, and thoughtlessly. Houses here for a year spring up faster than mushrooms, for mushrooms silently prepare for a year and more before they finally raise their house above the ground. The surface of the ground is barely scraped away, in some cases but a few inches deep, just enough to allow builders to find a level, and a house is tossed together with little thought of permanence, haste being the chief characteristic."[33] Was it surprising, therefore, that so many of the rapidly growing western cities in the twentieth century had an air of impermanence about them? Crass utilitarianism without any regard for esthetic considerations or beauty consequently was a major characteristic of the western architectural landscape in the twenties.

Perhaps the major architect in twentieth-century California was Richard Neutra, an Austrian who came to Los Angeles in 1926. Neutra was an advocate of modernism who had studied with Adolph Loos in Vienna. He was attracted first to Chicago by Louis Sullivan and Frank Lloyd Wright and later to Los Angeles by another Viennese modernist, R. M. Schindler, who had settled in the city in 1922, attracted by the hospitable environment that it offered for architectural experimentation. Neutra began to build striking modernistic homes, using new materials and methods made possible by machine technology. Seeking to take advantage of the brilliant light in southern California and the West, Neutra sought to blend indoor and outdoor living by vast expanses of glass—and sliding doors—and by the use of self-supporting slabs. During this decade, Neutra, Schindler, and the growing number of their disciples were laying the foundation for a new, highly original western architectural style that had deep roots in the physical as well as social and cultural environment of the twentieth-century West.

Elsewhere in the West architects were not so creative. They tended to stick with the Spanish colonial or Pueblo style, particularly in the Southwest. In New Mexico, for example, John Gaw Meem was the greatest exponent of the Pueblo architecture. In 1924 he founded the firm of Meem and McCormick, which executed many commissions in the region. Mary Austin used Meem as a character in her novel *Starry Adventure*. The campus of the University of New Mexico in Albuquerque and the railroad stations of the Santa Fe Railroad and the Southern Pacific were typical examples of Pueblo architecture, which—it must be admitted—was functional within its context.

The twenties, then, was a decade of lively architectural experimentation in the West. To be sure, there was considerable confusion as architects experimented with a bewildering array of different styles and designs, usually borrowed from elsewhere. But during these years two major trends indicated the development of a regional style. One was the extension of the Spanish colonial or mission style to twentieth-century conditions, the other a western modernism that grew from the West as it was in the twenties, not as it supposedly was at some earlier time. But the fact that western designers were gradually becoming aware of a sense of direction indicated an increased maturity that, in a way, reflected western society as a whole.

Music

To a considerable extent westerners were still "colonials" in music, since they depended largely on the East and on Europe for outstanding performers and composers. Perhaps the great musical event in the West during the decade was the founding of the San Francisco Opera Company in 1923, the oldest in the nation (with the exception of New York City's Metropolitan Opera Company). Under the direction of the Italian conductor, Gaetana Merola, it became one of the best opera companies in the United States. Meanwhile, the San Francisco Symphony Orchestra was emerging as a major organization. Under Alfred Hertz and Pierre Monteux it became the only truly first-rate orchestra in the West. By 1919, however, various patrons in Los Angeles were seeking to provide their city with an orchestra of similar quality. Perhaps the most active benefactor was William A. Clark, Jr., whose wealth had been acquired in Montana mining. He provided the Los Angeles Philharmonic with a major endowment. By 1922 the orchestra began to present its famous summer concerts in the Hollywood Bowl, the world's largest natural amphitheater. A series of distinguished conductors such as Otto Klemperer, Alfred Wallenstein, and Eduard van Beinum gradually made it into a major musical group, although it was not until after World War II that it moved into first rank. The programs of symphony orchestras in the West were very much like those in the East. Some composers in the West were influenced by regionalism, however. One of the most prominent was a San Franciscan, Ferdinand R. (Ferde) Grofé, who used a western setting for his *Grand Canyon Suite*. Elsewhere in the West, audiences looked largely to visiting performers from the East. During the 1916 season in Seattle, for example, Walter Damrosch and the New York Philharmonic, the Boston National Opera, and the Ballet Russe with Nijinski and Lopokove played to enthusiastic audiences. In this sense, a new region like the West was still colonial.

Education

The newness of the region made it a fertile field for educational innovation. In higher education the nineteenth century had been a growth period for new private collegiate institutions. In the twentieth century, on the other hand, the emphasis switched to new public institutions, and in this movement westerners made significant and imaginative contributions. California, in particular, became known for its educational experiments, especially in making post–high school training available to all of its citizens at low cost. The California university system was greatly strengthened when in 1919 the state legislature authorized the State Normal School at Los Angeles to become the University of California, Southern Branch, known by 1929 as U.C.L.A. at its new Westwood campus. During these years other state normal schools such as those at San Francisco and San Jose were transformed into state teacher's colleges (1921) to bring a four-year collegiate education within reach of these and neighboring communities. But perhaps the most striking innovation was the establishment of two-year, or junior colleges, usually under municipal or county auspices. They were originally authorized by the legislature in 1907; Fresno established the first such college in the United States three years later. By 1929 California boasted more than 30 such institutions, which were widely copied elsewhere in the nation in succeeding years.

The University of California, along with private institutions, first made the West Coast distinguished for scientific research during the 1920s. It was then that Nobel Prize winners in natural sciences were attracted to the Berkeley campus, partly because of the freedom for experimentation that such a new university offered, and partly because of climate and location. At the same time two distinguished scientists, the astronomer George Ellery Hale and the Nobel Prize–winning (1923) physicist Robert A. Millikan, were transforming the somewhat languid Throop College of Technology in Pasadena into one of America's leading scientific centers. Millikan was able to attract a remarkably brilliant group of young scientists to him in the twenties and by 1929 Cal Tech, the California Institute of Technology, was unmatched, except for its eastern rival, M.I.T. During these years Cal Tech was particulary strong in physics, biology, and genetics. It also cooperated closely with the nearby Mount Wilson Solar Observatory, administered after 1917 by the Carnegie Institution of Washington, D.C. No other institutions west of the Mississippi River could boast such scientific brilliance as California. The Lowell Observatory near Flagstaff, Arizona, was operated by Harvard University. It was founded by Percival Lowell, brother of President A. Lawrence Lowell of Harvard and of Amy Lowell, the poet. Lowell was particularly interested in planets, which could be studied effectively in the clear skies of the West. As a result of studies which he stimulated, in 1930 the staff at the observatory discovered the new planet, Pluto. In short, the West was beginning to have a national impact on scientific research on the eve of the Great Depression, reflecting its increasing cultural maturation.

Public educational facilities in the West were particularly strained in those areas where population was increasing rapidly. California's public school enrollments rose more than 70 per cent during the 1920s with smaller increases recorded in the Pacific Northwest. The school systems of other western states tended to be less innovative than those on the West Coast. Nevertheless, in relation to their total revenues, most of the states in the trans-Mississippi region were spending a higher percentage of public funds for education than states elsewhere, although some of the Rocky Mountain states and some in the Southwest, such as Arizona and New Mexico, stood low in national rankings. Population and wealth were often closely related to the quality of education that states could offer.

Popular Culture—Movies

The most striking cultural innovation in the West during the twenties in terms of national impact was the emergence of Hollywood as the film center of the world. Hollywood's rise was all the more dramatic because until World War I the West had had no particular theatrical or entertainment tradition. Theater groups had always been warmly welcomed in California and other western areas and there were community playhouses, such as at Pasadena, or the Padua Hills Mexican Players, as well as experimental theaters in the round. But, by and large, westerners had looked eastward for dramatic fare.

But beginning in World War I the whole world began looking to Hollywood for film entertainment. At the turn of the century Hollywood was still a sleepy little village, recently founded by Kansas prohibitionists, a crossroads on the way from Los Angeles to Santa Monica. In 1901 its population consisted of 166 males, living in a pleasant setting of orange groves and grain fields. Virtually no one had heard of it. Its sole claim to distinction was that the French artist, Paul deLongpre, made his home there. The big event each day was the arrival and departure of the Tolusa stage, which connected Hollywood with the San Fernando Valley. As late as 1910 the hamlet had no more than 4,000 souls.

Then came the movies. By 1929, 150,000 people lived in Hollywood, and at least half of them were employed in the production of motion pictures. In addition, the economic welfare of hundreds of thousands of others in surrounding areas was directly affected by the moving picture industry.

A variety of reasons help to explain the sudden change. Until 1907 most American movies were made in New York and New Jersey, and virtually none in the West. Thereafter, the scene switched to Hollywood. Partly, movie makers were drawn by the climate, which allowed uninterrupted year-round production. Moreover, the diversity of scenery available in southern California within a one-hundred-mile range of Los Angeles was another major attraction. The majority of pictures made after the success of "The Great Train Robbery"—the New Jersey film produced in 1903—were westerns, and in the West the scenery matched the plot. But the major reason for the wholesale exodus of eastern movie makers to Hollywood was the desire to escape legal suits for infringing on existing patents. Between 1900 and 1914 Charles Edison was filing a whole series of legal suits against movie producers for infringing on his patent rights. At his behest the New York legislature in 1907 had also enacted a very stringent motion picture patent law. Thus, most of the early movie moguls, men like William Selig or George K. Spoor, were attracted to the West Coast in the hope of escaping legal harassment. And in the unlikely event that process servers should find them, the Mexican border was not very far away, and quick escapes seemed assured.

Thus, in the decade after 1907, film makers began to flock to Hollywood. Since Los Angeles then was a rather sedate town, peopled by middle-aged retired middle westerners, they did not receive a rousing welcome. In fact, Angelenos considered them a nuisance because they shot many of their scenes on the public streets, near residences, and even in front yards. To the former small-town residents who lived in Los Angeles, the "movie colony" was a strange lot, indeed. "Over no decent threshold were they allowed to step," wrote a contemporary observer, Cedrick Belfrage. "They were unfit to mingle with respectable citizens." Many apartment houses displayed signs such as: "No Dogs or Actors Allowed." Some of the movie makers virtually camped out, retreated to out-of-the-way rooming houses and hotels, and spent their evenings in local bars, shunned by the local populace. But this local hostility began to change, for by 1915 the movie industry had an annual payroll of $20 million. From then on the movie crowd was increasingly accepted. And by 1929 the new industry employed more than 100,000 persons and had made Hollywood known throughout the world.

In the years before World War I Hollywood produced a succession of well-known motion pictures. Perhaps the first to be made there was "The Count of Monte Cristo," filmed in 1907 near Santa Monica by the Selig Polyscope Company. Within five years other movie makers moved in, including Essanay, Bison, Pathé, Biograph, Vitagram, and Edison. Some opened studios not only in Hollywood, but also in San Diego, Santa Barbara, and Long Beach. Seventy-three companies were producing films in California by 1914 and developing the "star" system. Mary Pickford, Douglas Fairbanks, and Charles Chaplin were the big names that supplemented the ever-popular westerns. Then, in 1915 director David Wark Griffith opened a new era in motion picture making with his full-length path-breaking film, "The Birth of A Nation." This was the first "great" picture produced by Hollywood, and it came at a most opportune moment. The outbreak of World War I led to the virtual ending of motion picture production in Italy, Germany, and Great Britain, and Hollywood stepped in to fill the void.

For more than a decade after 1917 Hollywood enjoyed a golden age. By 1920 many mergers and consolidations had taken place, and seven major companies emerged. Metro-Goldwyn-Mayer (MGM), Warner Brothers, Radio-Keith-Orpheum (RKO), and Twentieth-Century Fox were the giants, with Columbia, Universal, and United Artists not far behind. The men who became captains of the industry, men like Louis B. Mayer, Samuel Goldwyn, Marcus Loew, Adolph Zukor, William Fox, and Lewis J. Selznick, came from humble origins and rarely developed an esthetic feel for their work. They were primarily interested in commercial success, not in artistic endeavor. Most of their productions betrayed their philosophy, although on some occasions profit was joined with art or talent. This was true of "The Birth of A Nation," a story of the Reconstruction era which had technical brilliance but also a strong anti-Negro bias. The picture attracted more than 100 million viewers by 1929 and had grossed more than $20 million. Frank Norris' novel *McTeague*, when made into the motion picture *Greed* in 1923, was another of the early full-length successes. If the movie moguls were wedded to box office receipts, it must be remembered that, in a sense, they were still colonials. Although movies were made in Hollywood, the money needed to produce them came from New York. Eastern capital was still playing a major role in the development of this new industry, and also commanding a large share of the profits.

During the twenties Hollywood made its largest profits and developed its unique aura of commercial glamour. These were the years of the great matinee idols, of Greta Garbo, Theda Bara, Dustin Farnum, Harold Lloyd, Gloria Swanson, Pola Negri, Lillian Gish, and Rudolph Valentino, each of whom earned more than a million dollars annually. Western heroes such as William S. Hart, Tom Mix, and Ed "Hoot" Gibson became the idols of a whole generation of small (and often not so small) boys and girls. During the twenties approximately 60 million Americans visited a movie house each week, paying about $400 million annually for the privilege. Small wonder that the movie moguls, the producers, exercised as much power as ancient Oriental potentates, and often behaved accordingly. It was during this decade that Hollywood developed a fabulous life-style, astounding for its opulence and eccentricity. Hollywood personalities (who by 1925 were moving to Beverly Hills to live) built or bought palatial mansions, drove expensive motor cars, and accumulated personal adornments beyond belief. No beauty cream, perfume, or potion was too expensive for the movie queens, who often draped their dogs in fur coats costing thousands. In the words of one anthropologist, Hollywood became the dream factory of America.[34]

Despite crass commercialism, despite tastelessness and vulgarity, Hollywood had a far-ranging and profound cultural influence on the West. Certainly it made the region a center of popular culture in America, for better or for worse. For once the West was not following eastern cultural trends—as a good colony should; it was setting them. It was itself a pacesetter for popular culture in the United States, and influencing life-styles thoughout the nation. What movie stars thought or did or wore became prime public issues. If southern California became a new fashion center during the 1920s this was primarily because of Hollywood. The movie colony also attracted a number of talented writers and musicians, although some simply could not stomach the atmosphere they found. William Saroyan was one of these, and he stayed only briefly. Others, like Clifford Odets, Peter Kyne, Rupert Hughes, F. Scott Fitzgerald, Nathanael West, and William Faulkner stayed—and adapted. Musicians who went to work there in the twenties included Charles W. Cadman, David Rose, Vincent Youmans, and George and Ira Gershwin. Dance artists, set designers, decorators, and a wide variety of other professionals followed them. Along with the cheap and tawdry, with the lackluster and sensational, Hollywood also attracted some serious artistic talents who provided a firmer foundation for a more sophisticated cultural expression in the West.

Hollywood strengthened the stereotyped image of the West held by most Americans—and by people all over the world. It fed the nostalgia of an urban populace for a more primitive—and mythical—rural frontier of a bygone age. It made the cowboy into a national hero and celebrated his courage, his individualism, his moralism, and his freedom, national values that appeared threatened in the 1920s. The West represented that mythical America to which many Americans, living in the real world of a highly urbanized industrial society, wanted to escape. And Hollywood provided the visual means for the temporary satisfaction of such longings.

But the influence of Hollywood did not stop there. Without question, the growth of the movie community in southern California enormously accelerated population growth there and in other contiguous areas of the West. Hollywood tended to break down the pattern of rural values brought by so many of the new settlers to the West and may have contributed to the development of more tolerant urban attitudes. Hollywood furthered the increasing sophistication of Westerners and their cultural awareness. Certainly, the wealth accumulated in Hollywood was often simply squandered. But some of it found its way into the hands of patrons who energetically encouraged the development of art, music, architecture, and the dance along lines that had not existed in the West before. The architectural innnovations that came out of California in the twenties were perhaps the best example of the cultural impetus provided by Hollywood, as wealthy patrons commissioned new houses, although the seeds laid in other forms of culture did not germinate until succeeding decades.

By 1929, therefore, the West was gaining visible cultural maturity. True, as yet the West was making few substantial cultural innovations. But under the stimulus of regionalism westerners were beginning to look to themselves and the region rather than to the East for inspiration as well as for subject matter for cultural expression. Thus, the west became the home of significant colonies of writers, of artists and architects, of musicians, of actors, and of scholars and educators. On the eve of the depression the West was no longer a cultural desert as it had once been. Instead, it offered an increasing number of attractions for creative individuals in most fields of cultural endeavor.

And so, during the fifteen years after the start of World War I, the trans-Mississippi West continued its growth. Its population expanded and developed new life-styles that were attracting national attention. During this period the completion of the Panama Canal, and the extraordinary growth of automobile travel, ended western geographical isolation forever. These innovations in transportation not only consolidated the West internally as a region but increased its contacts with the East. Combined with the influx of millions of newcomers, transportation development provided an enormous boost to the western economy. It was still a colonial economy, primarily concerned with the production of raw materials for the industrial East, but during these years it was becoming more diversified than at any previous period. And the increasing importance of service industries loosened at least some of the colonial ties of West to East. That westerners were still conscious of their colonial status was clearly reflected in the politics of the region. Although at times individualistic and parochial, western politicians were united mainly in their efforts to ensure further growth of the region. Perhaps their feelings were whetted partly by significant strides in western cultural development, the self-conscious search to develop its own particular styles in literature, art, architecture, music, education, and the popular arts. True, the West in 1929 could not yet rival the East in many aspects of its civilization. On the other hand, it was no longer a barren frontier. From being a child of the East, it had grown to adolescence. On the eve of the Great Depression many westerners looked forward hopefully to another decade of intensive growth.

NOTES

1. Melvyn Dubofsky, *We Shall Be All: A History of the Industrial Workers of the World* (Chicago: Quadrangle, 1969), is informative on this aspect of the western labor movement.

2. An objective and detailed account of the Joe Hill case can be found in Gibbs M. Smith, *Joe Hill* (Salt Lake City: University of Utah Press, 1969).

3. Richard Frost, *The Mooney Case* (Stanford: Stanford University Press, 1968), contains an exhaustive description.

4. Robert L. Friedheim, *The Seattle General Strike* (Seattle: University of Washington Press, 1964), is a standard work on this incident.

5. Helpful on this subject are Eldridge F. Dowell, *A History of Criminal Syndicalism Legislation in the United States* (Baltimore: Johns Hopkins University Press, 1939), and Woodrow C. Whitten, *Criminal Syndicalism and the Law in California, 1911–1927* (Philadelphia: American Philosophical Society Transactions, 1969), Vol. 59, Pt. 2.

6. Among relevant books, readers will find James H. Shideler, *Farm Crisis, 1919–1923* (Berkeley: University of California Press, 1957), informative.

7. Louis Adamic, *Laughing in the Jungle* (New York: Harper & Bros., 1932), quoted in McWilliams, *Southern California Country*, p. 160.

8. Carey McWilliams, *North from Mexico* (New York: Greenwood Press, 1968), is a fine popular account.

9. The story of black Americans in the West still needs to be told.

10. Carey McWilliams, *Southern California Country*, contains a brilliant analysis of social trends in that region.

11. Charles M. Russell, *Trails Plowed Under* (Garden City, N.Y.: Doubleday, Page and Co., 1927), pp. 159–160.

12. Robert V. Hine, *California's Utopian Colonies*, rev. ed. (New Haven: Yale University Press, 1966), discusses the background of these groups.

13. Lately Thomas, *The Vanishing Evangelist* (New York: Viking Press, 1959), is a delightful and entertaining account of Sister Aimee.

14. Materials concerning the economic history of the West between 1919 and 1929 are widely scattered. C. R. Niklason, *Commercial Survey of the Pacific Southwest*, is helpful.

15. Interested readers can find many more details about this unhappy event in Charles F. Outland, *Man-Made Disaster* (Glendale: Arthur H. Clark & Co., 1963).

16. Beverly Moeller, *Phil Swing and Boulder Dam* (Berkeley: University of California Press, 1971), is informative on the Colorado River Project. See Hugh G. Hansen, *Central Valley Project, Federal or State?* (Berkeley: University of California, Bureau of Public Administration, 1955), on that subject.

17. Schlebecker, *Cattle Raising on the Plains, 1900–1961*, touches on these matters, while Carl Ubbelohde, *Colorado: A History* (Boulder: Pruett Press, 1965), and Elwyn B. Robinson, *History of North Dakota* (Lincoln: University of Nebraska Press, 1965), provide glimpses into farm problems of the era.

18. Tomasevich, *International Agreements*, and Nash, *State Government and Economic Development*, treat these matters at greater length.

19. Gerald D. Nash, *U.S. Oil Policy, 1890–1964* (Pittsburgh: University of Pittsburgh Press, 1968), provides an extended discussion of this subject.

20. As noted earlier, western tourism is a sadly neglected subject. On National Parks, readers will find Ise, *Our National Park Policy*, and Robert Shankland, *Steve Mather of the National Parks*, rev. ed. (New York: Alfred A. Knopf, 1971), instructive. Of dozens of detailed studies, H. Robison, *Some Economic Implications of the Tourist Industry for Northern Arizona* (Stanford: Stanford Food Research Institute, 1954), is illustrative.

21. Lewis Jacobs, *The Rise of the American Film: A Critical History*, Studies in Culture and Communication Series (New York: Teachers College Press, Columbia University, 1968), initiates readers into the subject.

22. Marquis and Bessie James, *Biography of a Bank* (New York: Harper & Row, 1956), tell this interesting story well.

23. Few books on western politics are available to general readers. Dean R. Cresap, *Party Politics in the Golden State* (Los Angeles: Haynes Foundation, 1954), and Thomas C. Donnelly, ed., *Rocky Mountain Politics* (Albuquerque: University of New Mexico Press, 1940), are informative.

24. Those wishing to learn more about this subject can consult Arthur E. Buck, *The Reorganization of State Governments in the United States* (New York: Columbia University Press, 1938), with profit.

25. State and local histories provide guidelines to politics in the Pacific Northwest, such as Gates and Johannsen, *Empire of the Columbia*, and Pomeroy, *The Pacific Slope*.

26. Robert L. Morlan, *Political Prairie Fire: The Non-Partisan League, 1915–1922* (Minneapolis: University of Minnesota Press, 1955).

27. The only available brief discussion of cultural regionalism in the West, especially in the Pacific Northwest, is by Carey McWilliams, *The New Regionalism in American Literature*)seattle: University of Washington Bookstore, 1930).

28. B. A. Botkin, *Folk-Say: A Regional Miscellany* (Norman: University of Oklahoma Press, 1929), pp. 14, 16–17.

29. John Gould Fletcher, *Life Is My Song* (New York: Farrar and Rinehart, 1937), p. 357.

30. Melba B. Bennett, *The Stone Mason of Tor House: The Life and Times of Robinson Jeffers* (Los Angeles: Ward Ritchie Press, 1966).

31. Consult Mabel Major and T. M. Pearce, *Southwest Heritage: A Literary History with Bibliographies*, 3d ed. (Albuquerque: University of New Mexico Press, 1972), and Thomas M. Pearce and Telfair Hendon, eds., *America in the Southwest: A Regional Anthology* (Albuquerque: University of New Mexico Press, 1933).

32. An excellent unpublished study on literature and arts is informative: James M. Gaither, "A Return to the Village: A Study of Santa Fe and Taos, New Mexico, as Cultural Centers, 1900–1934," Ph.D. Dissertation, University of Minnesota, 1958, available on microfilm.

33. Esther McCoy's books, *Five California Architects* and *Richard Neutra* (New York: Braziller, 1960), should interest most readers.

34. Hortense Powdermaker, *Hollywood, The Dream Factory* (Boston: Little, Brown & Co., 1950).

3

The West

in the Great Depression,

1929–1941

Few Americans were unaffected by the Great Depression that began in 1929. No other event in the twentieth century—not even World War I—changed the destinies of so many people so drastically. Its impact and effects appeared to linger and linger, apparently without end, throughout the following decade.

The Great Crash was like a roll of deafening and frightening thunder that heralded an approaching storm. Westerners, accustomed to extremes of weather, knew the pattern well. But little did they realize that this man-made storm would carry everything before it, would spare only a lucky few, and would leave wreckage that would take many years to rebuild. The depression abruptly curtailed the westward flow of population; dashed many western hopes for further rapid economic growth; it brought curious political alignments; it disrupted many promising cultural activities in the region that had just began to blossom. Yet by the beginning of World War II the West found itself less dependent on the East that it had been, less of a colonial appendage. During the depression the West changed masters. It became more dependent on the largesse of the national government.

The Great Crash and the West, 1929–1933

The immediate impact of the Great Crash varied in the West. It was most severe in those areas that were industrialized and in regions that were heavily agricultural. Its effects on regions with a diversified economic base were at first moderate, becoming severe only after 1931. But by 1933 all the western states were caught in the throes of acute crisis. Thus, California early felt the tremors of economic dislocations, along with the Pacific Northwest and the Great Plains. The Rocky Mountain states and the Southwest had a brief respite before the full brunt of the depression engulfed them, too. Of course, more moderate depression conditions had been with them ever since the end of World War I. But as the manager of the Wyoming State Department of Commerce and Industry wrote in December of 1930: "The . . . gloom and depression which has prevailed in the industrial and financial centers of the East . . . has been met with courage and optimism in Wyoming. This state has felt the effects the least of all the states."[1]

The Great Crash inaugurated a decade that witnessed the slowest rate of population growth in the West during the twentieth century. If we consider the entire trans-Mississippi West, its gain of people between 1929 and 1939 was less than 15 per cent. This figure requires qualification, however. The Pacific Coast states gained whereas those of the interior actually lost population. California increased the number of its inhabitants by about 1 million persons (or 20 per cent) and the Pacific Northwest states—despite some exodus—increased their total population by about 10 per cent. On the other hand, the Rocky Mountain states, the Southwest, and the Plains actually lost people, at rates ranging from 5 per cent to 10 per cent of their total numbers. Many of their native sons and daughters moved to the Pacific Coast or to large urban centers elsewhere in the country in their desperate search for employment.

The economic collapse of the industrial East understandably had a profound impact on the underdeveloped West. In general, the pace of economic activity in 1933 was less than half of what it had been in 1929. Whatever economic indicator one might choose—whether wholesale prices, income total value of goods produced, or wages—the pattern was the same. And it mattered little what industry one chose for comparison, whether agriculture, the extractive industries, the service trades, manufacturing, or finance. Everywhere western dreams for sustained economic growth lay shattered, victims of the nationwide economic collapse.

After 1929 a sense of gloom pervaded farmers in the West and those persons engaged in natural resource industries. By 1932 the incomes of farmers in the trans-Mississippi West had declined by almost one-half from their already low income in 1929. Even the highly mechanized corporate farms of California suffered severely, although their situation was far more advantageous than that of small farmers on the Plains. Whereas in 1929 the value of California farm products had been about $750 million, the figure had shrunk to a mere $372 million in 1932. The decline was even more precipitous in the western mining industry concentrated in the Southwest and the Rocky Mountains. The decline of manufacturing in the East drastically reduced the demand for minerals such as copper, lead, zinc, and alloy metals. Thousands of miners lost their jobs in the four years after 1929 and joined the ranks of the urban unemployed. And declining markets, combined with the rich new petroleum discoveries of these years in Texas and Oklahoma, produced the worst oil glut in the nation's history. By 1932 crude oil was selling for 10 cents a barrel, compared to $3 a barrel just a few years before. Pacific fishermen experienced a similar dilemma, for the more they increased their production, the lower the prices they received and their total income fell accordingly. Their neighbors, the lumber operators of the Pacific Northwest, fared no better. Cattlemen were also severely affected by the economic slump, as American meat consumption declined during the depression. With the raw materials industries of the West so closely geared to the manufacturing centers of the East, tremors on Wall Street were felt on every Main Street west of the Mississippi River.

Other sectors of the western economy were also slowed by the crash. Manufacturing enterprises in the region were directly affected by the shrinkage of purchasing power and laid off more than half of their employees. Since most concerns were small or medium sized they found it especially difficult to weather the crisis. The rate of business failures in many western states was higher than in the East. Particularly hard hit was the western tourist industry—a major source of income for most states in the region. The number of vacationing tourists and visitors dropped to less than one half of their 1929 totals. Thousands and thousands of small businesses such as gasoline stations, hotels, motor courts, and cafes were directly affected. And if their worsening economic situation led them to seek loans from a local banker, they often found his doors closed. More than one-third of the smaller banks in the region were forced into bankruptcy, and almost as many others escaped collapse only by merging with a large and distant institution.

Unfortunately the economic crisis had an immediate effect on many promising cultural activities in the West. Writers, actors, artists, and intellectuals were among the hardest hit by the crash, as, of course, were many of their patrons. Plummeting sales of books and paintings were but one result. One exception to the generally unhappy state of affairs was the motion picture industry. Weekly average attendance of 60 million patrons at the nation's 23,000 movie theaters did not decline significantly during the depression. Indeed, it seemed that an increasingly larger number of Americans were seeking some escape from the grim realities of their daily lives by slipping into their local theater. Hollywood, therefore, did not experience the same pattern of unemployment as most other industries.

The years following the collapse of the stock market were some of the worst ever experienced by educational institutions in the West. As state legislators frantically sought to economize between 1929 and 1933, they decreased their appropriations for all levels of education, usually by about 30 per cent. Most of the western state colleges and universities found survival possible only by reducing their faculties, and by cutting salaries of those who remained. An even worse situation prevailed in the public schools. By 1931 school boards drastically cut salaries, and pay day was often delayed or simply skipped. They increased teaching loads, shortened school terms, and simply eliminated "non-essential" subjects (usually anything other than the three R's) from the curriculum. Most school construction simply ceased. In 1932 the Wyoming legislature decreed a six-month instead of an eight-month term; Oregon lawmakers invalidated the minimum salary scale for teachers in their state, and Oklahoma required adoption of textbooks for 10 years or more and placed maximum limits on teacher salaries. But some western states resorted to even more drastic measures. They issued tax anticipation warrants to teachers instead of money. In Oklahoma only one such warrant could be redeemed in 1932; in Apache County in Arizona no warrants could be cashed. Communities in Idaho and South Dakota resorted to a form of barter as they "boarded around" local teachers at the homes of parents, much as Americans had done a century before. Some western communities were so hard hit that they simply had to close their public schools. In February 1933 it was reported that at least 8,000 children in New Mexico were unable to attend public schools that had been closed because of financial stringency, with larger numbers in the same predicament in Oklahoma.

Such desperate conditions did not have any immediate striking impact on the nature of politics in the West. To be sure, between 1929 and 1933 Republican strength began to wane, but electoral protests were of moderate proportions. Moderates dominated both major parties. Californians elected "Sunny Jim" Rolph to be their Republican governor between 1930 and 1934. Rolph was an erstwhile mayor of San Francisco who was a western counterpart of New York City's Jimmy Walker. With little comprehension of depression problems, Rolph stymied tax reform and concentrated on economies. Most western governors during these years advocated similar policies. If more serious, Democratic governors Clarence Martin of Washington and Charles E. Martin of Oregon (no relation) had like-minded outlooks. And moderate Democrats such as Utah's George Dern and Henry Blood, or U.S. Senators Key Pittman of Nevada and Carl Hayden of Arizona, were of the same stripe. What is indeed surprising is that the magnitude of suffering of westerners in the wake of the Crash of 1929 was not reflected in their electoral behavior between 1929 and 1932.

The crash of 1929, thus, stunned the West as it did other areas of the nation. It brought social disruption, economic chaos, and cultural vacuum, but as yet little change in political complexion. But let a contemporary tell his tale. As Oscar Ameringer, an Oklahoma socialist editor, reported to a congressional committee on his travels in 1931:

> During the last three months I have visited, as I have said, some 20 states of this wonderfully rich and beautiful country. Here are some

of the things I heard and saw: In the State of Washington I was told that
the forest fires raging in that region all summer and fall were caused by
unemployed timber workers and bankrupt farmers in an endeavor to
earn a few honest dollars as fire fighters. The last thing I saw on the
night I left Seattle was numbers of women searching for scraps of food
in the refuse piles of the principal market of that city. A number of
Montana citizens told me of thousands of bushels of wheat left in the
fields uncut on account of its low price that hardly paid for the
harvesting. In Oregon I saw thousands of bushels of apples rotting in
the orchards. Only absolute flawless apples were still salable, at from
40 to 50 cents a box containing 200 apples. At the same time, there are
millions of children who, on account of the poverty of their parents,
will not eat one apple this winter.

While I was in Oregon the Portland Oregonian bemoaned the fact
that thousands of ewes were killed by the sheep raisers because they
did not bring enough in the market to pay the freight on them. And
while Oregon sheep raisers fed mutton to the buzzards, I saw men
picking for meat scraps in the garbage cans in the cities of New York
and Chicago. I talked to one man in a restaurant in Chicago. He told
me of his experience in raising sheep. He said that he had killed 3,000
sheep this fall and thrown them down the canyon, because it cost $1.10
to ship a sheep, and then he would get less than a dollar for it. He said
he could not afford to feed the sheep, and he would not let them starve,
so he just cut their throats and threw them down the canyon.

The roads of the West and Southwest teem with hungry hitchhikers.
The camp fires of the homeless are seen along every railroad track. I
saw men, women, and children walking over the hard roads. Most of
them were tenant farmers who had lost their all in the late slump in
wheat and cotton. Between Clarksville and Russellville, Ark., I picked
up a family. The woman was hugging a dead chicken under a ragged
coat. When I asked her where she had procured the fowl, first she told
me she had found it dead in the road, and then added in grim humor,
"They promised me a chicken in the pot, and now I got mine."

In Oklahoma, Texas, Arkansas, and Louisiana I saw untold bales of
cotton rotting in the fields because the cotton pickers could not keep
body and soul together on 35 cents paid for picking 100 pounds. The
farmers cooperatives who loaned the money to the planters to make the
crops allowed the planters $5 a bale. That means 1,500 pounds of seed
cotton for the picking of it, which was in the neighborhood of 35 cents a
pound. A good picker can pick about 200 pounds of cotton a day, so that
the 70 cents would not provide enough pork and beans to keep the
picker in the field, so that there is fine staple cotton rotting down there
by the hundreds of thousands of tons.[2]

Herbert Hoover and the West, 1929–1933

Ironically, most westerners were not very sympathetic toward Herbert Hoover as he struggled to deal with the debacle. We say ironic because Hoover was the first American president in the twentieth century who could properly be considered a westerner. Although born in Iowa, he had grown up on his uncle's ranch in Oregon, and had been a member of the first class of Stanford University, in 1891 a new western institution. Although evincing public concern for many of the special problems that beset westerners, Hoover soon revealed that he was not well attuned to the realities of western politics.[3] By 1932 the various sections of the trans-Mississippi region had aligned themselves solidly against him, with that peculiar bitterness that comes from a feeling of having been betrayed.

Hoover's farm policies did little to solve the major problem of western farmers, especially those of the Plains and on the West Coast. That problem was insufficient markets. He declared himself resolutely opposed to the McNary-Haugen Bill, the favorite proposal to deal with surpluses supported enthusiastically by almost every western delegation in Congress. Instead, he favored the Agricultural Marketing Act of 1929 under which a new Federal Farm Board was to spend more than $500 million to purchase farm surpluses, thereby providing support for stable farm prices. But despite valiant efforts between 1929 and 1932, the Farm Board's program was a failure, for the more it purchased, the more farmers produced, thereby widening the gap between production and declining consumption. Even Hoover's effort to expand farm credit remained unappreciated. In 1932 he agreed to allow the Reconstruction Finance Corporation (a new government lending agency) to extend $200 million for agricultural loans. Yet, when all was said and done, the grain farmers on the Plains received only one-fourth as much for their crops in 1932 as in 1929 and fruit and vegetable growers on the West Coast received about one-half as much. And, rightly or wrongly, they blamed President Hoover, among others, for their plight.

Westerners also resented Hoover's conservation policies. Although himself a mining engineer, within three months after entering the White House Hoover had succeeded in angering various segments of the mining industry. In March of 1929, without much prior consultation with affected mining interests, he announced the suspension of oil prospecting permits by the Department of the Interior, which had been issuing them ever since the passage of the Minerals Leasing Act of 1920. This action affected the economies of Rocky Mountain states such as Colorado, Wyoming, New Mexico, and also that of Kansas. Their Republican governors were furious. But oblivious to the political storms he had aroused, Hoover called a conference of western governors to meet in Colorado Springs during June of 1929 to elaborate his conservation policies. The governors came, but instead of discussing conservation they used the conference as a platform from which to denounce the president. At the beginning of his presidential tenure, therefore, Hoover had already lost considerable confidence among the Republican leaders in the West.

Moreover, many westerners were dismayed and disheartened by Hoover's opposition to public power. Although Congress had authorized the construction of Boulder Dam on the Colorado River in 1928—before Hoover entered the White House—he himself did not encourage its completion. In fact, he opposed the building of electric power transmission lines of the federal government. With his curious logic he was willing to sell only falling water at the dam to a private utility company and to the city of Los Angeles, who in turn were to produce the power. Rather than conceive of the dam as a means of providing various benefits for the region in which it was located, Hoover urged the sale of federally owned water at a price designed to return a profit. Such a conception was a far cry from that of public power development for regional growth and prosperity then being advocated by Senator George Norris of Nebraska, whose bill for the establishment of a Tennessee Valley Authority the president bitterly opposed. Hoover's attitude was especially disappointing to many people in the Pacific Northwest who had been hoping for federal aid in the development of the basin around the Columbia River. Senator Charles McNary of Oregon—a staunch Republican but an even stauncher advocate of public power—reflected this mood in his criticisms of the president. Throughout the region westerners felt increasingly that, despite his background, President Hoover was not a firm advocate of their best interests.

Nor were western cattlemen happy with the Hoover Administration. They had suffered along with most farmers in the twenties, and now the depression only added to their miseries. Cattle prices in 1932 were only half of what they had been in 1929. American beef exports during these years fell to virtually zero, although the expenses of cattlemen remained the same. No wonder that their disposable income fell from a yearly $678 per capita in 1929 to $360 just three years later. Thousands of cattle growers went into bankruptcy, and private bankers in the Rocky Mountain and Plains states virtually ceased to make any loans to cattlemen after 1931. And drought plagued the growers in Texas, Oklahoma, Colorado, and New Mexico in 1930 and spread to the Dakotas and Montana a year later. Consequently, the Cattlemen's Association urged the Administration to extend large-scale help, only to meet with inaction. True, the Forest Service reduced grazing fees by 50 per cent in 1932, but this hardly touched the major problem. As a result, many smaller ranches disappeared during these years, along with many of the less efficient ones. By 1932 the size of the average ranch on the Plains had increased as these smaller holdings were absorbed by larger operators.

Western cattlemen found only one bright spot during the first years of the

Great Depression. This was the increasing amount of meat needed by Californians, who by 1930 had become enamored of hamburgers. By that time California cattlemen were unable to supply all the meat eaten by the state's growing population. And since hamburgers usually contained low-quality beef, producers on the Plains found a new and lucrative outlet for cattle of less than premium quality. As a source of food, hamburgers were peculiarly well suited to the needs of a society increasingly dependent on the automobile, such as California. To be sure, Californians did not invent hamburgers, destined to become America's national food. The broiled or fried hamburger sandwich was said to have first appeared in 1903 at the Louisiana Purchase Exposition, sold by vendors of German origin. Red meat had been eaten raw by people in Finland and Estonia in the early nineteenth century. From there it was adapted by sailors based in Hamburg, Germany, then Europe's largest seaport. At the beginning of the twentieth century German sailors from Hamburg who docked in New York City demanded chopped meat on a bun from the eating stands on the New York waterfront, insisting that they could carry their buns back aboard ship when they were in a hurry. Other people in a hurry, such as Californians toward the close of the 1920s, found the hamburger an economical and satisfactory meal. And since they were leading an even more mobile existence in their cars than German sailors in their ships, they considered hamburgers particularly well suited to their needs. Their popularity mushroomed in the twenties. As roadside stands became "drive-ins" during the 1920s, no longer making it necessary for customers to leave their cars to eat, the hamburger became an increasingly important new market outlet for cattlemen throughout the West.

Oil producers were another western group who became disenchanted with the Hoover policies. Owing to the discovery of new fields in Oklahoma and East Texas between 1927 and 1931, the petroleum industry experienced the greatest glut in its history. By 1931 producers were receiving 10 cents per barrel for crude oil—if there were any takers. This price was far less than their costs, and many of the smaller producers faced total ruin. The Independent Oil Producers Association repeatedly urged President Hoover to take effective action in reducing oil production and in stabilizing prices, but the administration in Washington remained inactive. In this crisis the oilmen turned to their state governments. In Oklahoma they prevailed on popular Governor "Alfalfa Bill" Murray to declare martial law in the oil fields and to close them, and to enforce his order by the use of state militia. Murray took such action in August 4, 1931, and kept the wells closed until October 10, when the price of oil stabilized at higher levels. Governor Ross Sterling in Texas took similar action, and on August 10,1931, shut down the flush East Texas field. There too troops patrolled the wells to prevent violations. It seemed that even economic chaos in the West seemed insufficient to prod the administration into action.

By 1932 greater restlessness swept the West. More clamor by the unemployed in California had led Governor Rolph in 1931 to allot small sums for relief from his contingent fund, although he told the inactive legislature to take whatever action it liked concerning relief for the unemployed. In the Pacific Northwest the jobless formed the Unemployed Citizens' League in Washington, which lobbied for direct relief. In Colorado, where unemployment had quadrupled between 1929 and 1932, private charities were exhausted and county poorhouses and state hospitals were filled to capacity. Whole families as well as young single youths could be seen moving along Colorado's highways; their abandoned farms became an increasingly familiar sight. In January of 1932 a small group of angry farm women stormed the Larimer County courthouse in the north-central portion of the state to demand tax reduction. Two hundred militant farmers stormed the Sedgwick County Courthouse for the same reason two months later. And then 1,500 angry farmers marched on the state capital in Denver to demand a reduction of state tax assessments, temporarily intimidating the lawmakers. All these incidents were significant in persuading unemployed war veterans that a march on Washington in support of a pending bill for veterans' bonuses might be desirable. Thus, one contingent of the Bonus Expeditionary Force (BEF) had its start in Denver in the summer of 1932 and then proceeded to the nation's capital. Moreover, in Colorado, New Mexico, Kansas, the Dakotas, Texas, and Oklahoma, the National Farm Holiday Association, led by Milo Reno, was active in organizing farmers to withhold crops from market to raise prices, and in interfering militantly in foreclosure proceedings and farm bankruptcies. Although he sent organizers to the states of California and Washington, Reno was less successful there than among the agrarians of the interior. But throughout the West, many individuals and groups looked to Washington for strong leadership and guidance. As Republican Governor Julius Meier of Oregon wired President Hoover on June 18, 1932: "We must have help from the federal government if we are to avert suffering . . . and possible uprisings." But little direct action came from the national leadership.

In fact, President Hoover was opposed to direct federal relief. Not that he was unsympathetic. In 1930 he had appointed an Emergency Committee for Employment, headed by Colonel Arthur Wood, to encourage private charities. In the following year he set up an Organization on Unemployment Relief chaired by Walter S. Gifford (president of American Telephone and Telegraph Company) to solicit voluntary relief contributions. Neither of these groups was successful in view of the magnitude of the problem they faced. And when Colorado's progressive Senator Edward P. Costigan introduced a bill for federal relief in Congress (Costigan-LaFollette Bill), Hoover vetoed it. He did approve the Emergency Relief and Reconstruction Act of 1932, which permitted the Reconstruction Finance Corporation to make up to $300 million in loans to the states to be used by them for relief expenditures, and another $322 million for public construction project grants, which would give employment to several hundred thousand persons. These sums were totally inadequate to aid more than a small fraction of the 15 million Americans then unemployed, more than 3 million of whom lived in the West.

Consequently, it was not surprising that in 1932 westerners turned away from Herbert Hoover to give their overwhelming support to Franklin D. Roosevelt. Before the major issues of unemployment and depression, all other problems paled in comparison, whether prohibition, administrative reform, or petty political rivalries. Throughout the twentieth century westerners had depended on easterners to provide an impetus to western economic growth, supplying the people, the skills, the capital, the ideas, and the markets necessary for development. Now the industrial East, prostrate economically, was unable to help, and so, many westerners looked instead to the national government for help, and voted for Franklin D. Roosevelt and his as yet inchoate New Deal.

Westward Migration During the Great Depression

To the poverty-stricken migrants of the thirties, the West was still the land of opportunity, even if only in their minds. For during these desperate years many had little to live for but a vision, a hope, which, real or fanciful, gave them courage to go on. The West thus performed a dual function for Americans.[4] It represented a real extension of their opportunities; and it continued to serve as a mystic symbol.

This dual function of the West was particularly noticeable in California. Many of the 350,000 refugees from the Dust Bowl (Oklahoma, Arkansas, Texas, the Dakotas, Kansas, Nebraska) hoped to find profitable homesteads there. If that was their goal, they had come to the wrong place, however, for that ideal was far removed from the realities of farming in the state. California, as we have pointed out, had become the nation's prime example of highly mechanized corporate agriculture. In 1939 it had 2,892 large farms (out of a total of 150,000) that produced a third of all produce and controlled almost two-thirds of all agricultural lands in California. Such a highly commercialized form of farming left little room—or profit—for the family-sized farm. Technology, which had set thousands of Dust Bowl migrants adrift, worked with the same inexorable effects in California to industrialize its great farming potential. The migrants were the weather-vanes of technological change, themselves pointing to the profound trans-formation of American farming by technology. No wonder that Californians afforded them a hostile reception.

Californians were not happy to see the newcomers because they usually arrived with very sparse funds. Attracted by the groundless rumor that jobs were plentiful in California, many of them soon swelled relief rolls and increased the burden of private charitable agencies. They came in their old jalopies, with children, dogs, and household goods. Some of the poorest families simply walked. They flocked to the giant farms in California's Central Valley, flooding the seasonal labor market, and depressing farm wages even further. Meanwhile, California farmers were themselves struggling under the impact of the depression and were in no mood to provide even minimal—let alone decent—working and housing conditions for the newcomers. Indeed, in 1936 California officials issued a warning to prospective migrants, urging them not to come in view of the scant employment opportunities. But the rumors of jobs in the West persisted throughout the United States, and so in 1939 the California legislature enacted a law prohibiting indigents from entering the state. During the next two years state police officers examined travellers at the borders, turning back many who could not give evidence of owning property or wealth. In 1941, however, the United States Supreme Court declared this act to be unconstitutional.

Not surprisingly, the influx of Dust Bowl refugees created many tensions in California. Between 1933 and 1939 more than 180 agricultural strikes were recorded, involving more than 90,000 workers. In addition, perhaps the most critical labor disturbance in the West Coast during these years was the great maritime strike of 1934 in San Francisco in which Harry Bridges, a reputed communist, led the longshoremen in a general strike that struck fear in the hearts of Californians not unlike the feelings loosed by the Seattle

Oklahoma Dust Bowl in 1936. Source: Farm Security Administration.

General strike of 1919. Without doubt, the communists were seeking to organize many of the migratory field workers on the Pacific Coast. For years both the IWW and the AF of L had sought unsuccessfully to organize agricultural workers in the West. The failure of major strikes in the Imperial Valley during January and February of 1930 only encouraged the communists, and in the following year they organized the Cannery and Agricultural Workers Industrial Union, the most active in California for the next four years. The militant leaders of this new organization pinpointed a succession of protests. In November 1932 they led the fruit pickers at Vacaville; in April 1933 they called out pea pickers in the Hayward area, and in October more than 18,000 cotton pickers in Corcoran. By then Governor Merriam called out the National Guard as increasing violence accompanied these disputes.

Such labor unrest brought a reaction from employers. Groups such as the California Farm Bureau Federation, the State Chamber of Commerce, and the American Legion organized a new "counter" organization, the Associated Farmers of California, which received ample financial support from the largest corporations and business enterprises in the West. Clearly an "open-shop" association, which frequently resorted to vigilante activities to break strikes, beginning in 1934 the Associated Farmers succeeded quickly in suppressing labor protest. During the Salinas lettuce strike of September 1936, for example, they mobilized a citizen army of more than 1,500, which effectively broke the work stoppage in the fields. By 1937 the California group took the lead in forming the United Farmers of the Pacific Coast, embracing not only Oregon and Washington, but also Arizona. Their strong-arm tactics were similar to those that had effectively stifled demands of workers in California. Many of the agricultural areas on the Pacific Coast, therefore, experienced considerable tension, violence, and unrest throughout the decade of the thirties.[5]

The living conditions of many of these new migrants were wretched. One investigator in 1935 reported that he found a two-room cabin in which 41 persons from southeast Oklahoma lived. Another described a one-room shack in which fifteen men, women, and children were huddled, living in unimaginable filth. On December 3, 1937, the California State Immigration and Housing Commission ordered thirty shanties near Visalia condemned as unfit for human habitation. Most camps had no baths, showers, or plumbing, and workers bathed in and drank from the same water supply found in nearby irrigation ditches. Near Kingsburg eighteen families were found living under a bridge. Other workers lived in cardboard cartons, or in tents improvised from gunny sacks, with coffee cans serving for chimneys. In such an environment health conditions were appalling. Six thousand cases of influenza were recorded in one county during February 1937. Scores of babies died of diarrhea and enteritis. Social worker Tessie Williams in 1937 reported the case of one woman who, upon leaving the county hospital, returned with her baby to live under the shade of a tree. A family of seven was reported to have eaten little more than bread and potatoes over a period of several months. Some ate nothing but beans and fried dough and oatmeal; one family of eight lived on dandelions and boiled potatoes. "I'm getting mighty tired of just beans and water," one woman moaned, "but even that may run out any day now."

Under such circumstances the education of children was all but forgotten. Schools tended to be jammed at the height of harvests, but less than half full in off-season. One schoolhouse, California State Board of Health inspectors found, was an old cow barn converted for the purpose. "There were no glass windows," they reported; "the only openings were sections of the wall which could be propped out, and since it was winter they were closed. Some small screened openings provided all the light and ventilation. Consequently the atmosphere was dense, especially as the effluvium of the recently washed floor mixed with other odors." In the rural schools of Kern County, 8,515 pupils entered in one season and 6,450 moved out. Five or six moves each season were not unusual for many students. The effect of this shifting was disastrous for youngsters who became increasingly mired in this culture of poverty. "There is a growing consciousness," wrote Dr. Paul Taylor, an economist with a special interest in the lot of migratory workers, "that for many of their kind the future portends, not progress from generation to generation, but retrogression." As one of the migrants reportedly told him: "My children ain't raised decent like I was raised by my father. There were no rag houses then, but I can't do no better.[6]

A large proportion of California's poor during the Great Depression were of Mexican descent, along with some Filipinos. About 250,000 Mexicans, mostly from Sonora, came in the 1930s, seeking unskilled jobs on farms or in factories, and swelling public relief rolls. At the same time it was estimated that perhaps 150,000 Mexicans who had been living in California returned to their native land, in view of the paucity of jobs. Many California farms began to employ the Okies and the Arkies instead of Mexican farm laborers, on whom they had depended during the preceding decade. Thus, many Mexicans sought work in factories, canneries, and farms. Many of them ended up on the relief rolls of Los Angeles. Another minority group were the 50,000 Filipinos who worked for extremely low wages, often as cooks, laundry workers, and houseboys. Frequently Californians accused them of being social undesirables, or homosexuals. The Watsonville Riot of 1930 and the Salinas Riot of 1934 reflected their intense hatred toward Filipinos, who were brutally attacked in both instances. In view of such hostility thousands of Filipinos in California returned to their native land during the depression, many of them fearing for their lives. Moreover, the state government of California officially acknowledged this racial prejudice by of-

Migrant mother in California during the Depression (1936), a classic photograph by Dorothea Lange. Source: U.S. Farm Security Administration.

fering to pay for the transportation of any Filipino in California who wished to return to his home. Thousands took advantage of the offer.

The Pacific Northwest

Migration patterns to the Pacific Northwest were not unlike those in California during the Great Depression. But the northern states were younger and not so fully developed as their neighbor to the south. Between 1930 and 1940 approximately 465,000 newcomers arrived from the Great Plains, from Texas, Oklahoma, Arkansas, and Missouri. Some came by way of California, not having found land or work there. Most of them were not drifters, but displaced farmers who were yearning for stable resettlement. Unlike the migrants of previous years, the majority were young, and had large families. The census returns showed that 85 per cent were under 45 years of age. A contemporary survey of the reasons why these newcomers went to the Northwest confirmed impressionistic accounts of journalists. Fifty-three per cent of one particular sample had migrated because of crop failures 25 per cent because they could find no jobs, and 20 per cent were seeking a better climate. The beauty and the climate of the Northwest were major attractions.

Many of the Dust Bowl refugees found the Pacific Northwest a land of greater opportunity than California. Agriculture in this region was mostly small-scale, and based far more on the family-size farm than in California. One-half of the newcomers found opportunities in farming, for the need for seasonal labor was greater here. Others tried to succeed with homesteads of their own. Their success was mixed, however, because some lacked the ability to manage farms efficiently. They were unaccustomed to the intensive specialized irrigated type of agriculture that flourished in the Pacific Northwest and soon joined the ranks of migratory field laborers picking hops or apples. Others sought jobs in the cities. Since the region was less heavily industrialized than California, it offered fewer nonskilled manufacturing jobs. But some of the newcomers eventually found openings in canneries. Whether on the farm or in the city, however, the Dust Bowl refugees tended to be attracted to green and rainy portions of the area. They swelled the populations of Portland and Seattle, Tacoma and Spokane, of the Willamette Valley or the Klamath region, and the Yakima Valley in Washington. Frequently they settled in groups. Thus, large groups of settlers from Arkansas settled down in McCleary and Manson, Washington, where they became a majority of the populace. Eighty of three hundred inhabitants of a small town in South Dakota moved to Kitsap County in Washington, where they constituted a homogeneous and close-knit community.

The Rockies and the Southwest

Not all the migrants during the Great Depression went to California, however. A significant number gathered in the Rocky Mountain area and the Southwest. These people included many of Mexican descent who were sugar-beet workers, especially for the Great Western Sugar Company of Colorado. In off-season they congregated in rural slums around Denver and other Colorado towns. "There is a human drama in Colorado," wrote Dr. R. W. Roskelley, a contemporary observer, "which is almost as spectacular as *The Grapes of Wrath.*" These workers were caught in a cycle of poverty that antedated the depression. The Colorado sugar producers had first brought in Mexicans in large numbers during World War I. In the twenty-five years thereafter, their descendants were caught in rural as well as in urban sweatshops. Mexican laborers were not restricted to Colorado, however. Along with Filipinos, Okies, Arkies, and Texans they plied the western roads known as "north of Highway #66" (the great east-west artery immortalized by John Steinbeck in *The Grapes of Wrath*). These were the thoroughfares leading north from Amarillo and Albuquerque to Wyoming, Montana, and the Dakotas. Although most historians have largely ignored them, many Mexicans frequented these routes during the thirties, working in sugar-beet, potato, and vegetable fields, often settling in communities near which they worked. As Carey McWilliams pointed out, little was said or written about them; no Steinbeck dramatized their lives.[7] But they constituted one of the most important migratory streams in the West during the thirties, totaling more than 100,000 people. They were among the poorest of the poor in the Great Depression, the "other America" of the trans-Mississippi West.

The thirties saw the growth of a Chicano population in most western states. The tendency of many Mexicans to stay near the sugar-beet fields was the result of various factors. Often they were in debt, for car, food, or medical bills, and so remained in a particular locality to work off their debts. Illness at times tended to lead them to settle near towns in sugar-growing areas, and access to public schools was a consideration in off-seasons. As a sugar-beet labor contractor in Billings, Montana, A. Halleck Brown, stated in a newspaper interview in 1940:

> Sure, we bring [them] in by the thousands. The big labor agencies in Kansas City and El Paso get 'em for us. A lot of Mexicans and Filipinos and lately more and more of these American floaters from the played-out farms in the dust bowl. They do pretty well by themselves, too. Wages are better than they used to be. Why, a hard-working family can now clean up as much as $240 in a season. Why, a lot of 'em go back where they came from. Some of them to Old Mexico, I suppose. But I shouldn't be surprised if we didn't have between 1000 and 2000 Mexicans right around Billings all the time now. But they don't make us any trouble. Matter of fact, I think they're less trouble and go on relief less than our own poor white trash.[8]

This pattern was not very different in the southwestern states. Arizona's rich irrigated farming lands as well as its extensive cotton fields required tens of thousands of field workers in the thirties. Indeed, the state became a "resort center" of the poor in these years as many migrants bound for California spent several months in the cotton fields of Arizona and in the labor camps and hovels that ringed many of its towns and cities and constituted the core of a new ghetto in Phoenix. In addition to dispossessed American farmers and Chicanos, Arizona's field workers also contained a sizable number of Indians. The low wages that the growers paid to Mexicans and Indians, however, tended to discourage white laborers, who moved further west. To a lesser extent, the conditions prevailing in Arizona also existed in the cotton fields of southern New Mexico, if on a smaller scale.

The agricultural revolution was also creating much social turmoil in Texas during the thirties. As farming—especially on irrigated lands—became increasingly mechanized, it tended to eliminate the need for manual labor.

Thus, it was disrupting the sharecropper and tenant-farming system that had developed during the previous half century. The depression—especially the shrinkage of farm markets—gave it a final blow. What happened to the 400,000 dispossessed tenant farmers? They were set adrift. And the cheapness of automobiles by 1933 made them more mobile than at any previous time. Yet their dream of finding a homestead elsewhere was rarely realized. Many migrated to cities in the hope of finding jobs. And thousands of others joined the migratory field forces who were in demand everywhere in the West. The displacement of so many farm families brought all too familiar social changes to the areas they left. It weakened the rural school systems, the tax structure of country governments, small businessmen in towns and cities, and even professionals who had catered to farm populations. White farmers who had been displaced by technolgical changes increasingly found that they could not compete with cheap Mexican labor in Texas, and so they constituted a significant percentage of the California-bound stream of migrants.

Perhaps as many as half a million Mexican migratory workers poured into Texas in the 1930s. Together with 80,000 black workers and 120,000 whites, they constituted the bulk of the labor force that brought in the large Texas cotton crop. Most of these workers were recruited by Mexican labor contractors. These *papacitos* were not unusual in Mexico, where they had functioned in various forms for over a century. The corporate managers of huge Texas cotton farms preferred Mexicans because large numbers could be brought in on short notice. Other migrant workers straggled in and out; the Mexicans could be supplied in disciplined crews, many of them families of fifteen to twenty persons, by just a telephone call. And instead of the administrative problems involved in dealing with thousands of persons—from wage payment to housing—one transaction with a contractor solved a wide range of problems, from the employer's viewpoint.

The growth of corporate farming in Texas, as in California, hastened the decline of the smaller towns. "Our merchants have no trading territory," complained one of them in Dimmit County. "Labor with $1.25 wages can't buy. Our lands of about 12,000 acres under cultivation are in the hands of about a dozen men. They live in hotels; they are not farmers; they are speculators in onions. The farms are practically uninhabited except by groups of Mexican laborers."[9] And how did these Mexican laborers live? The Texas Educational Survey Commission described the conditions of Mexicans in these rural slums and noted, "Many of them live in shacks that are hardly fit to shelter goats. They have not sufficient rooms to live decently. Frequently there are no outhouses, no gardens, no grass plots, no shade trees, nothing. . . . Here among the weeds the children grow up like weeds. . . . Passing through the same experience from year to year, he [the worker] loses courage, becomes despondent. He believes himself defrauded and is in sore temptation to defraud in retaliation, and more trouble ensues. He cannot clothe his children . . . keep them in good health, and in many cases children suffer from deficient nourishment. These children cannot attend school regularly and some of them hardly at all. . . . They grow up in surroundings that breed disease, ignorance, and crime."[10] So, in the place of declining small towns, large-scale agriculture was creating new rural slums.

Black ghettos in the Texas cotton fields during the 1930s also were not hard to find. Listen to the findings of the Texas State Employment Service in 1938:

> In March 1938 the County Judge of one of the principal cotton producing counties of the Amarillo District advised the Service that about three hundred Negro workers were stranded in a large cotton plantation in the adjoining county. The ranch in question was composed of 9000 acres. . . . The yield was great. The operator of this plantation preferred Negro labor and hired a number of truck owners to recruit Negroes from central Texas, paying approximately $5.00 per person, deducting the amount from the first money made by the pickers. The living quarters for these people are known as "dug-outs," about three feet in the ground with weatherboard side and roof . . . 80 feet long by 12 feet wide. Bunks were arranged in tiers and approximately 100 people were housed in each "dug-out". . . . The ventilation was extremely poor, and there were no toilet facilities except surface toilets. . . . These people were piled up like hogs in these places throughout the winter; having no transportation facilities, they could not get away, and the pay received was spent for food. . . . In February, it was said that there were 23 days of bad weather when no one could work and debt to the commissary was accrued. Their condition became unbearable.[11]

Here were the "invisible poor" of the 1930s, concentrated in rural slums created by industrial agriculture in many portions of the West, whose position was greatly worsened with the onset of the Great Depression.

Economic crisis also severely affected people on the Plains. If states such as Nebraska, the Dakotas, and Wyoming lost more than half a million persons during the 1930s this was owing to the severity of rural poverty in their midst. Probably many portions of the region should not have been farmed in the first place, but should have been left for grazing. Intensive farming denuded the soil, leaving the surface open to rapid erosion by high winds. Moreover, many of the settlers on the Plains after 1890 had little agricultural experience suitable to the climate there and followed dubious or unscientific farming practices. And the high wheat prices maintained by the U.S. Food Administration during World War I encouraged farmers to plant more wheat than they would have without such inducements, and their hopes were not dampened until the Great Depression. In short, many farmers had had a rendezvous with destiny, with the realities of an inhospitable environment for the type of farming in which they engaged before 1933. The depression only hastened the day of reckoning.

As if the woes of the depression were not bad enough, the worst weather in over a century came to plague the Great Plains in the thirties. In the period between 1929 and 1939 there were nine years in which the rainfall was below average. June 1929 was one of the driest on record; 1930 saw hot winds; July 1931 brought intensive heat. And then came 1933, the fourth driest year on record, in which less than 13 inches of rain were recorded. Thousands of farmers were unable to survive such disaster. But for those who still held out, who still hoped and prayed, 1934 finished their dreams, for it was the driest year ever recorded up to then, with less than 9 inches of rainfall. And those who survived that dreadful time witnessed the coming of severe dust storms in 1935. The year 1936 was the hottest (121°) and the coldest (−60°) on record. And for good measure, it was also the driest, with less than 8.8 inches of rain. Meanwhile the grasshoppers descended. They first came in the spring of 1931, eating everything in sight, crops and clothing, and infesting people, tools, and animals. By 1934 county governments on the Plains were spending close to $1 million in efforts to rid themselves of this scourge. In 1933 Congress came to their aid with more ample funds, and by 1938 state grasshopper commissions finally controlled the menace. These were bitter years on the Plains, years that shook the self-confidence that once had been so characteristic of the western farmer.

Thus, in the 1930s poverty gripped the Plains states. Approximately half a million persons moved during these years to the Pacific Coast; probably more than 1 million moved about within the region, seeking desperately to eke out a living, moving from failure to failure. And some were so poor that they could not move anywhere, and were riveted in place by their extreme poverty. Thus, the life of small towns and cities in the region became greatly depressed. Tax delinquency—often by as many as two-thirds of the population in a particular political unit—became common in the 1930s. Such shrinkage resulted in a decline of social services—in hospitals, institutions, and welfare facilities. Here, as in other areas of the West, large-scale absentee owners, suitcase farmers, took over delinquent properties and began to engage in industrial, large-scale farming.

North Dakota was especially hard hit. In 1932 wheat there sold for 36 cents per bushel, less than one-sixth of its World War I price. Moreover, the droughts of the 1930s diminished the size of crops, which rarely exceeded 100 million bushels annually, less than one-half of the 1929 total. The total income of North Dakota wheat farmers was $80 million in 1932 compared to $200 million just three years before. Their per capita personal income was $145 annually in the depression years, less than one-half of the national average ($375). By 1935, more than one-third of the farm acreage in North Dakota was tax delinquent. Land values declined, mortgage foreclosures increased along with tenancy and public ownership of land, and a vast exodus ensued. Almost half of the population on the Plains was forced to seek relief in those dreadful years.

What did this mean in the daily life of the average farmer in this region? A contemporary sociologist in the Dakotas wrote that "stoves are giving out; bedding is wearing out; curtains, carpets, and furniture becoming unusable; clothes have become shabby and indecent. . . . Along with these changes have come a decided loss of morale. Ambition has been killed, and there is little hope of ever being anything but a "WPAer." The children born into and reared in this situation are decidedly underprivileged. They are cut off from association with middle class children, feel themselves to be outcasts, and inferiors, have little or no recreational privileges, and come to absorb an atmosphere of defeatism and parasitism."[12] Thus did the depression contribute to the crushing of the human spirit in the West.

The New Deal and the West–Social and Economic Policies

Emergency Agencies

The overriding concern of most westerners in 1933 was the alleviation of massive unemployment. Private agencies and cost-conscious state legislatures had already shown themselves unable to cope with the problem in an effective manner. Most westerners, therefore, however reluctantly, looked to the federal government as a last resort for direct relief, and for help in dealing with the problem of economic recovery in the region.

Relief was the most pressing immediate issue that confronted Franklin D. Roosevelt as he assumed the hard burdens of the presidency.[13] Partly to alleviate hunger, deprivation, and suffering, Roosevelt created four agencies that were directly concerned with the problem. They included the Federal Emergency Relief Administration (FERA), the Civilian Conservation Corps (CCC), the National Youth Administration (NYA), and after 1935, the Works Projects Administration (WPA). In California, the Pacific Northwest, the Mountain states, the Southwest, and the Plains, these efforts were generally welcomed by the needy, but viewed with some skepticism by state officials. Throughout the West the CCC became the most popular emergency agency, engaged as it was in natural resource conservation.

During 1933 and 1934 the FERA created numerous small works projects designed to provide subsistence payments for about one-tenth of the unemployed. In California it met reasonable cooperation from Republican state officials who had shown little imagination themselves in providing relief for almost 1 million unemployed. A not dissimilar situation existed in Washington and Oregon, where state officials adopted a noncommittal but cooperative attitude toward FERA programs.

But in the Rocky Mountain area the FERA met a stormy reception. Throughout the West state lawmakers had shown themselves to be extremely reluctant to raise taxes and to appropriate revenues whereby states could supplement the FERA grants. The Colorado legislature's attitude was typical. When in January of 1934 that state's legislature was about to adjourn without making any provision for contributions to the FERA, a mob of 1,000 poor invaded legislative chambers in Denver to threaten violence. They also planned to pillage food stores in Denver. Under the pressure of revolutionary upheaval the reluctant legislators on January 22, 1934, increased the gasoline tax and diverted highway funds to match the federal FERA grants. Meanwhile, an intense power struggle ensued over the dispensation of relief funds between Roosevelt's assistant, Harry Hopkins, and Colorado's Democratic Governor Edwin C. Johnson. This conflict reflected the predilection of westerners for independent action, and minimal national control, and the harsh reality of their increasing dependence on federal largesse. A somewhat similar condition prevailed in Wyoming, which prided itself on not requesting federal relief funds until December 1933, when unemployment became so serious that state officials finally bowed to the inevitable. Over the next four years they accepted federal relief moneys, receiving—like most western states—about three times as much per capita as the national average. The southwestern states tended to be more receptive than the Mountain regions and on the Plains as many as one-third to one-half of the population subsisted on FERA funds during the first two years of the New Deal.

As successor to the FERA, the WPA proved somewhat more popular, perhaps because it was more selective in the projects it initiated as well as in its selection of relief recipients. In California and the Pacific Northwest it received a very warm reception. In Colorado the feud between Harry Hopkins and Governor Johnson continued until 1937, when the latter left the statehouse. In New Mexico the WPA was used by the Democrats, headed by U.S. Senator Dennis Chavez, to dispense patronage, leading to revelations of irregularities in 1937 that culminated in one of the worst WPA scandals in the nation. In areas that were primarily agricultural, such as the Great Plains, the WPA provided one of the few employment opportunities available to the jobless, more than one-third of whom went on WPA rolls between 1935 and 1940.

Both the CCC and the NYA proved themselves to be particularly popular in the West. In California, the CCC did important work in reforestation and flood control. In Idaho the CCC operated in 70 camps whose 20,000 young men built many miles of roads and fences and treated 2 million acres of white pine for fungus. Wyoming was more enthusiastic about the CCC than it was about most other New Deal programs, partly because it did not require matching funds. And for many of the farm boys of the Southwest and the Plains, who knew not where to turn, the CCC provided one of the few avenues available for the type of work to which they were accustomed. The NYA also was especially valuable for farm states in the West because, although school-age youths might find temporary jobs during the crop season, they often could find no employment during the winter. The supplemental funds provided by the NYA enabled many of them to pursue high school or college educations rather than join the ranks of transients. And in later years their educational training enabled them to follow nonagricultural pursuits. Thus, the NYA was helping to provide a reservoir of trained men and women that was quickly available to meet the demands of domestic mobilization on the eve of World War II.

Other New Deal agencies had less success in the West. Although initial enthusiasm for the National Recovery Administration (NRA) was high, in most western states it waned toward the end of 1933. Since industry and manufactures were of lesser importance in the West than in the East, most NRA codes affected the western economy only marginally. Hopes ran much higher concerning the potential employment to be offered by the Public Works Administration. But by 1936 most westerners were deeply disappointed with this agency, largely because Secretary of the Interior Harold Ickes, aided by the PWA executive secretary, Coloradan Oscar L. Chapman, was extremely slow in approving applications for new projects. In fact, very few large-scale projects were completed west of the Mississippi River before 1939.

Agricultural Policies

Far more popular were the farm programs of the New Deal in the West. They raised the income of western farmers while aiding them in reducing debts. Most beneficial were the production control programs of the Agricultural Adjustment Administration (AAA), which made benefit payments to farmers who restricted their acreage. The Farm Security Administration (FSA), the Farm Credit Administration (FCA), and the Rural Electrification Administration (REA) also enjoyed much support. As elsewhere in the nation, large- and medium-sized farmers were often the prime beneficiaries of federal farm programs. Certainly this was true in

California, where the 2,892 largest farms (of a total of 150,000) received 44 per cent of all benefit payments made in the state by the AAA. Between 1933 and 1936 California farmers were able to double their income while reducing their debts by about one-fifth. The wretched conditions of the migratory field workers were somewhat improved after 1937 by the Farm Security Administration, which built special camps for them, provided medical services, and sought to hold employers to minimum wage and housing standards.

The AAA likewise bolstered farm income in the Pacific Northwest states. But at least as significant there were the programs of the U.S. Bureau of Reclamation, of which the Columbia River project and Grand Coulee Dam after 1937 were the largest. By bringing down the price of electric power, and making new irrigated lands available for small farmers, the Bureau was substantially strengthening the basis of agricultural productivity in this area.

The AAA was not so successful in raising the income of farmers in the Rocky Mountain and southwestern states. There, however, the Farm Credit Administration was particularly important in saving thousands of farmers and cattlemen from bankruptcy. In Colorado, for example, virtually no private bankers were willing to extend loans to cattlemen after 1933 and very few would lend to farmers. Thus, cattlemen and farmers became dependent almost entirely on credit provided by federal agencies, of which the FCA was the most important. In these regions the REA also helped to improve the efficiency of some smaller farms.

On the Great Plains even federal support was often inadequate to save farmers from bankruptcy. With one-third of North Dakota's farmers undergoing foreclosures on their mortgages by 1935, federal agencies came to hold a substantial percentage—at least one-fifth—of producing farm lands in the state. Much of this was rented or sold to large corporate operators. At the same time the Resettlement Administration (after 1937 the Farm Security Administration) experienced moderate success in resettling some poverty-stricken farm families on more productive farms. On the Plains, also, the Department of Agriculture inaugurated a variety of soil rehabilitation programs that were extremely effective, although in the beginning they brought many scoffing smiles. This was especially true of the planting of tree belts on the Plains to lessen the destructive impact of blowing soil. They said that it couldn't be done. But it was done.

Water and Power Policies

Unlike Herbert Hoover, President Roosevelt gave his unswerving support to public power projects, thus endearing himself to many westerners. Four major enterprises in the West were promoted during the New Deal. They included the Central Valley Project in California, the completion of Hoover (Boulder) Dam, the Grand Coulee Dam on the Columbia River, and the Colorado–Big Thompson Project. Together, these development programs transformed portions of the semi-arid West of 1933 into thriving irrigated farmlands just eight years later, totaling more than one-third of all the irrigated farm acreage west of the 98th meridian. Through them the New Deal created 125,000 new family-sized farms as well as 125,000 new suburban houses.

Within the Roosevelt Administration there was considerable conflict over the expansion of federal reclamation in the West. Secretary of Agriculture Henry A. Wallace and his assistants were very much afraid that the opening of new farm lands would only add to the existing glut of farm products in available markets. Many newspapers in the East and the Middle West were strongly opposed to any extension of reclamation programs in the West. Congressman John Taber, Republican of New York—known by some of his colleagues as the Miser of the House—spoke for many of his fellow easterners when he charged that New Deal reclamation policies were but a prime example of waste by the Roosevelt Administration. But the western delegations in Congress insisted equally as strongly that the construction of new dams would not lead to an increase of agricultural production, but was designed to be significant primarily for the production of new electric power. Their most effective spokesman was Elwood P. Mead, the Director of the U.S. Bureau of Reclamation, who by 1935 had patiently won Secretary of the Interior Harold Ickes to his view. And westerners in Congress were becoming more aggressive in seeking funds for federal reclamation. As Congressman Charles J. Colden of California said in 1937: "We resent the implication that we are stepchildren of the older commonwealths. We but request the consideration which is legally, morally, and economically ours."[14] He saw irrigation as essential to diversified economic growth and the establishment of stable communities. And the western view prevailed. During the New Deal Congress authorized a fivefold increase in appropriations for federal power projects for the area.

After 1929 both state and federal officials in California had begun to make plans for cooperative water development for California's Central Valley. Essentially, the proposal presented by the California State Engineer to the legislature in 1931 called for the diversion of waters from the north to provide electric power and irrigation for the entire state, especially the populous south. The California lawmakers hoped that the implementation of this scheme would be undertaken by the federal government, since the cost was too heavy for the state to bear. Moreover, in the midst of the depression, they argued that besides providing new employment it would generate new income in California. The most powerful opposition to this public power project came—as might be expected—from private utility companies, especially the Pacific Gas and Electric Company. Nevertheless, in 1933 the California legislature enacted the Central Valley Project Act and at a public referendum two years later the voters approved it as well. Complicated negotiations with the federal Bureau of Reclamation stretched out over the next four years, and actual construction of the project began only then. In the decade after 1939 the Bureau built a series of three dams, five canals, and two power transmission lines, which came to constitute the nucleus of the most significant public power project in California.

The Roosevelt Administration also hastened the completion of Hoover Dam. Traditionally Secretaries of the Interior have had the privilege of naming federal dams. The project on the Colorado River, begun in 1928, had been known informally as Boulder Dam, but President Hoover's Secretary of the Interior, Ray Lyman Wilbur, took the liberty of naming it Hoover Dam before he left office. But this was something that his successor, that old curmudgeon Harold Ickes, could not stomach. One of his first concerns in 1933 was to change the name of Hoover Dam, and to designate it Boulder Dam. With President Roosevelt's consent, he did so. Thus, when Franklin D. Roosevelt dedicated the complete facility on September 30, 1935, it officially became Boulder Dam, although a Republican Congress in 1947 once again made the name Hoover Dam official. At the time of its completion it was the highest and largest dam in the world and contained the world's largest power house. Despite many disagreements among the participating states, the Colorado River project provided much new and essential power and water for southern California and many portions of the Southwest.

In the Pacific Northwest Republicans as well as Democrats were enthusiastic advocates of public power, especially the development of the Columbia River Basin. Partly because of the patient and persistent prodding of Oregon's U.S. Senator Charles McNary during the 1930s, the Roosevelt Administration by 1935 had been converted to support the construction of a multipurpose river development program in the Northwest not unlike the Tennessee Valley program already under way. The largest of a series of dams built by the Bureau of Reclamation for this project was the Grand Coulee, designed to generate more than 10 million kilowatts of power, to provide irrigation, flood control, and navigational improvements. Unlike President Hoover, Roosevelt sought to pass lower power costs on to the consumer by letting the Bureau of Reclamation's Bonneville Power Administration build its own transmission lines, and giving preference in its sales to public agencies and rural cooperatives. On the eve of World War II, this project had created more than 10,000 small farms (of less than 160 acres) from newly irrigated lands in the Columbia River Basin, encouraging family-sized units.

Meanwhile, in eastern Colorado, the Bureau of Reclamation was building the fourth largest reclamation project in the nation. Begun on a large scale in 1940, it was designed to make use of the source of the Colorado River at Grand Lake as the nucleus for another giant multipurpose river development program, but with an emphasis on the production of public power that would benefit a wide range of economic interests. The plan encompassed the transfer of water from Grand Lake through a 13-mile tunnel beneath the Continental Divide and the construction of a series of dams to harness it to a variety of constructive uses.

The New Deal thus promoted the most significant expansion of federal reclamation projects in the West during the twentieth century. Of the 25 million acres of irrigated lands in 17 states west of the Mississippi River in 1940, 7 million acres were being served by the Bureau of Reclamation. But these projects also contained the seeds of a bitter dispute over the allocation of new lands that were reclaimed or came under irrigation. The president himself believed that federal reclamation should also accomplish a restructuring of American society by stemming the trend toward large-scale corporate farming. This it could do by reasserting the necessity for creating 160-acre family-sized farms, and on them resettling Dust Bowl refugees. Thus, Roosevelt favored a 160-acre limitation on land leased or sold by the Bureau of Reclamation. On the other hand, Secretary of the Interior Harold Ickes felt that the 160-acre limitation in some cases would lead directly to inefficiency and that the most effective land utilization could only be made by large-scale enterprises. The conflict between these two divergent views was to become more heated after 1945 and would constitute one of the major issues in national reclamation policies in the two following decades. But there is no question that the New Deal brought electric power to the West and helped to provide the foundation for large-scale economic diversification after 1941. In fact, during World War II, 84 per cent of the new power needed for war production in eleven western states came from federal projects. Westerners may have been critical of many phases of the New Deal programs, but they overwhelmingly approved its significant expansion of public power.

Cattlemen and Miners

Like many other westerners, cattlemen in the thirties increasingly looked to the federal government for badly needed help. In 1933 most of them were producing at a loss, and then the terrible droughts of that year in Oklahoma, Texas, and the Dakotas added to their burdens. Moreover, no one who has not lived through a sandstorm can understand the terror that gripped many of them in that awful year as black blizzards of dust swept in to engulf man, beast, and land. And so the cattle-growers' associations—once the apostles of individualism—pleaded for greater assistance from Washington. Their pleas were not in vain as the New Deal embarked on a variety of measures that were of direct aid to the industry. In March of 1933 the Emergency Soil Conservation Act passed by Congress provided immediate programs to control soil erosion on the Plains. And by 1939 federal agencies had planted 11,000 miles of trees on farms and ranches as windbreaks. The Farm Credit Administration made immediate loans to cattlemen, many of whom could no longer secure credit at private banks. During November of 1933 the Federal Surplus Relief Corporation began buying up large quantities of beef, initially 50 million pounds, which were distributed to the poor by the Federal Emergency Relief Administration. The New Deal spent more than $500 million to buy up surplus cattle. Meanwhile, the Forest Service reduced its grazing fees, aware of low meat prices. The Division of Subsistence Homesteads in the Department of the Interior provided part-time work for displaced livestock ranchers. But as droughts and dust storms took a further toll in 1934 and 1935 it was estimated that at least 150,000 individuals who had been engaged in cattle raising moved from the Plains. Their animals and pastures were usually taken over by large-scale cattle ranchers who often were far more efficient than the operators they replaced.

With the passage of the Taylor Grazing Act of 1934 the New Deal met one of the long-standing demands of western cattle growers, large and small. For nearly half a century various cattle associations had pleaded for the establishment of some sort of system for allotment of federal grazing lands. Instead, much confusion prevailed until 1934 as most western cattlemen pastured their animals illegally on public lands. Moreover, the proposal of Nevada's Senator Pat McCarran that the federal government grant all of its public lands to the states did not enjoy wide national support. But congressional sentiment for the systematization of federal grazing policies was strong, and the result was the Taylor Grazing Act. This measure set aside 80 million acres of the public domain (which at the time totalled 143 million acres) for cattle and sheep grazing. The Secretary of the Interior was authorized to issue ten-year permits to cattlemen in return for their payment of low fees. Many cattle growers realized that the act strongly encouraged production control, since a reduction of available grazing lands would result in a smaller total amount of meat. By 1957 Secretary Ickes had issued more than 17,000 licenses under this law, which was of special benefit to large cattle growers in the West.[15] Throughout the region, however, the Taylor Grazing Act attracted widespread support and became one of the most popular measures of the New Deal insofar as cattle growers were concerned.

Since the western economy was so heavily dependent on the extractive industries it was not surprising that the Roosevelt Administration attempted to provide them with help. Mining was unmistakably among the most depressed industries in the Rocky Mountain states. Production in 1933 was less than one-half of what it had been in the 1920s. And already then the miners had faced a mild depression. Unemployed miners by the thousands in Nevada, Arizona, Utah, Colorado, and Montana flocked to towns and cities where they joined the ranks of the unemployed and often ended up on relief. Copper continued to be the queen of western metals as Arizona came to account for 40 per cent of national production, with Utah, Montana, and New Mexico producing significant amounts. After 1929 copper increasingly began to be used as an alloy for steel and aluminum, with large quantities also utilized for electric cables and power transmission lines. The difficulties of the depression without doubt fostered further concentration in the industry, driving out smaller producers and making the big ones bigger. By 1940 the Big Three of the copper industry—Anaconda, Kennecott, and Phelps-Dodge—controlled 80 per cent of the industry's output, compared to 40 per cent just a decade earlier. Meanwhile new metals were assuming greater importance during the decade, especially the ferro-alloys such as ferro-manganese. These were by-products of copper mining but rapidly equalled copper in value.

The depression stimulated the exploitation of various other minerals—for what sources of wealth did the Rocky Mountain states possess other than the riches of the earth? The Coeur d'Alene mines in Idaho became a leading supplier of the nation's lead in the New Deal Era. But most spectacular was the impact of the economic crisis on the revival of silver mining in the West. In 1931, only 4,069 silver mines were being operated in the West; by 1935 there were more than 12,000.

The increase of silver production during the New Deal was closely related to the administration's monetary policies and the political pressure exerted by representatives of silver producing states in Congress. After 1933 the silver bloc in Congress grew in influence. Ably led by Senator Key Pitman of Nevada—who, as chairman of the Senate Foreign Relations Committee, often had to be mollified by the president—it also counted such powerful spokesmen as Senators William E. Borah of Idaho and Burton K. Wheeler of Montana. Their prime aim was the remonetization of silver in the nation's currency, something they did not achieve. Other members of the bloc were satisfied with less, and included representatives from Utah, Colorado, Arizona, New Mexico, and California. Although the silver bloc could not persuade either the president or Congress of the merits of remonetization, it was instrumental in securing the passage of the Silver Purchase Act of 1934. Under this measure the Treasury Department was instructed to buy silver, thus providing the western producers with their major market. In the ensuing decade the Secretary of the Treasury bought $1 billion worth of silver before he suspended purchases during World War II. The program encountered savage opposition, in Congress and out, since easterners criticized it as a give-away.[16] Without doubt it did amount to a federal subsidy for western silver producers, yet the silver mines provided employment for several hundred thousand miners who otherwise might have been forced on relief programs. And since eastern business interests for over half a century had secured the major profits from the exploitation of western minerals it was hardly unjust for the federal government—acting as the great redistributor of wealth in America—to return a portion of that wealth to the West, whence it had sprung.

Western oil producers were also hard hit by the depression. The glut of petroleum in relation to available markets had already been a constant worry to them after 1927, and the inaction of the Hoover Administration only added to their woes. By 1933 they were so desperate that many of the executives of the major oil companies openly gave their consent to nationalization of the industry. Secretary of the Interior Ickes was a foremost proponent of such nationalization in the New Deal era, but after 1935 he found little sentiment for this proposal. Instead, most oil producers gave their support to the code that industry representatives framed under the National Recovery Administration and that was administered directly by Secretary Ickes himself. This code helped to get the industry back on its feet by 1935, when the U.S. Supreme Court declared the NRA unconstitutional. Nevertheless, many oil men continued the significant production curbs in the code by other means. Under the initiative of Governors Allred and Marland, of Texas and Oklahoma, respectively, all the oil-producing states in the West agreed through the Interstate Oil Compact of 1935 to use their state powers to limit production within their borders. Obviously Texas, Oklahoma, and California were the dominant members of the compact, but Colorado, New Mexico, Kansas, and lesser producers all cooperated. Congress supported these western states with the Hot Oil Act of 1935, sponsored by Senator Tom Connally of Texas, which prohibited the interstate shipment of oil produced in violation of state quotas. These various measures had succeeded on the eve of World War II in bringing a measure of stability to one of the most chaos-ridden industries in the trans-Mississippi West.

Lumbermen and Fishermen

Among the economic groups hardest hit by the depression were the lumber interests of the Pacific Northwest. By 1933 their production was only one-third of what it had been in 1926, as building construction slumped throughout the nation. Thousands of loggers were unemployed in the region, flooding the glutted labor markets of the towns and cities. It was not surprising, therefore, that the lumber operators welcomed any effort to raise timber prices. One way in which this could be done was through the curtailment of production. And so the interests of lumbermen, big and small, came very close to the demands of conservationists like Gifford Pinchot, who were also advocating a reduction of production and the elimination of waste. Conservation and stabilization thus became twin goals of the lumber industry by 1933, goals that industry representatives incorporated in the code that they formulated under the National Recovery Administration. This code contained many provisions limiting production and enforcing reforestation and fire-control policies to which most segments of the industry gave wholehearted support. And when in 1935 the United States Supreme Court declared the NRA unconstitutional, the lumber industry, too, continued to carry out most of its provisions through informal means, and through its major trade associations. But Congress also hastened to the aid of the timber men. Acting on the advice of a prominent consulting forester, David Mason, it voted in 1937 to limit timber cutting on the large California and Oregon Railroad land grant that it had taken over two decades earlier. By taking a vast amount of unmarketable lumber off the market, the New Deal legislators hoped to raise lumber prices and to nurse the industry back to health.

As much in need of stabilization as most other western natural resource industries were the Pacific fisheries. Throughout the thirties fishermen experienced serious difficulties because their annual catch was usually twice as great as the current demand for fish. Moreover, as fish prices dropped, fishermen tried to increase their catches, thereby adding the specter of rapid depletion to their price problems. In the decade after 1929 the fisheries along the Pacific Coast were facing exhaustion, and leading conservationists began to clamor for governmental controls and regulation.

In California the State Fish Commission tried to limit the annual catch of sardines and tuna. Each year it would meet with the fishermen as well as the packers to try to work out an agreement on the maximum total catch for the season, and then to distribute quotas. But just as regularly fishermen brought in more than they had been allotted and many of the smaller canneries simply ignored the restrictions. Thus, both the sardine and the tuna industry found themselves caught by depressed conditions throughout the New Deal era.

In the Pacific Northwest the efforts of state fishing agencies were supplemented by federal controls. The shrinking markets for salmon owing to the depression led to a decline in the production of canned fish by 1933, and industrial pollution on the Columbia River as well as in Puget Sound was destroying the salmon's spawning grounds. This deteriorating situation was worsened in 1931 when Japanese fishermen began to invade the salmon fisheries of the Pacific Northwest. By 1934 Japanese canned salmon exports were exceeding those of the United States and Canada and created a new source of friction between these nations. Then, in 1936 the Japanese aggressively invaded the Alaskan salmon fisheries near Bristol Bay. Meanwhile the Japanese government blithely announced the initiation of a three-year scientific study of Alaskan salmon. This action triggered a loud outcry from members of the congressional delegation from Washington and Oregon and from the delegate from Alaska. During the next five years they introduced a spate of bills to provide federal protection for American fishermen against the Japanese. At the same time, in 1937 the State Department sent a strong formal protest to Japan that undoubtedly added to the growing friction between the two countries. Temporarily the Japanese government yielded. It called off the projected scientific inquiry of Bristol Bay salmon and promised not to issue new licenses to its salmon fishermen in Alaskan waters. But the issue had not been solved by any means.

In the four years preceding Pearl Harbor A. J. Dimon, Alaskan delegate to Congress, proposed to extenUnited States jurisdiction over salmon by extending the customary mile-offshore limit. On the other hand, Senator Mon Wallgren of Washington sought to prevent the taking of any fish by foreigners in the North Pacific, including the Bering Sea and the northern Arctic. Congress, however, reluctant to accentuate existing tensions, did not enact these recommendations, and the outbreak of World War II temporarily put the dispute to rest.

Nor were the halibut fisheries prospering during the Great Depression. Alarmed by the rapid exhaustion of halibut fisheries in the Pacific, in 1931 the International Fisheries Commission drew up a new American-Canadian treaty that instituted strict controls to limit the annual catch of halibut by both American and Canadian fishermen. The commission worked closely with everyone involved in the industry—boat owners, fishermen, and canners—and in 1932 organized a Halibut Production Control Board in Seattle that allocated annual quotas. In fact, the Fishing Vessels Owners' Association prepared a draft code for the halibut industry under the National Recovery Administration in 1933. Although this was never put into force its provisions served as guidelines for the industry in the thirties. Administered by the International Fisheries Commission, the limitations on production achieved one aim—the conservation of the species. On the eve of World War II the Pacific halibut fisheries had been amply replenished.

One major problem of Pacific halibut fishermen during the depression decade was the increase of foreign interlopers, especially the British and the Japanese. As the Atlantic fisheries became increasingly exhausted, in 1936 and 1937 British and Norwegian halibut interests expressed a desire to send vessels to the Pacific Coast. Both the United States and the Canadian governments vigorously protested in London. And westerners in Congress sponsored bills to retaliate. In June of 1937 Congress as well as the Canadian Parliament enacted laws to prohibit their respective citizens from assisting any foreign ship that might fish for halibut. The British Foreign Office upheld the right of its fishermen to search Pacific waters, but the threat of retaliation led the owners of a British-Norwegian halibut vessel to abandon their ambitious fishing plans in Pacific Northwest waters. And the Japanese also temporarily withdrew from American-Canadian halibut fishing grounds in the Pacific. Thus westerners effectively used their political influence in Congress to eliminate foreign competition.[17]

Despite differences, the outlines of New Deal policies toward the natural resource industries of the West were similar. The major problem of farmers, cattlemen, miners, timbermen, and fishermen was the lack of markets. The Roosevelt Administration sought to assist these industries to restrict production, and to pay them subsidies besides. Limiting production would happily achieve another New Deal objective—the conservation of natural resources in the West. This was the major thrust of the thousands of laws and regulations that affected extractive industries in the West during the thirties. Yet although the New Deal aided the recovery of these industries and encouraged a less wasteful utilization of natural resources, it was not able by 1941 to bring them out of the depression. The significance of the New Deal for the extractive industries of the West, however, was profound. In the thirties the federal government was beginning to replace the East as the major source of capital for western development. The New Deal thus effectively altered the colonial status of the West.

Manufacturing and Service Industries

As in the case of raw materials, by 1939, manufacturing and service industries in the West revived, although they were unable to achieve the levels of 1929. Manufacturing in California, the Pacific Northwest, the Rocky Mountains, the Southwest, and the Plains remained static. Nor did the service industries recover their erstwhile thrust. Tourist expenditures did not regain the high levels they had reached in the 1920s, thus dealing another serious blow to the already injured economies of most western states. And since Congress drastically reduced its appropriations for the U.S. Army until 1938, this usually lucrative source of income for the more sparsely populated western states dried up as well.

The New Deal did much to bolster the stability of western banks. An index of the increasing importance of western banks was President Roosevelt's consultation with A. P. Gianninni of the Bank of America in March of 1933, concerning the national bank holiday. Indeed, Gianninni was perhaps the most important Californian during the thirties as far as many New Dealers were concerned. He consistently supported the Roosevelt policies, even after 1935, when most businessmen turned against the New Deal, and his great prestige calmed the fears of hundreds of smaller western bankers about administration policies. "We are on the right road," Gianninni said in 1933. "The system has to be changed. . . . There is something wrong with a system that lets 14,000,000 men get out of work." Gianninni received a reward for his loyalty in various provisions of the Banking Act of 1933, which greatly eased the establishment of branches by national banks, a right for which he had long contended. With this privilege, even during a decade of depression, he was able to double his bank's branches to more than 500 by 1939 and to emerge as the nation's largest banker. Elsewhere in the West the provisions of the Banking Acts of 1933 and 1935 helped to reduce the number of bank failures. Colorado, for example, did not experience a single bank failure between 1935 and 1939. And one of Utah's leading bankers, Mariner S. Eccles, became one of the architects of New Deal fiscal policies from his vantage point on the Federal Reserve Board.

The impact of the New Deal policies on the West was profound. It would not be exaggerating to say that the Roosevelt policies tended to benefit southern and western states more than they did the East. Certainly, on a per capita basis, the expenditures of the New Deal were higher in the West than in any other region. In general, western states received three times as much as the national average of government expenditures. Moreover, western states received at least three times as much money in federal funds as they sent back to Washington in revenues. To a large extent, this disparity resulted from the relative poverty of the West as compared with the industrial East, and its sparse population. If one examines a list of those states that received the greatest amount of federal funds in the thirties one finds that the first fourteen states were in the West. Such a compilation includes expenditures by the Reconstruction Finance Corporation, the Public Works Administration, the Rural Electrification Administration, and the Federal Emergency Relief Administration.

The New Deal transformed the West. What was most striking was that the West had become increasingly dependent on the national government rather than on the East for capital and skills to promote its economic growth. To be sure, such a trend was not entirely new, for throughout the nineteenth century the federal government had poured considerable funds and efforts into development of the West. After all, had not the U.S. Corps of Engineers built many western highways? And had not the impetus for western railroad building come from Washington? Nevertheless, in scope and scale, the conscious use of national resources in the development of a wide range of western economic activities was of special significance in the twentieth century. The New Deal also awakened the social consciousness of the West and prodded lawmakers, even if ever so reluctantly, to expand social services. Many western states, such as Wyoming, had not created statewide social welfare agencies by 1933, and established them in the thirties, if only to take advantage of a variety of federal grants that required such an institutional apparatus. And they became accustomed to increased dependence of many of their citizens on the national government for relief and employment. The New Deal lessened the political independence of the West as an increasing number of governmental activities were directed not from the state capital, but from Washington or one of its distant branch agencies. So, westerners felt—with some cause—that they had compromised a measure of their independence. But, since they had rejected other alternatives to the New Deal they had to live with their ambiance, leaning on the federal government while at the same time resenting their dependence. Some of them wondered, indeed, whether they were perennial colonials who had merely exchanged masters.

But let us examine the increasing opposition to the New Deal by westerners more closely. One reason was clearly the sparse western population. As a consequence, most federal agencies had few branches west of the Mississippi. Those that were operating were more often than not in Denver or on the Pacific Coast. The national capital therefore seemed far removed geographically for most westerners who, like colonials, felt a certain alienation because of the impersonality of distant federal agencies. Even worse, most government offices were staffed in the thirties by easterners and middle westerners, many of them from colleges in the Ivy League. By temperament and inclination, these men and women were not (and often still are not) very sympathetic to the West. Often they openly expressed contempt or hostility for western ways. Many westerners came to distrust the federal bureaucracy. This was also true of western state legislatures, which were still dominated by representatives from sparsely settled areas. Such feelings of distrust by the colonials in the West were well reflected in the Republican Party Platform of Wyoming in May of 1936 that preferred "states rights and responsibilities and the principle of home rule, as contrasted with an overwhelming and overpowering bureaucracy."

Other factors contributed to the lessening popularity of the New Deal in the West. Since the West had little industry, its tax base was extremely limited. Western states thus found it even more difficult than those in other regions to raise revenues required to match a great variety of federal grants. Almost without exception, state lawmakers in the West resorted to increasing sales taxes. With such a paucity of funds it was surprising, however, that they looked askance at governmental experimentation, whether in national or state politics. Moreover, westerners tended to favor the cult of local personalities more than easterners. Western politicians during the New Deal therefore were not very dependent on the national parties for their success. Even Democrats owed few political debts to President Roosevelt and were usually strong enough—if they so chose—to challenge him on particular issues. And amidst the chaos of depression, political factionalism flourished in the West as in few other areas, vitiating

strong organized support for the New Deal. Personal rivalries were perhaps
more rife in the West than elsewhere because the region had no Civil War
tradition that had encouraged party centralization in the Northeast, the
Middle West, and the South. So westerners voted for Roosevelt—to secure
federal moneys for irrigation, power development, and highways—but
strongly asserted their independence in other matters where they could.
Necessity, not choice, helps to explain their motivation.

Western State Politics During the New Deal Era

What about the impact of the New Deal on state politics in the West? In
general, its influence was limited. The depression stimulated few leaders in
the West. Indeed, perhaps the outstanding characteristic of western state
politics in the thirties was their mediocrity. Most state governors and
legislatures appeared helpless in the throes of economic crisis, and without
much imagination merely sought to continue in their accustomed ways. Few
western states had little New Deals to mirror the experiments being tried
out on a national scale.[18] Rather, most state governments sought to practice
economy, to raise sales taxes, and to secure a portion of federal largesse.

California

Politics in California were not unlike those of other western states during
the 1930s. Control of the statehouse was in the hands of conservative
Republicans like Frank Merriam (1934-1938), Iowa born and bred. Since he
had been elected with the aid of many Democratic votes, however, Merriam
lamely agreed to New Dealish policies. In 1935 he flirted with the advocates
of old age pensions, and signed a bill to increase benefits for the aged poor,
agreed to the repeal of sales taxes on food, and encouraged adoption of a
more progressive state income tax. His successor was Culbert L. Olsen, an
out-and-out New Deal Democrat who promised to bring a little New Deal to
California. But his hopes were greater than his accomplishments. Soon after
his election in 1938 he became seriously ill. Democratic factionalism in the
California assembly and Republican control of the state Senate prevented
him from doing much except to improve California's care for criminals and
for the mentally ill. It was he who pardoned Tom Mooney.

The general placidity of California politics was rocked early in the New
Deal, however. By 1933 many Californians were restive with the mediocre
do-nothing leadership of Governor James K. Rolph while all around them
suffering was increasing. Among the discontented was Upton Sinclair, the
well-known novelist and erstwhile muckraker of the Progressive era, who

had moved to California during World War I. A lifetime socialist, Sinclair hoped to provide an alternative to the early New Deal measures. In 1926 and 1930 he was the Socialist candidate for governor. In 1933 he published a volume, *I, Governor of California, and How I Ended Poverty,* in which he outlined his plans. To diminish unemployment he proposed government operation of idle factories, the establishment of communal farms, and welfare payments by the state government to old or needy persons, to be financed through bonds and scrip. Many of his plans sounded eminently sensible and generated great enthusiasm among thousands of Californians. More than 100,000 copies of his book were sold within a year, and his followers began to organize EPIC (End Poverty In California) clubs before the end of 1933. That was when Sinclair changed his party affiliation to enter the Democratic gubernatorial primaries. Soon EPIC speakers flooded the state, from its northern reaches to the borders of Mexico. EPIC handbills were everywhere, and to the dismay of conservatives, Sinclair had to be taken seriously. When the primaries were held in August 1934 they revealed that Sinclair had captured the Democratic gubernatorial nomination with the highest vote ever. More than two-thirds of his support came from southern California, where unemployment was higher than in other areas of the state. Sinclair's nomination thoroughly frightened conservatives in both major parties, and they combined to defeat him in the fall elections. Meanwhile, President Roosevelt declined to support Sinclair, but coyly sat out the California race for governor. This probably lost Sinclair the election, although the vast sums spent by Hollywood tycoons such as Louis B. Mayer to defeat him also played a role. Yet he received nearly 900,000 out of 2.3 million votes, a serious protest by the disaffected. Sinclair took his defeat in stride and promptly wrote another book, this one entitled: *I, Governor of California, and How I Got Licked.*

The defeat of Sinclair led hundreds of thousands of Californians to look to other messiahs for salvation, for the severity of the depression did not abate. In 1934 many of Sinclair's supporters turned to Dr. Francis Townsend, a retired dentist who was launching his own movement to secure pensions for the aged. Throughout his life Townsend had drifted from job to job, mainly in Montana and the Dakotas, without much success. In 1929, when he was 62 years old, like hundreds of thousands of other aging middle westerners, he left the harsh climate of the Plains to emigrate to California where he settled in Long Beach, the old folks capital of California. There he was fortunate to find employment as an assistant county health officer, and in this capacity he saw the suffering of the aged at first hand. He himself lost his job in 1933. Shortly thereafter, as he sat home, he looked down from his bathroom window to see three old, bent women searching the garbage cans in an alley below for scraps of food. Was this to be the fate of America's aged, Townsend thought? He became furious about the neglect of the elderly during the depression, and resolved to do something about it. Thus was born the Townsend Plan, first outlined by Townsend in a letter to the Long Beach *Telegram*, a local newspaper. Townsend proposed that all Americans over 60 receive federal pensions of $200 monthly, which they were to spend within 30 days. The federal government could raise the needed funds through the imposition of a federal sales tax. Not only would the elderly secure a comfortable existence, but much needed new money would be placed in circulation to revive the whole economy. This in essence was the famous Townsend Plan.

Townsend's proposals caught on like wildfire throughout the nation. His first public unveiling of the idea brought a response of thousands of cards and letters approving his scheme. Suddenly Townsend became a famous man, a national figure in his own right. By 1934 he had organized Old Age Revolving Pensions, Ltd., a national organization with almost 5 million members, organized in more than 5,000 local Townsend Clubs, often staffed by unemployed clergymen. Townsend organized the old people of America (over 60) and made them a potent political group, one which a neglectful president and Congress now had to recognize. Although Townsend was unable to secure congressional approval of his plan—which, it was estimated, would cost in excess of $2 billion yearly—he was directly responsible for securing the inclusion of old age pensions on a modest scale in the Social Security Act of 1935. Although that act satisfied few advocates of social welfare it weakened the Townsend movement. And when Townsend opposed Roosevelt's reelection in 1936 and flirted with third-party candidates such as Father Charles E. Coughlin and William Lemke (of the Union Labor party), he lost additional supporters.[19]

But the sentiment for increased old age pensions amongst the hundreds of thousands of old folks in California would not die. To receive a pension under the Social Security Act, for example, an individual was required to prove that he or she was without an income and without relatives who could provide support. No wonder that the aged of California, as elsewhere, still were not satisfied, and that they threw their support to any and all individuals who promised to secure more equitable pensions. Of the hundreds of schemes that attracted attention in the thirties the Ham and Eggs Crusade received greatest support. The idea of state-sponsored old age pensions was first publicized by two Hollywood public relations men, Willis and Lawrence Allen, who in 1936 began to advocate a "Thirty Dollars Every Thursday" scheme on a local Los Angeles radio station. Thousands of dollars in contributions from old people in support of the cause poured in weekly and soon the Allen Brothers had become rich. Actually, the Allens had no well-thought-out plan, but in 1936 they hired one Sherman Bainbridge, a professional organizer. It was he who formulated a program advocating monthly payments of $200 to persons over 60, to be financed by the sale of state bonds and a 3 per cent gross sales tax. It was Bainbridge who endowed the scheme with a slogan—Ham and Eggs—that became familiar throughout the state. Through the initiative process, the promoters of Ham and Eggs placed their proposal on the statewide ballot in 1938. Although the proposal received more than 1 million affirmative votes, it was defeated by a small margin. And U.S. Senator William McAdoo lost his seat because of his opposition to it. In 1939 it was placed before California voters for a second time, again to suffer defeat. Thereafter, the Ham and Eggs Crusade disintegrated, affected in part by improving economic conditions arising from defense preparations.[20]

The Pacific Northwest

The Pacific Northwest states during the New Deal also reflected the mediocrity of leadership that was so common in the West during the Great Depression. Although they voted for Roosevelt in large numbers after 1932, westerners in this area showed little penchant for reform in state politics. Third parties did not flourish during this decade, as they had earlier. Instead, old Wobblies, socialists, old age pension advocates, and members of the Unemployed Citizens' League (founded in the early years of the depression) combined in the Washington Commonwealth Confederation. This organization—the strongest New Deal faction in the state—was loosely affiliated with the National Commonwealth Confederation, formed by Selden Rodman and Hiram Bingham in 1931. A non-Marxist neo-socialist organization, it attracted many leading intellectuals by its advocacy of sweeping economic and social reforms. The Washington Commonwealth Confederation had a membership of more than 30,000 and exercised a potent influence on city and state politics. It helped to elect John Doar as mayor of Seattle in 1932, although he proved to be a big disappointment. Four years later the Confederation almost succeeded in capturing control of the state's Democratic party. Meanwhile its secured support from congressmen and U.S. senators such as Homer Bone, John Coffee, and Warren Magnuson. Nevertheless, the moderates were in control of both major parties between 1932 and 1940 and kept conservative Democrat Clarence Martin in the governor's chair.

Oregonians followed the same general pattern during the thirties. They voted for Roosevelt, but with increasing resentment. In this they were like many westerners who felt somewhat like poor relations—eager to accept a handout, but not without some resentment over the necessity that drove them to it. And so, while voting for more Democrats, they also rejected higher taxes that would have enabled them to match federal grants more readily. Democratic governor Charles Martin, a conservative Democrat, denounced most New Deal measures, from relief and labor legislation to public power. Oregon's Commonwealth Federation, under the able Monroe Sweetland until 1938, was the only visible progressive faction in the state, but its influence never matched that of the federation in neighboring Washington. By 1938 the Republicans had returned to a majority of state offices. Idaho's politics in this period were more colorful, largely because of the antics of Democratic Governor "Cowboy C. Ben Ross," who served for three terms. Something of a demagogue, he was the West's pale imitation of Huey Long. Ross was spectacular, but it was questionable whether his reform accomplishments equaled his penchant for political factionalism.

The Rocky Mountains, Southwest, and Plains

A few ripples of the New Deal could be observed in the Rocky Mountain states. Utah's Governor George Dern was a loyal New Dealer, but his moderation accurately reflected the temper of the voters. Much the same could be said for the regime of Governor Leslie A. Miller in Wyoming. In Colorado, Governor Edwin C. Johnson, although a Democrat, was consistently hostile to the New Deal and to many aspects of its program. The death of the progressive U.S. Senator Edward P. Costigan deprived Roosevelt of his ablest supporter in the state.

The southwestern states made few innovations but became more heavily dependent on the national government. Governor Arthur Seligman in New Mexico strove for an honest distribution of federal relief funds, but could accomplish little reform in his own administration other than the reorganization of state agencies. The pattern for Arizona and Texas was similar.

On the Plains the New Deal reinvigorated the Non-Partisan League. Moreover, some states like North Dakota had that flamboyant and highly personal form of leadership that so appealed to westerners. In North Dakota, Republican Governor William L. Langer became the dominant political figure despite intense factionalism there, as elsewhere in the West. Elected to the governorship in 1932 with the backing of the still influential Non-Partisan League, he undertook a series of dramatic steps to deal with the unprecedented economic crisis. In the fall of 1933, for example, he declared an embargo on wheat shipments from his state to raise wheat prices. At that time angry crowds were surging through the state capital at Bismarck, desperate for aid, for relief, and for a moratorium on farm foreclosures. Langer's drastic action, which was in effect for about two months, succeeded in raising wheat prices by about 23 cents per bushel. In addition, beginning in March of 1933 he used his executive authority to stop foreclosures of farms then under cultivation, exempting federally held properties. At times he sent in the National Guard to stop foreclosure proceedings. Although the Democrats opposed these measures, both the Farm Holiday Association and the Non-Partisan League enthusiastically supported them. Such actions inspired confidence in a majority of voters who felt that Langer was aggressively looking out for their best interests. Despite a federal indictment charging him with collecting political contributions from federal and state employees in 1934, Langer's popularity did not wane, nor did he change his style. In July 1937 he successfully ordered the state-owned mill and grain elevator to buy wheat at higher than market prices to force private purchasers to pay more to farmers. For most North Dakota farmers Langer could do no wrong, and in 1940 they elected him to the United States Senate.

In contrast to the great political changes on the national level, therefore, western state governments during the thirties underwent few startling visible changes. Beset by a lack of leadership, western state legislatures were more concerned with economy than with relief, with political factionalism rather than with reform, and with minor improvements in administrative reorganization. As far as state politics was concerned, this was not a sparkling era.

If not so obvious at the time, however, state governments in the West—as elsewhere in the nation—were adjusting to new relationships within the federal system. Despite much talk and oratory about their vaunted independence, despite loud protestations against the federal bureaucracy, most state governments in the West were quietly adjusting to taking their place as subdued junior partners of the federal government. If western state leadership was so mediocre during the decade, perhaps this was because the best talents in the West (such as Thurman Arnold of Wyoming and Marriner Eccles of Utah) were drawn off to Washington. Increasingly dependent on the federal government for new capital investment, for power development, highways, and internal improvements, most western states could not afford to bite the hand that fed them very hard. They had shown themselves unable to deal with sweeping problems of relief and unemployment. And so, for better or for worse, western states lost a measure of their independence in the thirties as their political life became secondary to the great tides of national politics.

Cultural Life in the West During the Great Depression

But if western political life was not terribly exciting in the thirties, the region's cultural life was far more interesting. To be sure, the economic depression of the Thirties also dampened the pace of western cultural development. But the emphasis on regionalism, which had been such a dominant trend during the twenties, was further developed in the succeeding decade, and, in fact, deepened in the throes of crisis to constitute a dominant leitmotif of various cultural expressions in the West. This was true of literature, art and architecture, music, education, and science. To be sure, these years were not so creative as the post–World War I period. Writers and other creative people—with few exceptions—tended to develop existing trends, rather than to innovate. One significant innovation of this decade was the temporary federal support for a wide diversity of cultural activities that enriched western cultural life immensely for half a dozen years, until Pearl Harbor. Thus, these were years of slow cultural development, but development nevertheless, since they saw a further growth of Western independence from the East in cultural affairs.

Literature

Some of the best-known western writers of the decade found themselves in the regional tradition. One of the most widely read was William Saroyan, a Californian of Armenian origins who used his familiar surroundings in Fresno, California, as a setting for many of his superb short stories, novels, and plays. Two of these works, *My Heart's in the Highlands* (1939) and *My Name is Aram* (1940), focused on the much publicized individualism and independence of people living in the West and their warm humanity. George R. Stewart, a writer and professor of English at the University of California, became another important interpreter of western life. His first successful novel was *East of the Giants (1938)*. His description of the dramatic impact of environment on the lives of westerners was especially vivid in *Storm*. One of the most widely read of the western novelists of this decade was Walter Van Tilburg Clark, whose *Ox-Bow Incident* (1940) Hollywood made into one of the major movies of the time. The distinguished literary critic Edmund Wilson believed at the time that Clark, better than most contemporary western writers, captured the mood, the feeling, and the problems of the West, while using literary techniques perceptively and uniquely developed to achieve his intended effects. But Wilson also felt that Clark transcended narrow provincialism and was using a local environment merely to write about major aspects of the national experience. Writing in *The New Yorker*, Wilson found the *Ox-Bow Incident* to be a far western book which, like the fiction of the Pacific slope, like John Steinbeck and William Saroyan, could not quite meet the requirements of an easterner. It seemed too easy-going and too good natured, too lacking in organization, always dissolving in even sunshine. It was one of the signs of vitality of writing in the United States, he noted, that the Pacific Coast should be producing a literature of its own, appropriate to its temper and climate, independent of New England, New York, and the South.[21] Wilson put it into a nutshell. Slowly the West was shedding its heavy cultural dependence on Europe and the East, and beginning, yes, just beginning to develop a literary style that was suited to its indigenous requirements of peoples and environment.

Although Hollywood had become the world's motion picture center after World War I and had attracted many able writers, no major literary figure emerged from the industry during its great days of glory. Not that some writers did not try. Nathanael West wrote *The Day of the Locust* in 1939 to portray the lives and foibles of Hollywood, and Budd Schulberg sought to accomplish a similar goal in *What Makes Sammy Run?* two years later. But these were successful contemporary best sellers rather than notable works of literature. And unfortunately not much more could be said of F. Scott Fitzgerald's unfinished *The Last Tycoon*, which did not show that author at his best. In fact, Fitzgerald's years in Hollywood during the thirties were the least productive of his career.

Perhaps the most notable western writer of the decade was John Steinbeck, whose *The Grapes of Wrath*, published in 1939, was unquestionably the Great American Novel of the depression years. Steinbeck was a native Californian, born in Salinas in 1902, and he was usually at his best in writing about his native region. But of course Steinbeck, like William Faulkner in the South, was using his locale merely as a tool with which to comment on the whole of human experience. The Salinas Valley provided the setting for his first successful books, *The Pastures of Heaven* in 1932, and *Tortilla Flat* three years later. Steinbeck's sympathies were with the underdog, the downtrodden, and the exploited. His passionate feelings for humanity were also starkly revealed in one of the most successful works in the regional tradition, *Of Mice and Men* (1938), which became a successful motion picture as well. After 1935 Steinbeck became increasingly concerned over the plight of migratory laborers in California, and of the Dust Bowl refugees who were just beginning to flood the state. In fact, he wrote a number of informative reportorial articles for San Francisco newspapers on these subjects before turning to write about his impressions in fictional form. From his labors came his masterpiece, *The Grapes of Wrath*, surely one of the great American novels of the twentieth century. In this familiar work Steinbeck chronicled the odyssey of the Joads, a fictional family of Dust Bowl emigrés whose pilgrimage to California represented Everyman during the Great Depression. Better than thousands of reported case studies, better than mountains of detailed statistics, Steinbeck was able to convey the tragedy and the suffering, the despair and the anguish, the faith and the hope of Americans during these terrible years. Steinbeck continued to be productive in later years, but never again was he able to reach the heights and plumb the depths that he probed in *The Grapes of Wrath.*

Steinbeck's book created a special furor in California. Having been born and raised in the Salinas Valley, Steinbeck was intimately acquainted with the nature of migratory labor there. The impact of his book was strengthened by the appearance of a hard-hitting journalistic study by Carey McWilliams, *Ill Fares the Land,* which in a way documented with specific detail many of the themes of Steinbeck's novel. Neither author had been aware of the work of the other, but together their books had an enormous impact.

The millions of Americans who read Steinbeck's moving work were touched no less than legislators and policymakers who read it in conjunction with McWilliams' searing indictment. Both volumes were severely denounced by the Associated Farmers of California, who prohibited their circulation in Kern County and in 1938 and 1939 carried on an extensive publicity campaign to denounce the works as the product of communist agitation. In fact, they encouraged the writing of a "counter-novel" portraying the delightful life of California farm workers. This was Ruth Comfort Mitchell's *Of Human Kindness,* a novel that was as quickly forgotten as it was written.

Regionalism as a literary trend was increasingly challenged by a group of distinguished foreign writers who began to settle in the West during the thirties. They urged Americans to adopt some of the standards that they brought with them and to adopt broad cosmopolitan perspectives. One of the most distinguished members of the foreign literary colony who settled in southern California was the great German author Thomas Mann, who was already world renowned by the 1930s as the creator of *Buddenbrooks.* Aldous Huxley, one of the most widely read British novelists and a man greatly influenced by Freudian themes, also settled in the area, which he found congenial to his work. His fellow countryman, Christopher Isherwood, lived not too far distant and added luster to the West's increasing literary stature. To be sure, his best-known work is set not in the West but in Berlin in the 1920s; his activities, however, added to the reputation of the West as the home of many talented writers, not only those confined to a regional idiom.

Nevertheless, regionalism continued to be a strong trend in western writing during the thirties. If the decade did not see the emergence of as many new talents in the post–World War I era, nevertheless it was a fruitful time. Among the younger talents, New Mexican Paul Horgan was distinctive. Sustaining himself as a librarian at New Mexico Military Institute at Roswell, Horgan first attracted attention in 1933 with his novel, *The Fault of Angels,* which won a Harper Prize. This book, as well as *Main Line West* (1936) and *A Lamp on the Plains* (1937), all had their settings in New

Mexico, although his themes were far from parochial. Oliver La Farge further developed his earlier promise with *The Enemy Gods* (1937), in which he examined the culture conflict between Indian and white civilizations. Conrad Richter, who lived in Albuquerque, New Mexico, during these years, revealed his talents in *The Sea of Grass* in 1937, which followed closely and skillfully in the regional tradition. Another of the younger writers to attract attention was George Milburn, whose *Oklahoma Town* (1931) was an extremely critical examination of small-town life. Not of the same stature as Sinclair Lewis's *Main Street*, it nevertheless sought to place social criticism within a western setting.

Some of the older writers continued in a more romantic vein. Eugene Manlove Rhodes continued his prodigious production—in tune with his established formulas—with *The Desire of the Moth*, which enjoyed a wide readership. The devotees of folklore were extremely active. J. Frank Dobie produced *Tongues of the Monte* in 1935 and *Tales of the Mustang* in 1936, substantial contributions to folklore and regional short-story writing. Stanley Vestal wrote a biography of *Sitting Bull, Champion of the Sioux* in 1932, a history of *Mountain Men* in 1937, and a novel, *Revolt on the Border*, in the following year. B. A. Botkin of the University of Oklahoma edited an anthology, *The Southwest Scene*, in 1931 and collected folklore in *Play Party in Oklahoma* six years later. Witter Bynner of the Santa Fe writer's colony continued as one of the nation's outstanding lyric poets, while his neighbor, Alice Corbin Henderson, published *Brothers of Light* in 1937, a glowing, if glorified, account of the Penitentes, a primitive Christian sect in the small Spanish-American villages of New Mexico. One of the younger romantic regionalists was Erna Fergusson, whose *Dancing Gods* (1931)—an account of Indian ceremonials—attracted a wide national readership. For a time in the thirties the playwright Maxwell Anderson joined the Santa Fe Colony; he wrote one of his more memorable plays there. His *Night Over Taos* in 1932 was a successful production that dealt with a favorite theme of the regionalists, the conflict of white and Indian cultures.

The regional movement in literature was also enormously strengthened in 1931 by the appearance of one of the most impressive historical works of the decade. This was Walter Prescott Webb's *The Great Plains*, an imaginative historical account of the region in which Webb developed the grand themes dealing with man's adjustment to the semi-arid environment of this region. Starting with the proposition that the flatness of the Plains and the lack of water determined the nature of American settlement and adaptation, Webb deftly described how various technological inventions such as the windmill, advanced irrigation techniques, and the six-shooter revolver allowed Americans to conquer what had once been considered the Great American Desert, a semi-arid environment unfit for human habitation. A professor of history at the University of Texas, Webb used a broad ecological approach to indicate that the impact of environmental influences on western civilization had been largely ignored, and that to understand the history of the region west of the 98th meridian it was necessary to have a fundamental grasp of the influence of nature there. To Webb the geographical rather than cultural influences determined the nature of western regionalism. His skillful delineation of the Great Plains as a separate entity within the American commonwealth did much to encourage various forms of distinct regional cultural expression.

Without a doubt, the extraordinary literary outburst that occurred in the West between the wars made a major contribution to the enrichment of western culture. Perhaps this can be considered the most productive period in the entire sweep of western cultural development. But like all creative movements it raised disturbing questions. Did the values of regionalism offer a viable alternative to the search for standards to guide writers in America? Or were the regionalists moving into a dead end? On the eve of World War II—as the vitality of regionalism dimmed—some critics, like Dudley Wynn, believed that the decline of the movement was directly related to its lack of depth, its failure to offer a new set of values for Americans everywhere.

Let us remember that the regionalists had become enamored of the West because it seemed to offer an antithesis to what they found wrong in American civilization. They disliked industrialism, standardization, and the phony or artificial sophistication of eastern esthetes, who were often aping European standards that were not rooted directly in American civilization. And so they became enthusiastic over Indian ceremonials or quaint Spanish-American villages. But did these life-styles really offer viable alternatives for the majority of Americans? Could a highly technological society adopt the ways of a pastoral people in a pre-industrial stage? Could American civilization turn back from the urban society it had created in the twentieth century? Most of the regional writers never came to grips with these hard questions. To them Indian ceremonials and Latin fiestas were strange, delightful, and exotic diversions, and they described them with verve. But were they able to move beyond description? Where they able to do more than to become futile romantics? Some critics believed that once they had told the world about the nature of southwestern culture in the 1920s, now in the 1930s it was time to analyze the relationship of the civilizations they had found and to relate them to American society in meaningful ways. For they said little about the relation of these differing culture values to those of the United States. Could Taos and Middletown be united? The regionalists had no ready or profound answers to this disturbing question.

Art and Architecture

As might be expected, many of the arts suffered during the depression as erstwhile patrons withheld their financial support. Western art during these years was represented by a significant number of painters who, like Thomas Hart Benton, were turned to social realism by the depression and who sought to portray America's problems on canvas. Nevertheless, regionalism as an influence on the work of many western painters was still prominent during the decade, especially in the art colonies of the Southwest. A distinctive western style in landscapes was developed by a number of talented men and women, including Joe Jones, John S. Curry, and Benton. After 1930 they were joined by Peter Hurd of New Mexico, who became known for his depiction of cowboy life and rodeos. Adolph Dehn, also a distinguished lithographer, was among those who were seeking to modify the regional tradition by interesting experimentation with colors and vistas affecting landscapes. Such experimentation was even more pronounced in the paintings of Ward Lockwood, whose brilliant use and juxtaposition of colors marked him as having been deeply influenced by John Marin. Some of the most striking innovative paintings to come out of the West were by Jerry Bywaters, whose Mexican cliffs and Texas deserts captured a haunting western mood. Maynard Dixon during these years became one of the foremost interpreters of western deserts in California, Nevada, and Arizona. And Alexander Hogue's works in the 1930s revaled something of the melancholy impact of the Texas Panhandle on the human spirit and succeeded in capturing the influence of environment on the moods of westerners.

Perhaps it was the environment, perhaps it was the majestic scenery, or the different cultures, or the brilliant light. Whatever it was, the West tended to appeal to some of the great photographers of the twentieth century, and many of them did some of their most outstanding work in the thirties. The photographs of Ansel Adams are too well known to require comment. Hardly less significant was Edward Weston, one of America's greatest interpreters in black and white, who made his home in the art colony of Carmel, California. Concerned with people, and the wonders of the western landscape, his special interest was in capturing the mood of individuals whose existence was rooted in the western soil. Angry over the ruinous impact of the depression on the lives of so many Americans, he often turned his lens on social problems during the depression, poignantly and effectively. Somewhat less far ranging but brilliantly effective was perhaps one of the greatest of western photographers, Dorothea Lange. For a time, from 1937 to 1941, she was attached to the Farm Security Administration and traveled throughout the West, visiting the camps of migratory laborers, Dust Bowl refugees, the dispossessed, the lonely, and the suffering.[22] In many ways, she was the John Steinbeck of the camera in the West during the Great Depression.

Western lithographers became especially distinguished in the thirties. Adolph Dehn and Boardman Robinson set standards in their art that won national acclaim—an imitation. And few photographers rivaled Paul Strand. His famous depiction of a ghost town on the Red River in New Mexico and his notable study of the church at Ranchos de Taos in 1930 created new artistic levels in American photography.

Western architecture showed increasing sophistication. Not that the neo-Spanish colonial or Pueblo style in California and the Southwest was abandoned. It continued in popularity. But architects in the West, notably Richard Neutra, R. M. Schindler, and their associates Gregory Ain and Harwell Harris, were developing striking new modernistic designs, blending interior and exterior settings, that were beginning to be copied in the East. The modern ranch house style was not yet fully developed in the decade, but its foundations were being laid. The conscious adaptation of ranch houses for suburban residence was first undertaken by Cliff May in California in 1936. It featured a ground-hogging silhouette fitted to its site, focused on the patio as a key feature of the house to combine outdoor and indoor living, and included a family room or den, which served at times as an outdoor living room. Another architect, John Funk, revealed the possibilities of large glass surfaces in conjunction with ranch design in his Heckendorf House in Modesto, California, which began this trend-setting pattern in the state, whence it spread to the entire nation. And by 1939 Neutra and his associates increasingly began to use the ranch house concept for their imaginative designs. At that time a listing of 136 of the most notable recently built homes in the United States revealed that almost one-third had been designed and constructed west of the Mississippi River. For a region still laboring under the onus of colonialism, that was a considerable achievement.

Music

Understandably, musical activities were especially hard hit by the depression. Most orchestras in the West, as elsewhere in the nation, suffered from a dearth of funds. But since those in the West had just begun to develop, they were particularly hard hit. Perhaps the only bright spot in this otherwise bleak situation was the opening in 1932 of the San Francisco War Memorial Opera House, which had been planned for almost a decade earlier. As the new home of the San Francisco Opera Company, it became the most distinguished opera house in the West, and the first municipal structure of its type in the nation. The rise of Nazism in Germany led many eminent musicians to settle in America, some of whom found southern California a congenial home. On the eve of World War II two of the greatest creative composers of the twentieth century settled there, Igor Stravinski and Arnold Schoenberg. Within a decade they had made the region famous as the center for experimentation with new forms of musical composition. Although it was not fully apparent at the time, the newness of the West and the freedom that it allowed for experimentation with new forms of cultural expression—a characteristic more apparent to foreigners than to Americans themselves—made it an ideal location for creative work in many spheres of culture. And so, quite unconsciously, the West was fostering experimentation with daring new forms of art and music. Less novel, and more in the tradition of French impressionism, was the French composer Darius Milhaud, who lived and worked in Oakland, California, during these same years.

New Deal Policies and Cultural Activities in the West

Some of this experimentation was fostered and encouraged by the federal government after 1935 through the WPA's cultural programs. These programs were designed to provide employment—and bare subsistence—for writers, artists, actors, musicians, and other persons engaged in the arts. To a considerable extent, the federal programs strengthened activities designed to develop regionalism and to plumb the depths of national existence, although this was not their exclusive emphasis. And so the WPA encouraged the writing of a series of guidebooks to the states, and to some cities; the study and collection of local folklore, painting and the execution of murals for public buildings; the collection of historical materials; concerts; plays; and the teaching of a variety of arts and handicrafts. Although created as an emergency measure, the cultural program of the WPA in the West was a great success, one that far transcended its immediate goal of providing sustenance for the unemployed.[23]

The WPA program in literature was particularly successful. Certainly the writing of guides to the individual states was a significant aspect of the program and employed more than 3,000 writers. The Idaho guide was the first to appear, and the high standards that it set were followed or transcended by the other volumes in the series. These books were a combination of history, folklore, travel description, and natural history. They were usually written in an easily read and delightful style and acquainted millions of Americans with their native land as they had never been acquainted with it before. Obviously set within the tradition of regionalism that had flourished for several decades in the West, these guides also provided emotional sustenance for many Americans in the midst of the depression crisis. As Lewis Mumford pointed out at the time: "Of all the good uses of adversity, one of the best has been the . . . American guidebooks; the first attempt, on a comprehensive scale, to make the country itself worthily known to Americans."[24]

The WPA's Federal Theater Project was also extremely important for the

West. Of the 13,000 persons who were at one time or another employed in the program, at least one-third were in Los Angeles, which had one of the largest concentrations of unemployed theater people in the nation. The Federal Theater presented plays for all kinds of community groups and provided an outlet for various types of new talents. In addition to serious dramas, the Los Angeles theater also presented circuses, marionette shows, musical comedies, and both light and classic operas. Dance groups were supported in Los Angeles, and, on a smaller scale, elsewhere in the West.

Musicians in the West also received support from the WPA. At least 4,000 of them were involved. Their organizations included symphony orchestras, chamber music groups, opera companies, dance orchestras, and black jazz ensembles, and their performances numbered in the thousands during the thirties. Some musicians gave lessons to school children under the program; others were engaged in copying scores or working in music libraries. In the West the Utah Symphony, and the Portland, Oregon, Philharmonic received strong WPA support. In addition, the WPA organized the Northern California WPA Symphony in San Francisco and the Los Angeles Federal Symphony in southern California.

Perhaps the WPA did not encourage distinguished art, but it did produce a large number of respectable art projects in the West, mostly in the realm of "popular art culture." More than 1,000 western artists were involved in this program. Creative work in the graphic and plastic arts graced many public buildings and was designed to bring art closer to the multitudes. Several hundred thousand works were produced. In addition to giving sustenance to the artists themselves, the attendance of millions of people at WPA art shows in the West seemed to indicate that this unprecedented federal program was attaining at least some of its objectives. It stimulated artistic production, revealed more of the heritage of American art, and brought art considerably closer to popular culture. Western artists who were "discovered" in the West included Eugene Trentham, a painter of Colorado landscapes, and Dong Kingman, a San Franciscan of Chinese parentage who, with unusual sensitivity, did striking studies of California mountains against the background of the Pacific. In New Mexico, the WPA encouraged the unique carvings in *piñon* wood of Patrocino Barela. The huge sculpture of an Aztec Indian by Donal Hord installed at San Diego State College was a direct result of WPA endeavors.

The WPA did a great deal to further the cause of historic preservation in the West. In almost every western state the WPA embarked on the restoration of historic shrines, old forts, homes, and monuments, which had been ignored for many decades. Many missions in California were restored, of which the San Gabriel Mission in San Bernadino County was but one example. The Mission San Jose in San Antonio, Texas, was also rebuilt by the WPA. Battlegrounds and forts, such as Fort Bridger in Wyoming, were reconstructed to acquaint visitors with their significance in the nation's history. Thousands of such projects gave the average American a more distinct awareness of the American heritage. In addition, thousands of WPA workers indexed unpublished manuscripts, classified valuable old state records, and prepared historical records so that they might be used by scholars and specialists. No inventory of county records such as the WPA undertook had ever been attempted, and such listings provided an invaluable catalogue of as yet unexploited source materials for the writing of the nation's history. As Charles A. Beard, one of the leading American historians at the time, wrote: "If you keep up the good work, we shall some day have the bedrock materials for a real history of civilization in the United States—and hence a deeper understanding of American life."[25]

The WPA also provided work for educators through a wide variety of programs. In the West it opened new adult education classes, especially on the Pacific Coast—vocational training, home economics, workers' education, correspondence courses, and leisure-time activities. Special classes were sometimes created to meet the needs of black Americans. In addition, the WPA created new nursery schools for small children from low-income families. In this pioneering educational venture the WPA not only provided employment for nurses, teachers, and nutritionists, but also a wholesome educational experience for children under six years of age for whom the public schools in the thirties made absolutely no provision. Although World War II brought a boom in the establishment of nursery schools, the WPA must be credited with taking the initiative in developing one of the new major forms of education in twentieth-century America.

If the depression slowed the pace of western cultural development, many westerners succeeded nevertheless in furthering greater sophistication and creativity in the region's cultural life. These years saw the rise of major figures on the western horizon, writers like John Steinbeck and Walter Van Tilburg Clark and architects like Richard Neutra, men who achieved national, and even worldwide, renown. At the same time the depression stimulated cultural nationalism in the West. The WPA especially encouraged thousands of writers, artists, musicians, or collectors of historical materials to delve more deeply into the rich historical heritage of the West. The net effect of their many-aided efforts was to give westerners a clearer sense of their past and a better appreciation of their potentials for the future. This cultural nationalism encouraged struggling western efforts to secure a greater degree of cultural independence from the East and led to more self-confidence and self-awareness. Indeed, the New Deal contributed a great deal to the changing self-image of the West from colony to pacesetter.

The Great Depression led to considerable suffering in the West, as elsewhere in the United States. During the first four years after the crash, perhaps the impact of the crisis was less severe in many parts of the West than in the more highly industrialized East and the mining areas of the Rocky Mountain states and agricultural regions of the Plains, for these western areas had been in the throes of a depression since the end of World War I. But after 1933 westerners felt the full impact of economic collapse. Profoundly disenchanted with the efforts of Herbert Hoover, westerners at the polls threw their support behind Franklin D. Roosevelt and the New Deal, although not among the most enthusiastic supporters. They resented the increasing power and influence of the federal bureaucracy, even while holding out their hands to secure federal largesse. Their suspicions were not entirely unwarranted, of course, for the depression crisis brought a change of masters for the West. Until 1933 the region had been largely dependent on Wall Street (and London) for the investment capital so necessary for its continued growth. During the 1930s, however, the federal government was displacing private investors as a major source of new developmental funds. This profound change, affecting virtually every sphere of life, was perhaps the most significant result of the depression crisis in the West. In the three decades after 1941, Pennsylvania Avenue displaced Wall Street as a headquarters for charting many directions for the future of the region's growth.

NOTES

1. Quoted in Alfred T. Larsen, "The New Deal in Wyoming," *Pacific Historical Review*, vol. 38 (August, 1969), p. 252.

2. U.S. Congress, House Subcommittee of the Committee on Labor, *Hearings on Unemployment in the U.S.*, No. 206, 72nd Cong., 1st sess., 1932 (Washington, D.C.: U.S. Government Printing Office, 1932), pp. 98–99.

3. Materials on the West during the Great Depression are widely scattered. Hoover's views are expressed in William S. Myers and Walter H. Newton, eds., *The Hoover Administration: A Documented Narrative* (New York: Charles Scribner's Sons, 1936).

4. Two instructive contemporary books on westward migrations during the 1930s include Carey McWilliams, *Factories in the Fields* (Hamden, Conn.: Shoe String Press, Inc., 1969, reprint of 1939 edition), and John Steinbeck's novel, *The Grapes of Wrath* (New York: Viking Press, 1939).

5. Detailed studies of farm labor in the 1930s include Lloyd S. Fisher, *The Harvest Labor Market in California* (Cambridge: Harvard University Press, 1953), and Paul S. Taylor, *Mexican Labor in the United States* (Berkeley: University of California Press, 1936).

6. Carey McWilliams, *Factories in the Fields;* p. 319.

7. Carey McWilliams, *Ill Fares the Land* (Boston: Little, Brown and Co., 1944), pp. 109, 110–129. This fine book surveys the lot of migrant workers in various parts of the West.

8. Quoted in McWilliams, *Ill Fares the Land*, p. 129.

9. McWilliams, *Ill Fares the Land*, p. 253.

10. McWilliams, *Ill Fares the Land*, p. 244.

11. A brief account of field workers in the Southwest can be found in McWilliams, *Ill Fares the Land*, pp. 187–256.

12. In addition to numerous contemporary government reports, readers will find the fine chapters on the depression years by E. B. Robinson, *History of North Dakota* (Lincoln: University of Nebraska Press, 1966), instructive.

13. In the absence of a comprehensive book about the New Deal and the West, the special issue of the *Pacific Historical Review*, vol. 38 (August, 1969), No. 3, "The New Deal in the West," is especially helpful.

14. *Cong. Record*, 75 Cong., 1 sess., Appendix, p. 1233.

15. A concise discussion of the Taylor Grazing Act can be found in John T. Schlebecker, *Cattle Raising on the Plains, 1900–1961* (Lincoln: University of Nebraska Press, 1963).

16. John Brennan, *Silver and the First New Deal* (Reno: University of Nevada Press, 1969), contains a good discussion of this issue.

17. Tomasevich, *International Agreements*, discusses these controversies in some detail.

18. A glimpse of federal relations with western states can be gleaned from James T. Patterson, *The New Deal and the States* (Princeton: Princeton University Press, 1969).

19. Francis E. Townsend, *New Horizons: An Autobiography* (Chicago: J. L. Stewart Publishing Co., 1943), and Abraham Holtzman, *The Townsend Movement: A Political Study* (New York: Twayne Publishers, 1963), discuss the movement in more detail.

20. A contemporary description is Winston Moore and Marianne Moore, *Out of the Frying Pan* (Los Angeles: De Vorss and Co., 1939).

21. Wilson's appraisals of California writers are gathered in his book, *The Boys in the Back Room: Notes on California Novelists* (San Francisco: Ridgeway Books, 1941).

22. Her impressions are in Dorothea Lange and Paul S. Taylor [her husband], *An American Exodus: A Record of Human Erosion* (New York: Reynal and Hitchcock, 1939).

23. A wide range of WPA publications provide scattered data on cultural programs in the West. Readers desiring a quick survey should consult Works Progress Administration, *Final Report on WPA Programs, 1935–1943* (Washington: U.S. Government Printing Office, 1943); more detailed are Works Progress Administration, *New Horizons in American Art* (New York: Museum of Modern Art, 1936), and Doak S. Campbell, *Educational Activities of the Works Progress Administration* (Washington: U.S. Government Printing Office, 1939).

24. As quoted in Works Progress Administration, *Inventory: An Appraisal of the Results of the Works Progress Administration* (Washington: U.S. Government Printing Office, 1938), p. 86.

25. Quoted in Works Progress Administration, *Inventory*, p. 62.

PART TWO

The Pacesetting Society, 1941–1971

4

The American West
During World War II

World War II inaugurated a new era in the growth of the West. In many ways perhaps the four years of frenzied wartime expansion compressed what might have been as many as forty years of peacetime growth. Thus, although the war itself occasioned few new changes, it did much to accelerate trends that had been developing at a more leisurely pace for more than half a century. In short, World War II brought about the maturation of the West.

Indeed, the war ended many vestiges of the colonialism under which westerners had been suffering for many years. The West emerged from the conflict as a pacesetter for the nation. Ironically, the underdeveloped character of the region in 1941 made it possible for Americans to use it as a vast testing ground for all kinds of new experiments, in living styles, economic development, science, new forms of cultural expression and education, and politics. Less stratified and less rigid than the older regions, more susceptible to change and experimentation, during World War II the West became the home of exciting new projects and ideas. As a result, in 1945 the West had become a barometer of American life, a role it was to play for the next three decades. Instead of continuing as a docile colony of the East, the West in World War II became an aggressive innovator, first to develop life-styles that, for better or for worse, in later years were to be widely copied throughout the United States, and eventually, in many portions of the world.

In the years between 1941 and 1945 the impact of the domestic mobilization program on the West was profound. It accelerated the flow of westward population and increased the already much vaunted mobility of westerners within the region. As a result, most western towns and cities grew appreciably in size, especially along the Pacific Coast and in the Southwest. On the other hand, many of the rural Plains states east of the Rockies lost population in the period. Most of these population movements were directly traceable to the wartime economic boom. The war significantly accelerated a tendency—already noticeable during the New Deal—for the federal government to assume a major responsibility for providing the capital necessary for rapid western economic growth instead of private financiers in the East. World War II thus facilitated a change of masters for the West, from Wall Street to Pennsylvania Avenue, from foreign and eastern financiers to the White House, Congress, and the administrative agencies in Washington, D.C.

Social Changes in Wartime

Like few other events during the twentieth century World War II accelerated the pace of social change in the West. Between 1941 and 1945 the rate at which newcomers arrived rose once again as the difficult depression years faded into the background. Although the rate of growth on the Pacific Coast tended to be greater than in other areas of the West, Texas and the entire Southwest also underwent a striking population boom. The

War workers in Richmond, California, 1942. Source: Dorothea Lange.

lure of new wartime jobs drew millions, especially large numbers of disadvantaged groups and ethnic or racial minorities. Thus the war years saw an increasing percentage of black Americans from the rural south drawn into western defense industries. Like the Okies in the thirties, black Americans and Chicanos were among the dispossessed who were displaced by the mechanization of agriculture. They poured into towns and cities, sometimes into hastily erected emergency housing in suburbs, creating new nucleii of slums and greatly complicating the urban problems of the West. Then, and in later years, their coming further diversified the composition of western population.

At the same time, mobilization laid the basis for a remarkable postwar population boom. More than 10 million servicemen and women at one time or another were stationed in the west, and a large number of them would return as permanent settlers with the end of hostilities. In addition, 3 million service personnel from the Pacific areas passed through the western states on their way home after the war, and a significant proportion of them were sufficiently impressed, too, to become residents in later years. Somewhat unexpectedly, therefore, the war provided the greatest spur to population expansion that the West had experienced in the twentieth century.

California experienced the largest growth, gaining 1 million newcomers (while the state of New York was losing 1 million), representing a 15 per cent increase in population. Washington (11 per cent) and Oregon (8 per cent) did not increase quite as fast, but nevertheless slightly more than other states west of the Rockies, and than Texas. On the other hand, western states east of the Rockies, such as Montana and the Dakotas, lost 15 per cent of their people, and Nebraska (11 per cent) almost as much. To put it in another way, the urban West grew greatly, while the rural West declined.

California

As in previous years, California's population increase was the highest in the nation. To be sure, the rate of growth was not so great as it had been in the first two decades of the twentieth century. But it was a more even growth in that a higher percentage of younger people (under 40) entered the state than in earlier years.

Although many areas of California were affected by the new migration, the southern portion of the state increased most rapidly. Of the more than 1 million new Californians who settled there during the war, at least 660,000 stayed south of the Tehachapi Mountains, the great majority in the Los Angeles area. Others flooded San Diego to change it from a sleepy town of 60,000 to a booming metropolis of more than a quarter of a million inhabitants. No doubt, many of the newcomers were attracted by the favorable climate of the region. But the enormous expansion of aircraft manufacturing and shipbuilding facilities in southern California and the attendant creation of more than 250,000 new jobs also provided a major incentive. Suddenly the depression generation of displaced people from Oklahoma and Arkansas, the poor and hopeless who had come from all corners of the land, found their labor in demand. In just a few short years the war boom dissolved California's problem of providing for the economically dispossessed. And the news traveled fast as the erstwhile unemployed wrote to their relatives and friends back home, causing hundreds of thousands of others to flock to the new war industries on the West Coast.

As might be expected, more than 90 per cent of the newcomers settled in towns and cities. The largest urban centers, such as Los Angeles and San Francisco, increased their populations by more than 25 per cent, although medium-sized towns like San Diego, Fresno, and Sacramento were transformed into metropolitan areas by the influx. Many smaller cities, Richmond and Vallejo in the San Francisco Bay area region, for example, were shipbuilding and oil-refining centers that grew from 25,000 people each to more than 100,000 each during the first year of the war. The federal government built temporary emergency housing projects in the area, which, unfortunately, degenerated into typical western urban slums in succeeding years.

A significant proportion of these war workers were members of racial or ethnic minorities. The number of black Americans in California doubled during wartime to 150,000. Already in 1942 both the Southern Pacific and Santa Fe railroads were importing many black workers from Texas, Louisiana, and Oklahoma to engage in maintenance operations on their lines. More than one-half of the new arrivals moved to the Los Angeles area. There they occupied a neighborhood once known as Little Tokyo, which they now rechristened Bronzeville. Los Angeles thus became one of the major new centers of black America.

Mexicans, Mexican-Americans, and Chicanos constituted another significant minority in California, outnumbering the blacks. By 1940 the teeming barrios of east Los Angeles already contained 300,000 Chicanos, swelled by perhaps more than 100,000 newcomers from Mexico during the war. Some of the Chicanos were second-generation Mexican-Americans who were inclined to be less docile than their parents. Moreover, many youths tended to be torn between Anglo and Chicano cultures, and grew sensitive and restive under added wartime strains. Juvenile delinquency and crime rates rose among the Chicanos, breeding increased prejudice against them. Throughout 1942 major newspapers in Los Angeles gave undue emphasis to crimes allegedly committed by Chicanos. The tensions of both the Anglo and the Chicano communities crystallized in the so-called Sleepy Lagoon case in Los Angeles during August 1942. The murder of a man named Diaz in an east Los Angeles mudhole known as Sleepy Lagoon led the city police to arrest more than 300 Chicano youths. The district attorney's office secured indictments against twenty-three of them for the murder and won seventeen convictions. An appellate court reversed these decisions for lack of evidence, but the incident was a clear reflection of prejudice against California's largest minority. These ethnic tensions were further reflected in the Los Angeles zoot suit riots of June 1943. Most of the major newspapers in Los Angeles had continued to reflect a strong bias against Chicanos and Mexicans. With tensions at a high pitch, on June 6, 1943, a band of about 3,000 white men in the downtown area set upon zoot-suited Chicanos, beating them unmerci-.fully. Other roving groups also attacked hapless Filipinos or black Americans who happened to be in the neighborhood. The city's mayor immediately imposed a curfew, and in the course of a week the disorders died down.[1] But the incident crystallized problems of discrimination and acculturation that had been simmering for decades and brought them into full public view. Before 1941 Chicano problems had been scattered in the rural areas of California; the war tended to concentrate them in the cities, where they became more highly visible and volatile than ever before.

Wartime tensions brought even greater strains to the lives of another of California's minorities—the Japanese-Americans. Their story is well known and can be summarized briefly. On the eve of Pearl Harbor the Japanese and Japanese-American (Nisei) community along the Pacific Coast numbered approximately 100,000 souls. By 1941 Oriental immigrants had already made an important place for themselves in western life. They were a significant element in the Pacific fisheries, dominating the San Pedro–Wilmington district; they had become a major factor in the state's fruit and vegetable farming industry; they were becoming famous as landscape gardeners; and some were beginning to enter various professions. But whatever their occupation or their status, all were regarded with suspicion by many Californians. Acting primarily on the advice of his military leaders—and under pressure from California State Attorney General Earl Warren—President Franklin D. Roosevelt in February 1942 ordered the internment of all Japanese and Japanese-Americans on the Pacific Coast, and in Arizona. Approximately 112,000 were rounded up and sent to ten new detention camps that had been quickly set up in remote areas of the interior in Arizona, Wyoming, Utah, Colorado, and Idaho, as well as California. There the internees remained for more than two years until, in December 1944, the War Department revoked its exclusion order and allowed them to go free. Many of their young men had served with distinction in the American armed forces and raised doubts about the wisdom of their internment in the first place.[2]

The Pacific Northwest, Rocky Mountains, and Plains

To a lesser extent, many of the strains of California's wartime population growth were reflected in the Pacific Northwest. Between 1941 and 1945 more than 500,000 new settlers arrived there, including almost 100,000 black Americans. Obviously the benign climate constituted one attraction. But wartime jobs provided the main magnet. Boeing's giant aircraft plants and the huge new shipyards operated by Henry J. Kaiser and others created several hundred thousand new job openings that beckoned to people in every corner of the nation seeking better employment opportunities.

Elsewhere in the West the population boom was less pronounced. Since businessmen in the Rocky Mountain states secured a relatively small portion of wartime contracts, a smaller number of new jobs opened up there. Thus, this region lacked the lure of the West Coast. One exception was the Denver area, which underwent significant economic expansion, and hence, population growth. Some of the Mexican farm workers who had come to work in Colorado's beet-sugar fields and factories in the thirties now migrated to Denver to take advantage of higher wages in manufacturing and other wartime industries. This pattern of urban growth was also typical of Nevada. There Las Vegas became one of the principal new smaller industrial cities of the West, largely because of its proximity to Hoover Dam and cheap electric power. In the Southwest a slower rate of population growth was

A Denver trailer company converts to war production, 1940. Source: Denver Public Library, Western History Department.

directly related to industrialization in towns and cities. Phoenix, Arizona, emerged during the war as the largest industrial complex in the region. This once sleepy town attracted a highly diversified population including Mexicans, Chicanos, and black Americans.

In the Plains states public officials worried greatly over their heavy loss of population. To be sure, that trend was not new, but it was accelerated by the war, as youths streamed into the armed forces and moved to lucrative wartime jobs elsewhere. Many young people did not return at the conclusion of the conflict. Moreover, unable to attract new manufacturing industries between 1941 and 1945, these states become more than ever dependent on agriculture. North Dakota's population, for example, declined from 642,000 in 1940 to 521,000 five years later. Many farmers simply gave up the land and went to work in factories. The 325,000 farmers of 1940 shrank to 285,000 in 1945. With the exception of urban centers such as Wichita, Kansas, which specialized in aircraft manufactures, the general population trend in the Plains states was one of decline. The twentieth century was the era of growth in the urban areas, not in the sparsely populated regions of the West.

Economic Impact of the War

If World War II fomented significant social changes in the West, these were often a direct result of its impact on the economy of the region. The domestic mobilization program led westerners to boost their output in virtually every sector of their economy. In manufacturing, especially, the Pacific Coast states and parts of the Southwest virtually doubled their capacity during wartime. What the Roosevelt Administration had been unable to accomplish during eight years of peace it was able to achieve in less than four years of war.

Not magic, but vastly increased federal expenditures, were responsible for this marvelous transformation. Between 1940 and 1945 the federal government spent more than $60 billion in the western states. Approximately $29 billion were expended for war orders, more than five times the value of all manufacturers in the region in 1939. To be sure, the geographical distribution of these funds was uneven, for California received the lion's share. Federal expenditures in wartime California totaled more than $35 billion, constituting about 10 per cent of all federal spending during the war, although the state's population was only 7 per cent of the national total. We can appreciate the extraordinary influence of this increase if we recall that in 1930 federal spending in California totaled $190 million; by 1945, it had risen to $8.5 billion.

These facts clearly revealed what had already been apparent in the New Deal era—that the federal government rather than private capital would be a major instrument in hastening the economic growth of the trans-Mississippi West. Government supplied not only the necessary capital for accelerated growth but also freed westerners from many of the artificial restraints often imposed upon them by eastern financiers eager to protect their own vested interests. And so the energies of westerners in many spheres of the economy were liberated. They boosted the output of their extractive industries, to be sure. But perhaps most significant was the remarkable expansion of manufacturing in the West, and the proliferation of new centers of scientific research and technological expertise.[3] The vast open spaces of the West and their remoteness encouraged innovation and experimentation. The war catapulted the western economy from a preindustrial stage into one characterized by technological sophistication.

Farmers, Cattlemen, Lumbermen, and Miners

Western farmers performed prodigious feats in wartime. True, the total production of most crops did not increase significantly between 1941 and 1945, but the yearly production records were achieved with a greatly diminished labor force. Farmers west of the Mississippi produced more than two-thirds of the nation's wheat, at least one-half of the national output of other grains such as corn, oats, and barley, and more than two-thirds of the nation's fruits and vegetables. Unlike the decade of the thirties, which had been characterized by drought, the war years were notable for their exceptionally good weather which enabled farmers to meet market demands without much difficulty. Rainfall was above average in most areas of the West between 1941 and 1945, years that were as wet as the thirties had been dry. Unlike World War I farmers, their descendants in World War II did not greatly increase their agricultural acreage, but relied on greater mechanization and improved scientific farming techniques to meet their production quotas.

Almost everywhere in the West the war brought great prosperity to farmers. In California and the Pacific Northwest the number of farms and the agricultural output remained rather stable during wartime. But the value of these farms virtually doubled between 1941 and 1945 as crop prices soared. In the Rocky Mountain states large-scale farmers increased the average size of their holdings while boosting their output by more than 20 per cent over prewar levels. In this region, with few exceptions, only irrigated farming was profitable commercially. In Plains states like North Dakota, the combination of plentiful rain and high crop prices brought farmers there the greatest prosperity they had ever known. Their personal income rose 145 per cent during the war (compared to the national average of 109 per cent), and with their bounty they paid off their debts, bought additional land at relatively low prices, and stocked away their surplus into savings. And for the first time since the Great Crash, North Dakota farmers produced wheat crops exceeding 100 million bushels annually.

The war also changed the fortunes of western cattlemen. As unemployment virtually disappeared in the United States during 1942, Americans began to eat more beef. More than one-half of the yearly production of cattle went to feed the more than 8 million men and women in the armed forces. For the first time in their lives many of these Americans were able to eat as much meat as they wanted. And that was about twice as much as they had eaten before 1941. Meanwhile, as an increasing number of Americans moved into the cities, and were gainfully employed, they also increased their meat consumption. As these new demands outran meat supplies, inflationary prices became a serious problem. Consequently, the Roosevelt administration beseeched Congress to authorize the imposition of price controls on meat. After some dawdling, in October of 1942, Congress finally enacted the Stabilization Act, which imposed price ceilings. Meat prices were not to exceed levels attained in March of 1942. Despite inevitable grumbling and complaints, these price limitations operated effectively throughout the war. And cattlemen themselves were not too perturbed since they made good profits and benefited from price controls on fodder.

As meat became scarcer early in 1943, however, the administration decided to institute rationing to wipe out the now flourishing black markets. And so, in March of 1943, the Office of Price Administration inaugurated a comprehensive meat rationing system. Older cattlemen who could remember the "Meatless Fridays" decreed by the Wilson Administration in World War I greatly preferred the rationing system used in World War II, since it ensured greater stability in their markets. And so they increased their production, often by enlarging the size of their ranches and by more sophisticated scientific farming methods.

Although western lumbermen strained mightily in wartime, they did not appreciably increase their output. They furnished the nation with more than one-half of its softwoods such as Douglas fir and Ponderosa pine. Yet the total production of the Pacific Coast remained stable as Washington's timber output shrank while that of Oregon increased. Rocky Mountain lumbermen slightly increased their production. As a whole, however, the contribution of the West to national lumber output declined in these years, from 42 per cent in 1938 to 37.5 per cent in 1945. The higher transportation costs associated with western lumber were one factor in explaining this trend.

Crucial to the entire war effort were the contributions of the western mining industry. The West was still America's treasurehouse of minerals, supplying the nation with more than 90 per cent of all its mineral needs. Most significant was copper, but increased production of lead, zinc, molybdenum, vanadium, manganese, chrome, mercury—and later uranium—was hardly less important. Wartime needs also boosted the output of new alloys such as ferro-manganese, ferro-chrome, and ferro-silicon to major proportions. The pressure for new production records tended to benefit large-scale mining enterprises. The Kennecott Copper Corporation, for example, increased its share of national production to a whopping 43 per cent during the war (compared to less than 30 per cent just a decade earlier). Similar trends characterized the petroleum industry, which reached new production levels to feed the worldwide war machine. The states west of the Mississippi River supplied more than one-half the nation's petroleum needs, making annual petroleum production a billion-dollar industry.

Manufacturing and Service Industries

But the most significant new departure in the western economy wrought by the war was the expansion of manufacturing and the creation of a vast new scientific-technological complex. Suddenly various areas of the West developed industries such as steel, shipbuilding, aircraft manufactures, aluminum, textiles, machine tools, and atomic energy. Mobilization uncovered hidden sources of western energy, opened up hitherto unrealized potentials of imagination, creativeness, managerial ability, and enterprise. The unused potential of America was being revealed and utilized in the West. And westerners helped to revolutionize the thinking of Americans in other regions. Until 1941 most Americans had been obsessed by a belief in scarcity, in the end of American frontiers, in the limitations on America's expansion. But the experience of World War II changed all that. It opened up new vistas, vistas of virtually unlimited potentials. The realization that seemingly limitless opportunities still lay in the future profoundly altered the thinking of most Americans in 1945, from a negative, pessimistic view of the future to one emphasizing hope and great expectations.

Much manufacturing expansion was triggered by federal funds. Of the total amount of $29 billion in war contracts awarded in the West, California secured more than its share—$1.8 billion. Other western states received smaller amounts. As a group, the western states secured 15 per cent of all war contracts awarded by the federal government, although in 1941 they had only 10 per cent of the nation's manufacturing capacity. Forty-five per cent of the total new war plants in the West rose in California, mostly in the Los Angeles and Bay Area regions. Other industrial centers that expanded included Phoenix, Arizona; Seattle, Tacoma, and Spokane in Washington; Portland, Oregon; Denver and Pueblo, Colorado; and Omaha, Nebraska. Smaller centers were located in Las Vegas, Nevada; Pocatello, Idaho; Carlsbad, New Mexico; Vancouver, B.C.; and Cheyenne, Wyoming. The dispersal of new manufacturing facilities was not accidental but rather was a conscious policy of federal wartime agencies. It was designed to ease labor shortages in some areas while lessening the potential destructiveness of possible enemy air attacks. Most of the new plants were financed by the Reconstruction Finance Corporation (usually through its subsidiary, the Defense Plant Corporation) after August 1940. Then the War Production Board supervised the expansion of new industrial facilities.

More than any other individual person, industrialist Henry J. Kaiser was responsible for the wartime manufacturing boom in the West. Kaiser, a human dynamo who made Oakland, Californa, the headquarters of his vast operations, had had considerable experience in the construction business before World War II. Among his major projects in the thirties had been the building of Hoover and Parker dams, the San Francisco Bay Bridge, and also the Bonneville and Grand Coulee dams in the Pacific Northwest. By 1940 he was planning to build the first large western steel making plant at Fontana, California, 50 miles east of Los Angeles, and also had begun construction of the largest cement plant in the world at Permanente, in California. Throughout these years he was a close associate of A. P. Gianninni and the Bank of America (which financed many of his ventures). It was Gianninni who urged President Roosevelt in 1941 to entrust new manufacturing responsibilities to Kaiser and who underwrote his success as the West's leading manufacturer.

One of the first tasks Roosevelt assigned Kaiser was shipbuilding. And although Kaiser had little experience with ships, his daring methods brought revolutionary innovations. With federal funds primarily, he built new shipyards at Richmond, Oakland, Sausalito, Vallejo, and San Pedro, California (where he controlled the Calship Corporation). Employing more than 150,000 men and women in his northern California yards, and an almost equal number in the southern portion of the state, Kaiser advertised for help in every section of the nation. By offering high wages, on-the-job-training, and medical care, and by soliciting black workers and other minorities, Kaiser was able to surmount the labor shortages that plagued other enterprises. His round-the-clock operations soon achieved remarkable production records; by 1943 he was building more than 800 ships yearly. Almost unbelievably, in that year the Kaiser shipyards were launching one new freighter every 10 hours. Kaiser reduced the time to build a Liberty Ship (freighter) to just 25 days, less than a third of the time required in the prewar period. By 1945 he had completed more than $4 billion of shipbuilding contracts for the federal government. Although other companies such as Todd Shipbuilding Corporation and the Bethlehem Shipyards at Richmond, Oakland, Sausalito, Vallejo, and San Pedro also contributed to the wartime shipbuilding boom, Kaiser's achievements seemed especially spectacular.

During the war aircraft manufacturing in California started the growth that would transform it into one of the major industries along the Pacific Coast in the next three decades. In 1940 aircraft manufacturing was a relatively small-scale enterprise in the state, characterized largely by skilled craftsmen numbering not much more than 1,000. The urgencies of war led to the development of mass production and assembly-line techniques in the aircraft industries. Between 1941 and 1945 the industry in California provided employment for more than 300,000 persons.

Indeed, during the war aircraft manufacturing became one of California's leading industries. More than 60 per cent of all federal monies spent in the state were related to airplanes. Although Detroit made most of the engines, the California plants built and assembled most of the frames. Much of this activity was centered in the southern portion of the state, in part because of its predictable and mild climate. Douglas, Lockheed, North American, Northrop, and Hughes erected huge plants in the Los Angeles area while Consolidated Vultee (Convair) and Ryan extended their San Diego operations. Douglas enlarged its Santa Monica plants and established major branches in Long Beach and El Segundo. Along with Lockheed, the company was one of the major cornerstones of the U.S. Air Force. Douglas built B-17 Flying Fortresses (on consignment for Boeing), Liberator Bombers (on consignment for Consolidated), and Havoc Nightfighters. Lockheed concentrated on P-38 fighters, Hudson bombers for Great Britain, and the Constellation Transport. The company built more than 20,000 planes during the war, about 6 per cent of the total production. Of the 301,000 planes built during the war, 60,000 (one-fifth) were assembled in California at a cost of a little more than $10 billion.[4]

Shipbuilding and aircraft manufacturing on such a vast scale also stimulated a host of other western industries, among which steel and aluminum were the most important. Kaiser was extremely anxious to construct new steel manufacturing plants in California to supply his shipyards, rather than rely on scarce eastern supplies. Late in 1941 his entreaties were successful and the Reconstruction Finance Corporation granted him a loan of $112 million to build an entirely new plant at Fontana, California, which became one of the West's largest steel manufacturing facilities. He also built a magnesium processing plant to facilitate airplane part and helicopter manufacturing operations. Meanwhile, California's airplane manufacturing plants were clamoring for greater aluminum supplies, since that metal comprised 75 per cent of most airplanes. In 1941 the Aluminum Corporation of America almost monopolized the industry, controlling more than 90 per cent of national production. Its ability to expand production quickly without federal help, however, was doubtful. Thus, the Reconstruction Finance Corporation extended more than $200 million in loans for the construction of six new major aluminum production plants in the West, most of which were operated by Alcoa. With a total capacity of 820 million pounds yearly, these plants were scattered on the Pacific Coast. One was at Torrance, California, another in Troutdale, Oregon, and four others were built in the state of Washington where access to the cheap power on the Columbia River was a major factor in determining location. Altogether, the total aluminum manufacturing capacity of the United States increased sevenfold during World War II.

Manufacturing activity in the Pacific Northwest was as greatly stimulated by the war as it was in California, if on a somewhat smaller scale. Employment in all industries increased twentyfold between 1941 and 1945, with shipbuilding and aircraft manufacturers as leaders. Shipyards in Seattle and Portland boomed. Henry Kaiser came to establish new shipbuilding facilities in this region, too. The contributions of the shipyards in the Pacific Northwest to the war effort were considerable. The naval repair yards at Bremerton, Washington, for example, repaired the fleet so heavily damaged at Pearl Harbor in December of 1941 and sent it back into action by the middle of 1942. Seattle brass foundries also manufactured ship propellers while iron works in Everett turned out engines. In short, shipbuilding activities were resulting in highly diversified manufacturing.

Airplane manufacturing also reached major proportions in the Pacific Northwest, largely because of the presence of the Boeing Company in Seattle. During the war the company employed more than 40,000 persons, not only at its main Seattle and Renton plants, but also at smaller shops in Bellingham, Chehalis, Everett, and Aberdeen. Boeing had long been a pioneer in the industry, having developed the B-17 Flying Fortress bomber as early as 1934, the first American four-engine bomber. During World War II Boeing built more than 10,000 B-17Fs, a larger version of the original model. By September 1942 Boeing engineers had ready designs for the B-29 Super Fortress, an advanced attack plane of which it built more than 4,000 for the army. Boeing's military contracts in 1943 exceeded $500 million annually and influenced the entire economy of the region. In addition to its own manufacturing activities Boeing also employed 67 major subcontractors who in turn made airplane manufactures a leading industry for the region, in addition to fomenting major auxiliary manufactures such as aluminum.[5]

If the expansion of manufacturing was not so dramatic in the Rocky Mountain states as on the Pacific Coast, it was nevertheless not insignificant. Perhaps Denver was an unlikely location for shipyards, but there they were. These shipbuilding facilities assembled hull sections for navy escort vessels as well as landing barges for the army. The launching of the U.S.S. *Mountain Maid* in the spring of 1942 established Denver's shipbuilding prowess. At the same time the federal government built the Denver Arms Plant, operated by the Remington Company and, later in the war, by Henry J. Kaiser. This factory employed 20,000 workers engaged in manufacturing munitions, shells, and fuses. North of Aurora, Colorado, federal initiative also resulted in the construction of the Rocky Mountain Arsenal, a chemical warfare manufacturing plant that employed 15,000 persons at the peak of the war.

Possibly the most important single new manufacturing facility in the Rocky Mountain states which was prompted by the war was the Geneva Steel Works in Provo, Utah. Indeed, the federal government virtually created a western steel industry with the establishment of this plant, and Kaiser's at Fontana. The Provo facilities were also the most important single project of the Defense Plant Corporation, which invested more than $200 million in its construction. Prior to the war the open-hearth furnaces of the Columbia Steel Company at Provo had been producing about 1 million tons of steel annually, laying a foundation for possible future expansion. Sensing their opportunity, in April of 1941 Utah's Governor Herbert Maw and U.S. Senator Abe Murdock went to see President Roosevelt in Washington to urge him to expand western steel-making capacity to aid in the defense effort. Roosevelt was sympathetic and suggested that they also discuss the matter with Henry J. Kaiser. Kaiser proposed the construction of new steel works in Provo, southern California, and the Pacific Northwest. Over the summer a large number of interested parties deliberated over these plans. Finally, in November of 1941 the Office of Production Management authorized not only Kaiser's Fontana plant, but large-scale expansion of the Provo works. During the war investment in plant expansion virtually quadrupled the steel ingot capacity of these Geneva Works (to about 4 million tons annually), although their capacity for finished steel was more restricted.[6] But the construction of major steel manufacturing facilities almost entirely by the federal government rather than by private capital was a major boon to the economic growth of the entire West, one more sign of the waning of colonialism.

The Plains states were far less successful in developing their manufactures. Kansas, with large airplane factories at Wichita, was an exception. In states such as North Dakota, for example, many businessmen and public leaders hoped that the war might provide them with an opportunity to diversify their economy. As early as December 1940 Governor John Moses of North Dakota and the Greater North Dakota Association (a group of businessmen) had presented briefs to the Defense Plant Corporation to make a case for the establishment of industrial plants in North Dakota. But their pleas were to avail little. Again, in March of 1942 a North Dakota War Resources Committee went to Washington in search of war contracts, with few results. By March of 1945 North Dakota had received only $9.6 million of war contracts (totaling $225 billion nationally), less than any other state. From the perspective of Washington, North Dakota could serve the national interest best by agricultural specialization. No wonder, therefore, that without federal funds, the state between 1941 and 1945 was unable to increase its manufacturing potential.

With the phenomenal economic growth of the western states during wartime came an expansion of its banking system. Commercial banks in California, such as the Bank of America, as well as banks in the Pacific Northwest increased their resources appreciably. It was a source of pride to western bankers that, apart from federal funds, they were able exclusively to finance expansion of the wartime shipping industry. No longer were they primarily dependent on eastern capital.

The war tended to bring western banks more directly into the mainstream of national finance. During the conflict large western banks such as the Bank of America not only had a part in financing western enterprises, but also engaged in investments throughout the nation. The Bank of America continued its policy of giving special attention to the needs of small businessmen. As workers were drawn to large plants in the bigger cities, small businessmen found it more difficult to secure necessary capital. The Bank of America also set up a special information office in Washington where small manufacturers desiring war contracts could secure guidance. The idea of proffering such guidance had come from Mario Gianninni, and by 1941 he had persuaded Donald Nelson, chairman of the War Production Board, of its desirability. By the middle of 1942 Congress created the Smaller War Plants Corporation for the express purpose of channeling war contracts to small businessmen.

But western banks had to work hard to secure a larger share of financing the expansion of wartime manufacturing. Large loans to aircraft industries were still largely in the hands of eastern syndicates. During the war the Bank of America was able to secure a bigger share of large-scale corporate financing, however, through its aggressive intervention. In addition, it participated in underwriting corporations throughout the nation such as Bendix, Chrysler, Westinghouse—as well as North American Aviation and Northrop Aircraft Corporation. In the process, the $2 billion of assets that the bank had in 1941 had doubled four years later!

Thus, western banks had matured sufficiently to provide a significant amount of the private capital needed to finance industrial expansion in the region. The Bank of America as well as the Crocker Bank of San Francisco were among the leaders. To be sure, while the federal government was expending $409 million for new shipbuilding facilities in California, private bankers supplied only $29 million. But the ability of western bankers to provide capital without eastern aid was a distinct step toward greater self-sufficiency. And of the private capital required to expand other industries, including aircraft, aluminum, and other auxiliary manufactures, western bankers provided a major share. More than the federal government, they also were largely responsible for underwriting the construction of much of the emergency housing that was needed to supply living accommodations for the hundreds of thousands of new war workers who poured into California. The Bank of America alone between 1941 and 1945 made more than 100,000 loans totaling $445 million exclusively for new housing. Indeed, in 1945 it emerged as the world's largest bank, a measure of western financial maturity, a turning point in the maturation of what had been for over a century, a colonial economy. By 1945 a more rounded economy, for, California and the West was at hand. As A. P. Gianninni noted in 1945: "The West has all the money to finance whatever it wants to; we no longer have to go to New York for financing, and we're not at its mercy. Wall Street used to give a western enterprise plenty of rope, and when it went broke it took over."[7] This phase was now past history.

Some of the West's major service industries, such as tourism, were virtually suspended by the war. But in their place came an enormous increase of armed forces facilities—training camps, supply depots, testing sites, and scientific installations—which channeled large amounts of federal funds into the region. California in 1941, for example, had only a few military bases, such as the Presidio in San Francisco, Fort Ord, the Mare Island Shipyard, March Field, and San Diego harbor. But by 1945 it contained huge army camps, virtual cities with troop populations over 50,000, such as Camps Beale, Cooke, Pendleton, Roberts, and Stoneman; the enormous Oakland Army Base, and the Oakland Naval Supply Center, Alameda Naval Air Station, Treasure Island Naval Station, the San Francisco Naval Shipyard; and vast new major air bases like Castle, McClellan, Parks, and Travis. And so it went in virtually every western state, in the Pacific Northwest, the Rockies, the Southwest, and the Plains. In the less densely populated areas the presence of federal installations was a major economic force in their economies. When the U.S. Army enlarged the Defense Depot at Ogden, Utah, for example, to make it one of the largest in the nation, or when it built its largest storage area for poisonous gases in the wilderness at Wendover, it became the largest employer in that state. And one could find similar parallels elsewhere, in New Mexico, Montana, Colorado, or North Dakota. Between 1941 and 1945 the federal government spent about $80 billion (about $20 billion annually) in the construction and maintenance of its military installations in the West. During World War II, not the ordinary tourist but G.I. Joe became a mainstay of the West's most important service industry.

The West and Science in World War II

Somewhat unexpectedly, the war made the West into one of the nation's leading scientific centers. As a region, the West offered various incentives to scientific research that other areas lacked. It had, for example, a nucleus of distinguished scientific talent clustered along the Pacific Coast, including oceanographers at La Jolla; outstanding physicists, chemists, astronomers, and others at Cal Tech in Pasadena; and the brilliant group gathered around Ernest O. Lawrence at his Radiation Laboratory at Berkeley. In addition, the recent completion of federal power projects in the West, on the Colorado and Columbia rivers, made cheap electricity readily available for a variety of new technological processes. And the very fact that the West was still so underdeveloped industrially made it more inviting for the establishment of new factories and projects. Moreover, the remoteness and isolation of many areas of the West, and their sparse population, made them ideally suitable for testing purposes while providing an additional measure of security. By 1941 some areas of the West also had skilled labor available, so necessary for transforming scientific theories into practical tools or weapons. Of lesser importance was the presence of many strategic materials important in scientific work, such as uranium ores, which were known to exist on the plateau of Colorado. Perhaps these various factors would have coalesced in peacetime, over many years, to make the West an important arena for American science. We will never know. But we do know that World War II crystalized these various advantages so that in four short years the West was transformed into one of the scientific centers of the nation.[8]

The Radiation Laboratory at the University of California in Berkeley, under the direction of E. O. Lawrence, by 1945 had become one of the country's leading research facilities in theoretical physics. Lawrence had built his first cyclotron in 1930, and in succeeding years made significant improvements that allowed for exciting new advanced research in physics. A man of extraordinary administrative talent as well, Lawrence also possessed the personal magnetism to attract one of the world's ablest groups of physicists to his Laboratory. By 1941 his staff included such distinguished men as R. T. Birge, L. W. Alvarez, Philip H. Abelson, Edwin McMillan, and J. Robert Oppenheimer. Moreover, as the persecutions of Mussolini and Hitler drove out many distinguished scientists from Europe, Lawrence and others found it possible to attract them westwards. Enrico Fermi came as a consultant, for example, while one of his distinguished coworkers, Emilio Sagre, secured a post at Berkeley. Supported by federal funds, by 1941 the Lawrence group concentrated on research dealing with elements 93 and 94, essential to the later fabrication of the atomic bomb.

Further to the south, at Cal Tech, scientists were engaged on a great variety of experiments directly related to the war effort. One of the most significant was the research in rocketry conducted by a team headed by Charles C. Lauritsen. This group constructed the world's largest torpedo tube during the war, worked on rocket motors and propellants, and was the nucleus of the Jet Propulsion Laboratory that was to become famous for missile research in the postwar decades. During World War II Lauritsen conferred frequently with J. Robert Oppenheimer, Director of the Los Alamos Scientific Laboratory, which was working on the A-bomb. The Cal Tech scientists developed some of the components essential to the weapon's explosive system. The importance of Cal Tech's diversified scientific research was attested by the fact that, next to M.I.T., it was the largest contractor for the Office of Scientific Research and Development, the major federal agency coordinating scientific research related to the war effort. Its contracts totaled $83 million while the University of California at Berkeley was fifth, with $15 million. Although these two institutions were the most important scientific centers in the West, they were not the only ones. The facilities of Boeing in Seattle harbored one of the most skilled groups of aircraft technicians and designers in the nation. Scientists at Stanford, the University of Texas, and the University of New Mexico did significant work on explosives. And late in 1943 the OSRD awarded more than $1 million to the University of New Mexico to operate a proving ground near Albuquerque on which to test mockup replicas of German V-1 robot bombs, which were just then beginning to threaten Great Britain.

To a considerable extent, much of the far-flung research conducted in scientific centers of the West, and elsewhere, was crystallized in the work performed at Los Alamos, in the remote wilds of New Mexico. Situated on a high, inaccessible plateau in northern New Mexico, prior to 1941 Los Alamos had been largely uninhabited. After World War I a portion of the site was occupied by an exclusive preparatory academy for the sons of wealthy easterners, the Los Alamos Ranch School. One of the youngsters who went camping there with his parents was J. Robert Oppenheimer, later a brilliant young physicist at Berkeley, who became enamored of the area in which he had spent part of his boyhood. When in 1940 President Franklin D. Roosevelt made the fateful decision to support research leading to a secret explosive nuclear weapon, and to establish a special weapons laboratory, his major scientific advisers, including Vannevar Bush, Charles B. Conant, and Karl T. Compton, pinpointed a number of possible sites for this super-secret project. At the same time they recommended the appointment of Oppenheimer as director. Oppenheimer's familiarity with Los Alamos was of course only one factor in its ultimate selection. The inaccessibility of the area and its proximity to vast empty spaces suitable for testing were also relevant considerations. Moreover, the fact that Los Alamos was only 40 miles from Santa Fe, a small city that could serve as an initial residential and supply center until an entirely new community could be constructed near the laboratory, was also conducive to its selection.

And so, during 1943, Los Alamos arose out of the western wilderness to become what was then perhaps the most important scientific research center in America. Under the aegis of the University of California, which administered the new city, and under the brilliant leadership of Oppenheimer, Los Alamos during the war drew to itself one of the most creative groups of scientists to be found anywhere in the world. Moreover, from Los Alamos Oppenheimer coordinated the research activities of scientists throughout the nation. At one time or another most major physicists, mathematicians, and chemists in the United States were drawn into the project, men like Edward Teller, Hans Bethe, John von Neumann, Isidor Rabi, George B. Kistiakowski, Edward U. Condon, Enrico Fermi, Niels Bohr, and Glenn T. Seaborg. As work on the project accelerated in 1943, the director of the entire project, Major General Leslie A. Groves, began seeking new sites for production plants. The West offered greater attractions for such facilities than other areas. One of the most important of those established was the huge new plutonium production plant built at Hanford, Washington. The easy access to electric power generated by the Bonneville dams was a major factor in the selection of this site. Throughout 1943 and 1944 a work force consisting of a small group of scientists and almost 40,000 technicians and other workers labored under great pressure on the thousands of operations necessary to produce plutonium, an essential ingredient of the projected new weapon. Their problems were many, and at times seemed insuperable, but by the beginning of 1945 the Hanford plant was finally producing plutonium in sufficient quantities. And so Los Alamos—the city on a hill—ensconced in the western mountains, affected the fate of mankind as much in three short years as Puritan divines once did in building their city on a hill three centuries before.

Thus the West during World War II became an essential element of America's war effort. It became arsenal, commissary, army camp, and scientific laboratory for all the United States. And the experience of war itself transformed western life-styles and the western economy. What might have been the ordinary progress of two generations was concentrated in a time span of less than half a decade.

Wartime Politics in the West

If the war had an enormous impact on the life-styles and the economy of the West, its influence on the political life of the region was far less pronounced. In view of the nation's preoccupation with the war, partisan politics remained largely muted during the conflict. If any one trend characterized western political life between 1941 and 1945 perhaps one should select political moderation or conservatism. Of course, greater aloofness from New Deal programs had already been apparent in most western states after 1937, and the war, especially the prosperity it induced, certainly strengthened such feelings.

In national politics, western influence on the president, Congress, and administrative agencies was far more potent during World War II than it had been in World War I. As we have already pointed out, western fears about a Japanese invasion in 1941 led President Roosevelt to intern Japanese-Americans on the West Coast. Increasing western influence in federal administrative agencies in Washington was revealed in the awarding of federal war contracts west of the Mississippi River by the Defense Plant Corporation, the Office of Production Management, and other agencies. The West as a whole received a larger share of such war contracts than the national average, measured by its population or industrial plant capacity. California and the state of Washington secured more than twice their share and states such as Oregon, Nevada, Montana, and Colorado placed well above national averages. Only the Plains states fell below.

On innumerable occasions during World War II western influence was evident in Congress. One notable example was the opposition of the western oil-producing states to any federally sponsored petroleum production and refining in the Middle East. In December 1943 Secretary of the Interior Harold Ickes secretly organized a Petroleum Reserves Corporation, a government corporation to exploit Middle Eastern oil reserves. Western senators, especially from California, Texas, Oklahoma, and Kansas, protested loudly and in unison. Senator Tom Connally of Texas and speaker of the House Sam Rayburn of Texas effectively led the strong opposition, which in March of 1944 forced Ickes to abandon the project. Thereupon, Ickes began negotiations with Great Britain whereby the two nations would enter into a treaty to allocate Middle Eastern petroleum supplies between them. Again, members of Congress from western states, speaking for independent oil producers in their region, who feared foreign competition, expressed bitter opposition. Although Ickes and his successors submitted various drafts of this proposed Anglo-American oil treaty to the United States Senate, westerners successfully prevented its ratification until in 1949 President Truman abandoned hopes for its passage.

Within the western states during wartime, moderation was the rule for successful politicians. In many ways, political conditions in California were similar to those in other western states. Before the war, in 1938, Californians had elected Democrat Culbert Olsen as their governor, on his promise to provide a new deal. But they also elected a placid Republican legislature, which effectively stymied almost all of his plans for reform. And when Olsen's term ended in 1942, Californians were in no mood to elect crusading reformers. Instead, both Democrats and Republicans flocked to the polls to give Republican Earl Warren one of the largest gubernatorial victories on record. Warren's muted partisanship and inoffensive blandness suited the mood of nonpartisanship that had become characteristic of many Californians. The state's cross-filing system had been encouraging this trend for over a decade. Warren's popularity was greatly enhanced by his extensive tax reduction programs during the war, coupled with healthy surpluses for the state treasury. But when Warren sought to take the stance of a reformer in 1945—when he recommended a compulsory state health insurance law—he found himself frustrated by a conglomeration of legislators similar to those who had impeded his predecessor, Culbert Olsen.

Elsewhere in the West this pattern was remarkably characteristic of state politics during wartime. Conservatives dominated political life in the Pacific Northwest. In Washington, Republicans as well as Democrats rallied behind conservative Arthur Langlie for governor, who struck a Warren-like pose of nonpartisanship. Similarly, his opponents in the legislature prevented him from carrying through much constructive reform. And for Congress Washingtonians elected only moderates. Republican moderates also seized control of politics in Oregon, stressing—with the exception of their advocacy of public power—a very muted type of partisanship. In Idaho conservatives came to dominate the Democratic as well as the Republican party. Moderation was the theme of Colorado's governor Ralph L. Carr, and of his more conservative Arizona colleague, Sidney P. Osborn. New Mexico governor J. J. Dempsey's conservatism was rarely challenged, nor was that of Texas' Pappy Lee (Pass the Biscuits) O'Daniel, first as governor, later as United States Senator. And on the Plains, more than ever, conservatism was predominant. In North Dakota, for example, wartime prosperity enabled Democratic Governor John Moses to reduce state debts between 1941 and 1945 and to ensure treasury surpluses. His caution reflected the mood of the voters, and was shared by his successor, Fred G. Aandahl. Even such moderate reforms as the reorganization of state government, which Governor Moses proposed in 1941, were neglected by suspicious state legislators. In most areas of the West, therefore, the war years were characterized by the cooling of reform ardor and an emphasis on moderation and conservatism.

In 1945 most westerners, young or old, could recall few events that had left such a profound impact on their region as had World War II. But they could not know then that the war had inaugurated a new era for the West—as for the nation—and that the war had created new patterns and life-styles for the next three decades. By ushering in an age of economic affluence the war laid the foundations for another western population boom. By their flexibility in accommodating millions of newcomers, westerners inaugurated new styles in urban and suburban living. By taking advantage of large-scale federal spending, westerners were able to liberate themselves from their dependence on eastern capital and to build a more diversified economy in which manufacturing and, above all, new technological and electronic industries became dominant. In 1945 westerners found themselves in a new role. They were no longer colonials; they had become pacesetters for the nation.

NOTES

1. General readers will find Matt S. Meier and Feliciano Rivera, *The Chicanos: A History of Mexican Americans* (New York: Hill and Wang, 1972), informative on the subject.

2. Morton Grodzins, *Americans Betrayed* (Chicago: University of Chicago Press, 1949), is informative.

3. Relevant to these subjects are Wendell Berge, *Economic Freedom for the West* (Lincoln: University of Nebraska Press, 1946), and the more technical account of Victor R. Fuchs, *Changes in the Location of Manufacturing in the United States Since 1929* (New Haven: Yale University Press, 1962).

4. Popular discussions include Frank J. Taylor and Lawton Wright, *Democracy's Air Arsenal* (New York: Duell, Sloan and Pearce, Inc., 1947), and the Boeing Company, *Pedigree of Champions; Boeing Since 1916* (Seattle: Boeing, 1963).

5. Washington State University, Bureau of Business Research, *The Impact of World War II Subcontracting by the Boeing Airplane Company Upon Pacific Northwest Manufacturing* (Seattle: University of Washington Press, 1955).

6. Leonard J. Arrington and Anthony T. Cluff, *Federally Financed Industrial Plants Constructed in Utah during World War II* (Logan: Utah State University, 1969).

7. Quoted in Marquis and Bessie L. James, *Biography of a Bank*, p. 476.

8. Unfortunately, readings on science in the West are scattered. Instructive are James P. Baxter III, *Scientists Against Time*, reprint of 1946 edition (Cambridge: M.I.T. Press, 1968), and Richard G. Hewlett and Oscar Anderson, *The New World, 1939–1946* (University Park, Pa.: Pennsylvania State University Press, 1962), the official history of the U.S. Atomic Energy Commission.

5

The West
and the Affluent Society,
1945–1960

Like other regions of the nation, the West was transformed by World War II. Between 1945 and 1960 the number of people living west of the Mississippi River rose from 32 million to 45 million. As in earlier years, the distribution of much of this growth was uneven. The largest increases were registered by California and the Southwest, the Pacific Northwest remained relatively stable, the Rocky Mountain area grew moderately, and the Plains states continued to decline. California's growth was spectacular, increasing from 9 million in 1945 to 19 million in 1960. Indeed, in 1962 California overtook New York as the most populous state in the Union. And more than half of the state's newcomers settled in Los Angeles County and San Diego, both of which more than doubled in population. The Pacific Northwest experienced a surge of population (40 per cent) in the immediate postwar years (1945–1950) but then settled down to a growth rate in the fifties that remained low-keyed and close to the national average (9 per cent). On the other hand, Arizona underwent a boom similar to that of southern California. Its population quadrupled from 1945 to 1960 as air conditioning and air transportation converted desert wastelands into thriving desert cities. Phoenix, just a town of 80,000 in 1945, became a bustling metropolis of more than half a million by 1960. Tucson increased from 40,000 inhabitants at the end of the war to 200,000 by 1960. New Mexico grew more slowly, but even there Albuquerque's population went from 50,000 in 1945 to over 200,000 in 1960. In Texas, Fort Worth and Houston saw enormous population increases. Metropolitan areas of Dallas grew from 434,000 in 1950 to 680,000 in 1960 and 1.5 million a decade later. Houston jumped from 591,000 in 1950 to 1.2 million in 1960, and almost 2 million by 1970.

A much smaller proportion of the newcomers settled in the Rocky Mountain states. The rate of increase there was about 16 per cent, somewhat above the national average of 13 per cent. And the Plains states continued to lose population as many of their ablest young people left in search of greater economic opportunities elsewhere and many senior citizens departed for more balmy climates. In historical perspective, these various western population patterns did not vary greatly from those of the preceding 100 years. What the new influx between 1945 and 1960 did bring was a leveling of the age composition of westerners, eliminating high percentages of young and old persons and bringing the age composition of Westerners more closely in line with the national averages.

Population Growth– Urban Society and the West

Obviously, economic opportunity proved to be the major magnet of newcomers, who still saw the West as a land of opportunity. As an underdeveloped region the West could still use a greater variety of talents, perhaps, than the East. But, in addition, federal expenditures of more than $150 billion in the West opened up a vast new reservoir of jobs. These government funds were largely channeled into growth industries like aerospace and electronics, which transformed the fabric of western life. Federal expenditures were closely related to the Cold War and increasing American involvements in the Far East. But the creation of a vast technological complex in the West held implications for peacetime uses as well. Thus, economic opportunities were a main attraction for millions of new settlers.

There were, of course, other forces at work. The increasing mobility of Americans between 1945 and 1960 undoubtedly was a factor in the growth of population in the West. The doubling of automobile ownership and usage in these years greatly facilitated the westward flow of people. Hardly less significant was the great expansion in air travel, which added considerably to the conquest of time and distance, something for which westerners had striven for over a century. Many of those who moved West had first come into the region during World War II as members of the armed forces, as many as 3 million of them. There still were open spaces in the West in 1945 and population density was relatively low, an undeniable attraction for millions in the increasingly congested urban centers of the East and the Middle West. And now technology made great stretches of the once vaunted Great American Desert habitable and pleasant. Air conditioning, for example, removed a major barrier to settlement in Arizona or California's Imperial Valley. And the mild healthful climates in many portions of the

West, especially along the Pacific Coast and in the Southwest, and the natural beauties of the area were a strong pull for the scientists, doctors, engineers, technicians, and educators—who chose to come West to live and work because the environment and job opportunities made possible an attractive life-style.

The new influx of people had a significant impact on the existing social structure of the West. It brought a large group of highly skilled and well-educated persons westwards—but a significant proportion of poor people as well. This was somewhat similar to the historical pattern that had begun in 1890 which had seen new immigrants drawn from progressively lower rungs on the socioeconomic scale. Recall that the wealthy boosters of the 1890s were followed by the prosperous middle-class retirees of the World War I era; lower-middle-class whites and Mexican braceros came in the twenties; Okies and Arkies in the thirties; and poor rural whites and blacks were drawn westward during World War II. The new cycle of migration between 1945 and 1960 included a large group of well-educated scientists, technicians, and executives, on the one hand, and a large group of unskilled, uneducated, and displaced poor, on the other. A survey of newcomers to Arizona in 1960 revealed that more than 50 per cent of the heads of families were professional people, skilled workers, or managers. And in that year Albuquerque, New Mexico, had more Ph.D.'s per capita than any other city in the nation.

A new Del Webb housing tract development in Tucson, Arizona, in 1948. Source: *Arizona Highways.*

Ethnic Minorities

Among the poor were a large number of persons belonging to ethnic or racial minorities, especially black Americans, Mexican-Americans, and American Indians. Indeed, the postwar era saw the first significant large-scale movement of black Americans into the West during peacetime. Of the million and a half black Americans who left the South between 1945 and 1960, more than 600,000 went west. The focal point of this migration was Los Angeles, where the black population rose from 97,000 in 1945 to 460,000 in 1960, almost one-half of all blacks in the state. Like California, most of the western states doubled their black population during this period, especially Washington, Arizona, Colorado, New Mexico, and Nevada. Black Americans came for reasons similar to those that lured whites—greater economic opportunity and a more pleasant life-style. With some exceptions, they also found a higher rate of tolerance in the extremely fluid society of the West than elsewhere. As one black mother commented at the time: "I would rather take a little insecurity than no security at all which we have been used to. At least my kids can go to good schools here. We see opportunity all around us here, whether we can grab hold of it or not. We smell freedom here, and maybe soon we can taste it."[1] Los Angeles was one of the first cities in the United States to establish a Human Relations Commission in 1943—in the wake of the zoot-suit riots. During the fifties it was one of the first large cities in the nation to elect black members to the city council, including ill Mills, Thomas Bradley, and Gilbert Lindsey. And California state legislators in 1959 authorized creation of a Fair Employment Practices Commission. Most of the black men and women who came West fared better than they had before. Nevertheless, in these years their incomes were significantly lower than those of whites. Although constituting less than 10 per cent of the population of Los Angeles, in 1960, for example, black persons made up 40 per cent of the unemployed.

Among poor people in the West, Mexican-Americans (native U.S. and Mexican born) were also prominent. At least 2 million lived in the West (1960). California had more than 1 million, from 10 to 15 per cent of its populace; another 500,000 resided in Arizona, New Mexico, and Colorado; and more than 800,000 could be found in Texas, where they also encountered the strongest prejudice. A minority in California, in Texas, and more in New Mexico traced their ancestry back to the Spanish and Mexican periods; a larger number were relatively recent immigrants from the Mexican peasantry, and hence without much formal education or training. Indeed, American farmers had consistently encouraged the importation of *braceros*, the "strong armed ones." At the behest of large California agriculturists, in 1942 Congress had authorized an agreement with Mexico under which the United States Department of Agriculture assumed responsibility for recruiting, contracting, and housing temporary farm workers. Thinking the United States Department of Agriculture too favorably oriented toward the growers, President Harry S Truman transferred the bracero program to the Department of Labor in 1948 to supervise the importation of approximately 500,000 wetbacks annually, a program greatly resented by most American workers. In 1951 Congress authorized a revised agreement, in force until 1964. Under this agreement the Mexican government assembled workers and the Department of Labor transported them to the United States and provided reception centers. There labor contractors from the growers' associations made contracts according to standards set by the Mexican government concerning wages, hours, housing, transportation, and working conditions. In 1960, 100,000 braceros entered the country. The pressure of American unions led to the abandonment of the program by 1964. Although many of these temporary workers were assumed to have returned to Mexico once their field work during harvest seasons was completed, in fact large numbers remained in the United States, crowding into the barrios of Los Angeles and the Southwest.[2] Reflecting their background and recent experiences, many of them became farm workers, providing reliable labor for low wages. Others worked as unskilled laborers on the railroads, in restaurants, and construction work. As a group, Mexican-Americans were poor, with incomes significantly below those of white Americans. Language problems often worsened their situation, partially explaining their high drop-out rate in public schools and the less than 1 per cent attending college.

Ironically, among the western poor were some of the oldest inhabitants of the region—the American Indians. During these years the Indian population increased significantly, for the first time in more than a century. The 343,000 Indians in the West in 1950 grew to 525,000 a decade later. Most of them lived in Arizona, but Oklahoma, New Mexico, and California also held significant numbers, with others scattered in various western states. These years saw a reawakening of Indian culture and ethnic consciousness that had begun after World War I. Of all the tribes perhaps the Navajos made the greatest economic progress. They benefited from mineral royalties, from gas, oil, and uranium found on their lands, which encompassed more than 30 million acres in Arizona and New Mexico. Extensive timber on the Navajo reservation led the tribal council to construct new sawmills, including the $17 million Snowflake Pulp and Paper Mill. They also received $30 million yearly (1959) from the Bureau of Indian Affairs for the establishment of model farms, soil conservation programs, and the construction of new roads, schools, and tourist facilities.

Most other Indian tribes did not fare so well, and lived in poverty. True, the Utes in Utah and Colorado also secured royalties from oil and gas and the Klamath Indians in Oregon increased income from their lands. But the majority of Indians found it difficult to prosper in what was now the white man's land, this despite the Indian Claims Commission Act of 1946 in which Congress declared that Indians were entitled to federal payments equivalent to the original value of their lands. The settlement of claims by the Indian Claims Commission extended for more than twenty years. In 1965, for example, the California Indians voted to accept the Commission's award of $29 million—a sum that was hardly adequate to eradicate the poverty among them.[3] Meanwhile, between 1945 and 1960, fully 170,000 Indians in the West moved away from their reservations, many of them settling in towns and cities. In fact, Los Angeles became the largest Indian city in the nation, with more than 50,000, but sizable communities could also be found in Phoenix, Tucson, Albuquerque, and Denver. Sometimes the move resulted in improved economic status; more often than not, for the majority, it was an exchange of rural poverty for urban poverty, and additional problems of cultural conflict and adjustment.

It should not be assumed, however, that all the minority groups in the West were mired in poverty. As the most cosmopolitan region of the nation, the West harbored a great variety of minority groups, including more than one-half of America's Orientals. Their progress was remarkable, despite racial prejudice and persecution. During World War II the Japanese-Americans had perhaps fared worse than other minorities as a result of their internment in detention camps. Most of the more than 100,000 who began to trickle back to their erstwhile homes in 1944 found them occupied, often by black Americans who had been drawn west by war jobs. So many of the Japanese-Americans turned to build new lives. But their progress between 1945 and 1960 was as remarkable as it was unusual. In income as well as educational levels in this period they ranked higher than any other ethnic group, even exceeding national norms. And significantly, their crime rate was far below the national average. Although prime objects of suspicion in World War II, the Japanese succeed in gaining widespread social acceptance in the West, and in securing virtually full integration into American society. Congress in 1948 offered to compensate for losses suffered due to wartime detention and granted $38 million (about one-tenth of claims made) to the 44,000 Japanese-Americans who had sought compensation. And the McCarran-Walters Immigration Act of 1952 finally made Japanese eligible for naturalization, thus removing what many Japanese had long regarded as a racial slur. In that same year the California Supreme Court declared the Alien Land Act of 1915 unconstitutional, an act which had prohibited the ownership of land in California by aliens ineligible for citizenship. Few other minorities had met such strong discrimination—and had achieved such remarkable integration—in as short a period as the Japanese.

Most Chinese-Americans in the West also improved their status. In 1943 Congress had repealed the Chinese Exclusion Act of 1882, leading to the influx of several thousand Chinese immigrants yearly thereafter. Most settled in Los Angeles and in San Francisco, where the Chinese population increased by 50 per cent. Despite language difficulties many of the newcomers excelled in mathematical and scientific studies. A significant percentage of Chinese and Chinese-Americans between 1945 and 1960 entered scientific and engineering careers in which they were markedly successful.[4] Their assimilation and integration into American society was greater than at any previous era in western history.

Like Americans in general, many minorities discovered the economic opportunity in the West that had lured them there in the first place.

Western Life-Styles

Primarily, the postwar immigration contributed to the growth of metropolitan areas, of cities ringed with suburbs. These suburban communities were unlike the small towns and cities in the West before World War I. They lacked vital downtown areas, but consisted instead of dispersed residential areas interspersed with clusters of shopping centers. Los Angeles first developed this pattern soon after 1920, but in the fifteen years after 1945 it spread rapidly throughout the West. Soon after World War II many of these suburbs were beginning to be connnected by a grid of freeways—limited access highways that bypassed settled communities and speeded traffic. But the enormous growth of traffic, congestion, and pollution created by this increasingly ubiquitous pattern brought problems of such enormous dimensions that by 1960 urban planners began to experiment anew with various alternate ways of living, from urban core clusters to retirement villages. They knew that westerners had greater mobility than people elsewhere, and that their high per capita ownership of automobiles made them sympathetic to experimentation with new life-styles.

Suburbs

Indeed, the proliferation of suburban communities with scattered residential areas and clusters of shopping centers became one of the outstanding characteristics of western social development between 1945 and 1960. The residential areas of Los Angeles, San Francisco, Seattle, Denver, Phoenix, Albuquerque, El Paso, Dallas, and Houston—not to mention scores of smaller towns and cities—tended to sprawl horizontally, with a predominance of middle-class neighborhoods consisting of assorted types of individual one-family dwellings and small apartment complexes here and there. As the acquisition of the 160-acre homestead had once constituted the dream of many western settlers in the nineteenth century, now ownership of a split-level ranch house became a prime goal of their successors. Federal tax policies and procedures of the Federal Home Administration (FHA) encouraged individual home ownership rather than communal (or apartment) living. Only as land prices skyrocketed after 1950 and as desirable home sites became scarcer did the trend toward the construction of apartment buildings accelerate. Los Angeles first heralded this newly emerging pattern emphasizing group living in 1958 when the number of building permits for apartment units exceeded that for individual houses. Meanwhile, the downtown areas of older towns and cities rapidly deteriorated as their former middle-class inhabitants flocked to the suburbs to escape high taxes, congestion, and an increasing crime rate. "Downtown" became increasingly synonymous with "slums" as many of the poor newcomers were forced to seek housing there. Office buildings and areas that were populated during the day but deserted at night became typical of downtown areas.

Los Angeles was a pacesetter for the development of metropolitan areas in the West. What central downtown core there was—around Pershing Square—had become a dreary slum with a prominent Skid Row in 1945. In 1950 the city council authorized a large-scale redevelopment program for this neighborhood, to be dominated by a sprawling 260-acre civic center. By 1962 this vast area encompassed seventeen buildings, including a music center, a city hall, and a federal building. Extending in all directions from this nucleus was a motley array of suburban residential areas stretching out farther than fifty miles and loosely strung together by unsightly strips of roads. Highways began to acquire the appearance of arcades, dominated by cheap and tawdry shops and establishments catering to motorists. Here, as in many areas of the West, were hot-dog stands and hamburger joints, coffee huts, fruit stands, automobile service stations and repair shops, motels, souvenir stores, and junk yards. And in order to attract the attention of motorists in this vast jungle of ugliness the various entrepreneurs erected increasingly garish signs, billboards, blinking lights—anything that appeared sufficiently bizarre or garish to arouse attention. And everywhere there was trash, among the weeds or on the roads as motorists—like medieval householders—heaved garbage out of their windows.[5] This was the new face of the more heavily congested metropolitan areas in the West. It was repeated almost everywhere, in San Francisco, Portland, Seattle, Denver, Albuquerque, El Paso, Houston, and in thousands of smaller western towns and cities. America the Beautiful was being transformed into America the Ugly by this newest population surge.

Related to the suburbanization of the West was the construction of shopping centers to satisfy the needs of suburban dwellers. These clusters of arcades with shops, offices, plazas, and fountains were not unlike self-contained small medieval cities—although their vast blacktopped parking lots geared to the needs of a motoring public made them peculiar manifestations of the twentieth century. As we have already seen, the first successful shopping centers arose in Los Angeles during the 1920s when realtor A. W. Ross built his famous "Miracle Mile" on Wilshire Boulevard. Between 1945 and 1960 approximately 10,000 new shopping centers were constructed west of the Mississippi River. Initially, downtown merchants had opposed their development. By 1955 the trend was clear as downtown stores opened suburban branches—and eventually closed their downtown locations.

Between 1945 and 1960 an increasingly complex system of freeways came into existence to connect the new bedroom communities of the West. Indeed, an increasing proportion of western land was being paved over to become freeways, streets, or roads. Los Angeles, perhaps, was an extreme manifestation of this trend, for there, by 1960, one-third of its land area had been paved over for streets and freeways, and an additional third of its area was devoted to parking lots or automotive service facilities. Thus, at least two-thirds of the land in the Los Angeles vicinity was fully devoted to the automobile! If the proportion of land set aside for the use of cars was not so high in other western metropolitan centers, nevertheless a similar trend was becoming apparent in them during this period. The concept of freeways was first formulated in 1937 by E. E. East, chief of the Automobile Club of Southern California's Engineering Division. East realized that the new industrial metropolitan areas of the West such as Los Angeles were based on highway rather than on railroad transportation. Reliance on motor transport created a much wider dispersion of factories and warehouses than was true of older communities, which had clustered about railroad tracks. In 1945 few western cities or states as yet had freeways; but under East's prodding Los Angeles built forty-five miles over the next fifteen years. By 1960 the concept came to dominate roadbuilding everywhere in the nation.

The greatest impetus to freeway construction, however, came with large-scale federal aid. This was provided by Congress in the Federal Highway Act of 1956, which authorized the expenditure of about $15 billion of grants to the states over the next twenty years for the building of a vast national interstate highway system. During the ensuing decade virtually every western state legislature authorized development of new state highway plans and appropriated approximately an additional $6 billion for their completion. In 1957, for example, the California legislature created the first of these comprehensive freeway plans, appropriating (1959) $10 billion for a ten-year program. By 1960 Los Angeles had more than 250 miles of freeways and then the pace of construction quickened further, approximately tenfold. During this period freeways made their first appearance in sparsely populated states such as Idaho, Montana, and the Dakotas as well as in more heavily populated areas like Denver, Phoenix, or Salt Lake City. Highway commissioners began to take on awesome powers, literally moving men, women, and mountains. They redid the landscape everywhere, fashioned new political alignments, created new economic interest groups, leveled hills, and reshaped valleys—undoing the work of Nature. In the name of the public welfare they ruthlessly obliterated historic sites, buildings, and landmarks, not to mention farms and pleasant vistas. Traffic movements and their practicality, not beauty or aesthetic pleasure, became their primary objective. And in their determination to cover the countryside with Portland cement they assiduously denigrated other considerations. And so, between 1945 and 1960 freeways became the most notable public space open to the movement of people in this automotive age, just as streets and boulevards had been in an earlier era.

Already by 1960, however, many of the new problems created by the new metropolitan area–freeway complex were beginning to disturb the people who lived within it. Traffic congestion, air and water pollution, and also mental strain, depression, and alienation were only a few of the products of the new order. One of the earliest critics was Harrison Salisbury, a noted journalist with the *New York Times.* After a visit to Los Angeles in the 1950s and some harrowing experiences on its freeways Salisbury wrote, "I have seen the future and it doesn't work." Of course, freeways did work in their particular context, and Salisbury was expressing the bias of an easterner accustomed to a central city. But by encouraging an increasing volume of automobile traffic, and by further encouraging the dispersion of homes, schools, offices, and factories, freeway advocates were unwittingly providing the foundation for a serious air pollution problem. Los Angeles first experienced serious smog problems in 1950, and before the end of the decade most large western cities such as Seattle, Phoenix, Denver, and even Albuquerque, New Mexico, were forced to confront the same unwelcome issue.

It could be argued, too, that freeways tended to have a dehumanizing effect on urban and suburban dwellers. Many commuters found driving on freeways to be a sterile and solitary task, allowing little human contact, or any form of physical exercise. Driving on a freeway allowed individuals little time for relaxation, self-expression, reading, or the discovery or contemplation of nature. Drivers were *on* the land but were not *of* it. Their major responsibility was to exercise caution by keeping their eyes glued on seemingly endless white or yellow road (dividing) lines, broken occasionally by traffic signs. In this world of the motorist other drivers—or rare pedestrians—became faceless anonymous figures rather than individual human beings. And constant movement of a car on freeways sometimes fostered a sense of rootlessness in suburban commuters in suburbopolis. This type of existence—according to public relations men of the period—was the Good Life offered by the Affluent Society. But was it?

Urban Clusters and Retirement Villages

The burgeoning problems of the expanding western metropolitan areas in the West during the 1950s led urban planners to propose various alternatives to suburban commuter living. Among the most notable proposals by 1960 were designs for new urban clusters, and for the building of retirement villages for the elderly. Just as the Puritans of Massachusetts Bay in the seventeenth century had planned new townships in the wilderness, so westerners during the second half of the twentieth century were experimenting with new types of urban communities. One was the urban cluster—a self-contained city—with subdivisions embracing homes, offices, stores, and entertainment and educational facilities, each within walking distance of the other. Among the first—and in 1960 the largest—of such subdivisions was Century City in West Los Angeles, sponsored by the Aluminum Corporation of America. Designed to house 12,000 persons, the complex consisted of twenty-two apartment buildings, whose dwellers could walk to work in any of the twenty-eight office buildings that were part of the development. In addition, it included several three-level shopping centers, two hotels, and several theaters. By 1960 the concept of a self-contained community designed to avoid suburban commuting was being actively developed in California and Arizona—and watched with much interest elsewhere in the West. Similar urban complexes arose in California at Conejo Village, near Ventura, Vandenbergh Village, and at California City in the Mojave Desert. Under construction were complexes at Irvine and San Diego. During the sixties the concept led to the construction of Lake Havasu City in the wilderness of western Arizona and Cochiti Lake in New Mexico, with plans for other such settlements being readied in Colorado and Montana (by former newscaster Chet Huntley).

To serve the increasing proportion of older people in the population some urban planners began to design communities exclusively for their use. The years between 1945 and 1960 saw the construction of dozens of "retirement villages" in the West. Such developments provided special living accommodations for the elderly, often substituting ramps for stairways, offering medical facilities and health care, food services, and a variety of recreational opportunities. Usually they were designed for persons with relatively high incomes. The pattern was set in 1960 by Ross Cortese in his Rossmoor Leisure world at Seal Beach, California. Within two years he sold 6,370 cooperative apartments and created a small city of 11,000 people. Similar communities in California, with 5,000 residents or more, included Panorama City (near Hemet), and Sun City, with others planned in Scottsdale, Arizona.

Most older persons were unable to afford life in these "villages," however, and some of them went to live in trailer parks or villages. This trend, first

An urban oasis in the twentieth century: Intersection in Phoenix, Arizona, in 1907 and in 1960. Source: *Arizona Highways*.

Changing Arizona highways in the twentieth century: 1910, 1920s, and 1960s. Source: *Arizona Highways*.

significant in the West in 1960, was to take on the dimensions of a boom in the ensuing decade. Before World War II most Americans considered trailer parks to be a temporary abode for drifters, or migrant workers. During World War II, however, auto trailer parks became a vital form of temporary housing for thousands of war workers in the West. And from 1945 to 1960 the travel trailer, and its more luxurious successor, the mobile home, became home for 3 million Americans in the West. By 1960 mobile houses often measured as much as 10 x 50 feet with comfortable and even luxurious interiors and appliances. It was estimated that in 1960 the western states had more than 30,000 special trailer parks—unique communities often featuring paved streets and landscaping with mores and rules all of their own. California alone had 16,000 such trailer parks in 1960. At the same time, the inhabitants of these trailers formed dozens ·of new social groups and organizations that reflected their special interests. These associations provided them with a sense of identity, companionship, and community. One of the best known of these groups was composed of owners of Airstream trailers who organized caravans each year that visited various interesting sites in the United States, Mexico, and Canada.

The entire conglomeration of settlements that developed in the West between 1945 and 1960 created the foundations of megalopolis. In its simplest form, megalopolis is a string of continuous metropolitan areas. Although not a utopia, a megalopolis was likely to be an autopia, based on thousands of miles of freeways. California was the first western state to develop a megalopolis, stretching from San Diego in the south to Sacramento in the north. In 1960 planners were predicting that thirty years later more than 90 per cent of the state's estimated 40 million people would be living in this new form of urban community. If Los Angeles was the prototype of the future, of the new urban order, other western cities in 1960 were just beginning to be conscious of this new form of growth. Planners in Portland, Oregon, for example, envisaged a megalopolis in their region by about the year 2000, from Olympia, Washington, across the Columbia River to Portland, and down through the Willamette Valley to Salem and Eugene in Oregon. Urban planners were speaking of similar complexes in Seattle, Denver, Phoenix-Tucson, and elsewhere. Historically, the West had been the weathervane of impending change in twentieth-century America, and so still seemed to be.

The Barbeque Culture

In this complex of communities westerners developed life-styles between 1945 and 1960 that set patterns often imitated by Americans elsewhere. The new suburban life-style one contemporary sociologist dubbed the "barbeque culture." This particular form of sybaritic life was first developed in the West, and became symbolic of the good life in the affluent society. Among its characteristics was a great measure of mobility, much emphasis on leisure and leisure-time activites, on outdoor life, and also a general air of informality.

Mobility was one of the pronounced characteristics of westerners. Even after they arrived in the West, the new immigrants kept on the move, not unlike their predecessors in earlier eras. They were not likely to be tied down as much to land or houses as easterners, but felt freer to roam, usually in their automobiles, in search of new opportunities, or for new pleasures. In 1960, for example, two of three Californians were no longer residing in the same house in which they had lived five years before. In northern California, one of three persons changed his or her residence annually; in southern California it was one out of two. To be sure, in other areas of the West (especially in the Pacific Northwest) these ratios were not so high, but they did tend to be higher than in the East. In New York City only one out of twelve individuals changed his or her residence annually; in Chicago, one of ten. Moreover, tallies of transcontinental air travelers in the fifties revealed that twice as many westerners were passengers on the Los Angeles–Chicago route as easterners. And the number of passports for foreign travel issued to residents of the Pacific Coast in these years was about 50 per cent above the national average. It was no accident that the American propensity for light and portable goods was born in the West. Here, people on the move were developing items as diverse as portable buildings, radios and television sets, paperback books, portable barbeques, and plastic movable flowers. U-Rent trailers and U-Rents for virtually anything were originally western phenomena as well—the product of a mobile people.

An emphasis on leisure living was developed most fully in the West during these years. This casual, easy manner—not for the few, but for the many— became characteristic for the middle classes. It included ownership of a ranch house with picture windows, perhaps with a backyard swimming pool, and with an indoor-outdoor patio allowing year-round outdoor activities. Close by was the garage housing usually more than one car for various members of the family. And frequently the automobiles were in use, carry- ing their occupants to some outdoor activity. In California surfing became distinctive. In Oregon and Washington boating and fishing were popular with hundreds of thousands of workers; hunting and mountain climbing were favorites in the Rocky Mountain areas, as was skiing. And almost every- where in the West virtual year-round golf under the clear western sky was possible. For many the scenic extravaganzas and magnificent landscapes of the West provided a soothing balm, an escape from crowding for a harassed generation of urban and suburban dwellers. Ironically, in their frenzied pursuit of leisure, many westerners re-created the very problems

An urban oasis on the Plains in the 1950s, Minot, North Dakota. Source: North Dakota State Soil Conservation Committee.

they were seeking to escape—crowding, pollution, and desecration of the landscape. But in the 1950s ranch houses, cars, and leisure were but some of the symbols of the new affluent society. Of course, this was true of Americans in various sections of the United States, but in the West the attainment of these material benefits seemed closer to realization for the average wage earner than anywhere else. If westerners seemed crassly materialistic, they were only peculiarly representative of a contemporary national mood.

Informality became another keynote of the western life-style. Not that this western characteristic was new—only its particular manifestations. Outwardly it was expressed by wearing sports or leisure clothes. Sport shirts for men and slacks for women were first accepted in the West, years before they were considered appropriate elsewhere in the nation. And by 1955, blue jeans or Levis, long worn by blue-collar workers in the West, were widely adopted, not by the poor, but by the sons and daughters of the affluent middle class. Jeans became the most ubiquitous western garment—and swept the nation in the sixties. This development was not without its paradox. Just as the remote West of the cowboy was on the verge of disappearing, the new generation of suburban westerners adopted a romanticized version of his outfit, including western shirts and bandanas, cowboy boots, belts, and bolo ties. Informality in the dress of westerners was also a reflection of their manners, which tended to be open and friendly, more so than in many other sections of the country. After 1960 western life-styles were widely imitated throughout the United States—and indeed the world—as young people as far away as Japan, or western and eastern Europe, developed a craze for going "western."

And so western society between 1945 and 1960 remained a weathervane of American society. In the wake of another large influx of population westerners built new metropolitan areas that bore within them the seeds of megalopolises in the future. Their patterns of settlement were largely determined by the automobile—as they had been by the railroads a hundred years before—for this was a major instrument for the conquest of time and space. It helped to create the suburb—tied together by a growing net of freeways—merging into vast metropolitan areas that spread to become megalopolis. And the mobility fostered by many of these communities created informal life-styles that were reflected in leisure and outdoor activities and a general air of informality. These characteristics were widely admired by millions of Americans east of the Mississippi River eager to imitate the Good Life first pioneered by westerners, and appeared like the beacon of America to many foreigners. The way of the West in the 1950s was to become more common in the rest of the United States during the succeeding generation.

The Eco-Technostructure in the West, 1945–1960

Of course, a sybaritic life-style for the many was possible only in a society characterized by economic affluence. And between 1945 and 1960 the West experienced another burst of economic growth, the product of a chain reaction. It began with the receipt of more than $150 billion of federal expenditures and contracts, largely for national security purposes. This was the era of the Cold War with Russia, and of "Hot" wars, as in Korea (1950-1953).[6] Such vast sums facilitated the creation of vast new scientific and technological centers in the West, with special emphasis on the aerospace and electronics industries. The stimulus that these new glamour industries gave to the existing economy—and the new markets they created—was felt throughout the entire West. Millions of new jobs were created, and the total income of the region more than doubled during the period.

If western market areas expanded so extensively during this period it was in large measure because of vast improvements in transportation that made the region a more integrated economic unit. The significance of the automobile for western growth between 1945 and 1960 was hardly less significant than railroads had been in the nineteenth century. It was not surprising that in these years the per capita ownership of automobiles was higher in the western states than in any other section of the nation. This was true of every state west of the hundredth meridian. The high mark of car ownership was in Los Angeles County, which had more automobiles than any of 43 states in the Union! California alone counted 8 million motor vehicles in 1960; the other states in the trans-Mississippi West had more than 16 million. Consequently, this period saw a frenzied road, highway, and freeway building boom. In California, the Collier-Burns Act of 1947 gave birth to a $3 billion freeway system which by 1960 was already being vastly extended. Even sparsely populated states such as Idaho or North Dakota built more roads between 1945 and 1960 than in any comparable period up till then. By 1960 California had about 200,000 miles of roads—about one-fifth of the mileage in the West. This effort by the state legislatures was greatly encouraged by the federal Highway Act of 1956 which, we have already seen, provided more than $15 billion for the interstate highway system.

The enormous expansion of air transportation between 1945 and 1960 also did much to integrate the western economy. Private air carriers such as United Air Lines, Trans-World Airlines, American, Continental, and Western, as well as scores of smaller companies, encouraged by federal tax laws, invested heavily in new aircraft and equipment. They established extensive, frequent transcontinental air service as well as thousands of new local routes. Much of this expansion was aided by the construction of new airports in virtually every western town or city, effectively ending their erstwhile isolation. Although localities contributed sums for this construction, the major burden was borne by the federal government. Thus, as in the nineteenth century, the federal government assumed a large share of the responsibility for the development of "internal improvements" in the West. And such improvements were a necessary prelude to further economic growth.

Let us briefly examine some other reasons for this growth. The enormous outlay by the federal government was a crucial factor, for at least one-half of all federal expenditures for aerospace development were made in the West. This stimulus was most pronounced in California but affected virtually every other state in the area as well, including Alaska and Hawaii. The West was the recipient of such contracts because during World War II it had developed into a major aircraft manufacturing center, and still provided some of the best testing sites for new aerospace and scientific devices anywhere in the nation. During the war the West had attracted notable scientific talent, and this in turn provided a magnet for attracting others in the postwar years who contributed to the creation of one of the most sophisticated scientific-technological complexes anywhere in the world. The U.S. Census revealed that the number of scientists, engineers, and technicians in the trans-Mississippi West tripled between 1945 and 1960, when it exceeded 400,000. Many of these persons were attracted by unusual economic and scientific opportunities and also by the favorable western climate and ways of living. Meanwhile, this large influx of population resulted in the creation of vastly expanded western markets for a wide variety of goods, providing a strong stimulus for the economy as it emerged from World War II.

The new aerospace industries that grew in the West during these years—supplanting aircraft manufactures—became the most spectacular sector of the economy. Unlike industries of previous years, they were not dependent on raw materials, location, pivotal market areas, or even availability of electric power. The vast open spaces of the West—especially mountains, which minimized the noise of missiles—beckoned the aerospace manufacturers more than other regions. And the beautiful scenery of the West made its economic opportunities even more attractive and drew many scientists and engineers from elsewhere. Moreover, by 1945 the West had cities that could provide adequate educational training and a labor force that was attractive to many new or expanding companies. The combination of such advantages made the West the space age center of America.

California secured the lion's share of the new aerospace industries. It garnered 40 per cent of all federal aerospace research and development contracts in the United States and more than two-thirds of all those awarded west of the Mississippi River. At least one out of ten working Californians was directly dependent on defense contracts for his job. By 1960 the federal government was disbursing at least 24 per cent of *all* of its defense expenditures in California. By then, one-third of all missile workers in the country were in California, more than 1 million. The bulk of the aerospace complex was centered in the south, in San Diego and the Los Angeles vicinity and in the north on the San Francisco Peninsula, a one-hundred mile strip between San Francisco and San Jose.

These years saw California's transition from a leading aircraft manufacturer to a research and development complex for missiles and space vehicles. Among the giant corporations that wrought that change were North American Aviation, which produced the B-70 bomber and the X-15 supersonic plane. By 1955 it was also making guidance and control systems for Boeing's Minuteman Missile. Its Rocketyne Division was fabricating Hound Dog air to surface missiles, Tiros weather satellites, and engines for spacecraft. Douglas Aircraft developed the Thor Able booster rocket, the Nike-Zeus, and the Skybolt ballistic missile for the U.S. Navy, and the Midas Intercontinental Ballistic Missile (ICBM). Hughes Aircraft built a multitude of missiles, including the Falcon. The smaller Convair Corporation in San Diego manufactured the Atlas ICBM in the 1950s. Important research was conducted at the U.S. Air Force's Space Technology Laboratory at Inglewood, not far from the Jet Propulsion Laboratory at the

Seattle plant of Boeing Aircraft Corporation in the 1950s. Source: Boeing Aircraft Corporation.

California Institute of Technology at Pasadena.[7] No wonder that southern California was sometimes called a "federal city." Seventy-eight per cent of San Diego's manufactures were related to national defense, as was fully one-half of all manufacturing in the Los Angeles vicinity.[7] To be sure, other western cities, especially Seattle, Salt Lake City, Denver, Phoenix, Tucson, and Albuquerque, secured a significant share of income from federal defense expenditures—more than 25 per cent—but not quite to the extent of Los Angeles.

Elsewhere in the West the aerospace industries were also significant. The giant facilities of the Boeing Company in Seattle and other Washington cities produced the B-52 bomber and Minuteman missiles. In 1957 the Martin Company chose the Denver area (Littleton) as the new production site for the Titan missile. In Utah the Thiokor Chemical Corporation in 1956 constructed a new plant near Brigham City for the manufacture of solid fuel for the Minuteman missile. At Ogden the Marquardt Aircraft Company opened a plant to make Bomarc Missiles, not far from another Boeing plant that assembled Minuteman missiles. In Arizona both the Goodyear Aircraft Company at Litchfield and Hughes Aircraft at Tucson sparked a remarkable business growth in the state while an electronics firm—Motorola—became the largest single employer in Phoenix. Neighboring New Mexico secured the Bell Telephone–operated Sandia Corporation, under contract with the Atomic Energy Commission, a missile research and manufacturing facility employing more than 10,000 persons.

A Western space age industry: Assembly Division of the Boeing Aircraft factory in Seattle during the 1950s. Source: Boeing Aircraft Corporation.

Federal expenditures were not only funneled through private enterprise, however, but were also pumped into the western economy directly through military bases and installations. Increasing American interest and involvement in Pacific and Far Eastern affairs made western military bases and supply depots more crucial than ever. Almost without exception, the areas of greatest population growth in the West of this period were close to military sites. Some of them were military bases, such as the giant Vandenbergh Air Force Base in California. Others were scientific facilities such as the Atomic Energy Commission's nuclear reactor test station and plutonium plant near Idaho Falls, Idaho. Colorado's economy—as well as its tourist trade—was significantly bolstered by the construction of the Air Force Academy in Colorado Springs, built at a cost of more than $250 million during the 1950s. Nearby the U.S. Army Corps of Engineers blasted one of the world's most expensive tunnels ($66 million) into a mountain to serve as the combat operations headquarters for the North American Air Defense Cmnd, which was completed in 1965. Proportionately, defense installations in Utah made a greater economic contribution to Utah's total income

Missile testing at White Sands, New Mexico, proving grounds in 1950s. Source: U.S. Air Force.

than in any other state. Utah's geographic position in the center of the West, and between Canada and Mexico, made it ideal as a base for supply depots such as the huge facility at Ogden. And Hill Air Force Base was the largest single employer in the state, engaging between 12,000 and 20,000 persons during these years.

This pattern was repeated in most others western states during the 1950s. Congressman Lee Metcalf of Montana noted at the time that his state's economy was kept going primarily through the federal expenditure of several hundred millions of dollars. The Minuteman Missile Complex in central Montana and the great Malmstrom Air Force Base at Great Falls were but two of the installations without which, Metcalf felt, the state would have stagnated. This was true of New Mexico as well, where the Atomic Energy Commission spent one-sixth of its total annual budget between 1945 and 1960. The Los Alamos Scientific Laboratory in 1960 represented a government investment in excess of $350 million. And the Alamogordo and White Sands rocket and missile testing and proving grounds were additional beneficiaries of federal largesse.

Large-scale federal expenditures also flowed into the West through grants for natural resource and transportation development. These exceeded $500 million annually for the western states, or about $35 billion for the period from 1945 to 1950. Some of these went into expansion of facilities at Hoover Dam, which supplied the increasing power needs of Los Angeles and the Southwest. California did suffer a setback over water allocation of the Colorado River in 1960 when a Water Master appointed by the U.S. Supreme Court awarded Arizona a larger share of the river's flow than it had been receiving, and denied California's claims. In fact, the continuing controversy over allocation of Colorado River waters had led presidents from Truman to Kennedy to seek a treaty with Canada to control the Colorado River's flow at its point of origin. Perhaps the U.S. Supreme Court's decision in 1960 gave the negotiations urgency, for in 1961 a Canadian-American treaty was signed and ratified. Meanwhile, Congress poured large sums into the Bonneville Power Administration and the Grand Coulee project in the Pacific Northwest. By 1960 these facilities were supplying one-half of all power consumed in the Pacific Northwest, and even produced a surplus. Throughout the 1960s the Department of the Interior as well as western states themselves were negotiating about various plans to transmit the surplus power from the Pacific Northwest into other regions of the West where it was needed. The most acute demands were in growing California. Consequently, the pace of construction for the Central Valley project was accelerated during these years. With congressional appropriations the Trinity River Dam was begun in 1955, and the Feather River project two years later. Within California many groups feared that the project would benefit mainly the large corporate farmers and consumers in the state. Thus, by 1960 Congress provided a 160-acre limitation on purchases of irrigated lands in the Central Valley project. The newly elected governor in 1958, Pat Brown, hoped that this would remove some of the objections to the project, the implementation of which he made a major goal of his administration. In 1960 he achieved his goal when the California legislature approved a $1.75 billion state bond issue for completion of the elaborate network of dams designed to transfer the ample waters of the north to the parched southern sections of the state. The congressional contribution to the project was expected to be upward of $10 billion. The Central Valley project represented one of the largest as well as most significant investments in the development of western water and power resources ever made. And when these were added to the expenditure of more than $10 billion for highway improvement and new airports, the crucial role of federal investment to the western economy is starkly evident.

Burgeoning Economic Growth

The impact of such huge federal spending stimulated the entire western economy, but other factors also spurred the advance. The West continued to

U.S. Air Force Academy cadets marching in front of interfaith chapel. Source: U.S. Air Force Academy.

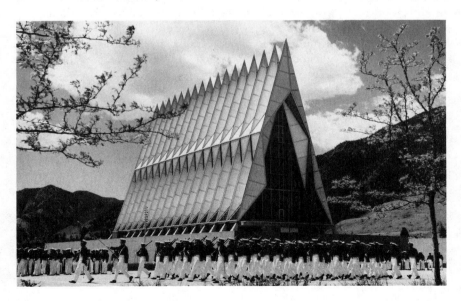

Western cotton fields: harvesting cotton in California in the 1960s. Source: University of California, Agricultural Publications.

be one of the nation's major producers of raw materials. It was an important purveyor of agricultural produce and cattle and the prime producer of minerals. But most of these activities were dramatically affected by technological change and by mechanization, which tended to stimulate large-scale rather than small-scale enterprises, whether in farming, stock breeding, mining, or lumbering.

California between 1945 and 1960 continued to be the West's—and the nation's—leading farm state. A large producer of at least 300 agricultural commodities, it was a leading producer also of 41. It supplied fully one-fourth of all the table foods consumed in the United States, and more than one-third of all fruits and vegetables. The total value of California's farm products in 1960 was more than $3 billion—equalling the glamorous aerospace industries. But this sum did not include the value of canning, processing, or related industries, which boosted the total value above $12 billion. Despite the glamour of the space-age industries, the most important sector of California's economy was still farming.

California's farmers achieved record production levels largely because of their continued emphasis on mechanization of their operations. If cotton became a major crop in the Imperial and San Joaquin valleys between 1945 and 1960, it was largely because of sophisticated new methods of irrigation and large-scale use of mechanical cotton pickers. Inventors perfected lettuce-picking machines with feelers to determine ripeness, and built-in memory devices, programmed to select only certain heads. Other machines to pick asparagus, tomatoes, grapes, and melons were in the process of development. Meanwhile, scientists in the laboratories developed new crop strains so as to make them more adaptable to mechanical pickers.[8] Yet in this period some of the harvesting was still being performed by stoop-labor, by as many as 200,000 migratory field workers. In 1962 many of these were first effectively organized in the National Farmworkers' Association, headed by the charismatic Cesar Chavez. One result of this unionization was to hasten pressures making for farm mechanization.

In the Pacific Northwest farming and lumbering also continued to provide a major source of income for the region, even if manufacturing income rose above World War II levels. Wheat and fruit were still major products. As in California, the average size of farms increased, reflecting the influence of mechanization and specialization. Although lumbering was still a dominant industry of the Pacific Northwest, the amount of timber cut in Oregon and Washington between 1945 and 1960 was only one-half of what it had been in 1930. The competition of new construction materials was one factor in this decline, which led to a stubstantial decrease of employment opportunities in the lumber regions. Expansion in the paper and pulp industry was insufficient to take up all the existing slack.

Wherever there was water, western farmers prospered. In the Rocky Mountain area farmers on Colorado's irrigated lands were securing some of the most profitable vegetable crop yields in the nation.[9] The owners of Arizona's large-scale irrigated farms were among the wealthiest agriculturists in the United States. In these years Arizona became one of the nation's largest cotton growers as its big California-style corporate farms produced a fine quality of long-staple cotton. Arizona farmers had one of the highest average net farm incomes in the United States. During these years cattle growers on the Plains enjoyed considerable prosperity as increasing meat consumption in the affluent society raised price levels for beef and cattle, stimulated also by pressing world needs in the decade after World War II. As in farming, the size of the average ranch increased during these years as large-scale cattle operations became more common.

Mechanized agriculture on the Plains: Grain harvest in the Red River Valley during the 1950s. Source: North Dakota Soil Conservation Committee.

The West continued to be America's main mineral producer. But mining was not a particularly profitable venture for any but the largest producers during these years, and production of few minerals, except for petroleum, increased. One of the major changes in the industry between 1945 and 1960 was the shift from underground to vast open-pit or strip mining operations, characterized by a high degree of mechanization. The copper mining industry was one of the first to be so automated, especially in Arizona and Utah, leading producers in the nation. In thousands of mining tunnels of Montana—such as those at Butte—a strange silence prevailed, for soon after the Second World War they became the newest—and largely invisible—ghost towns of the twentieth-century West.

Even in the atomic era, however, mining booms in the West were not unknown. One of the most dramatic—if shortlived—was the Uranium Rush of '49, or more properly, between 1945 and 1952. After 1946 the Atomic Energy Commission became a prime purchaser of uranium and stimulated hundreds of prospectors to search for the ore. Few found much of value until one day, in 1948, a New Mexico Pueblo Indian named Sanchez found some yellow rock near Grants, New Mexico. This stimulated active development, mostly by large companies, in the Grants area for the next four years. Meanwhile, an unshaven prospector named Charlie Steen made a lucrative uranium find near the small Mormon farming community of Moab in the remote southeastern portion of Utah. The Mia Vida mine that was developed there had a value of more than $150 million and set off another rush of prospectors. After 1952 the uranium rush subsided as the Atomic Energy Commission decreased its purchases of the mineral.

The most valuable mineral resource of the West was petroleum. In this period the production of California and Oklahoma declined as Texas and Louisiana became the major producers. At the same time, the large integrated oil companies made major discoveries in Alaska, which came to supply an increasing percentage of petroleum, particularly for California and the West. A significant trend in western oil production was the enormous increase of off-shore oil drilling, in the Gulf of Mexico as well as off the California coast. Although off-shore drilling had been begun by some California operators in the World War I era, exploitation of the tidelands did not become extensive until after 1945 when new technology made such operations profitable.

Such development also precipitated a clash between the coastal states and the federal government for nearly a decade after 1945 over ownership of the tidelands. Under international law federal jurisdiction extended three miles offshore. But both California and Texas claimed that their jurisdiction extended ten miles out to sea. As early as 1941 California had leased some of its tidelands to private companies and was intent on receiving lucrative revenues from such leases. But at President Truman's behest the U.S.

Attorney General sued California in 1945 for damages and challenged the state's claim to ownership. Two years later the United States Supreme Court upheld the federal government's contentions. Thereupon, the representatives of the oil producing states embarked on an extensive lobbying campaign in Congress to secure legislation that would confer ownership on them. The Republican party was sympathetic to their pleas, and in the presidential campaign of 1952 Dwight Eisenhower pledged himself to seek necessary legislation. The result was the Submerged Lands Act of 1953, which ceded federal claims to the tidelands within the three-mile limit to the states and allowed them to make further claims. Between 1953 and 1961 California extended its jurisdiction as far as thirty miles off shore and in 1961 the United States Supreme Court awarded Texas tidelands twelve miles into the ocean. Thus, some of the western states benefited extensively from the profitable oil leases that they awarded to thousands of off-shore drillers. The western frontier had moved out into the ocean!

At the same time westerners discovered that they possessed another—and hitherto little utilized—valuable energy resource—natural gas. Before World War II the consumption of natural gas—a by-product of petroleum—had been insignificant. But between 1945 and 1960 demand boomed as never before. Production rose from 4 trillion cubic feet in 1945 to more than 12 trillion cubic feet in 1960, as natural gas became a major form of energy for urban dwellers in the West and the Middle West. By 1960 the natural gas industry had become one of the largest in the West, and fifth largest in the nation. Major sources were Texas, Louisiana, New Mexico, and Kansas. But appreciable amounts were also produced in California, Wyoming, Colorado, and Oklahoma.

Raw materials, then, were still a major component of the western economy. Crops, cattle, and minerals continued to be symbolic of western wealth between 1945 and 1960 as they had been in earlier years. But the West was no longer as dependent on its earthly riches as it had once been. Its growing maturity was increasingly reflected in the diversification of its economy.

Manufacturing and Service Industries

That diversification was greatly stimulated, of course, by the further growth of manufacturing. In this period the value of western manufacturing income—exclusive of the aerospace industries—*more than tripled.* The production and value of hundreds of different lines of manufactures rose considerably. This development was most marked in California—and also in Texas. In the Pacific Northwest, the Rockies, and the Southwest (except

Arizona) manufacturing activity grew only slowly, and very little on the Plains, despite action by the Interstate Commerce Commission in 1947 to lessen the impact of discriminatory freight rates on the western states.

Although the West made progress in the development of its manufacturing potential, it still had not caught up with the older eastern states. Of the 200 largest corporations in the United States between 1945 and 1960, no more than 10 per cent had their headquarters west of the Mississippi River. Located in San Francisco were Standard Oil of California, Crown-Zellerbach Paper, California Packing, and Foremost Dairies. In Los Angeles were Lockheed Aircraft, North American Aviation, Douglas Aircraft, Litton Industries, Hunt Foods, and Union Oil. Elsewhere in the West such large companies were few and far between. Boeing was in Seattle, Weyerhaeuser in Tacoma, Washington, and Georgia-Pacific was in Portland, Oregon. And then there was the peripatetic western entrepreneur, Howard Hughes, whose industrial empire was worth more than $1 billion, encompassing Hughes Aircraft of California; companies manufacturing armaments, missiles, space vehicles, and petroleum; and other firms engaging in recreation and real estate in California, Arizona, Texas, and elsewhere in the West.

As in earlier years, California continued to be the leading manufacturing state in the West. It accounted for a little more than one-half of all manufacturing west of the Mississippi River. Most western steel production was centered at the Kaiser Steel works in Fontana, the only integrated producer in the West. There, Edgar Kaiser, Henry J.'s son, continued his father's policies of aggressive industrial expansion. In 1962 Kaiser Steel made the crucial decision to cut its prices to levels of eastern companies to best their competition; it had more than tripled its output since 1945. From the new twenty-eight-story Kaiser Center beside Lake Merritt in downtown Oakland, California, Edgar Kaiser supervised sixty affiliated companies engaged in aluminum and concrete production, gypsum mining, construction, and for a time, even the manufacture of automobiles and jeeps, with operations in more than a dozen western states.

Perhaps the most remarkable manufacturing center of the West was Los Angeles. By 1950 it had surpassed San Francisco in the value of its manufactures and had become the third largest manufacturing city in the United States, outdistancing Detroit, Cleveland, Pittsburgh, Philadelphia and ranking behind only New York and Chicago. Between 1950 and 1960 its manufacturing employment grew at ten times the national rate, and by 1960 it had also become the second most important retail market area in the United States. In certain newer industries, such as synthetics and lightweight plastics, it became preeminent. It was the home of Mattel Industries—America's largest toy manufacturer—and was the sports fashion center of the United States. Indeed, the garment industry, with more than 50,000 employees in 1960, grossed more than $700 million. Catalina

Swimwear and Cole of California made Los Angeles the bathing suit capital of the world, supplemented by Jantzen factories in Oregon. And women's clothing brands such as Ardee of California, Marusia Originals, and DeDe Johnson (inventor of the pedal pusher) gave Los Angeles and California a national reputation as a major style center.

Other areas of the West witnessed only a slow growth of manufacturing. The Pacific Northwest attra ted some of the new electronics manufacturers. The state of Oregon built an industrial park on the Columbia River to attract new manufacturers, but its hopes were not fulfilled. Manufacturing in Washington was on a modest scale. Dow Chemical built a new plant on the Columbia River, near the Oregon line, and Kaiser Industries erected a gypsum factory near Seattle, while leasing two government surplus aluminum plants near Spokane. But the assumption of many northwesterners that cheap power would attract large-scale industry to the area was not realized during these years.

In the Rockies and the Southwest, manufacturing continued on a small scale. An exception was the manufacturing complex around Denver, Colorado, which grew impressively. The steel manufacturing facilities built by the federal government at Provo, Utah, during World War II were gradually expanded by the United States Steel Company, which in 1945 had bought them for less than one-fifth of their cost. Beginning about 1950, however, industry in Texas began a growth that was only slightly less impressive than that of California.

If the West by 1960 had not yet fully developed its manufacturing potential, it did make more rapid strides than the older East in the expansion of its service industries.[10] Reflecting a national trend, each year between 1945 and 1960, service industries in the West came to provide a larger proportion of income as well as employment. One of these important service industries was banking, where the Gianninnis continued to influence the financial growth of the region profoundly. Their philosophy of a bank as a money store for small depositors was distinctly western and was widely imitated during this period. Between 1945 and 1960 the Bank of America expanded to more than 800 branches. Its total assets exceeded $12 billion by 1960, making it the largest bank in the world. Its impact on other western bankers was reflected in the development of branch banking in most of the states west of the Mississippi River in the two decades after 1945.

But of the various service industries, perhaps tourism was most exclusively associated with the West. The emergence of affluence in America between 1945 and 1960 provided a strong impetus for western tourism. This tourism was on a massive scale, involving the millions of affluent Americans who had not only more money, but more leisure, who wanted to fish, hunt, hike, ski, and swim, or perhaps just view the beauties of nature, seeking an escape from the pressures and tensions of big-city life.

More than ever, in these years, the West served as America's playground. As automobile ownership increased, tourist traffic in the West reached an unprecedented volume. In 1945 approximately 5 to 7 million tourists had visited the West; in 1950, 20 million; and in 1960, 50 million. Some of this traffic beat a bath to national parks and monuments, which were rapidly developed and expanded by the National Park Service. Already, by 1960 automobile traffic had become so dense at Yosemite, Yellowstone, the Grand Canyon, and Mesa Verde that the Park Service at times had to restrict the number of visitors.

But perhaps the most extraordinary manifestation of tourism in the West was the startling rise of Las Vegas, Nevada, as the entertainment center of America. Until 1945 Las Vegas had been nothing but a small, little-known railroad town. Founded in 1905 by the San Pedro, Los Angeles and Salt Lake Railroad, it grew very little until 1931, when it became a supply center for the nearby Hoover Dam construction project. During the next 14 years its population was rarely more than 10,000. Near the end of the war, however, a group of enterprising promoters bought up land in the area with the hope of making it into a convention center that could rival Reno. They reasoned that with the expected increase of automobile traffic the geographical location of Las Vegas was unique—situated at the hub of a wheel whose spokes extended to Los Angeles, San Diego, San Francisco, Denver, Salt Lake City, Phoenix, and Tucson. The desert could become a playground for these cities' urban multitudes. Perhaps they could not foresee the great expansion of air travel between 1945 and 1960, but it extended the spokes of the geographical wheel and added to the success of their venture. And so, in 1945, they embarked on the construction of the Strip—the main thoroughfare of Las Vegas—which contained large and luxurious hotels, bars, restaurants, a myriad of entertainment facilities, and specialty stores catering to tourists. The special attraction, of course, was the casinos, which sprang up everywhere, for ever since 1931 gambling had been legal in Nevada. By 1960 over 300 casinos were operating in Las Vegas and their annual profits exceeded $200 million. Throughout the fifties promoters were building some of the largest luxury hotels in America and indeed, in the world—hotels such as the Sands, Caesar's Palace, and the Flamingo. Between 300,000 and 500,000 convention delegates yearly came to Las Vegas in the fifties, where they spent more than $650 million. The number of other annual tourist visitors exceeded 2 million and their expenditures, $2 billion.

Las Vegas' population increased tenfold during these years. In 1960 the census takers counted 130,000 residents. By that time Las Vegas had largely outdistanced its rival, Reno. Las Vegas, an oasis in the desert, appeared to provide an outlet for the inhibitions of Americans. It glamorized gambling, provided a gloss for commercialized sex in various forms, and left very little to the imagination. For better or for worse, in the middle of the twentieth century it provided standards for accommodations, food, and entertainment which much of the rest of America sought to emulate. Americans liked Sodom and Gomorrah in their midst, as long as it was not located in their own home towns.

The economic significance of tourism for the West cannot be over-emphasized. Next to federal expenditures, those of tourists were most essential for the region. Thus, westerners built more than 15,000 new motels and hotels during this period, at a cost of more than $8 billion, hundreds of thousands of new restaurants, and an elaborate network of automobile service facilities that provided income and employment for more than 1 million westerners. Tourism was important even in diversified states such as California, but it was crucial in less-developed states like Arizona, New Mexico, Colorado, Wyoming, and Montana, where it constituted a major source of income.

Between 1945 and 1960, thus, the western economy was greatly diversified. The major influence in the acceleration of the region's rate of economic growth was obviously the infusion of federal monies, totalling more than $150 billion. This influx of capital boosted the rate of growth three to four times as much if it had not been expended, and had a trigger effect in creating millions of new jobs. To be sure, by 1960 the West was still a major producer of raw materials—but it was also becoming an increasingly important manufacturer. Thus, the net result of large scale government expenditures during this period—in conjunction with the efforts of private enterprise—was to leave the western economy more diversified than it had been at any previous time. This diversification was reflected in various spheres of western life, and was especially noticeable in the realm of politics.

Politics in the West, 1945–1960

Whether the West as a region constituted a distinct regional entity in American politics between 1945 and 1960 was highly questionable.[11] Unlike the nineteenth century, when western sectionalism had been a distinct and potent force in Congress and in national political life, in the twentieth century such regionalism was rarely expressed. The interests of a sparsely settled agricultural community were relatively homogeneous, as Frederick Jackson Turner aptly discerned, and could be molded into a clearly formulated political consensus by able leaders. But in the twentieth century the diversity of western life was increasing so rapidly that it tended to obliterate clear-cut regional political issues. And the constant stream of new settlers only blurred political affiliations further. To a considerable extent, the decline of political sectionalism in the West during the twentieth century may also have reflected the nationalization of American politics. As the major parties became more highly centralized after 1890, they exercized increasing control over their rank and file. Thus, party loyalty and party affiliation sometimes came to replace local loyalites in determining the votes of western legislators.

But, of course, western regionalism in politics was not completely dead during these years. The one common cause to which virtually all western politicians subscribed, irrespective of political party or affiliation, was increased federal aid for accelerated economic development. In the years between 1945 and 1960 this meant federal funds for defense purposes, for transportation development, and for the development of natural resources—water, power, land, and forests. This strong desire for greater economic diversification also permeated state politics in the West. If western governors and state legislators showed an even greater penchant for balanced state budgets than their eastern brethren, this was not really surprising in view of the underdeveloped economies of most western states. Since their political leaders were simply seeking to attract outside capital to their particular states, they hoped to offer financial solvency as one incentive to prospective private investors.

Western politics during this period thus reflected three characteristics. In the first place, it was characterized by increasing diversity, reflecting the multitudinous growth of the region in the previous decades and the continued high rate of population growth. But no simple generalizations can accurately designate western political life at this time. Diversity not only resulted from the flux of shifting populations, but also from the prevalence of primaries in the West, which often tended to blur party lines and party responsibility. In view of this flux, and in the absence of rigid party lines, the role of personality was perhaps more important in the West than in other regions of the nation. The well-publicized western penchant for independence and for individualism probably furthered the cult of personality.

National Politics

It was obvious that the vastly increased population of the West between 1945 and 1965 would result in increased political power and representation. Moreover, two new western states entered the Union during these years, Alaska in 1958 and Hawaii in 1959, giving the West greater strength in the United States Senate. There the West was stronger than in the House, although the West was the only region to secure increased representation in the House between 1945 and 1965. The forty-three House seats held by eleven western states in 1940 had increased to sixty-nine in 1960, not enough to give western states a preponderant voice in Congress, but reflecting a decided shift in power. Although three westerners, Key Pittman, William H. King, and Carl Hayden, had been president *pro tem* of the Senate, no westerner served as Speaker of the House from 1945 to 1960. Nevertheless, westerners became increasingly visible in national congressional politics during these years. The Republican Minority Whip in the U.S. Senate was Thomas Kuchel of California. Wayne Morse, the Neubergers, and Mark Hatfield from Oregon were in newspaper headlines frequently, and Barry Goldwater from Arizona was well on the way to assuming titular leadership of conservative Republicans. The majority leaders of the Senate Democrats were authentic westerners, namely, Lyndon Johnson of Texas during the fifties, and Mike Mansfield from Montana during the sixties and early seventies.

In the executive branch of the federal government westerners also became more numerous. Eisenhower, Lyndon Johnson, and Richard Nixon had all been born and bred west of the Mississippi River and never gave up their loyalties to the region. To be sure, westerners were not too well represented in cabinet posts. Harry Truman appointed Charles Brannan (Agriculture), Oscar Chapman (Interior), Clinton P. Anderson (Agriculture) and Lewis Schwellenbach (Labor). Eisenhower chose Douglas McKay (Interior) and Ezra Benson (Agriculture). Kennedy chose Edmund Day (Post Office), Johnson, and Stewart Udall (Interior). Westerners fared better at the subcabinet level in executive departments. In 1940 western states counted 1

Western politicians: U.S. Senator Carl Hayden, Arizona's senior statesman, with Vice President Lyndon B. Johnson, in 1962. Source: *Arizona Highways.*

undersecretary, 3 assistant secretaries, 4 commission chairmen, and 14 commissioners. In 1960 they had 2 undersecretaries, 6 assistant secretaries, 7 chairmen of commissions, and still 14 commissioners.

Within the major national parties a similar trend could be observed. The Republican convention of 1960 revealed a decided western touch. The nomination of Richard Nixon for the presidency was made by Mark Hatfield of Oregon. Barry Goldwater became chairman of the Republican Senate Campaign Committee. By 1960 he was also becoming a leading potential presidential candidate. And the vice-chairman of the Republican National Committee was Jerry Jones of Utah. Among the Democrats at their 1960 national convention Senator Frank Church of Idaho gave the keynote address. Lyndon Johnson was nominated as the party's vice-presidential candidate and Senator Henry Jackson of Washington became the chairman of the Democratic National Committee. Even more striking was the growth of western influence on the Senate Democratic Policy Committee in 1959, at which time five of the nine men in the group were from western states.

On many national issues during this period, westerners did not vote according to regional patterns as much as along party lines. Various westerners attempted to organize the region's representatives during these years, usually with scant success. Thus, in 1947 Senator Pat McCarran (Nevada) formed a "Conference of Western Senators," a bipartisan group, that in succeeding years became largely moribund. Then, in 1959 a group of western senators formed a conference, headed by Senator Murray of Montana. This group met on four occasions during 1959 to discuss water problems, but gathered only sporadically thereafter. The Republican party formed a similar group in 1965, which also met only intermittently. But the looseness of regional alignment was perhaps well expressed by Senator Thomas Kuchel in 1968 when he said that: "During my more than fifteen years in the Senate there has been no bloc effort I can recall to exert political strength on behalf of western states in the direction of influencing distribution of federal monetary aid. I have cooperated on occasions with California colleages, of course. . . . Similarly, I have joined Senate colleagues from other western states from time to time in pressing legislation we felt was of major significance to the area, such as in regard to water problems, maritime matters, other nature resources development or activity, and the like."[12]

Only on economic development issues, therefore, did westerners stand together. In the vote on the St. Lawrence Seaway Project in 1954, which opened up possibilities of increased western commerce, only seven senators from the West were in opposition. Similar unanimity could be discerned in the vote on the Mineral Stockpiling Program of 1955. All westerners, with one exception, voted for increased federal purchases of a variety of minerals. And the Malone Amendment of 1955 to the Mutual Security Authorization

Act, which eliminated presidential authority to use this agency's funds to purchase strategic raw materials in foreign countries, received all but 2 western Senate votes. In 1956 more than three-fourths of western senators voted for the Natural Gas Act in the hope that it would benefit producers. Roll-call analysis also revealed that when Senator Bennett of Utah offered an amendment to the Defense Production Act of 1956, proclaiming the desirability of industrial dispersal in the development of defense industries, he secured almost unanimous support from western representatives with the exception, quite understandably, of those from the Pacific Coast. And when the Airport Construction Bill came up in 1959, providing for large-scale federal funding for constructing new airports, westerners voted almost as a unit for its passage. This was also true of the Silver Purchase Act repeal of 1963, for which easterners had striven for almost a decade. As the increased demand for silver led to an increase of its price, easterners sought to end the program of federal purchases, a move opposed virtually unanimously by senators from western states. This act also reduced the silver content of half-dollar coins from 90 per cent to 40 per cent, further limiting the market of silver producers in the West. But perhaps the issue that most united western politicians was—as might be expected—water. Analysis of the *Congressional Record* between 1945 and 1965 reveals that in the House as well as in the Senate westerners talked more about water than about any other subject and cast more votes in unison in regard to water issues than on any other subject.

So diverse had western interests become that they found increasingly fewer common bonds, bonds strong enough to provide the basis of long-range regional alliances. But what they did share was remoteness, rugged terrain, and of course lack of water. Historically the western states had always been unable to cope with these problems without some federal aid, and the years between 1945 and 1960 were no exception. Although the West was a land of great natural riches, capital was required for their development. As in the past, since the early nineteenth century, private investment often was insufficient, or unwilling. So the one major political goal upon which most westerners could agree was the desirability of large-scale federal investment to develop transportation, industry, and natural resources.

Moreover, the federal government served the important function of equalizing opportunity for the West as a region. In effect, it redistributed regional income. Some of the profits secured by easterners from the exploitation of western natural resources were taxed away by the federal government through its levies on manufacturers and corporations. In 1958, in eight of eleven western states, federal expenditures were greater than the taxes collected. The three exceptions were Nevada, Idaho, and Oregon. Western states secured a significant proportion of federal expenditures for highways, reclamation, public education, and public assistance. In 1960 the federal government had more than half a million employees in the West, owned more than 50 per cent of the lands in most western states, and spent more than $6 billion there annually, not to speak of $7 billion in defense contracts awarded west of the Mississippi.

Politics in the Western States

In the western states during these years politics revealed much of that same diversity that was so apparent on the national level. Such diversity came not only from shifting populations—whether increasing or declining—but also from the predominance of primaries in the West. Of thirteen western states, eight used the closed primary and five, the open primary. Washington had a blanket primary in which voters were not required to identify their party affiliation. The effect of these primaries was to blur party lines and to encourage the cult of personality in state politics.

Virtually any western state could be used to illustrate these trends, but California provided a prime example. Although since 1936 the majority of voters there had registered as Democrats, they elected a majority of Republican legislatures and officials between 1942 and 1958. The increase of Democratic power came in part from the influx of thousands of southerners after 1940 who brought their Democratic party preferences with them. California's cross-filing system encouraged the reelection of Republican incumbents, however. A candidate's political affiliation did not appear on ballots. Many of the newcomers, somewhat bewildered in their new home, thus voted for incumbent officials, with the result that between 1945 and 1958 more than three-fourths of the incumbent state officials were reelected in California. Such blurring of party lines encouraged a peculiar brand of personal blandness in politicians, who wooed voters from both parties. One of the office holders best suited for this unique kind of politics was Earl Warren, chosen for a second gubernatorial term in 1946 after capturing both the Republican and Democratic nominations. He retained his popularity by taking a moderate stance on most issues and won a third term in 1950. Two years earlier he won national prominence as the vice-presidential candidate of the Republicans. A similar cloak of blandness helped his successor in 1954, Goodwin Knight. As party responsibility became weaker in California lobbies for special interests increased their influence in the state legislature. The most important lobbyist in the state between 1937 and 1953 was Arthur Samish, who was ultimately convicted of federal income tax evasion.

Warren also initiated a trend in American politics in 1942 by hiring Campaigns, Inc., a new public-relations firm that specialized in applying the techniques of advertising agencies to political campaigns. Headed by Clem Whitaker and Leone Baxter (later husband and wife), the firm specialized in political image building through the use of the mass media and the "slick" new technology of mass communications. In a state like California—with a multitude of new and not very well-informed voters, and a weak party structure—this kind of image building and mass manipulation was extraordinarily effective. It presaged a pattern that was to affect much of the rest of the nation after 1950, as California once again became the pacesetter for new trends.

One of the most heated issues in postwar California as well as along the rest of the Pacific Coast and in some other western states was the Communist issue. Popular feeling was reflected in young Richard Nixon's campaign for a House seat in southern California in 1946 when he bested Jerry Voorhis with charges of being "soft" on Communism. Four years later he used the same techniques to triumph over Helen Gahagan Douglas for a seat in the U.S. Senate. Meanwhile, the California legislature encouraged the work of its "Un-American Activities Committee," first established in 1941 and headed by Jack Tenney. This committee embarked on a number of well-publicized hearings that critics dubbed witchhunts because Tenney accused various individuals of Communist sympathies without producing much evidence for his charges. Then, in 1949, Tenney introduced legislation to give the legislature power to ensure the loyalty of employees with the University of California. The comptroller of the university, James H. Corley, made an agreement with Tenney whereby he would withdraw his proposal while the Regents of the University would require the staff to take a special loyalty oath in which they had to swear that they were not and had not been members of the Communist party. Thus began the notorious loyalty-oath controversy in California. Many among the faculty rebelled, not so much because they opposed an oath, but because members of the university staff alone were being singled out for suspicion and were being implicitly accused of disloyalty. The Regents insisted on the implementation of the oath, and amid much controversy dismissed thirty-two professors in 1950 who refused to sign it. Only in 1952 was the issue settled when the legislature adopted such an oath for all state employees, not only those of the University. Meanwhile, in 1952 the California Supreme Court in *Tolman* v. *Underhill* ordered the reinstatement of the ousted professors. During this same period a similar controversy was rocking the University of Washington, where the Canwell Committee, a legislative committee investigating un-American activities, was also intent on unearthing Communists on campus, although it found very few.[13]

In fact, the pattern of state politics was similar in the entire Pacific Northwest. In the state of Washington Arthur Langlie was reelected as governor in 1948 and 1952 largely because, like Earl Warren, he made his major appeal to the independent voters. And the blanket primary used in the state, which allowed voters to participate without divulging their party affiliations, led to the same blurring of party lines that cross filing did in California. The primary system in Washington also favored incumbents. From 1914 to 1960 only four incumbents for U.S. Senate seats were defeated, and in 101 House contests between 1932 and 1962 only eight incumbents lost! Blandness was also the key to Governor Robert Smylie's success in Idaho, where he maintained himself in office from 1954 to 1966. His affable personality united divergent factions in that geographically divided state. As for Oregon, the resurgence of independence was characterized in the highly personal campaigns of Wayne Morse, Richard Neuberger, and Mark Hatfield.

In the Southwest, Arizona politics reflected the increasing social diversity of the state by the same increasingly even match of the major parties, the blurring of party lines, and the emphasis on personalities. The result was often moderation, in fact if not in theory. In the Arizona legislature, the terms "Republican" or "Democrat" were rarely heard. Freedom from party control was endemic in the midst of an unprecedented era of population growth. Many of the new younger settlers were Republicans, unlike the original Arizona settlers who, as southerners, had been loyal Democrats. Large numbers of the migrant Republicans early registered as Democrats so that they might wield some influence in the primaries. Thus the 6 to 1 ratio of Democrats to Republicans was transformed into a 2 to 1 ratio by 1960. Yet the white-collar workers tended to be individualists and to vote for personal choices rather than according to party affiliation. Republicans like U.S. Senator Barry Goldwater (1952), Governor Paul Fannin (1958 and 1960), and Congressman John Rhodes (1954) won office with large state-wide majorities. Arizona voters admired Goldwater for his outspokenness and independence. Whether they took him seriously in his talk about the need for state independence from federal subsidies is doubtful. In 1960 one-half of the expenditures of the Arizona state legislature were devoted to supplementing federal programs for highways, education, and social welfare. And residents of the state could well indulge in talk against "federal interference" because their venerable senior Senator, Carl Hayden, was chairman of the powerful Senate Appropriations Committee. There, as he had for half a century, unobtrusively he made sure of directing a large flow of federal funds to his state. As in other western states, moderation was the keynote of state policies in Arizona as a great variety of state programs became increasingly dependent on federal funds.

Thus, the growth of population and the diversification of the western economy decidedly affected the nature of the region's politics. Western influence in national politics increased—reflecting the significant increase of new population. Yet, westerners were less conscious of strong, unified interests than they had been in earlier years. Most likely, this western trend was presaging a nationwide trend of the 1970s and 1980s.

Culture in the West

Greater economic opportunities in the West brought not only more people but a more selective populace with a diversity of cultural backgrounds and talents. Especially significant was the large intellectual migration from the East, composed of scientists (including twelve Nobel laureates), researchers, university professors, executives, and a wide array of skilled workers, artists, and other talented persons in their prime. In many cases these people had been accustomed to higher cultural standards than those they found on their arrival in the West between 1945 and 1960. Soon after arriving at their new homes many of them set about energetically to enrich the cultural life of the communities in which they settled. In fact, often they found the opportunity to experiment—to try out something new—exhilarating and exciting. Howard Chandler of the Los Angeles *Times* noted that at the time many of those who came after 1945 were people of superior caliber, and thought about cultural horizons which might make western cities great. They wrought a cultural explosion in this period when western cultural life ceased to be merely derivative—a pale reflection of the East—but instead became a pacesetter for the nation.

Of course, the levels of achievement in various fields varied. Literary accomplishments during this period were not distinguished, but respectable. The stage, however, flourished more, perhaps, than at any other time in the twentieth century. Musical activities achieved a new sophistication. And in architectural innovation westerners distinguished themselves and were widely copied elsewhere. Artistic endeavors flourished as never before as Los Angeles, second only to New York, became the major art center of the nation. During this period, also, the West became the home of a substantial number of America's most eminent scientists and of major scientific installations. At the same time, the West pioneered in various educational innovations, such as community colleges, which were widely imitated throughout the United States. Western cultural life thus transcended the regionalism that had been its hallmark in the two decades before World War II and came to be characterized by exciting experimentation and innovation.

Literature and Drama

The literary scene in the West became increasingly cosmopolitan, although the regional tradition was still strong. Writers of such worldwide renown as Thomas Mann, Aldous Huxley, and Christopher Isherwood continued to make Los Angeles their home, although millions of their less-talented fellow citizens they were *on* the land, rather than *of* it. At the same time, a group of younger writers and critics were making their reputations during these years. One of the best known was Eugene Burdick, the author of several immensely successful novels that became national best sellers. These included *The Ninth Wave* (1956); with William J. Lederer, *The Ugly American;* and with Harvey Wheeler, *Fail Safe* (1962). All of these books were effective satires of contemporary American foreign and domestic policies. Burdick's insights were possibly deepened by his professional training as a political scientist, although few of his students at the University of California in Berkeley, where he taught, were always aware of his double life. In contrast to earlier years, the West now also came to harbor distinguished literary critics of national stature. In California Mark Schorer—with the University of California—not only wrote novels and short stories himself, but in *Society and the Self in the Novel* (1956) made it clear that westerners were not necessarily Philistines. His biography of Sinclair Lewis (1961) was a masterpiece. Meanwhile, the eminent critic and writer Joseph Wood Krutch settled in Tucson, Arizona, in 1950, a vantage point where he found it possible to commune with nature and to criticize the materialistic urban society that was becoming so characteristic of America.

Other well-known western literary figures continued to develop the regional tradition established in earlier years. In California Wallace Stegner, who also taught at Stanford University, was one of the most productive. Some of his perceptive short stories were collected in *The Women on the Wall* (1950). His *The Preacher and the Slave* (1950) dealt with the Mormons and Mormonism in the West. His western orientation was also revealed in *Beyond the Hundredth Meridian: John Wesley Powell and the Second Opening of the West* (1954). Also read widely was Dale Van Every, a former Hollywood script writer who became a fine historical novelist and popular historian of the old West. His novels such as *Bridal Journey* (1950), *The Captive Witch* (1951), and *Trembling Waters* (1953) captured the spirit of eighteenth- and nineteenth-century western settlers in superb fashion. During the 1960s he completed in four volumes one of the finest popular histories of western settlement before 1848 ever written. Another author with a wide audience was David Lavender. *The Big Divide* (1948) dealt with the Rockies in the romantic vein that so appealed to readers in all parts of the country. *Bent's Fort* (1954), *One Man's West* (1956), about Colorado, and *Land of Giants: The Drive to the Pacific Northwest, 1750–1950* (1958) continued the romantic popularization that found a seemingly unlimited audience.

But the spirit of freedom and innovation was restless in the West, and in California, during these years, found an outlet in the writings of the Beat generation. The North Beach section of San Francisco became the headquarters of these Holy Barbarians who drew youths from all parts of the nation eager to experiment with new life-styles. Rejecting the prevailing materialism and affluence so predominant in the contemporary United States, instead they opted for ways of living that would be beatific—hence they became known as Beats or Beatniks. Sometimes they indulged in use of drugs such as marijuana, or practiced free love, or homosexuality. Their heroes on the streets of North Beach during the Fifties were such characters as the Reverend Bob, Dr. Fric-Frac, or Mad Marie, who as likely as not might be found in such Beat hangouts as the Co-Existence Bagel Shop or the Bread and Wine Mission.

On a more intellectual level, the leading writers of the Beat movement sought to turn it into a serious critique of materialism in the United States, and its crass neglect of human values. Allen Ginsburg became the poet of the Beat generation, and one of its most loquacious spokesmen. Some critics considered him to be a minor Walt Whitman while others thought him to be primarily a clown. His work during these years perhaps mirrored the movement itself—a mixture of talent and superficiality. One of the most prolific writers among the Beats was Jack Kerouac, who wrote at least seven books during the 1950s through which he acquainted Americans with the major suppositions of the Beats. These included *On the Road* (1957), *The Subterraneans* (1958), *Mexico City Blues* (1959), and *Doctor Sax* (1959). Many literary critics questioned his talent—and that of Gregory Corso, another Beat writer—but they provided the movement with publicity. Meanwhile, in Sausalito the poet Lawrence Ferlinghetti operated the City Lights Bookstore which carried the largest collection of "Beat" literature in the world, including little magazines, pamphlets, erotica, homosexual literature, and the like.[14] In retrospect, the Beat literary contribution was less distinguished than it appeared at the time, generating more heat than fire.

In the Pacific Northwest writers tended to follow more closely in the regional tradition. The "Puget Sound" school included Stewart Holbrook, who turned out well written narratives by the dozen, including *Burning an Empire: The Story of American Forest Fires* (1943), *The Promised Land: A Collection of Northwestern Writing* (1945), *The Rocky Mountain Revolution* (1956; about mineworkers' unions), *Yankee Loggers* (1961), and *The Wonderful West* (1963). Murray Morgan was not so prolific, although a more careful writer. His *Bridge to Russia–Those Amazing Aleutians* (1947), *The Dam* (1954), and *Century 21: The Story of the Seattle World's Fair* (1963) were well received. Among the more talented novelists was Nard Jones, whose *Still to the West* (1946) was often cited as a fine example of northwestern fiction of these years.

The New Mexico literary colony was perhaps not so distinguished between 1945 and 1960 as it had been after World War I. Yet it continued as a literary oasis in the desert West. One of its best-known figures was Paul Horgan, an extremely versatile and imaginative craftsman. He justified his early promise in a variety of novels such as *The Devil in the Desert* (1952), *Give Me Possession* (1957), *A Distant Trumpet* (1960), *Things as They Are* (1964), and *Memories of the Future: A Novel* (1966). His interest in the

Southwest as a region did not abate, however. His two-volume work, *Great River: The Rio Grande in American History* (1954), won him a Pulitzer Prize in history that year. He also wrote *The Centuries of Santa Fe* (1956), and *Conquistadores in American History* (1963). Another New Mexico writer who used the region as a basis for his work and who was well-known nationally was Frank Waters. His books on *The Colorado* (1946), *Masked Gods: Navajo and Pueblo Ceremonialism* (1950), *The Earp Brothers of Tombstone* (1960), *Book of the Hopi* (1963), and a novel, *The Woman at Otowi Crossing* (1966) acquainted nonwesterners with some of the ancient as well as modern charms of the Southwest. Among the most creative of the New Mexico group during these years was Winfield T. Scott, poet, novelist, and story writer. His *Mr. Whittier and Other Poems* (1948) and *Collected Poems* (1962) won wide acclaim. *Exiles and Fabrications* (1961), *Change of Weather* (1964), and *A Dirty Hand: The Literary Notebooks of Winfield T. Scott* (1969) revealed his imaginative efforts and mastery of language. Notable literati of the Santa Fe colony also included Ruth Laughlin Alexander, *The Wind Leaves No Shadow* (1948), and Peggy Pond Church, *The House at Otowi Bridge* (1960).

Other areas of the West were by no means literary deserts. One of the most gifted novelists in the trans-Mississippi West was A. B. Guthrie, who made his home in Montana. Certainly he was able, better than most twentieth-century novelists, to capture and portay the moods and feelings of the West as these sprung from the impact of the environment on the human beings who settled there. *The Big Sky* (1947), *The Way West* (1949), *These Thousand Hills* (1956), and *The Big It, and Other Stories* (1960), captured the vastness of the West and the exhilarating feelings of freedom that it engendered. This same theme was explored in somewhat different fashion by Irving Stone, prolific author of biographical novels, in *Men to Match My Myths: The Opening of the Far West, 1840–1900* (1956).

The increasing cultural maturation of the West in this period was also revealed in a lively expansion of theatrical activities. The West became the scene for some of the most creative and most interesting experimentation in American drama. In California, the UCLA theater group under John Houseman was experimenting in play writing, acting, and producing. Some of its graduates carried out their ideas in the more than forty active theaters that functioned in the Los Angeles area during the 1950s, more than at any other time in the twentieth century. Other western cities did not have as many such groups, but in contrast to the 1930s, most western towns and cities now had at least one respectable community theater, and in addition, several experimental theaters, little theaters, and theaters in the round. The quality of western stagecraft rose appreciably as well. Manifestations of the increased sophistication of theater in the West was reflected in the distinguished annual Shakespeare Festival in San Diego, which critics ranked as among the best in the country. Equally famous was the yearly Shakespeare Festival in Ashland, Oregon, which gained worldwide renown.

Art and Architecture

The spirit of excitement, creativity, and willingness to experiment that ran through western drama in this period was also apparent in the world of art. The greater freedom that the West still offered to younger artists led to an outburst of activity. Most western towns and cities established new art galleries between 1945 and 1960, undertook new and innovative art acquisitions, and hired some of the ablest young art talent in the nation. Western art galleries and museums no longer exhibited pale reflections of traditionalism; they pioneered with the introduction of new artists and new forms of expression, especially in Los Angeles, Seattle, Denver, and Phoenix. In part this was because of the increasing economic wealth of the West, which produced new art patrons—men like Norton Simon of Hunt Foods in California, who actively supported museums as well as artists. By 1960 the extraordinary influx of new artistic and critical art talent into California had made Los Angeles the second leading art center of the United States and one of the great art centers of the world. Here were the most notable art galleries and auctions, the most reputable critics, appraisers, and experts—the tastemakers who set standards for the West and for the nation. The varied tapestry of artists, connoisseurs, patrons, galleries, technical experts, dealers, and entrepreneurs was primarily a post–World War II phenomenon and gave the West a worldwide image of sophistication and creativity. As Henry Dreyfus, a Los Angeles industrial designer, noted at the time: "New York is knowledgable in the realm of *know-how,* and California has a zestful climate of *why-not?*"[15] Subtly and imperceptibly, the West created an atmosphere more sympathetic and receptive to artistic innovation. Moreover, new patrons, galleries, and museums meant that the market for art was expanding.

This creative surge was reflected in interesting experimentation by some western painters. In San Francisco some of those in the post-Impressionist vein included Richard Van Diebenkorn and E. Bishop, who also moved into abstractionist work. Nathan Oliveira founded a new art dimension in the 1950s, the New Figurative style, which attracted various disciples. In Los Angeles James Strombotne was one of the most distinctive Abstractionists in the West and Rico Lebrun's experimentation with abstract painting aroused much comment. Santa Barbara became something of a center for photographers during this period, largely because of the presence of two of the most innovative camera artists in America, Ansel Adams and Josef Muench.

Other portions of the West participated in the wave of increased artistic activity. Seattle in 1952 established a Municipal Art Commission to encourage the creation of new work and the wider display of existing holdings. During these years the Seattle Art Museum built one of the best collections in the West. Some of the sustained interest resulted from the presence of a small colony of nationally known painters. Mark Tobey, one of the great figures in American Abstractionism, made his home in Seattle. The curator of the Seattle Art Museum between 1935 and 1953 was Kenneth Callahan, not only an able museum administrator, but a talented artist in his own right, who won many prizes for his experimentation in modernistic styles. Another nationally known abstractionist in the region was Morris C. Graves, who exhibited extensively in the Seattle Art Museum until 1956 when he went to live in Ireland.

The art community of New Mexico was perhaps not so well known as it had been in the 1920s, but Santa Fe and Taos continued to attract large numbers of young artists. Clearly the most eminent painter in New Mexico was Georgia O'Keeffe, who by mid-century had received recognition as one of the most imaginative and sensitive painters in the United States. She made her home in Abiquiu, New Mexico, inspired, as she noted, by the grandeur of the landscape and the brilliance of the colors around her. Many of the New Mexicans further developed the regional tradition—artists such as Peter Hurd (in Roswell), a student and son-in-law of Newell Converse Wyeth; Theodore Van Soelen (who also wrote stories for hunting magazines); and Randall Davey, one of Robert Henri's pupils. A widely known western painter (though not a New Mexican) was Thomas Hart Benton, who captured the western mood on many of his canvases and who was also known for his extensive murals depicting the settlement of the West—such as his work at the Harry S Truman Library in Independence, Missouri.

Not only art, but architecture benefited from the surge of creative energy in the west between 1945 and 1960. The innovations of western architects—men like Richard Neutra, Pietro Belluschi, William W. Wurster, Eldridge T. Spencer, Ronald R. Campbell, Donn Emmons, Welton D. Becket, William L Pereira—were widely imitated throughout the United States. The ranch house style, as already mentioned, was one of the most distinctive western architectural innovations to find wide acceptance in other regions of the country. When it is remembered that American architecture during the first half of the twentieth century was highly eclectic rather than original, the distinction of the western architectural contribution can be better appreciated. Western architects also developed unique garden apartment complexes that created new standards for similar projects elsewhere. In addition, unlike the older regions of the United States, the West provided a laboratory for architectural experimentation. Creative pioneers such as Neutra, Craig Ellwood, A. Quincy Jones, Fred Emmons, Edward Killingsworth, and Wayne R. Williams used new materials as well as new designs. They experimented with arc-welded steel skeletons, exposed steel or concrete, aluminum frames and beams, glass walls, picture windows, sliding partitions, fluid room arrangements, and split levels. Above all, their work revealed unfettered minds willing to experiment.

Western architecture also came to serve as a bellwether to the nation for changing architectural styles. The boxlike effect of commercial buildings between 1945 and 1960, for better or worse (many think, for worse), was much experimented with in the West. In fact, Los Angeles voters, who since 1911 had limited buildings to a height of 150 feet (13 floors), ratified an amendment in 1956 to remove this restriction, leading to a new skyline for the city. In 1957 Los Angeles issued more building permits for the construction of new apartment units than for single family dwellings, heralding a trend toward more communal living that was to become nationwide during the second half of the twentieth century. California was also the home of a talented group of landscape architects, men like Thomas Church, John C. Warnecke, and Joseph Eichler, whose concepts led to a "California style" that was to be copied in many other regions of the country.

Music

The thrust toward creativeness also reached into western music. Almost every western city—and most western towns—established new symphony or community orchestras, while the larger cities did much to upgrade the quality of their existing musical organizations. The Los Angeles Philharmonic reached the stature of one of the nation's major orchestras during these years under the guidance of Alfred Wallenstein and Zubin Mehta. The greatness of the San Francisco Symphony under Pierre Monteux was unfortunately not matched by his successor in the 1950s, Enrique Jorda. In Seattle the Seattle Symphony under Milton Katims secured an elaborate new opera house and reflected increasing interest in good music throughout the Pacific Northwest by extensive concert tours into every part of the region. The Utah Symphony under Maurice Abravanel achieved a new level of distinction during this period and played to packed houses, not only in Salt Lake City but in every locality in Utah. At the same time, the Mormon Tabernacle Choir in Salt Lake City achieved a reputation as one of the best such musical organizations in the world. The Orpheus Male Choir in Phoenix, although perhaps not quite so well known, was highly regarded. In 1954 a young wealthy easterner, John Crosby, founded the Santa Fe Opera. Securing the services of the renowned composer Igor Stravinsky for his summer season, Crosby rapidly built the Santa Fe Opera into one of the major opera companies in the United States, known not only for its high quality, but especially for its imagination, innovativeness, and daring, which reflected very well indeed the western cultural spirit of this era. And in Los Angeles, Arnold Schoenberg, Igor Stravinsky, and other giants of innovation

Opera in the West: Interior of San Francisco Memorial Opera House in the 1950s. Source: San Francisco Opera Association.

in modern musical composition found a receptiveness and freedom to experiment that was not quite matched by the more stratified musical world of the East.

Education

The cultural explosion in the West could not fail to affect education in the region. One of the innovations was the development of research and development centers, or "think tanks." The Institute of Advanced Study at Princeton, New Jersey, had been operating since before World War II, but its efforts had been largely devoted to pure research. With a characteristic western bent for practicality, in the years between 1945 and 1960 the West developed think tanks alyo concerned with applied research. One of the first such institutions was the Rand Corporation (Research and Development), a non-profit research corporation founded in 1946, a brainchild of General Hap Arnold. The Douglas Aircraft Corporation offered it a temporary home in Santa Monica, California. Arnold believed that such an organization should be as far away from Washington, D.C., as possible to avoid undue influence and pressure, especially since much of Rand's early work consisted of studies for the U.S. Air Force. Other think tanks included the Center for Advanced Study in the Behavioral Sciences at Stanford, California, created

The spectacular outdoor home of the Santa Fe Opera in the 1960s. Source: Santa Fe Opera.

in 1954 under a $5 million grant from the Ford Foundation, and the Center for the Study of Democratic Institutions under Robert M. Hutchins at Santa Barbara, largely devoted to philosophy and political theory. A novel think tank founded in 1950 was the Aspen, Colorado, Institute for Humanistic Studies established by Walter Paepcke, chairman of the board of the Container Corporation of America, designed to broaden the vistas of top business executives in the nation. It also gave rise to the Aspen Music Festival and Music School, both of which acquired national reputations during the 1950s.

Meanwhile, new standards for higher education were being created in California. Throughout the 1950s California lawmakers talked much about adjusting the state's system of higher education to their newest population influx. They were sympathetic, too, toward experimenting with a system that would make a college education available for every resident of the state who was qualified and desired one. In essence, they looked toward attainment of an open admissions policy. The legislature in 1959 appointed a special commission headed by President Arthur Coons of Occidental College to prepare a specific proposal to achieve this aim. The recommendations of this group gradually took form as the California Master Plan, which the California lawmakers adopted in 1960. Representing an effort to combine quality with quantity, the Plan provided that the state university, and its branches, assume prime responsibility for research and for graduate training, and also for teaching the upper 12 per cent of the state's high school graduates. It would become a "multiversity" satisfying a variety of needs. In addition, the Plan proposed that the sixteen state colleges in 1960 concern themselves primarily with teaching, serving the upper third of California's high school graduates. As for remaining high school graduates, they would have an opportunity for further training in more than seventy local community or junior colleges, inexpensive, and conveniently located. Successful community college graduates were entitled to transfer to state colleges or to the state university after satisfying certain minimum requirements. This plan provided a pattern for higher education that was widely copied during the 1960s not only in the West, but throughout the nation. Oregon, Idaho, Nevada, New Mexico, Colorado, Montana, and Kansas adapted it to their own needs, not to mention eastern states like New York and Massachusetts and Florida. The concept of junior—or community—colleges was distinctly western in origin—and was one of the most significant innovations in higher education during the twentieth century.[16]

California's experience in public education in this period also provided certain guidelines for schools everywhere. As one of the first states to be beset by very large increases in school enrollments, California was virtually forced to pioneer with the financing of public school expansion. Immediately after World War II it became clear in California that school districts by themselves would be largely incapable of financing extensive expansion. Beginning in 1947, therefore, the California lawmakers provided state allocations for school districts. In 1949 that sum was $250 million, but over the next thirteen years the amount virtually quadrupled. Education was the largest item in the state's 1960 budget, totaling 43 per cent of all expenditures, or $1 billion. The California experience was to be repeated in virtually every western state.

Particularly in the sciences, but in other professional fields as well, western universities and research faculties were acquiring new distinction during these years. The raiding of Ivy League colleges and universities—or eastern corporations—became common. By 1960, 37 per cent of the world's Nobel Prize winners were living in California. The University of California boasted eleven, Stanford University, five, and the California Institute of Technology, three. More than one-fifth of the members of the prestigious National Academy of Sciences lived in California. That western scientists were often innovators in their fields was revealed by the fact that 28 per cent of American Nobel Prize winners had earned academic degrees in California. And a survey of Great American scientists undertaken by *Fortune* magazine in 1960 revealed that more than 40 per cent lived and worked in California.

California was not typical of the entire trans-Mississippi West. But California did represent in more extreme form a trend that was reflected in other western states. The West outside California was certainly not a scientific desert. In Boulder, Colorado, Walter O. Roberts headed the High Altitude Observatory, and the National Center for Atmospheric Research, one of the foremost research facilities of its kind in the nation, innnovating with and applying interdisciplinary pure research to atmosphereic conditions. Here too was the new main laboratory of the U.S. Bureau of Standards, which acquired Walter U. Condon, a well-known physicist, as first director. In New Mexico, the Los Alamos Laboratories of the Atomic Energy Commission continued to be one of the nation's principal nuclear energy and missile research laboratories, with supplementary facilities in Hanford, Washington; Idaho; and other Western sites. At Albuquerque, New Mexico, was the Lovelace Clinic, one of the country's foremost pioneering research institutions for high altitude medicine and studies of human life in space. Just beginning to achieve worldwide renown in various fields of medicine was Houston, where Dr. Michael DeBakey of the Baylor University School of Medicine was in the process of developing new open heart surgery techniques that revolutionized the frontiers of medical research. In Houston, too, after 1960, the National Aeronautics and Space Administration (NASA) established its major space center to supervise space exploration. In science, and other fields as well, westerners during these years were revealing imaginativeness and daring innovation, prompted in part at least by great freedom to experiment.

Popular Culture

In the realm of popular culture the West also initiated new trends in music, art, sports, and drama that became models for much of the rest of the nation. The great days of Hollywood had ended with World War II. In the years between 1945 and 1960 the number of movies made in Hollywood shrank each year. From an average of 750 annually in the 1930s it diminished to less than 300 yearly in the 1950s and the shrinkage continued in the 1960s. Box office revenues from moving pictures shrank accordingly, while antitrust suits by the U.S. Department of Justice against large movie makers further lessened the profitability of the industry. A major reason for the decline of Hollywood was the great growth of television between 1945 and 1960. Some of the people who had helped to make Hollywood a movie center shifted to this new medium. In the 1950s more national network programs originated in Los Angeles than in New York, largely because of the concentration of popular entertainment talent in Hollywood. In a way, the triumph of television over motion pictures was symbolized in 1959 by the Music Corporation of America's purchase of Universal and International Studios. The West was still a major tastemaker of popular culture in America but no longer primarily through the movies.

And so, between 1945 and 1960, a major characteristic of western culture was an enormous outpouring of energy—a cultural explosion unprecedented in the history of the region during the twentieth century. Obviously, not all of this burst of energy was positive, and energy did not always result in quality. Still, the high levels of achievement attained in many fields perhaps mark this period as a Golden Age of western culture. In art, architecture, and music, in science, technology, and some of the social sciences, and in the field of education, the contrast between western achievements in 1945 and in 1960 was astounding. No longer was the West an intellectual or cultural desert, a poor imitator of the older East. By 1960 the West had become a major oasis in the cultural life of America, perhaps the most innovative segment of American civilization—a pacesetter for the nation.

Pacesetter for the nation. That phrase aptly describes the course of western growth from 1945 to 1960 in literature, art, architecture, and education. The West had made giant leaps since 1945, and had come of age. And yet, it paid a price for the loss of its innocence. In becoming a pacesetter for the nation, it lost some of its regional distinctiveness, and became more like the older regions.

NOTES

1. Quoted in Neil Morgan, *Westward Tilt* (New York: Random House, 1961), p. 67. This is one of the few books that attempts to analyze western development in the decade after World War II.

2. The subject is discussed in greater detail by Ernesto Galarza, *Merchants of Labor: The Mexican Bracero Story* (San Jose, Cal.: McNally & Loftin, Publishers, 1966).

3. Kenneth M. Johnson, *K 344, Or the Indians of California Versus the United States* (Los Angeles: Dawson's Book Shop, 1966).

4. Instructive are Shien Woo Kung, *Chinese in American Life* (Seattle: University of Washington Press, 1962), and William Petersen, "Success Story, Japanese-American Style," *New York Times Magazine* (January 9, 1966), pp. 20 ff.

5. Richard G. Lillard, *Eden in Jeopardy* (New York: Alfred A. Knopf, 1966) provides an interesting contemporary appraisal of urban problems in Los Angeles.

6. James L. Clayton, ed., *The Economic Impact of the Cold War* (New York: Harcourt, Brace, Jovanovich, 1970), contains some essays relevant to the West.

7. H. O. Steckler, *The Structure and Performance of the Aerospace Industry* (Berkeley: University of California Institute of Business and Economic Research, 1965), deals with the more technical economic aspects of the subject.

8. The Autumn 1964 issue of *California*, published by the California State Chamber of Commerce, contains an excellent report on California agriculture.

9. Morris Garnsey, *America's New Frontier: The Rocky Mountain West* (New York: Alfred A. Knopf, 1950), focuses mainly on economic growth.

10. Data on this trend can be found in Victor Fuchs, *The Service Economy* (New York: National Bureau of Economic Research, 1968), distributed by Columbia University Press.

11. Efforts by political scientists to survey western politics are included in Frank H. Jonas, ed., *Western Politics [1940–1960]* (Salt Lake City: University of Utah Press, 1961), and, by same editor, *Politics in the American West [1960–1969]* (Salt Lake City: University of Utah Press, 1969).

12. Quoted in Frank H. Jonas, *Politics in the American West*, p. 20.

13. California politics are discussed in James Reichly, ed., *States in Crisis: Politics in Ten American States, 1950–1962* (Chapel Hill: University of North Carolina Press, 1964). Detailed on the oath controversy are Edward L. Barrett, *The Tenney Committee* (Berkeley: University of California Press, 1951), David P. Gardner, *The California Oath Controversy* (Berkeley: University of California Press, 1967), and Vern Countryman, *Un-American Activities in the State of Washington* (Ithaca: Cornell University Press, 1951).

14. Lawrence Lipton, *The Holy Barbarians* (New York: Julian Messner, Inc., 1959), provides an entertaining discussion of the Beats.

15. Quoted in Morgan, *Westward Tilt*, p. 152.

16. Merton E. Hill, comp., *The Functioning of the California Public Junior College* (Berkeley: University of California Press, 1938), and Clark Kerr, *The Uses of the University* (Cambridge: Harvard University Press, 1963), deal with these trends in education.

6

Western Problems in the 1960s: Ethnic Minorities and Environmental Imbalance

The fifteen years of rapid growth after World War II not only presented enormous opportunities for westerners but also confronted them with a variety of problems. The surge of population to the West between 1945 and 1960 gradually slackened in the ensuing decade. And although expansion continued to be much in evidence throughout the region, nevertheless these years saw increasing stocktaking, increasing concern about the future of the West and possible directions of growth. In part such introspection was fostered by a growing awareness of major problems that became a concern of Americans everywhere. Although of national scope, these issues had a regional context, whether relating to population growth or natural environment. During the 1960s two central issues that absorbed westerners were the acculturation of minority groups in their midst, and the alarming pollution of the natural environment. The West harbored a majority of Mexican-Americans in the United States, most of its Indians, and an increasing proportion of black Americans. And although in 1900 few westerners had expected the wilderness to disappear, by 1970 the bulldozing of much of the trans-Mississippi West had actually been accomplished. Problems such as air and water pollution, land subdivision, wanton destruction of animals and plants, and the disappearance of wilderness areas assumed crisis proportions. At the beginning of the century the land and resources of the West may still have appeared inexhaustible to the average American, but by 1970 his dream of securing an empty piece of land or a valuable natural resource had become more a dream than a reality.

Minority Groups

Like Americans everywhere, westerners in the 1960s became increasingly conscious of stirrings among minority groups in their midst. The largest ethnic minority were Mexican-Americans, or, as they increasingly liked to refer to themselves, La Raza, or Chicanos. More than 5 million were concentrated in California, Arizona, New Mexico, Colorado, and Texas, with others scattered throughout the West. Some of them were proud to call themselves descendants of Spanish settlers who had peopled the region for more than ten generations; others were the offspring of Mexican immigrants who came during the twentieth century, proud of their Indian blood. American Indians themselves revived strong feelings of racial pride during these years. Perhaps as many as 500,000 lived in the trans-Mississippi area, about one-half on their reservations, the remainder in towns and cities. Meanwhile, the decade of the sixties saw a continuation of the large-scale exodus of black Americans from the rural South, and an increase of the black population in the West. During the decade, approximately 900,000 made the westward trek in search of greater opportunity.

Chicanos

Chicanos, or Mexican-Americans, as we have noted, were the most numerous ethnic minority in the west.[1] They shared some of the problems faced by other minorities, yet within their own unique cultural context. And within La Raza, variations were also significant. In California, a large number of Chicanos were descended from Mexican immigrants who had come after the turn of the century. To some extent this was also true of the Southwest and of Texas. On the other hand, in New Mexico and parts of Texas, Chicanos were fifth- or sixth-generation settlers—or of even older origins—whose ancestors had moved there before the days of American ownership or occupation. Many of these were farmers. They lived on marginal lands in poverty-stricken villages and felt that United States violations of the Treaty of Guadalupe Hidalgo (1848) had deprived them of lands rightfully theirs. Although well-adjusted to life in their own particular communities they felt a keen sense of alienation from the mainstream of American life.

Economic problems of Chicanos came to the fore in the 1960s. In California, the urban poverty of Mexican-American *barrios* became an issue; in New Mexico and Texas it was rural poverty in Chicano villages. Many of the Mexicans who had migrated to the United States after 1900 came from the poorest strata of Mexican society. More than 90 per cent were landless

A Chicano student protest in the 1960s. Source: Chicano Student Newspaper.

peons. In Veracruz at the time of World War II, for example, 98.9 per cent of the population was landless. Many men and women labored for wages of less than 15 cents per hour. To such people American wages, even as low as 50 cents per hour, seemed munificent. And so they often brought their poverty, and the culture of poverty, with them when they moved into the barrios of western American cities. After their arrival they were handicapped by lack of skills, by language barriers, and by discrimination.

A Chicano movement of the 1960s: girl of the Brown Berets in Los Angeles. Source: Chicano Student Newspaper.

The U.S. Census of 1960 revealed that Chicanos were on the lowest rungs of the nation's economic ladder. Only 4.6 per cent of Chicanos were professional people (compared to 15 per cent of Anglos), and only 19 per cent were classified as white-collar workers (compared to 46.8 per cent of Anglos). Most fell into the ranks of unskilled workers. In many *barrios* of the West more than 50 per cent of Chicano men were unemployed. Thus, in 1966 the United States Department of Labor reported that although the official unemployment rate in the San Antonio, Texas, *barrios* was 8 per cent, the subemployment rate (less than full-time employment) was 47.4 per cent. Family incomes in the *barrios* averaged $2,760 annually in 1966, compared to the national average of $6,300. Hunger and disease were common. In San Antonio, a Citizen's Board of Inquiry into Hunger and Malnutrition reported in 1967 that perhaps as many as 150,000 persons in that city were undernourished, most of them Chicanos. And other evidences of urban poverty abounded in the Chicano sections of many western cities. Clusters of shacks and hovels, abandoned cars or furniture, and outhouses all bore witness to the persistence of Mexican-American poverty in the United States during the sixties.

In many portions of the Southwest Chicano poverty tended to be as much rural as urban. In the Spanish-American villages of northern New Mexico—such as San Cristobal, for example—most families had small plots, often ten acres or less. Water was scarce in these semi-arid regions, and their acreage was too small to allow much grazing by livestock. Thus, to secure pasture these farmers had long let their cattle roam, often on forest and mountain lands owned by the United States government and administered by the United States Forest Service. And already for several decades before 1960 the Forest Service had been increasing the acreage it included in National Forests. Moreover, between 1945 and 1960 in some areas the Forest Service had been drastically reducing the number of grazing permits it issued. In San Cristobal, for example, it issued 350 in 1947, but only 140 twenty years later. Some Chicano leaders felt, rightly or wrongly, that their poverty was the creation of the United States government.

But the causes of rural poverty went deeper, of course. Some families in northern New Mexico had been on public welfare for several generations and were mired in the culture of poverty and its vicious cycle. Some of the semi-arid or marginal lands they tried to till simply were not remunerative within the context of the highly mechanized agriculture characteristic of the United States. Like the Okies before them, the Chicanos were being ruthlessly displaced by technological progress.

Chicanos often felt that poverty was at the root of most of the social problems they faced in their struggle for existence. Lack of education, of skills, of pride, and a high rate of illegitimacy could often be traced to economic want. The constant stream of new migrants kept some of the *barrios* in continual turmoil. New migrants were sometimes ridiculed by older settlers, were cowed by the affluence they saw about them, by new life-styles, by fast freeways, strange clothes, and unfamiliar customs. Little wonder that they found it difficult to secure decent employment or housing in the cities they were drawn to. In the 1960s housing problems were intensified—ironically—by urban renewal programs of the federal government, which often destroyed portions of existing *barrios*. In Los Angeles, for example, in 1961 bulldozers destroyed Chavez Ravine, one of its oldest *barrios*, to make room for new freeways, parking lots, and the new Los Angeles Dodgers baseball stadium. In San Antonio during 1965 its oldest *barrio* was torn down to provide room for the Hemisfair in 1968. And in Phoenix, the new Interstate Highway 80 cut directly across the *barrios* in the southern part of the city.

Economic and social problems of Chicanos were compounded by cultural conflict. Particularly the younger generation of Mexican-Americans in the 1960s felt a keen sense of cultural clash—of a tug between American and Chicano cultures. Beginning in the 1960s the divergent values of Chicano and Anglo cultures often conflicted in the public schools. In California and Texas, especially, some teachers discouraged Chicano children from speaking Spanish, and urged them to use the English language only. Indeed, sometimes they made Chicano students feel ashamed of their background or their use of spoken Spanish. Thus, in the spring of 1968, at the Sidney Lanier High School in San Antonio, authorities paddled a student for speaking Spanish since the Texas State Penal Code (Section 288) required teachers to use English solely—custom had led this rule to be applied to students as well. Only after a series of student strikes over the incident did Chicano students win the right to use Spanish in the San Antonio public schools. The same was true in other communities. Until 1966 few western schools placed much emphasis on Mexican or Chicano culture. Without question, the clash of cultural values compounded the economic and social difficulties that many Chicanos faced in adjusting to predominant life-styles in America.

The increasing severity of these problems awakened Chicano consciousness after 1960 and paved the way for the emergence of new leaders, and new organizations. The oldest association of Spanish-speaking people in the Southwest was the League of United Latin-American Citizens (LULAC), which was founded after World War I to combat the nativism of the Ku Klux Klan. In the years before 1941 LULAC acted largely as a social organization for predominantly middle-class Mexican-Americans, who often were barred from Anglo country clubs or fraternal groups. It sponsored barbeques and picnics, innumerable teas, and special events to celebrate patriotic holidays. One of the major concerns of LULAC members during this period was to demonstrate to their Anglo-American neighbors that their patriotism rivaled, if it did not exceed, their own.

But after World War II LULAC became more of a civil rights organization, striving to secure a greater measure of equality for Chicanos. Even so, its membership declined, as it found less support among the younger generation. After 1945 it increasingly stressed racial pride, charitable and educational activities, and legal action to lessen discrimination. In the sixties, under the leadership of George Sanchez, a professor of education at the University of Texas, LULAC increasingly supported the demands of more militant Chicano groups.

Among these, the Alianza Federal, founded by Reies Tijerina, became a militant advocate of Chicano rights in the Southwest during the decade. Something of a mystic, Tijerina recalled that about 1957, God, by divine revelation, urged him to become the prophet of New Mexico's mountain villagers. A former evangelical Baptist preacher, Tijerina was born in Texas in 1927, the son of Mexican migratory field workers. He grew up with little schooling, but with an intense interest in the Bible. By World War II he had become a circuit preacher for the Assembly of God Church, a fundamentalist sect. Thus he came into contact with thousands of Mexican-American farm workers in Texas and Arizona, and ultimately in New Mexico. Tijerina soon decided that the primary means of reducing poverty among his people would be to secure them land. Driven by a mixture of motives, including mysticism, romanticism, and realism, Tijerina came to feel that the Chicanos of the Southwest were entitled to the land grants once owned by the Spanish and Mexican governments. Tijerina maintained that Chicanos had been deprived of their rightful heritage by Anglo land frauds and irregularities in the implementation of the Treaty of Guadalupe Hidalgo, and began advocating that Chicanos should demand the return of much of the land in the Southwest that was rightfully theirs.

In accordance with this objective Tijerina founded the Alianza Federal de Mercedes in a small store in New Mexico on February 2, 1962. Emphasizing the racial and ethnic nature of the struggle for land, Tijerina stressed the mingling of Spanish and Indian blood in the veins of Mexican-Americans, the native peoples of the Southwest whom he designated as La Raza—the New Breed. Like the Hebrew prophets of old, Tijerina envisioned himself as a Messiah who would lead his people from bondage to freedom—to a Promised Land.

Tijerina secured national prominence because of various Alianza activities. In October of 1966 the organization sponsored a picnic in the Carson National Forest in New Mexico—in the Echo Amphitheater, the site of the old San Joaquin del Rio de Chama land grant. There Alianza members "liberated" the forest and "arrested" two Forest Rangers for trespassing, "confiscating" their jeeps in the process. In the ensuing months Tijerina urged the small villagers of northern New Mexico—alarmed over the shrinking of their grazing lands because of expansion of the National

Forests—to assert their ancient rights. In May of 1967 the approximately 500 citizens of the hamlet of Tierra Amarilla gathered to hear one of Tijerina's fiery speeches. Proclaiming the Free State of Tierra Amarilla, they promptly voted to establish local self-government as it had functioned before 1882. To celebrate the event the Alianza sponsored a picnic in the little village of Coyote on June 2, 1967. But when Tijerina followers arrived, they were met by the New Mexico State Police, who prevented the meeting and also arrested eleven of them. They were to be arraigned in the Tierra Amarilla Courthouse on Monday morning, June 5, 1967. But then the Mayor of the Free City-State of Tierra Amarilla ordered a citizen's arrest of District-Attorney Alfonso Sanchez. In the midst of this emotional atmosphere, Tijerina was said to have driven into the village on June 5 with about twenty followers who allegedly pointed their guns at the presiding judge, the sheriff, and other officials, and captured the courthouse—the county seat of Rio Arriba County. In the fray they wounded State Policeman Nick Saiz. And Deputy Sheriff Elogio Salazar was later found murdered on a lonely mountain road. Soon the State Police arrested Tijerina and his twenty followers and charged them with kidnapping, assault with intent to kill, and with attacking the courthouse. At his trial Tijerina swore that he was not present when the shooting started, and was acquitted of these charges. Sometime later, however, on June 8, 1969, he was detained by Forest Rangers at the burning of a National Forest signpost near Coyote, New Mexico. Ultimately a jury convicted him on charges of obstructing United States Forest Service officials at the June 2, 1967, picnic. In 1969 the courts remanded Tijerina to prison where he served for two years before returning to New Mexico.[2]

In neighboring Colorado, Rodolfo "Corky" Gonzales became the most popular spokesman for Chicano rights. Born of a Mexican father in the Denver *barrio* (1931), Gonzales became a prominent professional featherweight boxer, a genuine crowd pleaser, who won 65 of 75 professional bouts during his career. In 1960 he quit the ring for other activities. He liked to write poetry, and became a general agent for the Summit Fidelity and Surety Company of Colorado. He was also active in local Democratic politics, rising to become a district captain in Denver and serving as chairman of Los Voluntarios, a Chicano political action group. A young man on the make, by 1965 he was also chairman of the board of Denver's war on poverty. But about that time he became disillusioned with the "system" and resigned his various offices in federal anti-poverty programs. Instead, he founded the Crusade for Justice, La Crusada Para la Justicia, a racially conscious Chicano community action group. In an old downtown Denver church the Crusade established a cultural center where "liberation" classes were held, Mexican arts and crafts were taught, and a Chicano library, an informal police review board, and health and social services were available.

A Chicano leader of the 1960s: Rodolfo "Corky" Gonzales of Denver. Source: Denver Public Library, Western History Department.

The center also sponsored a revolutionary theater. The purpose of the Crusade was to foster a spirit of Chicano nationalism among Mexican-Americans. Such a feeling, Gonzales held, could be channeled into improved conditions for Chicanos in the Southwest inasmuch as total social revolution was not a realistic short-range goal. His program thus encompassed demands for better housing, education, economic opportunities, land reform, and the distribution of wealth. During the Poor People's march on Washington in 1968 Gonzalez led a Chicano delegation. On Palm Sunday of 1969 he convened a national conference of Chicano *barrio* youths at his Denver headquarters attended by more than 1,500 representatives. A realist, Gonzales worked assiduously to develop a distinct Chicano cultural identity.

Other Chicano leaders were active in California. In the Los Angeles area a militant organization that called itself the Brown Berets rose after 1966. Whether its founders were influenced by the Black Power movement and the Black Panthers was often debated. But they chose Brown Berets as a symbol because of racial pride and skin color, according to one of their manifestos. Starting in 1966 as a self-defense organization against alleged police brutality in the *barrio*, some Brown Berets in these early years stressed military training and revolutionary tactics. Other members were less militant, but sought to use the group to develop a strong sense of Chicano racial pride and cultural nationalism. The Berets developed out of a Young Citizens for Community Action group in Los Angeles in 1966. One of the founders was David Sanchez, a sixteen-year-old high school student whom Los Angeles Mayor Sam Yorty's Advisory Youth Council chose as the outstanding high school student in the city during 1966. Sanchez became prime minister of the Brown Berets. They sponsored education classes, theatre performances, and music and poetry readings, all designed to develop pride in La Raza.

But perhaps the most charismatic Chicano leader in California, if not the nation, was Cesar Chavez, head of the National Farm Workers Association. Chavez was born in Yuma, Arizona, in 1926 and grew up on his father's farm. During the 1930s the family became migrant workers, ultimately settling in San Jose, California. Through much of his life Chavez' father was a union man, and his son followed in the tradition. As a youth Chavez labored in the fields, but by 1944 he met Fred Ross, a social worker. After World War II, Ross became an organizer for the Community Service Organization, a community action group formed by Chicago organizer Saul Alinsky. Ross hired Chavez as a community organizer for the CSO in various parts of California. In the decade after 1950 he dealt with a wide range of welfare problems among Chicanos. Eminently successful, by 1958 Chavez was a director of the national Community Service Organization. But two years later Chavez said that he was becoming dissatisfied with the middle-class orientation of the Community Service Organization and resigned his position. Others wondered whether his own political ambitions, and a lust for power prompted his decision. In any case, by 1962 he had organized his own group, the National Farm Workers Association, designed to unionize migratory field workers. In the ensuing decade he carefully nurtured an image of himself as a Mexican peasant with saintlike attributes, an image that provided him with considerable influence in the union—and in the nation's mass media.

Chavez was extremely effective as a leader. By 1962 he had settled in Delano, California, in the midst of great vineyards where he had worked in his youth. His wife had relatives in the town who provided Chavez and his family with room and board. During the summer of 1962 Chavez and his coworkers patiently began to sign up field workers in local labor camps. At first he had no more than several hundred followers, but by 1965 the number had risen to thousands. At that time the bracero agreement between the United States and Mexico had just expired. Thus, the time was propitious for a strike in support of higher wages. In 1965, therefore, Chavez called a strike against the large grape growers of Delano who, as expected, adamantly refused his demands.

But Chavez was adept in focusing national publicity on his struggle. Soliciting the support of national union leaders, he secured the ear of Walter Reuther, president of the powerful United Automobile Workers. At Christmas 1965, Reuther came to Delano to march down its main street in support of Chavez. In addition, he pledged $5,000 monthly from his union funds to aid Chavez. At the same time Chavez approached Robert Kennedy, who became one of the most enthusiastic supporters of his cause. When Chavez organized a national boycott against Delano grapes in early 1966 Kennedy gave the boycott national prominence through his statements. With an acute sense of drama, Chavez, in March in 1966, organized a 300-mile march from Delano to Sacramento, California's state capital, to urge legislators to support farm workers. In the spring of that year some of the large vineyard owners like Schenley, Christian Brothers, and Gallo signed contracts with the National Farm Workers although other employers still held out. Nevertheless, by this time Chavez counted more than 20,000 members in his union. Further to dramatize his struggle, and to attract the attention of the mass media, in 1968 Chavez embarked on a 25-day fast. As network television cameras eagerly covered the ordeal, Senator Kennedy flew out to Delano on the twenty-fifth day to break bread with Chavez, riveting the eyes of the entire nation on what had been, in its inception, a local strike. Meanwhile, Chavez sent union organizers to Texas and to other states. Proclaiming itself a descendant of the Mexican Revolution, the National Farm Workers Association sought to become more than a union, sought to become a spokesman for the poor, seeking bread and justice. Chavez sought a social revolution—a revamping of California's structure of large-scale farms—and a return to individual small-scale land ownership. Although Chavez did not confine his appeal to Chicanos, they constituted the bulk of his membership.

In part prompted by the various Chicano protest movements, both state and federal governments between 1965 and 1970 strove to improve the condition of Chicanos. In addition to general anti-poverty programs in the cities, they made certain special efforts. One of these—designed to strengthen communal village life in sparsely populated areas such as northern New Mexico—was the Home Education Livelihood Program (HELP) there. Sponsored by the New Mexico Council of Churches, the Ford Foundation, and the Office of Economic Opportunity, this program helped to develop more than fifty village industries and cooperatives. It provided job training for villagers and aid to small businessmen, and helped agricultural cooperatives. Its director, Alex Mercure, was convinced that many other federal anti-poverty programs that unwittingly dumped rural Chicanos in urban *barrios* were producing more harm than good.

The movement for greater economic and cultural rights for Chicanos was bound to increase their political consciousness. Until 1964, it was estimated that 95 per cent of the Chicanos in the West had voted for Democratic candidates. But thereafter, Chicanos became politically more independent. Already in 1963 a local La Raza Independent ticket appeared in the Rio Grande Valley in Texas. In that year Texas Chicanos formed PASO, Political Association of Spanish Speaking Organizations. In California they organized a Mexican-American political association. Such Chicano influence soon made itself felt. In the United States senatorial race in Texas in 1966 a significant number of Chicano voters deserted the Democratic candidate, Waggoner Carr, whom they distrusted, to support the victorious Republican, John Tower. In Arizona, Democratic gubernatorial candidate Sam Goddard was defeated, most likely by a shift of *barrio* voters whom he had angered by his views on housing. And in New Mexico Chicano villagers helped vote in Republican governor David Cargo (1966). President Lyndon B. Johnson was sensitive to this political shift and on June 9, 1967, created an Inter-Agency Committee on Mexican-American Affairs. Composed of four cabinet officials and the director of the Office of Economic Opportunity, this agency held hearings on special problems of the Mexican-American community. Many Chicano leaders criticized this group, however, and demanded more direct action. In the election of 1968 the Mexican-American Political Action group withheld support from candidates of each major party, reiterating, instead, the political independence of La Raza. One thing was sure by 1970—the allegiance of Chicano voters was no longer safe for the Democratic party, or for the Republicans either.

American Indians

Although American Indians were largely "invisible" to the majority of Americans during the first half of the twentieth century, they became an object of prime concern to Congress and the federal government during the 1960s. Partly this was because of the civil rights movement of the 1950s, which spotlighted the plight of ethnic minorities in America; partly it may have reflected increasing guilt feelings on the part of many Americans; but to a considerable extent it was also because of the reawakening of racial consciousness among Indians themselves. Moreover, the affluence of white America highlighted the poverty of red America. And the almost chronic failure of federal Indian policies before 1960 to improve the condition of a majority of Indians in the United States invited new programs or possible solutions. Not that federal Indian policies had been a complete failure, of course. Perhaps it was the slow improvement among a minority of Indians that whetted their desire for further gains. Between 1930 and 1960 the Indian population of the West increased at a rate greater than at any time since the Civil War as various health and sanitation programs cut infant mortality and lengthened the life span of adults. Such factors underlay the emergence of a vocal Indian rights movement in the sixties.[3]

If the condition of some Indians in American society was improving in the 1960s, the majority were still beset with serious problems. Poverty was obviously a central concern. The U.S. Census estimated that the annual income of the average Indian family in 1960 did not exceed $1,200, less than one-fourth of the national average, and less than that of any other minority in the United States. According to some estimates, approximately 53 per cent of adult Indians were unemployed in 1962. Of course, the Indian attitude toward work was quite different from American concepts. Many Indians preferred seasonal or part-time work simply because of their cultural heritage, and a very different value system. They did not stress materialism like Americans, and consequently their life-style did not embrace the industrial discipline and routine accepted by most people in the United States. With the end of World War II many Indians found that the new jobs that they had held during that conflict quickly disappeared. Indians who had become wage earners in cities were forced to return to reservations where only hunger and hopelessness awaited them. Symbolic of the Indian's fate was the career of Ira Hayes, the famous U.S. Marine Corps hero of World War II who had helped raise the American flag on Iwo Jima in 1945. Hailed at the time as a national hero, within two years after the war he wandered poverty stricken and forgotten on the Pima Reservation in Arizona. Weakened by alcohol, he died by drowning in a drainage ditch, putting an inglorious end to a glorious career.

Nor had federal Indian policies between 1945 and 1960 done much to improve the average Indian's lot. In the immediate period after World War II the attitude of Washington swung back to emphasize integration of Indians into American society. This was somewhat of a reversal if compared to the stance of the Bureau of Indian Affairs in the 1920s and during the New Deal, when it had emphasized cultural pluralism. But in a task force report of 1947 the Hoover Commission urged the most rapid integration policy possible, to be achieved in part by the rapid termination of many existing federal economic and social programs designed for Indians. In 1950, President Eisenhower's Commissioner of Indian Affairs, Dillon Meyer, sought to put this recommendation into effect by encouraging—or sometimes forcing—reservation Indians to emigrate to cities. Meanwhile, the Bureau inaugurated numerous training programs for Indians designed to equip them for jobs as urban dwellers. The large urban migration of more than 200,000 Indians in the ensuing decade was a consequence of this short-sighted policy, which brought misery and despair to the lives of a great majority.

In addition to their economic problems many Indians were also deeply concerned over acculturation into American society. Varied forms of discrimination hampered their adjustment, but the conflict of white and Indian cultural values was profound and created a major dilemma for all Indians, especially the younger generation. It was the youths who were keenly conscious of their lack of political power and who sought to turn ethnic and cultural consciousness into political clout when bargaining with federal as well as state and local governments.

Two cultures of the twentieth-century West: Oglala Sioux dances in downtown Denver in the 1960s. Source: Denver Public Library, Western History Department.

The conflict of white and Indian cultures in the 1960s crystallized in western cities as well as on reservations. Urban Indians were primarily a postwar phenomenon. In 1946 perhaps no more than 20,000 Indians lived in towns; in 1956 Ralph Nader estimated that 100,000 had moved there; and by 1970, Vine DeLoria guessed that as many as 250,000, or roughly one-half of American Indians, had become urbanized. This policy—which, it had been hoped, would hasten acculturation and integration—actually sharpened cultural conflicts experienced by many Indians, and merely moved their poverty from the country to the city. In the cities Indians established "native quarters." Los Angeles, with more than 50,000 in 1970, was the largest Indian city in the nation. But sizable communities could also be found in San Francisco, Seattle, Denver, Phoenix, Albuquerque, and many smaller western towns. Appreciable numbers also went East, settling in New York, Cleveland, Detroit, Chicago, and Saint Louis. More often than not their lot was a very unhappy one. More than one-half were unemployed and lived in squalid poverty. In addition to the problem of finding well paid jobs, of "making it," Indians often found adjustment to the unfamiliar complexities of urban life overwhelming—and defeating. As Richard McKenzie, a Sioux activist in San Francisco, pointed out during the 1960s, reservation Indians had a difficult enough time in adjusting to city life in the 1860s, but were even less well prepared to adjust to the demanding, fast-paced, and cold blooded city of the 1960s. Indeed, probably more than one-half of the Indians who migrated to the cities in the 1960s eventually returned to their reservations, many broken in spirit and body. By 1970 it was clear that the federal policy of relocating Indians in cities did not necessarily result in much improvement of their lives. As President John F. Kennedy's Commissioner of Indian Affairs, Philleo Nash, aptly said, relocation was often only a program that transported people from one poverty pocket to another.

During this same period, the efforts of the Bureau of Indian Affairs to secure more rapid acculturation of Indians on reservations also met with scant success. The underlying assumption of many federal officials—that acculturation required Indian adoption of the white man's ways—came under increasing criticism during the 1960s. This assumption was reflected in scores of federal programs that simply ignored the cultural traditions of Indians. Thus, in 1960 the Bureau of Indian Affairs built a group of garden apartment complexes on the Turtle Mountain (Chippewa) reservation in North Dakota, on the Wind River Indian Reservation in Wyoming (1966), and on the reservation of the Oglala Sioux in South Dakota. But in many cases these Indians were reluctant to move into such communal settlements. To be sure, they were sparkling new and had many modern conveniences. Still, many of the Indians looked, pondered, and then decided that they really preferred to remain in their traditional individual and dispersed huts and dwellings, which were not so alien to their life-style. After all, a house is not a home. And the white man's concept of affluent living was not necessarily congenial to the Indian.

By 1960 the various vicissitudes of federal Indian policies had convinced an increasing number of Indian youth that they wanted a greater voice in controlling their own destinies. No longer did they wish to be subject to white man's control. The first stirrings of such sentiment surfaced at an American Indian conference at the University of Chicago in 1960 at which several young Indian college graduates, including Herbert Blatchford (a Navajo) and Mel Thom (a Paiute from Nevada), derided traditionalists as Uncle Tomahawks. They urged the organization of Indian youth to demand Red Power, militantly, if necessary, and to strive for cultural identity and independence. Rejecting assimilation into American society, they desired instead the adaptation of white society to their Indianness. At the Inter-Tribal Indian ceremonial at Gallup, New Mexico, that year (August 1960) ten of these "Red Muslims" met to organize the National Indian Youth Council, by 1970 to include more than 5,000 members under the presidency of Mel Thom.

During the sixties Thom articulated the goals of the Council in lectures throughout the nation. The modern Indian, Thom felt, had to understand modern America in order to secure his rights, and better education was therefore essential. And Indians needed to use direct political action to secure their goals. The United States was like an enemy that had scattered the Indian people and had divided them against themselves. The Red Power movement hoped to unite them, partly through its emphasis on racial consciousness that would enable Indians to close ranks and to unify for defense of their rights. The goal of the New Indians, Thom repeated many times, was to retain and adapt Indian culture so as to partake of American economic affluence, but without losing the Indian's unique cultural heritage and identity.

During the 1960s the Indian activists relentlessly pursued their cause. Through their organizations they constituted a very vocal, militant, and influential pressure group on the Bureau of Indian Affairs and other federal agencies. Their skilled public relations programs won them increasing national support among both Indians and non-Indians in positions of influence. They also sponsored highly visible "protest demonstrations." One of these was the fish-in in the state of Washington during 1964. There the Yakima Indians rebelled against the declining number of fish and fishing rights available to them because of new dams and power projects in The Dalles, Oregon. As Indians sought to fish in the Columbia River after 1960 they were increasingly fined or arrested for violation of state laws. By 1964 the Indians were thoroughly aroused. Consequently, several leaders like Mel Thom and Bruce Wilkie (of the Maha tribe) organized a fish-in. Hundreds of Indians left their reservations and went out to fish on Puget Sound in defiance of state game wardens and state police, who began to make mass arrests. Taking a cue from the Puget Sound demonstrations,

Leaders of the National Indian Youth Council, in 1964. Left to right, they are Bruce Wilkie, Clyde Warrior, and Mel Thom. Source: National Indian Youth Council.

other Indians in the area conducted fish-ins on five other rivers (Quillayute, Puyallup, Yakima, Nisqually, Columbia). The Maha Indians also conducted war dances in the rotunda of the Washington State capitol in Olympia to celebrate the fish-ins and to focus national attention on the plight of the Northwest tribes. Nevertheless, Governor Albert Rossellini, and his successor Daniel J. Evans, refused to recognize Indian fishing rights, pleading instead the necessity for fish conservation. But the Indians ultimately won their case. In 1967 the United States Department of Justice announced that it would support recognition of Indian fishing rights as defined by old federal treaties with them and would support them in taking the issue to the courts.

Another protest took the form of a raid on Alcatraz, in San Francisco Bay, led by Sioux activist Richard McKenzie and a band of his followers. They "occupied" the abandoned prison to reinforce their demand for utilization of the site as a university of the American Indian. This they did not achieve, but they gained much national publicity and won considerable public sympathy.

One of the prime aims of the Red Power advocates was for Indians to utilize their political rights more fully. As late as 1956, less than 17 per cent of the Indians in the West exercised their right to vote. The militants hoped to change all that by urging Indian unity in state and local elections. One of the most vocal activists, Vine DeLoria, felt that in many of the western states a well-organized Indian bloc of votes could provide an effective balance of power in local, state, and even national elections. Until 1948 such states as Arizona and New Mexico had actually disfranchised Indians, and consequently, during the 1950s the great majority of native Americans was unaccustomed to active participation in politics. But DeLoria and his aides began an effective organizing campaign in the sixties that lured more than 40 per cent of western Indians to turn out to vote, with Indian leaders hoping for more in the future. Meanwhile, Indians began to campaign for local

Indian leaders of the 1960s: Mel Thom *(left)* and Herbert Blatchford *(right)*. Source: National Indian Youth Council.

offices. In 1964, Monroe Jymm and James Atcitty won seats in the New Mexico House of Representatives. Other Indians were elected in Arizona, Idaho, South Dakota, Montana, and Alaska. In 1966 fifteen Indians won seats in six of these western legislatures. Western Indians were on the warpath again, but this time in the role of politicians.

The New Indians also contributed to changing traditional Indian attitudes toward education in the 1960s. Until the middle of the twentieth century, the great majority of Indian parents were distrustful of education. They often refused to send their children to school, or did so only with great reluctance. But by 1960 Indians began to seek out educational opportunites in earnest as they came to recognize that more education could win them an improved place in American society. Between 1950 and 1960 the number of Indian high school students more than doubled, from 24,000 to 57,000. College attendance during this period virtually tripled, from 6,000 to 17,000. But the real surge began in the 1960s when more than 80,000 Indians were attending high schools, and even more significantly, over 30,000 were enrolled in institutions of higher learning. The message of the Indian activists had struck a responsive chord—education meant power.

Throughout the 1960s the Indian militants were loud in their criticisms of federal Indian programs. Although the Office of Economic Opportunity won more Indian support than the Bureau of Indian Affairs, it was not immune to harsh protests. Indian leaders like Thom and DeLoria felt that the white "experts" who were hired by the OEO to operate tribal anti-poverty programs were not at all well versed in Indian culture or psychology. They felt that they themselves could wage a far more effective war on poverty. In support of their claims they pointed out that the average Indian family income in 1965 of $1,200 annually would not increase under current federal programs to much more than $1,500 annually by 1975. The war on poverty between 1965 and 1970 brought hope but not solutions to the problem of Indian poverty in the West.

The demands of Indian activists for greater self-determination won solid support from the Nixon Administration. In 1970 the Indian tribes were authorized to establish their own tribal Offices of Economic Opportunity, with full powers to plan and administer their own projects, underwritten by federal funds. But their greatest victory under Nixon came with the Indian Affairs Act of January 1972, which undertook another major redirection of federal Indian policies. Reflecting the view of the Red Power advocates, it was designed to give Indians a greater degree of self-determination. The relocation program of 1957, under which Indians were trained on reservations to equip them for work in cities, was now abandoned. Instead, training was to be directed toward skills that could be used on or near reservations. The Bureau of Indian Affairs also undertook an accelerated economic development program for the reservations and promoted far greater tribal control of educational activities than in prior years. Included in the act were provisions for the establishment of three new reservation junior colleges. The act responded to many of the demands of the young Indian activists of the 1960s, who saw it as a tribute to their work.

During the 1960s, therefore, westerners became more concerned than at any other time in the twentieth century with the improvement of life for American Indians in the region. No longer could Indian problems be consigned to remote reservations, as in the past. In the technological society of the 1960s the dilemmas of the American Indian entered squarely into the mainstream of western life.

Black Americans

Another important minority group in the trans-Mississippi West during the decade of the sixties were black Americans. Since the literature about black Americans in the 1960s is large and readily available, no extensive discussion of their special problems is included here, to avoid repetition. In most western states—apart from the Pacific Coast—they constituted no more than about 5 per cent of the population. The largest influx during the decade was into California. Los Angeles alone increased its black population from 450,000 to 700,000, and in California as a whole their numbers rose from about 1.1 to 1.8 million. Their problems in the West were similar to those in other sections of the nation—job discrimination, poor housing, and substandard educational facilities. In Los Angeles, San Francisco, Seattle, Denver, Phoenix, Albuquerque, Houston, and El Paso the details differed, but not the problems.

The situation in California was not unrepresentative of conditions elsewhere in the West. Partly to help ease the pressing housing shortage for newly arrived black westerners, as well as for the older settlers, in 1963 the California legislature enacted the Rumford Act. This legislation prohibited landlords from engaging in racial discrimination in rentals. The law seemed designed to secure equity, but incurred hostility from the California Real Estate Association. In sponsoring an initiative proposition (#14) for its repeal by voters at the 1964 election, the Association also supported a state constitutional amendment that guaranteed persons the right to sell, lease, or rent real estate to any person they chose. At the November 1964 elections the California voters approved Proposition #14 by an overwhelming (2 to 1) vote. In later years the California Supreme Court (1966), and the U.S. Supreme Court (1967), declared this measure to be unconstitutional as a denial of the equal protection of the laws. But in the glum winter of 1964 this action by white Californians deeply embittered many of their black fellow citizens.

A Black Panther leader in the West: Lauren F. Watson at the University of Colorado, 1969. Source: Denver Public Library, Western History Department.

Much of their frustration found an outlet in the Watts riots in Los Angeles during the following year. Many dwellers of this predominantly black ghetto felt deprived by the restricted housing available to them. Moreover, Watts had a large number of unemployed, more than twice as many as among whites. In addition, many of the poorer inhabitants found it difficult to secure public transportation, and so to take advantage of employment opportunities in other portions of the city. And they lacked the means to purchase their own cars. And so, when on August 11, 1965, a California State Highway patrolman arrested a black youth for drunken driving, a scuffle between the two ensued, which provided the spark for a large-scale riot. Within hours thousands of persons roamed the streets, setting fires to hundreds of buildings and engaging in widespread looting. After more than three days of disorders, tempers cooled. But thirty-four persons had been killed in the riot, hundreds injured, and more than 200 buildings worth more than $40 million destroyed. Watts was one of America's worst race riots in the twentieth century, and certainly the worst in the annals of the West.

Pent-up resentment against job discrimination by black citizens of San Francisco resulted in a smaller riot there during the following year. Some of the San Francisco labor unions had discriminated against black workers for many years, and were loath to change their practices. In the summer of 1966 a riot broke out in the Hunter's Point section of San Francisco, where many newly arrived black immigrants had clustered. The disturbances were on a small scale, but were a register of some of the special problems that black Americans faced in western cities.[4]

Black Americans, then, did not always find that their experiences in the West differed markedly from those elsewhere in the United States. Lack of economic opportunity, discrimination, poor housing, education, or social welfare services were becoming almost as common in the larger western cities as elsewhere. Nevertheless, some black newcomers found that the West still provided them with some improvement of their lives, whether in respect to a better job or less congested housing.

Environmental Problems

Hardley less serious than the problem of minorities in the West during the 1960s were pressing issues of environmental imbalance. The spiraling population in the trans-Mississippi West during the first half of the twentieth century had placed enormous burdens on the area's natural resources. To be sure, this strain was not entirely new. Since the first white settlers had come to the frontier they had ruthlessly exploited its resources. But the seeming plentitude of natural riches had allowed westerners the luxury of waste for several centuries. In the sixties, however, it seemed that they would no longer be able to indulge themselves. Not only did new and serious environmental crises signal an end to the era of reckless waste, but the large number of people in the trans-Mississippi West, and the shrinking availability of resources per capita, as well as the increased pace of exploitation resulting from technological advances, created a new context for man's endless struggle with his environment. As if to herald a new era, pollution of air and of water, decimation of wildlife, and desecration of wilderness areas appeared like Cassandras in the sixties. Meanwhile, continued wanton subdivision of lands by profit-conscious developers provided a warning to many westerners that a change in attitudes (and policies) toward natural resources was necessary.[5]

Air Pollution

Although the West had once been the Mecca of tuberculosis sufferers because of its clean, fresh air, by 1960 many portions of the region were suffering from severe air pollution. Los Angeles became the first western city to experience serious smog, but in the sixties San Francisco, Seattle,

Denver, Phoenix, Colorado Springs, Tucson, and Albuquerque—to name only a few—were beset by similar problems. Industrial wastes such as those emanating from chemical or power plants were a primary source of air contamination, in addition to the burning of natural gas, trash, fuel oil, and timber. Nevertheless, the major cause of air pollution came from the ever increasing number of automobiles in operation. And since so many western cities had been built in or near river valleys or mountains, their topographical features accentuated the retention of large masses of foul air and encouraged air inversion. Cars, mountains, and smog went together. Los Angeles alone in 1960 registered more than 4 million motor vehicles. Exhaust from jets added to the problem. The beauty of the western sky, and of the western mountains, came to be shrouded in an ugly, dirty, brownish pall. Westerners of this generation could aptly be described as the "coughing generation" as thousands of persons suffered from eye irritation and many new respiratory ailments traceable directly to increasing smog. In 1950 only one death per 100,000 people could be attributed to emphysema (a disease stimulated by smog), but by 1963 the incidence of the disease had increased sevenfold.

The efforts of westerners during the 1960s to deal with their air pollution problems came gradually. As the first large city to be beset with intensive smog, Los Angeles in 1947 created a County Air Pollution District to cope with this new menace. Chemists working for this new agency discovered that smog contained sulfur dioxide that irritated eyes, nose, mouth, and bronchial tubes. It also contained lead, which caused anemia and colic in some persons. Nitrogen oxide in smog also caused blood poisoning and heart palpitations. Thus, in the decade after 1950 the District imposed a variety of

Los Angeles freeway interchange in the 1960s. Source: California Division of Highways.

restrictive regulations on industrial polluters under its jurisdiction. By 1960 its orders had significantly reduced the use of smudge pots by orchardists, ended most trash incineration, and required mills to install filtering devices. In addition, they ordered oil refineries to reduce their emission of sulfur dioxide into the air. The District estimated that by 1962 industrial enterprises in its area had installed at least 90,000 air pollution control devices that caught more than 4,600 tons of contaminants daily. By 1960, therefore, rigid local regulations had succeeded in significantly reducing the emission of industrial air pollutants in southern California.

But it was clear by this time that the automobile had become the major source of air pollution in the West. The damaged alfalfa and vegetable crops of southern California and the sad destruction by smog of beautiful white pine trees in the San Bernardino Mountains were mute evidence of the fact that the smog problem still was a severe threat. Paradoxically, automobile manufacturers during the sixties built increasingly heavier vehicles with high compression engines that required extremely toxic, high-lead content gasolines. And hydrocarbon leaks from fuel tanks, carburetors, and exhaust pipes were adding to the poisonous load. Many areas of the West were balmy, and motorists generally were less accustomed to keeping their cars tuned than were drivers in the Northeast and the Middle West, where quick starts on cold mornings were more essential. And in areas where daytime temperatures ranged over 90 degrees, many tons of gasoline evaporated from the gas tanks and carburetors of automobiles in motion.

In a pioneering effort to deal with automobile air pollution in 1961 the California legislature enacted a law requiring the use of special smog-control devices on cars registered in the state. Although not foolproof, these mechanisms were designed to carry crankcase fumes back into the combustion chambers of automobiles. Certainly the new attachments helped reduce exhaust fumes, but unfortunately could not totally eliminate them. Although the California effort represented only a minimal step, other western state legislatures were extremely loath to take similar action. The elimination of air pollution in the West—it was clear by 1970— awaited a rather profound change of values on the part of westerners and in their concern for their environment.

Water Pollution

During these same years water pollution in the West became increasingly serious. The problem was manifold in its manifestations and varied with the topography of a particular region. On the Pacific Coast the contamination of the ocean became a major issue. In the interior the problem involved pollution of streams, lakes, and rivers. And everywhere in urban areas the

A typical freeway complex of the 1960s: Valley Highway in Denver, 1967.
Source: Denver Public Library, Western History Department.

disposal of sewage and waste by growing populations created serious problems of water pollution and water supply. Another source of pollutants were the oil wastes resulting from offshore drilling activities in the Pacific off the coast of California. The most glaring, but by no means only, example of oil seepage occurred at Santa Barbara, California, in 1969 when four oil companies (Gulf, Mobil, Texaco, Union), spilled millions of gallons of fuel into the ocean, killing most forms of sea life in the area. The result of such dumping was the veritable destruction of the ocean. The introduction of wastes in large amounts led to the growth of photoplankton and other small animals and plants, which multiplied so intensively that they produced effluent yellow-green or reddish-brown stagnant water masses characterized by a foul smell. Thus, in the 1960s one after another of the beaches along the Pacific Coast became unfit for swimming or water sports and fish and other marine life were slowly dying from lack of oxygen.

The ever-present fear of westerners that population increase would outrun their meager water supplies was particularly prevalent in the 1960s. By 1962 many metropolitan areas in the West were even then engaged in maximum utilization of their available water reserves. The Chief Engineer of the Colorado River Board of California noted, for example, that already 97 per cent of the Colorado River's waters was committed to particular users.

Under the prodding of western congressmen and President Lyndon B. Johnson, Congress in 1964 enacted the Water Resources Research Act, which supplied federal funds for universities and research centers engaged in water resources research. At the same time the United States Department of the Interior established an Office of Water Resources Research to carry out this mandate—so vital to the growth and future of the West.

Wilderness Destruction

The rapid growth of urban centers in the West during the sixties also resulted in the increased desecration of wilderness areas. Intrusion of a steadily increasing stream of tourists—in cars, campers, motorcycles, or snowmobiles—threatened wildlife in those wilderness regions still remaining. To be sure, a big-game inventory made by the U.S. Bureau of Sports Fisheries and Wildlife in 1963 revealed that the deer population of the West had increased steadily after 1945, and that the number of antelope, elk, and buffalo had grown as well. What worried conservationists were not the absolute numbers of animals, however, but the imbalance among species wrought by abrupt intrusions of people into their native habitat. One of the most concerned groups of environmentalists, in addition to the Sierra Club, was the Izaak Walton League. Its concern had already resulted in the Dingell-Johnson Act of 1950, which provided invaluable federal aid to the states for fish restoration. In the ensuing two decades it had an enormous impact in furthering the cause of fish conservation methods in most western states and enabled them greatly to expand their activities in this sphere. To a large extent its influence was responsible also for the Fish and Wildlife Coordination Act of 1958, which authorized the United States Fish and Wildlife Service to undertake river-basin studies to evaluate the effects of water diversion projects and dams on fish and wildlife and to recommend appropriate protective laws. President Johnson threw his support behind these efforts and, prompted in part by the urgings of the Executive Secretary of the Wilderness Society, Howard C. Zahneiser, persuaded Congress to enact the Wilderness Act of 1964. This act created a National Wilderness Preservation system (not unlike the National Park system of 1916). Almost immediately President Johnson reserved 9 million acres for the purpose while making plans for additions in the future.

Another serious environmental problem to face westerners in the 1960s was the chaotic subdivision of lands in the region, in part caused by the proliferation of highways. In these years most of the metropolitan areas of the West were engulfed by a crazyquilt hodge-podge of residential areas, freeways, industries, and commercial businesses. Westerners had replaced the natural beauty of their region with manmade ugliness. A growing number of western communities by 1970 were characterized by garish signs, unsightly housing tracts, jerry-built business establishments, a notable absence of landscaping or tasteful decoration, unsightly power lines, and wanton destruction of trees and greenery. And still, in 1970, the vast fleets of bulldozers, scrapers, tractors, and earth movers were on the march, a mighty army that displaced or flattened mountains to make more room for a teeming population. The desecrations of earth-moving equipment on the land—in the name of new housing projects or new freeways—lay like open sores upon the western landscape. Similar spoilage was occurring in the mining regions of the Mountain West—in Utah, Arizona, New Mexico, and Colorado—where huge new digging machines inaugurated a new era of vast strip mining operations.

Indeed, as in western cities, so in the less sparsely populated areas of the West, the armies of land developers were on the march. By 1970, in states such as Oregon, Washington, Wyoming, Idaho, Arizona, New Mexico, Colorado, and Montana the land developers stood poised for a large-scale invasion, carefully marshaling their heavy earth-moving equipment and machinery, coolly organizing their manpower—including their lawyers, bankers, accountants, and engineers, all led by their public relations personnel. The anguished protests of environmentalists were usually in vain. In the name of progress the mighty horde sought to move on. Montana provided a specific case in point. There a giant developmental company, Big Sky of Montana, headed by former National Broadcasting Company newsman Chet Huntley, in 1971 planned to develop a 10,467-acre recreation complex at a cost of $20 million. Locating a tract 40 miles south of Bozeman along the western fork of the Gallatin River, the Company, backed by funds from the Chrysler Corporation, the Burlington Northern Railroad, the Continental Oil Company, and other corporate giants, planned to build two new villages with 1,200 condominiums and 800 homes. In addition, it planned tourist lodges, restaurants, and shops to accommodate upward of 10,000 people. This project aroused the wrath of Montana environmentalists, who not only objected to the inclusion of former National Forest lands in the planned communities but greatly feared the diversion of Gallatin River waters, the disruption of wildlife, and the collapse of unstable mountain slopes because of the construction of new roads, heavy buildings, new dams, and the accumulation of a huge volume of sewage. The conflict in Montana was but a reflection of similar struggles in most of the sparsely populated western states. And although Congress in the Classification and Multiple Use Act of 1964 had directed the Secretary of the Interior to develop criteria for classifying residential, industrial, and grazing lands coming under the Taylor Grazing Act, by 1970 existing laws were wholly inadequate to protect large areas of the West from the type of spoliation that had been so characteristic of preceding decades.

The rapid pollution of air and water, the disappearance of wilderness areas, and vast ugly sprawls in many cities and towns of the West contrasted starkly with the beauty of the region's natural environment. During the 1960s Congress as well as some state legislatures made first beginnings in an effort to halt the pace of pollution. The Los Angeles Air Pollution District (1947), the California Smog Control Act (1961), the Water Resources Research Act of 1964, and the Wilderness Act of 1964 were only a few illustrations of such efforts. But by 1970 it was clear that a far-reaching change of values on the part of millions of westerners (and Americans) was needed if the West's environmental balance was to be improved. For centuries westerners had regarded their environment as an object of spoliation, primarily for private profit. Unless they changed this view and began regarding their natural habitat as a thing of beauty—useful for rest, solitude, and contemplation, or other non-material goals of human existence—the future of the West's remaining natural resources was uncertain.

America had lost its innocence by 1970. And as the newest region of the United States, the trans-Mississippi West was profoundly affected by that change. Increasingly the problems of the West were no longer local or regional, but manifestations of national issues. For centuries Americans in the older areas had hoped for a second chance, for a new start, in the West. In 1970 that West was no more. No longer did the West provide an escape, a renewed lease on life, a career, or economic opportunity. The West had become much like other parts of the nation. Surely this represented a paradox, because in their very effort to escape from disturbing problems in the East, Americans re-created those very same problems in the West. The difficulties westerners encountered in the 1960s with the acculturating minorities and with maintaining balance in their environment were mute evidence of the irony.

NOTES

1. A short historical survey by Meier and Rivera, *The Chicanos,* is useful. Stan Steiner, *La Raza* (New York: Harper & Row, 1968), is a lively contemporary estimate. Both works provide guidance to further readings.

2. A more detailed account of these events is in Peter Nabokov, *Tijerina and the Courthouse Raid* (Albuquerque: University of New Mexico Press, 1969).

3. A lively and fast paced account is by Stan Steiner, *The New Indians* (New York: Harper & Row, 1968), which also contains further references.

4. An urgent need exists for historical works dealing with black Americans in the West. Meanwhile Jerry S. Cohen and William S. Murphy, *Burn, Baby, Burn: The Los Angeles Race Riot, August, 1965* (New York: Dutton, 1966), and Robert Conot, *Rivers of Blood, Years of Darkness* (New York: Morrow, 1967), are informative.

5. Raymond F. Dasmann, *The Destruction of California* (New York: Macmillan, 1965), is an interesting introduction to the subject, and suggests additional references. Roderick Nash, *Wilderness and the American Mind* (New Haven: Yale University Press, 1967), and this author's anthology, *The American Environment: Readings in the History of Conservation* (Reading, Mass.: Addison-Wesley, 1968), are excellent.

Conclusion:
The Influence of the
Twentieth-Century West
on American Civilization

Throughout its history the American West has exerted an important influence on the rest of American Society. In the eighteenth and nineteenth centuries the settlers who poured into the trans-Allegheny region did much to contribute important elements of what came to be known as the American character. They introduced and strengthened characteristics such as individualism, egalitarianism, democracy, optimism, and competitiveness. They exhibited a spirit of restlessness that helped them conquer constantly expanding frontiers. And they displayed a pioneering spirit of enterprise that served as an inspiration for succeeding generations. If the West strengthened many national ideals, however, it is also true that to a considerable extent it was formed by eastern influences, for it was a colony of the older regions. In short, during the eighteenth and nineteenth centuries the West was the child of New England, the Middle states, and the South.

During the twentieth century—even more than in previous years—the American West has exercised a significant influence on many phases of American life. Indeed, during the twentieth century the West has been ahead of the rest of the nation by about one generation. To give meaning to our theme let us explore five characteristics of western life that subsequently affected the rest of the nation. Let us take a closer look at social patterns, technology and science, economic development, politics, and a few selected aspects of cultural life. Obviously, not all of these developments were unmixed blessings, and before concluding it might be well for us to pause and to reflect some of the problems that arose out of rapid western growth, problems that later emerged more fully blown in our national life.

In the twentieth century, as the West goes, so goes the Nation! The American West today is America tomorrow.

Without doubt the West has left an imprint on the social outlook and structure of the United States. Forty years before the rest of the nation the West revealed population trends that were to become characteristic of the United States as a whole. One aspect was the higher percentage of the young—and the old—which the West contained. Perhaps it was this population pattern—including a relatively large group of persons who were consumer-oriented rather than functioning as producers—that gave rise to the particular life-styles for which the West became known. For this particular western life-style of the twentieth century stressed informality and outdoor living. Whatever its sources, evidence is abundant that after 1945 the entire nation enthusiastically embraced the western style. This style includes informality of behavior, in dress, and also in food. Western jeans—originally invented by Levi Strauss in 1860 to suit the needs of gold miners panning in California—became the national garb. Cowboy boots were sported in every section of the nation, and became as familiar on the sidewalks of New York as in Cheyenne, Wyoming. Sportswear, once largely confined to the West for everyday attire, was eagerly adopted by Americans everywhere, and California and Texas, not New York, set the national style. The outdoor barbeque became a national institution. It even graced the White House lawns during the 1960s. And the western predilection for outdoor living became a national characteristic by mid-century. Western foods—whether barbeques or tacos—have found wide acceptance in the Northeast and Middle West, where their consumption is often greater than in the trans-Mississippi region.

As a relatively young region, the twentieth-century West has shown itself hospitable to social dissent, setting precedents that were increasingly followed by the older regions. It is no accident that so many protest movements in America have started in the West. San Francisco was the home of the Beat movement in the 1950s that challenged the prevailing American concern for material wealth. Again, San Francisco—the end of the line—saw the birth of the Hippie movement during the 1960s, and Berkeley became the first home of student radicals. From the West these protest movements moved east to take on national dimensions.

Few would argue that the West made wholly satisfying responses to the challenges posed by integrating minorities, especially the Chicanos and the Indians. But beginning in the 1920s various western states such as California and New Mexico placed a greater emphasis on cultural pluralism than many eastern states. Their purpose was to encourage the fuller development of cultures and subcultures in the region without imposing the dead hand of conformity and total assimilation on them. During the 1920s, therefore, both federal and state Indian officials began to encourage the celebration of traditional rites and ceremonies, the practice of native handicrafts, and the more intense study of local dialects and folklore. By the 1950s these experiments in cultural pluralism aroused intense interest in other sections of the nation preoccupied with finding viable solutions to problems requiring the blending of acculturation and cultural independence.

The west first developed the urban-suburban pattern of living that was to become characteristic of twentieth-century America, especially in the three decades after 1945. This pattern was a result of the combination of cultural and environmental influences. The very large migration of middle westerners who entered the trans-Mississippi region between 1900 and 1930 went largely to towns that until then had served primarily as distributing centers for their surrounding areas. In 1900 the West had few "old" cities on the pattern of Boston, New York, or Philadelphia. Upon these towns the middle westerners often imposed the village or small-town pattern they had recently known in their former homes. And so the West simply skipped one stage of urban development that eastern cities were undergoing. Between 1900 and 1970 the metropolitan areas of the East spread out from inner city nucleii to successive rings of suburbs. But western cities evolved from the huge villages that grew between 1900 and 1930 into huge suburban areas thereafter. Los Angeles was a prime example. Already by 1930 its pattern presaged the new shape of Boston, New York, Philadelphia, and other eastern cities in the 1960s. This peculiar sprawl created wholly new life-styles for its inhabitants. They became increasingly mobile and accustomed to a life on wheels. Their homes and their places of work were usually separated by relatively long distances; they made their purchases at new marketing clusters—the shopping centers—and a whole new range of service facilities geared to automobiles appeared. This new way of life made its first appearance in the West, a generation before it affected the rest of the nation.

During the past seven decades the West also led the nation in demonstrating the possibilities inherent in the application of science and technology to modify the environment. The reasons for western pioneering in this sphere are not hard to find. The presence of mild climates in some areas of the West, such as Texas, New Mexico, Arizona, Washington, and California, provided special attractions for the establishment of scientific laboratories. These provided year-round facilities for testing new scientific instruments and inventions, while vast stretches of uninhabited land provided necessary testing grounds that few other regions of the nation could offer. Moreover, these attributes of climate and location also served as a magnet in attracting able scientists and technicians, who often became enamored of western life-styles and so added to the strengthening of scientific research centers in the West.

Between 1900 and 1970 westerners also pioneered in technological innovations that revolutionized American agriculture. They developed the most advanced methods for the scientific eradication of diseases in the nation. The irrigation works constructed in California and other parts of the West in 1900 were on a size and scale that had rarely been witnessed elsewhere. The highly commercialized form of horticulture developed by Californians and other westerners at the turn of the century was adopted by other regions a generation later.

Yet in many ways the West still is not unlike a foreign underdeveloped region. Even now its economy is not so highly developed or diversified as many older areas. Its economic growth has been far more selective. But in its own peculiar way the West developed new industries that the rest of the nation came to embrace 30 years later. A few examples will help us to illustrate the point.

The peculiar form of highly mechanized large-scale commercial agriculture that developed in the twentieth-century West set the pace for farmers everywhere in the United States if not, indeed, throughout the world. Perhaps this form of agri-business, as it came to be known, was most highly developed in California and along the rest of the Pacific Coast, but it was also prominent in Colorado, parts of Utah, New Mexico, Arizona, Texas, and the Dakotas. Between 1900 and 1940 these states came to supply 90 per cent of the fruits and vegetables consumed in the entire nation. By 1970 the total value of western agriculture exceeded $10 billion annually. Its diverse climates and terrain allowed for year-round production, and for the most diverse array of crops to be found anywhere on the globe. Moreover, the rationalization of production by the utilization of scientific methods capitalized on the advantages offered by the environment. Carey McWilliams aptly termed western farms "factories in the fields." The creation of Big Agriculture in America, for better or for worse, was a distinct western contribution.

As a pioneer in scientific advances the West also became a harbinger of future America in its development of space-age industries. The West became the leading aerospace center in the United States, to a considerable extent because of the annual expenditure of more than $20 billion by NASA in California, Texas, and other western states. In these areas North American Aviation, Lockheed, Douglas, General Dynamics, and the Hughes Aircraft Company became giant employers of more than 2 million westerners. Military expenditures also did much to stimulate the growth of large-scale electronics and automation industries in the West. During the 1950s these industries showed a much higher growth rate than any other type of manufacture. The West came to take on a significant role in the manufacture of communications equipment, electrical machinery, and scientific instruments. Facilities such as the U.S. Air Force Space Laboratory at Inglewood, California, IBM's huge research complex at San Jose, and the Sandia Laboratories in Albuquerque were prime examples of pub- lic and private space industries in the West becoming pacesetters for many other parts of the nation.

Another characteristic of the western economy in the twentieth century that was a harbinger of things to come was the growth and importance of service industries. One of the major national economic trends since 1955 has been the increasing importance of the service industries. In this development the West, by a generation, far and away paced the rest of the country. In 1930 only 4 out of 10 Americans worked in a service industry, with the increasing leisure provided by an affluent society by 1970 this figure had risen to 6 out of 10, and by 1980 it will be 7 out of 10. What do we mean by service industries? We include services such as those provided by banks or educational institutions, and above all, the tourist industry. The favorable and healthful western climates and the spectacular scenery provided a most favorable environmental context for the growth of tourism—now the major source of income for many western states. Already by 1900 a number of first-class hotels had been built in the West. But they were designed mainly for the wealthy. The most significant boost in tourism came in the 1920s when the automobile revolution made the West a vacation center not only for the upper classes but for the masses as well. Almost every western state legislature seized on the opportunity to construct an excellent system of roads and highways and to encourage the construction of a vast net of service facilities such as gasoline stations, motor courts, restaurants, and hotels. Westerners also showed their innovativeness by inventing the convention center. The so-called tourist complex embracing hotels and motels, automobile service facilities, restaurants, and convention centers since 1945 has been widely copied by every other section of the country, for in an affluent society the new leisure has boosted tourism into a major industry.

Finally, a word should be said about the enormous impact of the West on American financial and banking practices. Until 1914 the West was largely dependent on eastern as well as on foreign capital. Shortly after 1919, however, a group of imaginative western bankers sought to end this colonialism. Perhaps the most brilliant of the group was A. P. Gianninni, who in 1904 had founded the Bank of Italy in San Francisco. By skillful and adroit use of the technique of branch banking Gianninni made the Bank of Italy (after 1933, the Bank of America) the largest in California by 1929; by 1939 it was the largest in the trans-Mississippi West; and by 1949 it was one of the greatest banking giants in the world. The expansion of the Bank of America helped to free much of the West from its reliance on outside capital and its operations were widely imitated. The flexibility of branch banking, which the Bank of America demonstrated, was widely adopted in the decades after 1945 by bankers everywhere in the nation.

Another area in which the West has bequeathed a diverse heritage to the rest of the nation is politics. Both in defining the role of government in our national life, and in the elaboration of new political techniques, the West has had a profound impact during these past 75 years. Among the major political trends first worked out in the West was a new cooperative relationship with private enterprise that was widely accepted by the middle of the twentieth century. As we well know, despite myths and legends, the West was not solely a product of individual initiative and enterprise, but a prime example of mixed enterprise, of a partnership between private individuals and federal, state, and local governments. Theodore Roosevelt first aptly characterized this relationship early in the century when he dubbed it the New Nationalism. Between 1900 and 1970 the federal government alone spent more than $300 billion in the development of the trans-Mississippi region. These funds were distributed in the form of defense contracts; river, harbor, and highway improvements; aid to agriculture, mining, and livestock interests; and in many other ways. To this amount must be added another $50 billion expended by state governments for public works, social services, or for attracting new industries. Nor can the contributions of local governments be ignored, for they totalled at least another $25 billion. When added up, these expenditures total almost one-half of the capital investment that was needed to settle and develop the region west of the Mississippi River.

Westerners turned to government to promote the growth of their region largely because in a highly industrialized society the amount of capital needed for economic development is enormous. And private individuals as well as corporations found themselves unable to generate all the capital needed for rapid growth, especially in a region that in 1900 was still largely undeveloped. So westerners pioneered in working out a myriad of cooperative relationships between themselves and federal, state, and local governments to hasten the growth of their region. And in this endeavor they were ahead of the rest of the nation by at least a generation. By 1945 westerners had demonstrated the potentialities and the efficacy of government pump-priming techniques that the rest of the nation came to adopt in the quarter century after 1945.

Throughout the twentieth century the West has been a prime laboratory for experimentation with new political techniques designed to improve the functioning of democratic political institutions. Wyoming in 1890 was the first state to grant voting rights to women. By 1910 the western states were also the first to adopt the initiative and referendum, designed to bypass legislatures that appeared unresponsive to public opinion. William U'Ren in Oregon became one of America's pioneer political reformers early in the century, and his influence spread into every corner of the nation. Similarly, the West first developed the direct primary as a means of democratizing the political electoral process, to give the individual citizen a voice in party nominations instead of leaving the process entirely in the hands of party caucuses and conventions. And it was western states, like Arizona in 1912, which were the first to adopt provisions for the recall of public officials who appeared derelict in their public duties.

Westerners also made many innovations in the field of local government. They invented the city commission form of government. In 1900, in Galveston, Texas, after a huge tidal wave had destroyed parts of the city and wrought much havoc and destruction, citizens of the city created a commission of experts to handle the job of reconstruction after the city council had been unable to handle the problem. Within ten years 400 other cities in every section of the country had adopted the idea. Already by 1914 the West was beginning to pace the nation.

If the contributions of the West to the nation's cultural life were not always profound, nevertheless they became increasingly significant in the course of the twentieth century. One major contribution came in the form of regionalism, the effort to ground various modes of cultural expression in native soil. In the West (as in the South) regionalism blossomed in the 1920s, received an enormous boost from the crisis of the Great Depression, and continued to reflect much vitality in the ensuing three decades. Regionalism was reflected in the growth of western literature, art, architecture, and to a lesser extent, music. The persistence of regionalism as a cultural influence over the course of half a century was in part due to its great diversity, for it appealed to high-brows as well as low-brows, to devotees of sophistication as well as to adherents of popular or mass culture. The regional tradition was able to contain writers as diverse as poets like Robinson Jeffers or Witter Bynner, on the one hand, and popularizers such as Owen Wister, on the other. Indeed, it could be argued that "western" inaugurated an era of popular literature a generation before mass culture assumed nationwide importance.

And the laborers in the vineyards of western culture—writers, artists, musicians, folklorists, and others—helped to enshrine the western cowboy in the mythology of American folklore by making him one of the authentic folk heroes of Americans in the twentieth century. Whether in books, magazines, moving pictures, television, or art, the image of the cowboy which they created made him a symbol of the traditional values embraced by the Protestant Ethic in America. Beset by rapid changes in their lives and values, successive generations of urbanized Americans in the twentieth century looked longingly back to a simpler—and supposedly golden—age which they often associated with the frontier West. Then man had triumphed over nature and seemed to have mastered his environment—in stark contrast to an industrial society where impersonal forces seemed increasingly to dominate the lives of men and women. Then Americans had shared many common values such as individualism, simplicity, adventure, morality, courage, self-reliance, personal freedom, and virtually unlimited opportunities, beliefs personified by the western cowboy. To many Americans western regionalism represented the ideals once personified by the United States, ideals which were rudely disrupted by technology and industrialism and which—despite wishful thinking— were perhaps no longer attainable. In the twentieth century, therefore, western regionalism came to constitute a significant part of the nation's culture.

Another major contribution of the West to American culture was its function as an arena for experimentation. Less stratified than the older regions—and more responsive to new ideas and concepts—the West in the twentieth century appeared especially hospitable to new forms of cultural expression. This was especially true of the world of art, as spectacular natural scenery and brilliant coloration drew creative and innovative artists to California and the southwest. In 1900 these areas had counted for little in the nation's art circles; by 1970 they constituted one of its major components. This was equally true of architecture. At the turn of the century most western buildings were characterized by a crude eclecticism; but in the course of the twentieth century the West developed new styles that resulted in making the region one of the most distinctive centers of architectural innovation, not only in the United States, but in the entire world.

The West during the twentieth century also provided rare opportunities for a wide range of experimentation in education and science. Once a backwater in the field of education—even as late as 1900—westerners took giant strides during the twentieth century to transform the region into a center of creative educational experimentation that was widely emu- lated elsewhere. This was true not only of innovations in primary and secondary schools, but also in higher education. The growth of state and municipal colleges and universities designed to offer low-cost advanced training for the many—rather than the few—was distinctly western. The phenomenal growth of public institutions during the twentieth century was directly related to the implementation of this concept. Along the way westerners innovated with new types of institutions such as the junior colleges and the "multiversity" institutions that were to be copied throughout the country.

Much of the creativity in western education was bound to the region's development as one of the distinguished science centers of the nation. When it is remembered that in 1900 science in the West had barely begun, and enjoyed no special distinction, the magnitude of this achievement stands out even more. By 1970 the West harbored more

Nobel laureates and eminent scientists than any other part of the United States. More than one-half of the leading scientists and engineers in the United States lived west of the Mississippi River during the second half of the twentieth century. The West had also become the home of scores of distinguished scientific laboratories and installations—from Cal Tech to Los Alamos. The freedom for experimentation and testing, the vibrant spirit of innovation, the opportunities for experimentation spurred the creative capacities of several generations of scientists in the West during the course of the twentieth century.

But enough. We have spoken about the diverse influences which the American West in the twentieth century has had on many spheres of national life. We have glanced at social behavior, at science and technology, at economic patterns, at politics, and at cultural life. In every instance the West heralded national patterns by about one generation.

One cannot leave the subject of the West in the twentieth century without taking cognizance of some of the grave problems which its growth has produced. If the West mirrors the attainment of the affluent society in America, it is at the same time a prime example of some of its most elemental flaws. This is not the occasion for a catalogue of errors. But it would not be amiss to note that three of the most fundamental weaknesses of American society during the second half of the twentieth century were first revealed in the West a generation before they seriously became visible elsewhere in the nation.

Western culture and society have always revealed a sense of anomie in many individuals, a feeling of rootlessness and alienation. Considering the enormous growth of the West during the last 70 years and the great mobility and diversity of a portion of its population, perhaps this was inevitable. Some westerners early felt a loss of that sense of community which in 1970 nagged Americans everywhere. Long before the rest of the country the West had its colonies of drop-outs, utopians, and non-conformists. That sense of spiritual insecurity, of loss of community which is one of the by-products of a culture in a condition of constant flux was clearly reflected in the West several decades before it turned into a national malaise. In this sense, too, the West mirrored the America of the future.

The problem of acculturating its Indian and Chicano minorities which the twentieth century West faced by the time of World War I heralded a broader national problem which the rest of the country faced after 1945. If the West as a region made some contributions in the resolution of this issue, nevertheless its shortcomings, even after many decades of effort, revealed the deep dimensions of the problem and the difficulties attending its resolution. For good or ill, the West as a region reflected the special difficulties attending a pluralistic multiracial and ethnic society a generation before the rest of the nation became absorbed with similar issues.

Western development has also resulted in serious physical problems. By the middle of the twentieth century the West had already become an almost classic example of environmental imbalance brought about by wanton and unplanned applications of science and technology. Smog and air pollution, contamination of rivers and streams and vegetation, and the destruction of wilderness areas and wildlife were more apparent in California in 1950 than elsewhere. The western predicament was not unique, however, but only served as a showcase for a problem that plagued the entire nation. But nowhere else were environmental problems brought about by a technological society so starkly revealed as in the West.

And so, for better or for worse, the impact of the American West on twentieth-century America has been important. Unlike the nineteenth century, however, this was not the influence of a moving agricultural frontier. Rather, this was an expanding technologically oriented urban oasis—a West consisting of vast stretches of wilderness—yes—but also of a growing network of urban centers. By 1970 these metropolitan centers were already on the verge of further expansion into megalopolises. Not the frontier but the urban oases came to have a significant influence on shaping many phases of life in the United States during the twentieth century.

In the broad context of human history the experience of the twentieth century West has not been unique, of course. Throughout recorded time, man has built cities in the midst of deserts, reflecting a wide range of adaptability. Whether in Turkestan, Iran, Arabia, or the Sudan—or in Arizona and southern California—the restless vagrant life encouraged by dry lands has centered upon urban clusters. Much of human history has been written in tales of desert cities and their errant denizens. Just recall Kalgan and Kashar, Tashkent and Samarkand, Bokhara and Teheran, Baghdad and Damascus, Jerusalem and Bethlehem, Mecca and Medina— these names fill the pages of old Asia's chronicles. And have not Cairo and Khartoum, Kordofan and Bekodoka, Kimberley and Mafeking shaped the destiny of Africa as Tucumán and Potosí, Mendoza and Cochabamba have that of South America? These have been cities of drought, of sunshine, of cool nights and torrid noondays, of adobe and brick, of nomads and shepherds, of warriors and priests, of learning and faith, of fair women and seers, the cities spawned by the desert. It has been there that much of the drama of human life unfolded, where much of man's recorded history was made. So in the United States the towns and cities of the trans-Mississippi West played a major role in shaping the course of American civilization during the twentieth century.

Bibliographical Note

The literature of the twentieth-century West is widely scattered and contained in thousands of specialized books, monographs, and articles. No general survey of the history of the region during the years since 1900 is as yet available. Rather than present a detailed list of works used in the preparation of this volume, this bibliography merely lists several works that will be especially useful to general readers.

An interesting general introduction by a journalist is Neil Morgan, *Westward Tilt: The American West Today* (New York: Random House, 1961), one of the few works to survey the trans-Mississippi region. Various appraisals have dealt with special problems of the area. One of the most stimulating is Walter P. Webb, *Divided We Stand: The Crisis of a Frontierless Democracy* (New York: Farrar & Rinehart, 1937). Webb focused on the colonial status of the West in the Union. Also of interest are Ladd Haystead, *If the Prospect Pleases: The West the Guidebooks Never Mention* (Norman: University of Oklahoma Press, 1946), and A. G. Mezerik, *Revolt of the South and West* (New York: Duell, Sloan & Pearce, Inc., 1946), who develop the theme of colonialism further. The point is made persuasively in regard to western economic growth by Wendell Berge, *Economic Freedom for the West* (Lincoln: University of Nebraska Press, 1946).

Much has been written about California and the Pacific coast. Earl S. Pomeroy, *The Pacific Slope* (New York: Alfred A. Knopf, 1965), is one of the best general books, concentrating on political and social developments. Competent textbooks about California include Andrew F. Rolle, *California: A History*, rev. ed. (New York: T. Y. Crowell, 1969), and also Walton E. Bean, *California: An Interpretive History* (New York: McGraw-Hill, 1968). Brilliant in insight are the essential works of Carey McWilliams. These include *The New Regionalism in American Literature* (Seattle: University of Washington Bookstore, 1930), *Factories in the Field* (New York: 1969 reprint of 1939 edition, by The Shoe String Press Inc.,) and *Ill Fares the Land* (Boston: Little, Brown & Co., 1944); dealing with migratory farm labor problems, *Southern California Country* (New York: Duell, Sloan & Pearce, Inc., 1946), and *California, the Great Exception*

(New York: Current Books, 1949). His essays in Ray B. West, ed., *Rocky Mountain Cities* (New York: W. W. Norton & Co., Inc., 1949), and a book he edited, *The California Revolution* (New York: Grossman, 1968), are also well worth reading. The best survey of the California economy during the first three decades of the twentieth century is a U.S. government publication by C. R. Niklason, *Commercial Survey of the Pacific Southwest* (Washington: U.S. Government Printing Office, 1930). The Pacific Northwest is admirably surveyed in Charles M. Gates and Dorothy O. Johansen, *Empire of the Columbia: A History of the Pacific Northwest*, 2d ed. (New York: Harper & Row, 1967). A brief evaluation is in Benjamin Kizer, *The United States–Canadian Northwest* (Princeton: Princeton University Press, 1944).

Readers will find some good books about other areas of the West. General introductions include Robert G. Athearn, *High Country Empire: The High Plains and the Rockies* (Lincoln: University of Nebraska Press, 1965). Morris E. Garnsey, *America's New Frontier: The Mountain West* (New York: Alfred A. Knopf, 1950), emphasizes economic development. One of the first books in the sadly neglected field of western urban history was Ray B. West, ed., *Rocky Mountain Cities* (New York: W. W. Norton & Co., Inc., 1949). Carl Ubbelohde, *A Colorado History* (Boulder: Pruett Press, 1965) is a readable state history. Indispensable are the monographs of Leonard J. Arrington and associates, including *The Changing Economic Structure of the Mountain West, 1850–1950* (Logan: Utah State University, 1963), *The Richest Hole on Earth: A History of the Bingham Copper Mine* (Logan: Utah State University, 1963), and with Anthony T. Cluff, *Federally Financed Industrial Plants Constructed in Utah During World War II* (Logan: Utah State University, 1969). Surveys of the Southwest include Eugene T. Hollon, *The Southwest–Old and New* (New York: Alfred A. Knopf, 1961), and his *The Great American Desert* (New York: Oxford University Press, 1966), Odie B. Faulk, *Land of Many Frontiers–A History of the American Southwest* (New York: Oxford University Press, 1970), Lynn Perrigo, *The American Southwest: Its People and Culture* (New York: Holt, Rinehart & Winston, 1971), and Howard R. Lamar, *The Far Southwest, 1846–1912* (New Haven: Yale University Press, 1966). On the Plains region Walter P. Webb, *The Great Plains* (Boston: Ginn and Co., 1931) is still instructive. Perhaps the best history of a Plains state is by Elwyn P. Robinson, *History of North Dakota* (Lincoln: University of Nebraska Press, 1966).

INDEX